WITHDRAWN

JEWISH LAW ASSOCIATION STUDIES IX
The London 1996 Conference Volume

THE JEWISH LAW ASSOCIATION
Papers and Proceedings

Jewish Law Association Studies I: The Touro Conference Volume
    B. S. Jackson, Editor

Jewish Law Association Studies II: The Jerusalem Conference Volume
    B. S. Jackson, Editor

Jewish Law Association Studies III: The Oxford Conference Volume
    A. M. Fuss, Editor

Jewish Law Association Studies IV: The Boston Conference Volume
    B. S. Jackson, Editor

Jewish Law Association Studies V: The Halakhic Thought of R. Isaac Herzog
    B. S. Jackson, Editor

Jewish Law Association Studies VI: The Jerusalem 1990 Conference Volume
    B. S. Jackson and S. M. Passamaneck, Editors

Jewish Law Association Studies VII: The Paris Conference Volume
    S. M. Passamaneck and M. Finley, Editors

Jewish Law Association Studies VIII: The Jerusalem 1994 Conference Volume
    E. A. Goldman, Editor

JEWISH LAW ASSOCIATION STUDIES IX
The London 1996 Conference Volume

Edited by
E. A. Goldman

Scholars Press
Atlanta, Georgia ©1997

© 1997 Scholars Press
ISBN 0-7885-0418-5

THE JEWISH LAW ASSOCIATION
Papers and Proceedings

Jewish Law Association Studies I: The Touro Conference Volume
  B. S. Jackson, Editor

Jewish Law Association Studies II: The Jerusalem Conference Volume
  B. S. Jackson, Editor

Jewish Law Association Studies III: The Oxford Conference Volume
  A. M. Fuss, Editor

Jewish Law Association Studies IV: The Boston Conference Volume
  B. S. Jackson, Editor

Jewish Law Association Studies V: The Halakhic Thought of R. Isaac Herzog
  B. S. Jackson, Editor

Jewish Law Association Studies VI: The Jerusalem 1990 Conference Volume
  B. S. Jackson and S. M. Passamaneck, Editors

Jewish Law Association Studies VII: The Paris Conference Volume
  S. M. Passamaneck and M. Finley, Editors

Jewish Law Association Studies VIII: The Jerusalem 1994 Conference Volume
  E. A. Goldman, Editor

Printed in the United States of America
on acid-free paper

THE JEWISH LAW ASSOCIATION OFFICERS 1996/98

Hon. President: B. Lifshitz
Chairman: C. Povarsky
Membership Secretaries: N. Rakover
D. Cobin

Executive Committee: J. Bazak, B. Berkovits, M. Broyde, D. Cobin, A. Fuss, E. Goldman, B. A. Greenberger, B. Jackson, A. Kirschenbaum, S. Passamaneck, N. Rakover, E. Schochetman, D. Sinclair, H. Sprecher.

Publications Committee: E. A. Goldman, *Chairman,* M. Broyde, E. Dorff, B. S. Jackson, B. Lifshitz, S. Passamaneck, D. Sinclair.

The Association seeks to promote the research and study of Jewish law through biennial international congresses, the publication of a *newsletter* and of a yearbook series, *Jewish Law Association Studies,* and making other publications in Jewish law available to its members at concessionary rates. For further details of membership, please contact the appropriate membership secretary:

For Israel: Prof. Nahum Rakover, Ministry of Justice, 29 Salah a-Din, P.O. Box 1087, Jerusaelm 91010, Israel.

For the rest of the world: Prof. David Cobin, Hamline University Law School, 1536 Hewitt Avenue, St. Paul, MN 55104, USA.

Contents

1. Jacob Bazak
   People Usually Don't Watch Their Steps on the Roads / 1

2. Leah Bornstein-Makovetsky
   Rabbinic Scholarship: the Development of Halakhah In Turkey, Greece and the Balkans, 1750–1900 / 9

3. David M. Cobin
   Jews and the Medieval Slave Trade: The Law and Its Historical Context / 19

4. Elliot N. Dorff
   "Legislated Spiritual Disciplines:" Jacob Agus' Philosophy of Jewish Law / 25

5. Hillel Gamoran
   The Tosefta in Light of the Law against Usury / 57

6. Ben Tzion Greenberger
   Mental Capacity and the Deathbed Will / 79

7. Moshe Ish-Horowicz
   The Problem of Iggun *And Its Solutions* / 91

8. Jonathan M. Lewis
   Insolvency in Jewish Law / 103

9. David Novak
   Parental Rights in the Marriage of a Minor / 131

10. Stephen M. Passamaneck
    Remarks on Pesquisa *in Medieval Jewish Legal Procedure* / 143

11. Chaim Povarsky
    The Law of the Pursuer and the Assassination of Prime Minister Rabin / 161

12. Laurence J. Rabinovich
    Hidden Interest And Risk Management in Sixteenth Century Mediterranean Commerce / 199

13. Nahum Rakover
    Preventing Apostasy by Violating the Sabbath / 213

14. Yosef Rivlin
    Consecutive Gifts / 231

15 Jeffrey I. Roth
    Inheriting the Crown in Jewish Law: The Question of Rabbinic Succession   /   237

16 Daniel B. Sinclair
    Genetics and Jewish Law   /   261

17 Hannah Geldwerth-Sprecher & Stanley Sprecher
    Refusing the Milk of Human Kindness   /   273

18 Peter Zaas
    *The (Double) Vision of the Divine Picnic (Acts 10:1–11:18):
    The History of New Testament Kashrut III*   /   289

1

People Usually Don't Watch Their Steps on the Roads

(The responsibility in torts, under Jewish Law and Israeli Law, for damage incurred from an obstacle on the road)

Jacob Bazak*

The Duty of Local Councils to Repair Roads

The subject of the responsibility for damage incurred from an obstacle on the road is better known in Jewish Law under the title of בור ברשות הרבים.[1]

In modern times such claims are in most cases brought against local councils who under law are responsible for keeping the roads within their jurisdiction safe from any obstacle. As was held by Justice Agranat in the case of ישראל ראש חודש ד עירית תל אביב: ". . . Where there is a pit on a road, and the road is within the bounds of a municipality, or where part of such a road sinks down or endangers passengers in any other way, that municipality is obligated to take reasonable steps to protect the public against such dangers."[2]

---

* Jerusalem.

[1] ראה רמב"ם, נזקי ממון יג ב-"וכל המניח תקלה הרי זו תולדת הבור ואם הוזק בה אדם או בהמה-משלם זה שהניח התקלה נזק שלם."

Strictly speaking, the term *bor* refers to cases when a person or an animal fell into a pit (depth ten *tefachim*) on the road, and, as a result, is killed. It is commanded in the Torah that in such cases, the owner of the pit must pay damages for an animal that was killed thereby, though not for a man who was killed and also not for damage caused to property thereby. R. Baruch Epstein (in *Torah Temimah*, Exodus 23:33 s. 263) explains that the reason for that differentiation is that the death of a man as a result of falling into a pit in the road is so rare that one must conclude that if death did occur, it was not because of the pit but because of some personal reasons of the deceased himself that have nothing to do with the falling into the pit.

When however the result was an **injury** to the person or to an animal, then the owner of the pit (whether ten *tefachim* deep or less) is liable in damages. When the damage was a result of an obstacle, not a pit, the technical halachic term used is *Toladat ha'bor*, and the law is that the person who put the obstacle on the road is liable in damages for the resultant injury, to a man as well as to an animal.

[2] ע"א 176/59 פד"י ט"ז p. 301.

In the case of *Gursky v. The Mayor of the City of Tiberias*[3] the plaintiff was seriously injured as a result of slipping down on sewers' water which had accumulated on the sidewalk from a cistern in the neighboring house. It was proved in court that the cistern was under constant supervision of the municipality and in fact had been cleaned on the same day that the accident occurred. The claim was dismissed because the court held that the municipality did all it could do, within the limits of its budget, to prevent that nuisance.

It is interesting to compare this case with a more modern one (decided more than 30 years after the previous one): *Levi Sternberg v. the City of Bnei Brak*[4] where although the facts were almost the same, the decision was completely different. This time the municipality was found—on appeal—liable. The court cited an American case[5] which held:

> The duty of a municipality to keep its sewers in repair, involves the exercise of a reasonable degree of watchfulness in ascertaining their condition from time to time and preventing them from becoming dilapidated or obstructed where the obstruction or dilapidation is an ordinary result of the use of the sewer which ought to be anticipated and could be guarded against by occasional examination and cleansing.

In this case, the court held that when such leakages occur frequently, the municipality must take more radical steps and not be content with occasional repairs. The modern view, as presented in the case of *The City of Hedera v. Aaron Zohar*,[6] is to increase the liability of local councils for damages. The court remarked that in some jurisdictions the liability of local councils in such cases is even a strict one, i.e., not dependent on the proof of any fault on the part of the local council.

In Israel, however, at present, the liability of the municipality in such cases depends on proving negligence on the part of the local council. Moreover, if the municipality can convince the court that what was needed to prevent the damage was completely beyond its budgetary limits, the claim for damages will be dismissed. Take for instance the case of *Rachel and Abraham Grubner v. The Municipality of Haifa*.[7] An old lady was walking in a public park on a way intended for pedestrians only. Suddenly a child riding a bicycle came from behind and kicked the plaintiff, injuring her. The old lady

---

[3] C.A. 406\61 Padi, 16, p. 834.
[4] C.A. 78\86 Padi 43 (3) 1989.
[5] M.F.G. Co. v. City of Portsmouth Mitchell Ohio St. 250, 148 N.E. 846.
[6] Padi 37 (3) 1983.
[7] C.A.343\74 Padi 30 (1) 141.

sued the municipality for damages and claimed that since riding bicycles in that park, contrary to the sign prohibiting it, had become customary, the municipality should have sent an inspector to that park to see to it that children with bicycles would not enter the park and would not endanger pedestrians. The court dismissed the claim and held that placing an inspector constantly on the spot would have been beyond the financial resources and manpower of the municipality. (It seems that the court did not consider the possibility that what in fact was needed was not a full-time inspector, for inspection from time to time combined with fines levied on offenders might have deterred bicycle riders from entering the park.)

The Duty of Local Councils Under Jewish Law to Repair Roads

The duty of a local council to keep the roads and the sewer system in good condition has been recognised in Jewish law as early as in the time of the Mishnah. In *Mo'ed Katan* (1:1) the Mishnah enumerates several urgent works that may be performed on חול המועד in spite of the general prohibition on the performance of any work on these festive days. The Mishnah states as follows:

> ... and the defective cisterns are repaired on Hol Hamo`ed, and the sewer systems are repaired and cleansed, as well as the roads and the highways.

The Talmud[8] cites the following *Baraita* which very sharply condemns local authorities who did not fulfill this duty:

> ... and where is the source from which we learn that if the local authority (the *Beth Din*) did not perform all these repairs, that any blood that is shed as a result thereof will be considered blood shed by that local authority itself? The source is found in Deuteronomy 19:10: 'That innocent blood be not shed in the midst of thy land ... and **so blood be upon thee**' (והיה עליך דמים).

The General Principle

The general principle that can be deduced from the ancient sources of Jewish law is similar to that found in modern judgments decided by Israeli courts: that anyone who puts or leaves an obstacle on the road must be aware of the fact that **while going on the road, pedestrians do not usually**

---

[8] Ibid., 5a.

watch carefully to detect whether a potentially dangerous obstacle is there. Therefore, the person responsible for the obstacle is liable for any damage incurred thereby. On the other hand, a pedestrian may not close his eyes while walking, or look to the sky and pay no attention whatsoever to the road. When the obstacle is big enough so that it would have drawn the attention of an ordinary pedestrian, or when the circumstances in a neighborhood are such that ordinary people would expect an obstacle in that specific place, then the pedestrian should exercise due care not to be hurt by such an obstacle. If injured, he would not have any claim for damages against the person who put that obstacle there.

Jewish Law

The rule as stated in *Baba Kama* (27a) is that one who left a pitcher on the road is liable in torts for damages incurred to a pedestrian who stumbled on that pitcher, fell and was hurt as a result. The reason stated for that rule is "**because people regularly do not look down at the road,**" i.e., because it is human nature not to look down at the road while walking. *Therefore one should take this fact into consideration and not leave any obstacle on the road* that might endanger pedestrians.[9] Rabbi Shlomo Lurie (Poland, 16th century) who cites this rule in one of his responsa (s. 96) gives a psychological explanation for it: "for a man is a thoughtful being," i.e., people, when walking, are regularly occupied with their thoughts and therefore do not look carefully at the ground to watch the road. Rabbi Moshe Sofer uses a slightly different expression: (סי' יח) "מתוך שאדם הוא בעל שכל, לכן אין דרכו להתבונן בדרכים".

Maimonides states that in the case of an **animal** injured in daylight by a similar setback on the road, the law is different: "For the nature of a normal animal is to look down and to avoid setbacks on the road." Rabbi Josef Karo[10] opines that the source for this ruling of Maimonides is in the above-mentioned dictum. "For only a man, not an animal, is a thoughtful being . . ." Accordingly Karo rules in the *Shulchan Aruch* that because an animal goes with its head bent down, watching the road, if it stumbles on a pitcher left on the road by Reuben, Reuben is not liable in damages for losses caused to the animal thereby.[11] The reasoning for this rule, it seems, is that in such a case the cause of the accident is not the obstacle but the conduct of the animal.

---

[9] Maimonides, Damages to Property 13:5; Ḥoshen Mishpat.

[10] *Magid Mishne*, ibid.

[11] Maimonides, Damages to Property 12:16; Ḥoshen Mishpat, 412,3; *Aruch Hashulchan*, 412, 5.

Rabbi Shlomo Lurie opines[12] that the general principle (that people do not watch the roads) relates only to a person walking in an ordinary way, but not to a person running away from someone chasing him. For in such a case, argues Lurie, the plaintiff can not claim that he was "absorbed in thoughts," for it is obvious that when running away, a person is not absorbed in thoughts and therefore can and should watch his way. (R. Moshe Sofer,[13] however, does not agree with Lurie on that point.)

Another exception to the rule occurs when the location of the accident is a neighborhood where one should have expected a pitcher to be left on the road: for instance, near a place where people come with pitchers to buy olive oil. It is customary in such places to leave pitchers on the road; therefore, pedestrians should be cognizant of that fact and take special care not to stumble on such a pitcher.[14] See also in the commentary *Be`er Ha`gola*: "in spite of the general rule that people are not looking carefully down at the road, in a neighborhood where it is customary to leave pitchers on the road, people should look down carefully."

We have seen that in one instance—a man walking on a road—Jewish law accepts the tendency of human beings not to watch the road as a given fact and puts the responsibility on the owner of the obstacle. Yet in another instance—in the neighborhood of a factory for olive oil—Jewish law demands that one should overcome human nature and pay attention to the road. The reason for the difference is that law must always decide between conflicting values and give preference to one of them according to moral and practical considerations. In the present case the two conflicting values are the right, on the one hand, to walk on the road safely without constantly watching the road for hidden dangers, and the right, on the other hand, to leave a pitcher on the road. It seems that the attitude of Jewish law is that in the case of walking on the road, there is no moral justification to demand that one should constantly watch his steps. On the other hand, in particular places, for instance in the neighborhood of a place where olive oil is manufactured and it is customary—out of necessity—to put pitchers on the road, it is justified to favor the right of those coming to the factory to leave their pitchers there and, hence, to demand that pedestrians watch their way in this limited area. Therefore if damage occurs as a result of not noticing the presence of a pitcher in such a place and stumbling on it, the responsibility belongs to the pedestrian, not the one who left the pitcher there. Similarly, a driver of a car who was involved in an accident can not claim as a defense

---

12 Ibid.
13 Ibid.
14 *Baba Batra* 27a; Ḥoshen Mishpat 412,2.

that the accident occurred because he had been absorbed in thoughts. A car is a dangerous thing, and a driver, while driving, must overcome the human proclivity to be absorbed in thoughts. He must pay constant attention to the road so that he will not hurt anyone while driving his car. This demand is morally justified under **these** circumstances, though it is not justified when a pedestrian walks on the road. In the case of the pedestrian it is more reasonable to demand that no one put an obstacle on the road considering the human inclination not to pay attention to the road.

The decision in *Heln Shorr v. The State of Israel* 299 (א) פד"י לא was based on a similar principle. The plaintiff was walking one night on an open highway out of town and reached a place where local barriers indicated construction. An arrow was also placed there to divert traffic to a detour. The plaintiff proceeded in the darkness and suddenly fell down into a deep ditch and was seriously injured. The court found the contractor liable in damages, for he should have anticipated late-night pedestrians and should have put barriers on the sides of the deep ditch so that passers-by would not fall down. But the court also found the plaintiff liable for contributory negligence at a level of 50%: "The existence of ditches and pits and other sorts of danger **in a place where repairs on the road are conducted** is common knowledge and a reasonable man should take cognizance of it, especially when walking in darkness." As we have noted, there is an exactly similar principle in Jewish law, i.e., that in a place where one should have expected a danger (in a neighborhood where people come with pitchers to buy olive oil), a passenger should take special care to avoid potential hidden dangers.

Similarly, in the case of *Menachem Shacham v. The Municipality of Kiryat Ono*,[15] the court found that a pedestrian is not obliged to watch carefully to detect any obstacle in the road. Briefly, the facts were as follows: The plaintiff was walking one evening on a sidewalk and stumbled on a low fence of 30 cm. height. The small fence surrounded a plant. The plaintiff did not notice the fence and the municipality claimed therefore that he was negligent. The Court of Appeals dismissed that claim and, citing the above mentioned talmudic rule, found the municipality fully liable for the damage done. On the other hand the court dismissed the claim that the municipality was also negligent on account of a non-functioning light near that plant. The court held that bulbs are known to burn out from time to time without any fault of the municipality. It was not demonstrated that, under the special circumstances of the case, the municipality should have been found liable in damages for negligence by not changing the electric bulbs

---

[15] C.A. 2004\92 Takdin 92 (1)1011.

(as would have been the case, for instance, if it would have been proved that the bulb had not been functioning for several days before the accident occurred).

The division of liability between the parties according to moral considerations and the principle: "One should be careful not to injure others, even more then not to injure oneself"

In the case of Allen Shorr, just mentioned, the court decided to divide the responsibility in equal shares between the two sides according to "moral standards," citing the dictum of Justice Denning in the case of *Davies Motor Co. v. Swan*:[16]

> While causation is the decisive factor in determining whether there should be a reduced amount payable to the plaintiff, nevertheless the amount of the reduction does not depend solely on the degree of causation. The amount of the reduction is such an amount as may be found by the court to be "just and equitable," having regard to the claimant's "share in the responsibility" for the damage. This involves a consideration, not only of the causative potency of a particular factor, but also of its blameworthiness. The fact of standing on the steps of the dustcart is just as potent a factor in causing damage, whether the person standing there be a servant acting negligently in the course of his employment or a boy in play or a youth doing it for a "lark," but the degree of blameworthiness may be very different.

In the case of *Levi Sternberg v. the Municipality of Bnei Brak*,[17] previously mentioned, the plaintiff, a young Yeshiva student, was on his way to the synagogue one morning of Ḥol Hamo`ed Succot. In one hand he was holding the *lulav* and the *ethrog* while in the other hand he was holding his *talit* bag. On the corner of Rashi street he saw in front of him a pond of sewage water collected near the sidewalk that obstructed his way. He jumped over the pond but slipped and fell down, seriously injuring himself. On appeal the Supreme Court found the defendant liable. The court also found the plaintiff liable for contributory negligence, for he should have anticipated that it was dangerous for him to jump over the sewage when both his hands were holding the *lulav* and the *talit* bag. He should have anticipated that under such circumstances he was less stable and therefore unable to maneuver so as to avoid falling in so harmful a way. The court found the plaintiff liable to

---

[16] 1949, 1 All.I.R. 620,632.
[17] Padi 43 (3) 1989.

the degree of 50% (not just 30% as in the case of *Hotel Ramada Shalom v. Amsalem*[18] where the plaintiff, a chief cook, ran in the large kitchen of the hotel while holding a big, heavy dish in both his hands. He slipped on cooking oil that had splattered from a nearby frying pan. The cook was seriously hurt and the court found the hotel guilty to the degree of 70% and the cook guilty to 30 %). The court held that in the case of the Municipality of B`nei Brak[19] the probability of a serious injury as a result of jumping over the sewage was very small and that therefore the liability should be divided between the plaintiff and the defendant in equal parts.

One should be more careful not to cause damage to others than not to cause damage to oneself

Regarding the division between the parties of the responsibility for the damage done, it seems that a more justified result would have been achieved had the court included in its "moral" considerations another one, the one that was concluded by the Tosafists from the discussion in *Baba Kama* 23a as follows: ". . . it seems that one can deduce from the present talmudic discussion that one should be more careful not to injure others than not to injure oneself." Imposing a greater degree of responsibility on the tortfeasor than on the injured party is justified by considerations of judicial policy, i.e., to educate people to anticipate the possibility that by their action or default someone might be injured. Clearly, people should also be educated to be careful so that they themselves will not be injured through carelessness; however, that educational aim is achieved through involvement in the accident itself: the injury and the physical pain and the mental suffering caused thereby. That very point serves also as a moral consideration justifying the placing of a greater onus on the tortfeasor. For the losses caused to the injured party through the accident are always much higher and more painful than the losses caused to the tortfeasor through the amount of damages paid by him for it. Dividing the responsibility for the accident and its consequences between the tortfeasor and the injured party in equal parts does not therefore seem fair. The judicial policy mentioned above—that one should be more careful not to injure others even more than he should be careful that he himself avoid injury—should also be considered and, consequently, a greater amount of responsibility should be imposed on the tortfeasor than on the injured party.

---

[18] Padi 38 (1) 72.
[19] Ibid.

2

Rabbinic Scholarship: The Development of Halakhah in Turkey, Greece and the Balkans, 1750–1900

Leah Bornstein-Makovetsky[*]

This lecture will analyze the various halakhic writings that were composed during this period by the Rabbis who flourished in the communities of Turkey, Greece, and the Balkans. The period that will be discussed is the middle of the eighteenth century until the beginning of the twentieth century and is characterized by the political and economic decline of the most important and established Jewish center in the Ottoman Empire. This halakhic literature is comprised of about 450 books which exist today; most of them have been printed while a small percentage remain in manuscript form. This analysis will not include the numerous halakhic works that were written in other parts of the Ottoman Empire.[1] Most of the authors of these halakhic writings were of Sephardic descent, a minority of Romaniot (Byzantine) origins, and only some individual authors of Italian or Ashkenazic descent. During this period most of these halakhic works were written in communities that attempted to preserve their traditional lifestyles that had been practiced for centuries. At this time cracks threatening traditional observance appeared within the community frameworks. From the middle of the nineteenth century an acute decline in religious observance can be traced within Jewish society. This erosion in orthodox observance steadily increased throughout the remainder of the nineteenth century and had a clear influence on the realm of halakhic literature. Throughout

---

[*] Senior Lecturer in the Department of Jewish History, Bar-Ilan University, Ramat-Gan, Israel. This article is based on my research on the halakhic works in Turkey, Greece and the Balkans, which was supported by the Memorial Foundation for Jewish Culture. In a forthcoming publication I survey this phenomenon as portrayed by many rabbis.

[1] See Y. Barnai, "The Jews in the Ottoman Empire," in S. Ettinger, ed., *History of the Jews in the Islamic Countries*, II (Jerusalem, Zalman Shazar Center, 1986), 238–267 (Hebrew); A. Rodrigue, *French Jews, Turkish Jews: The Alliance Israelite Universelle and the Politics of Jewish Schooling in Turkey 1860–1925* (Bloomington, IN, 1990).

this entire period there were large Jewish elementary schools and rabbinical academies (yeshivot) within the large cities. These educational institutions were focal points of Jewish intellectual life within Jewish society. The yeshivot of Istanbul, Izmir, and Salonica, most of them newly established, were especially famous, and many of their students wrote halakhic works. Many sages served as lecturers in these yeshivot, as rabbis in the various communities, and also authored halakhic writings.

In the yeshivot of the Ottoman Empire, from the sixteenth century through the end of the nineteenth century, two types of methodologies were employed, both part of the Spanish heritage from before the Expulsion of 1492: 1. Analysis of *Halakha*, in order to provide the student with an analytical aptitude, thought processes and methods of conceptualization of the Talmud, the Rashi commentary and the Tosafot dialectics. 2. A course of study of *bekiyut* or expansive knowledge, to provide the student with a broad knowledge of the Talmud. For the most part, these students studied the Talmud with the Rashi commentary, without the *Tosafot*.[2] The continuity of the talmudic methodology employed for generations in the Sephardic Diaspora throughout the Ottoman Empire resulted in the fact that halakhic creativity in these areas from the second half of the eighteenth century onwards preserved the characteristics of the halakhic writings of the sixteenth and seventeenth centuries.

The examination of about 450 volumes that were written in the Jewish communities of Turkey, Greece, and the Balkans reveals that they had been composed by about 275 authors. Most of them were penned in the large cities, a minority in medium-sized communities, and a very small number authored in the smallest of Jewish communities. Furthermore, most of them were printed, with a small minority still in manuscript form. Finally, there is evidence of many compositions that had been completed, but unfortunately were not published, and subsequently were lost through the passing years, usually in the conflagrations that plagued the communities from time to time.

The following is a breakdown of authors and books.

Istanbul: In the second half of the eighteenth century until the beginning of the nineteenth century, seventeen authors wrote twenty books.

---

2 See H. Bentov, "Methods of Study of Talmud in the Yeshivot of Salonica and Turkey after the Expulsion from Spain"(Hebrew), *Sefunot*, XVIII, (1971–1981), 5–102; D. Boyaren, "On the Talmudic Method of the Exiles from Spain" (Hebrew), *Pe'amim* 3 (1980), 75–82; J. Hacker, "Patterns of the Intellectual Activity of Ottoman Jewry in the 16th and 17th Centuries" (Hebrew), Tarbiz LIII (1984), 569–604; H. Z. Dimitrovsky, "On the Pilpulistic Method" (Hebrew), S. W. Baron Jubilee Volume, Hebrew Section (Jerusalem 1974), 111–122.

Throughout the entire nineteenth century until the beginning of the twentieth century, twenty-six authors composed forty books.

Salonica: In the second half of the eighteenth century until the beginning of the nineteenth century, thirty-eight authors wrote forty-five books. Throughout the entire nineteenth century twenty-five authors penned about thirty books.

Izmir: From the middle of the eighteenth century until the middle of the nineteenth century, one hundred fifty-three books had been written by sixty-five authors. In the second half of the nineteenth century, twenty-four rabbis authored about fifty-five treatises.

Edirne: In the second half of the eighteenth century, seven authors composed eight works. In the nineteenth century, only four sages wrote eight compositions in that city.

Bursa: At the end of the eighteenth century, there was only one author who wrote a single book in this city. However, in the nineteenth century, three rabbis who composed five books lived there.

Rhodes: In the second half of the eighteenth century, seven rabbis wrote twenty-four books that were published; other works still exist in manuscript form. In the nineteenth century, six rabbis authored eight books.

Other communities: Out of about fifty rabbis who were active in other Jewish communities, about sixty works have survived in published and manuscript form. Most of these works were composed in other Jewish communities in Greece and Turkey, while a minority had been authored in the cities of Serbia, Herzogovine, Bosnia and Bulgaria.

Halakhic Literature

During these centuries, the main concentration was in the realms of halakhic creativity, especially within the framework of halakhic monographs such as the *Mishneh Torah* by Maimonides, the *Turim* by Rabbi Jacob the son of Rabbi Asher (Rosh), and Rabbi Joseph Karo's *Beit Yoseph* commentary to the *Turim* and his *Shulḥan Arukh* code. Compared to previous decades, there was a sharp increase in the number of commentaries to these codified works. Many of the authors employed these authoritative monographs as springboards for their own compositions, writing commentaries or critical notes to these codes and at times even formulating their own halakhot within the framework or according to the order of these works of Jewish law. Moreover, one can note a sharp increase in homiletic works. There were also various books of an explanatory nature written, albeit less so than in previous generations, especially in comparison to books written in this literary genre during the sixteenth century.

From the middle of the eighteenth century until the beginning of the twentieth century, twenty-three commentaries to the *Tur*, *Shulḥan Arukh*, and the *Beit Yoseph* commentary of the *Tur* were composed. To this should be added an additional number of commentaries to these major halakhic codes that were published as pamphlets in eleven different works or as part of compositions that contained various genres of literature in different fields by varying authors.

Most of these works dealt only with part of the *Turim* code. It should be noted that attention was given almost equally to the entirety of the *Tur*, and comprehensive compositions were authored on the volumes of *Ḥoshen Mishpat* that dealt with civil law, laws that served especially as a focal point for much interest in these generations.

The literature of *Ḥidushim* (novellae) on Jewish law, called by the sages of these centuries *Piskei Dinim* (Determination of Laws), *Ḥidushei Dinim* (Novellae on Laws), or *Likutei Dinim* (Selected Laws), also flourished. Sometimes these volumes were organized into conspectuses, usually according to the Hebrew alphabet or according to the arrangement of the *Shulḥan Arukh*. Many were actually called *Ma'arakhot* (Arrangements); this genre includes about thirty-five compilations.

The crown of creative halakhic literature was the responsa literature which also flourished during the period under discussion, and the number of volumes in this field reached almost one hundred. From a numerical point of view, fewer volumes of responsa were composed during this period in comparison to the sixteenth and seventeenth centuries. The reason may be that many of the solutions that the sages of previous generations had put forth to answer the problems had proved to be the final word on those issues; hence, the Rabbis of the period under discussion were intensively involved in the genre of novellae on Jewish Law. There are thirty-six compilations of responsa in the second half of the eighteenth century. During the nineteenth century, fifty-one compilations of responsa were collected. In the beginning of the twentieth century, five collections of responsa were compiled.

Most of these books of responsa were written in Izmir, Salonica, and Istanbul, while a small number were edited in the smaller towns and villages. Furthermore, many groups of responsa by additional authors appear in more than thirty other works. In addition to these responsa, numerous single responses were published by different authors in dozens of other works.

In the responsa literature, more than in other halakhic literature, the problems of the periods are well reflected, especially those of Jewish society. Certainly, most of the authors of the various responsa were rabbis of communities and congregations. Many were considered to be the greatest of halakhic *posekim* among Sephardic Jewry, and from the farthest reaches of the Sephardic Diaspora, people appealed to them to answer their various queries.

Homiletics and Commentaries on the Bible

There exists a mutual relationship between homiletic literature and commentaries to the Bible, mainly because homiletics are based upon comprehensive commentary. Homiletic literature warrants a discussion by itself. One should note that biblical commentary had been in decline in comparison to this genre's flourishing in the sixteenth century. Most volumes of homiletics from the eighteenth and nineteenth centuries contained sermons that had actually been delivered in congregational synagogues in various cities. The rabbis would deliver these sermons on the Sabbath and at public and private social gatherings. The sermon usually touched upon the weekly Torah portion and actual events in the communities. There were some rabbis who composed and assembled their sermons in special collections or in different chapters arranged according to the nature of the sermons. The *darshanim* were obligated to be experts in Torah and *Halakhah*, in the midrashic and talmudic literature, and in the writings of Medieval and modern commentators. Many used earlier volumes of sermons and discussed halakhic issues within the framework of their sermons. The sermon had to accommodate all members of the community, both the masses and the intellectual elite who also attended. During this period, the *darshan* was expected to be original but not to the extent found in the sixteenth century when there were greater tendencies to be creative and an exaggerated pursuit of originality.[3] Perhaps this was a result of the great amount of homiletic literature that was found among the rabbis and general public and these volumes had already employed most of the possibilities for originality and creativity. Similar to the Medieval Sephardic sermon, the eighteenth and nineteenth century sermon became more anthological in nature. The sermons are essentially built upon the words of Midrash, legend and occasionally upon a *Halakha*. Philosophical/theological analysis is almost nonexistent during these two hundred years whereas it is prominent in the Sephardic sermons composed in the sixteenth and seventeenth centuries. The essential reason for this was the decline in the study of philosophy in general and specifically, of Jewish philosophy. One should note that the Kabbalah did not play a central role in the homiletic literature of these centuries despite the fact that a majority of the sermonizers were familiar with

---

[3] J. Hacker, "The Sephardi Sermon in the Sixteenth Century: Between Literature and Historical Source" (Hebrew), *Pe'amim* 26 (1986), 108–127.

the basic concepts and symbols of the Kabbalah, and among them were scholars of the Kabbalah. Nonetheless, it is clear that in this period the Kabbalah replaced the philosophical speculations that had been present in the Sephardic homiletic literature of the sixteenth and seventeenth centuries. There were also a small number of books of sermons that were composed solely upon the methodology of the Kabbalah.

The homiletic literature on the Bible is in many cases called "Commentaries to Scripture" or "A Commentary to the Torah" and the like. We have at least fifty-five complete compositions of homiletic literature written throughout the discussed period. From homiletic literature for special occasions including eulogies written in the eighteenth century, there are sixteen books. From the nineteenth century, we have thirty-one books of this type. These sermons have a significant historical value, for they include important data concerning the communities in which the sermons had been delivered, their institutions, their political, economic, social and spiritual problems, and much information concerning different personalities that lived in those communities.

Commentaries on the Mishneh, Tosefta and the Midrashim

An important branch of the explanatory literature written by the sages of these centuries was the commentaries to the legends of the Sages. This genre includes books of commentaries according to the Mishneh or Talmud, and they serve to explain the halakhic and aggadic material found there. Sometimes the titles of these works of commentaries are *Peirushim* (Commentaries), *Berurim* (Explanations) or *Ḥidushim* (Novellae). It is evident that the numbers of such works increased in contrast to previous centuries.

There are only two comprehensive commentaries to the Mishneh from this period. One of them was composed by Rabbi David Pardo who also composed the only comprehensive work on the Tosefta: *Ḥasdei David*, which contains more than a thousand pages. In contrast to the sixteenth century, in which many Sephardic scholars would explain Tractate *Avot*, in the eighteenth and nineteenth centuries, only a few such commentaries addressed it. Only one comprehensive work in three volumes was written on *Avot de-Rabbi Nathan*, that of Rabbi Nissim Yitzḥak Palache.

Most of the compilations on the Midrashim were written in the nineteenth century. Most prominent in this field is the Palachi family in Izmir.[4]

---

[4] The members of this family composed more than one hundred compositions. On Tabbi Ḥayim Palachi see Y. Hasida, *Rabbi Hayim Palachi and his Books* (Hebrew), (Jerusalem, 1968); S. Ekstein, *The Religion and the Autonomous Halakah of the Jews in Smyrna in the Eighteenth and*

The *Sifrei* aroused great interest among three well-known rabbinical scholars in the eighteenth and nineteenth centuries.[5] Only a few commentaries were composed to other midrashic works, such as *Pirkei de-Rabbi Eliezer* and the *Pesikta*.[6] Finally, some compositions of *Likutei Aggada* (commentaries on anthologies of legends) were written in Izmir, most of them by rabbis of the Palachi family.

Commentaries on the Babylonian Talmud

The Sephardic Rabbis of the eighteenth and nineteenth centuries wrote many volumes of *Hidushei Torah*. This phenomenum reflects the spirit and atmosphere that could be found in the yeshivot, especially the desire to struggle with difficult comments by the sages of the *Tosafot* school, in order to comprehend correctly the opinions of *Tosafot*, explain their positions, and reach proper conclusions. Thus they continued in the paths of their mentors of the sixteenth and seventeenth centuries. The compositions on the Talmud bear the title *Sheeta* (Position) or *Hidushei Massekhtot* (Novellae on the Tractates); sometimes they would be entitled *Pilpulim* or *Hidushei Gefet*.

During this period under discussion, in Turkey, Greece, and the Balkans, twenty-three complete sets of *Hidushim* or *Sheetot* were written either on specific tractates of the Talmud or on a number of tractates in one volume. These commentaries are on a wide range of tractates. Among these works are many comprehensive ones, including three volumes on Tractate *Ketubot*, *Heena ve-Hisda*, authored by Rabbi Joshua Solomon Ardite in Izmir in the nineteenth century. In addition, commentaries on individual pages of many different tractates were included in forty-three other books. Furthermore, some compilations were written containing explanations of talmudic legends, in which essays on ethics were usually included.

Commentaries on the Jerusalem Talmud

The Jerusalem Talmud, which from the seventeenth century onwards has increasingly interested scholars of *Halakha* throughout the world, did not inspire much literary activity by the Ottoman Rabbinical scholars of the

---

Nineteenth Centuries as Reflected in the Activities and the Decisions of Rabbi Hayim Palachi, a doctoral dissertation (Yeshiva University: New York, 1970) (Hebrew).

[5] Rabbi David Pardo, *Sifrei Devei Rav* (Salonica, 1759); Rabbi Yitzhak Pardo, in his book *To'afot Re'em*; Rabbi Hayim Palachi, *Sifrei Hayim* (Smyrna, 1881).

[6] Rabbi Hayim Palachi wrote only nine pages on Pirkei de-Rabbi Eliezer, *Par Ehad* (Smyrna, 1880); Rabbi Abraham Palachi wrote his book *Shemo Abraham*, Vol. II on the Pesikta (Smyrna, 1896).

eighteenth and nineteenth centuries. Only a few individuals were involved in its study. In the eighteenth century, Rabbi Binyamin Kazish, one of the sages of Istanbul, wrote a commentary to the Jerusalem Talmud which has yet to be published. In nineteenth century Izmir, Rabbi Nissim Avraham Ashkenazi summarized his comprehensive literary endeavors in four volumes on the Jerusalem Talmud (*Zera'im, Mo'ed, Nashim*, and *Nezikin*) entitled *Nechmad le-Mar`eh*. His fellow townsman, Rabbi Shmuel Krispin, also wrote in the nineteenth century the book *Ben Meshek*, which includes, in alphabetical order in its beginning, various principles concerning the Jerusalem Talmud.

Literary Works of the Geonim

It is well known that the Sephardic Rabbinical scholars of these centuries demonstrated a growing interest in the responsa of the Geonim. They even took the time to publish some sets of Geonic responsa that had been buried in manuscripts over the centuries. A primary example of such interest is the activity of Rabbi Ḥayim Moda'i. Notwithstanding, they almost never wrote commentaries on these works of the Geonim.

Only one commentary was composed on the *She'iltot* of Rav Achai Gaon and that was by Rabbi Yitzchak Pardo in Sarejevo and was included in his book *To'aphot Re'em*. Similarly, on the *Halakhot Gedolot* only one commentary was written and that was by Rabbi Shlomo Shalem, the rabbi of the communities of Sofya and Belgrade in the eighteenth century.

In contrast, the *Sefer Mekah u-Mimkar* by Rav Hai Gaon, enjoyed great popularity. This compilation is the greatest of Rav Hai's works and one of the classics in halakhic literature. It was often quoted by the Sephardic sages through the last generations. It is known that at least two scholars, Eliyahu Hazan and Eliyahu Israel, wrote commentaries on this work, but these compositions have since been lost.

Commentaries on Maimonides, Rishonim and Acharonim

Maimonides' Mishneh Torah also enjoyed tremendous popularity among the Sephardic Rabbis from the time of the Expulsion onwards. This did not lessen in the eighteenth century and in the nineteenth century and the number of complete or partial commentaries on Maimonides' magnum opus amounts to dozens. These include some comprehensive works in many volumes on the *Mishneh Torah* and its classical commentaries.

From the middle of the eighteenth century until the beginning of the nineteenth century, twenty-four books were written on the *Mishneh Torah*.

During the nineteenth century, twelve volumes were compiled. Furthermore, many partial works were composed on the Mishneh Torah, usually in the form of pamphlets or part of another book.

Explaining the opinions of Maimonides was quite popular among the sages, but other halakhic works by *Rishonim* and *Acharonim* also inspired the interest of these sages. The Rabbis of the eighteenth century were especially interested in these works. On the *Sefer Mitzvot Gedolot (SeMaG)*, only three treatises were written, all in the eighteenth century. Also in this century, two significant works were written on the *Mordekhai* and another two on the *Sefer Ha-Terumot*. Likewise, a few books were composed on the works written by other *Rishonim*. On the *Acharonim* only a scant number of commentaries were written.

The Literature Concerning Rules and Monographs on Various Halakhic Topics

The literature concerning rules was quite widespread among the sages of those generations who compiled books of rules on the Tosefta, the Babylonian Talmud, the Jerusalem Talmud, the Geonim, the *Rishonim* until the generation of Rabbi Joseph Caro and Rabbi Moses Isserles (Rama). During the nineteenth century, four books about the rules of the Babylonian Talmud (*Klallei ha-Shas*) were written. Moreover, some monographs on various halakhic topics were authored. The topics include sacrifices, writs and deeds, and laws of kashrut (dietary laws).

I would like to note some additional points in regard to the nature and development of the halakhic literature which was surveyed in this presentation. Alongside the halakhic literature, many works in Jewish mysticism, the Kabbalah, were written during this period. However, their numbers are quite small when compared with the quantity of halakhic literature that was produced. It should be noted that the intense involvement in Halakhah and Kabbalah brought an acute reduction in the study of philosophy and the sciences, realms of study that had still comprised the intellectual world of many rabbis in the sixteenth century. Consequently, philosophical/theological speculation is almost non-existent during these two centuries in Sephardic Halakhic literature. In contrast to this, during the eighteenth and nineteenth centuries the Masters of Halakhah extensively quoted Kabbalistic literature, concepts, or commentaries throughout their halakhic works.

It is striking that in the last centuries Izmir had become the center where most halakhic books were compiled. Next came Istanbul and Salonica, cities that originally had been the center for halakhic culture. The growth and flourishing of Izmir can be simply explained by the Jewish community's relatively good economic circumstances in comparison to her sister communities. Hence, it was her rabbinical academies that were flourishing during this period of decline in the Ottoman Empire.

It is also important to note the total concentration of the rabbis of these generations in halakhic creativity as they prepared themselves for the study of the *Halakha* itself. Their intellectual talents were essentially channeled into creative halakhic thought and original formulations of Jewish law and these endeavors were the source of their fame among contemporaries. A perusal of their responsa literature demonstrates that they attempted to meet the challenges of the problems of their generations and tried to offer the best possible halakhic solutions.

Many of the rabbis of this period had a developed sense of the importance of bibliographical information and hence included extensive bibliographies in their works. As an example, mention can be made of the bibliographical achievements of Rabbi Hayim Palachi who noted in every one of his writings dozens of earlier compilations.

Although there had been contact between some Sephardic sages and their Eastern and Western European contemporaries, and despite many well-known Ashkenazic books that had made their way to Sephardic libraries, it should be further noted that until the second half of the nineteenth century, Sephardic Jewry would generally not accept European Ashkenazic spiritual influences. One more striking fact should also be emphasized: only a part of this great harvest of late Sephardic halakhic literature was constantly employed by the Sephardic Rabbis from the second half of the nineteenth century to the present day. The reason for this was the decline of Torah study in the Jewish society of the Ottoman Empire during this period and the sharp drop in Sephardic yeshivot which resulted in the fact that most of the books mentioned herein were relegated to a deserted corner, unwanted and unused.

3

JEWS AND THE MEDIEVAL SLAVE TRADE: THE LAW AND ITS HISTORICAL CONTEXT

DAVID M. COBIN[*]

Allegations that the Jews played a dominant role in the African slave trade to the Americas have been effectively disproved.[1] Too few Jews lived in the New World and too few Jews were involved in slavery to give Jews a significant role.[2] However, there was a time and a place when Jews were dominant in the slave trade: Europe in the ninth and tenth centuries. This paper will focus on the historical circumstances that led to such dominance, in both the Jewish and non-Jewish world, and the legal decision that enabled Jews to engage in the commercial trade of human beings.

Our study must begin in the non-Jewish world. Charlemagne died in the year 814. During his remarkable nearly fifty-year reign, the inhabitants of Western Europe enjoyed a new prosperity. The unification of Europe and good relations with the East under Charlemagne had brought spices and luxuries to the backward lands of Europe. Following his death, however, weak and divided leadership brought an end to prosperity. Charlemagne's only son, Louis the Pious, was incapable of keeping the kingdom together. He unsuccessfully attempted to arrange a succession plan and divide the kingdom among his three sons, Charles the Bald, Lothair and Louis the German. His plan was to give the title and bulk of the estate to Lothair, the eldest. However, the younger sons would not agree and, from 829 onward, the younger sons fought against each other, their elder brother, and their father. Louis died in 840, and the younger brothers combined against

---

[*] Professor, Hamline University Law School, 1536 Hewitt Avenue, St. Paul, MN 55104.

[1] For an example of such allegations, see *The Secret Relationship Between Blacks and Jews*, Vol. 1 (The Nation of Islam, 1991). For a refutation, see David Brion Davis, "The Slave Trade and the Jews," *New York Review of Books* Vol. 41, No. 21 (December 12, 1994) 14.

[2] The total Jewish population in the United States in 1820 has been estimated as a maximum of 2,750. Ira Rosenswaike, "The Jewish Population of the United States from the Census of 1830," in *The Jewish Experience in America*, vol. 2 (American Jewish Historical Society, 1969) at 19c.

Lothair. Following a great and bloody battle, in 843 the brothers signed the Treaty of Verdun and divided the kingdom into three roughly equal parts. The empire, however, would continue to disintegrate for another thirty years. The end result was a region, weak, poor and divided.[3]

The inhabitants of Europe wanted a return to prosperity through trade with the East, but circumstances made such trade next to impossible. A devastated Europe had little to export in exchange for Eastern luxuries. Their best commodity was slaves, available from conquests in Slavic lands and desirable to Muslims.[4] Relations with the Muslim East, however, had deteriorated. Christians and Muslims were no longer speaking with one another. Furthermore, the Mediterranean region, at the center of the trade, was fraught with danger. Vikings raided from the west, Muslims from the south, and Magyars from the east. All three converged on the Mediterranean Sea, which separated East and West.[5] The Europeans could not, would not do the trade themselves. How then could they engage in trade with the East? Use the Jews.

Why the Jews? First, Jews were living virtually everywhere along the desired trading routes. A diagram showing the distribution of Jews in the middle of the sixth century indicates Jews living in cities such as Lutena (Paris), Orleans, Nantes, Avaricum, Dijon, Chalon, Macon, Trevoux, Lugdunum, Vienne, Clermont, Bordeaux, Auch, Tolosa, Narbonne, Agde, Avignon, Arles, and Marseilles in the region known as France today.[6] Jews lived in nearly every city in Byzantium, as far east as Shiraz in Persia, and as far south as Aden in Arabia.[7]

Second, the ninth century was a rare time of reduced anti-semitism in Europe. During this period Christians were willing to look to Jews for help. Testimony of Jews' position comes from the great enemy of Jews at the time, Agobard, the Bishop of Lyon. He complained that many favors were granted Jews by the court, and Jewish women paraded around displaying the fine dress they wore. He further complained that some Christians said the rabbis were better preachers than the priests. As a result of actions that Agobard took against Jews, he was dismissed from court.[8] Another ex-

---

3 For a discussion of the turmoil which followed Charlemagne's death, see, e.g., "Collapse of the Carolingian Empire: Civil Wars and the New Invasions," in Robert S. Hoyt, *Europe in the Middle Ages* (New York 1966), 167–172; See also B. Tierney and S. Painter, *Western Europe in the Middle Ages*, 300–1475 (New York, 1970) 11–113.

4 See H.H. Ben-Sasson, ed., *A History of the Jewish People* (Harvard, 1976) 395.

5 For a diagram showing the confluence of the three invasions on the Mediterranean Sea, see B. Tierney and S. Painter, *Western Europe in the Middle Ages*, 300–1475 (New York 1977), 114.

6 Haim Beinart, *Atlas of Medieval Jewish History* (Jerusalem, 1992), 14–15.

7 Ibid.

8 Edward James, *The Origins of France* (London 1982), 103.

ample of Jews' acceptance comes from Charlemagne himself. He chose a Jew named Isaac to serve as his ambassador to Baghdad.[9] Still another comes in the case of Bodo, a nobleman destined for high clergy. In the year 838 Bodo converted to Judaism and took the name Eleazar.[10] These examples all suggest that, at this time, Jews were acceptable trading partners for European Christians.[11]

Third, mutual hostility meant that western Christians had little contact with either Muslims or Byzantine Christians in the East. Jews, on the other hand, traded with all of them. Thus, Jews could make deals between the East and West that neither Christians nor Muslims could make independently.[12]

Fourth, the dominant merchants of the period were a group of Jews known at the time as 'Radhanites'. A book written at the time by the Arabic traveler Ibn Khurdadhbe, wrote that "Jewish Merchants called Radhanites" operated along several routes stretching from Western Europe to China.[13] These merchants spoke six languages: Arabic, Persian, Greek, French, Spanish, and Slavonic.[14] While there is some dispute,[15] most modern scholars agree that the Radhanites originated in Iraq.[16] Radhanites were willing to continue the trade—despite the Viking, Muslim and Magyar raiders—because they had established relatively safe routes and, if captured, were most likely to be redeemed by fellow Jews. The rabbis considered providing ransom for captive Jews a greater *mitzvah*, a religious duty, than giving charity for the poor.[17] All of these factors made Jews logical agents for the Christian trade with the East, using slaves as items for exchange.

The only thing that stood in the way of Jews playing a prominent role in the European slave trade was the law. Under Talmudic law if a Jew purchased a non-Jewish slave that slave must be converted within the first day.[18] An exception in the Talmud was made for a male Jew who was not

---

[9] Id. at 102.

[10] Id. at 104.

[11] See H.H. Ben-Sasson, ed., supra n. 4 at 410–510.

[12] Id. at 397.

[13] Ibn Khurdadhbe, *Geographie*, ed. De Goeje, *Bibliotheca Geographorum Arabicorium VI* (1889), 153. See Moshe Gil, "The Radhanite Merchants and the Land of Radhan," *Journal of Economic and Social History of the Orient*, Vol. XVII, part 3 at 299.

[14] Id. at 299–300.

[15] See Charles Verlingen, "Les Radaniya et Verdun: a propos de lat traite des esclaves slaves vers l'Espagne musulmane aux IXe et Xe siecles," in *Estudios en homenaje a Don Claudio Sanches Albornoz en sus 90 anos* (Buenos Aires, 1983) Vol. 2, 105–32. Verlingen maintains the position that the Radanites originated from Europe.

[16] See Gil, supra n. 13; Mark R. Cohen, *Under Crescent & Cross—The Jews in the Middle Ages* (Princeton, 1994) 79.

[17] *B.B.* 8a and 8b. See *Encyclopedia Judaica*, vol. 5, 154–155.

[18] *Yev.* 48b.

sure he was willing to be circumcised. The master could wait up to a year for the slave to make his decision.[19] Once converted the slave could not be sold to a non-Jew. If such a sale were made, the master would have to pay up to ten times the slave's value, some said a hundred times, to reacquire the slave.[20] If a converted slave were freed, he or she became a full member of Jewish society.

Under these principles, Jews could not legally purchase non-Jewish slaves from Christians, convert them, and then sell them to Muslims; nor could they sell the slaves to Muslims without giving them the opportunity to convert. So, after being engaged in the trade for some time, the Jewish merchants sought a ruling.

Despite Jews' dispersal across Eurasia, in the ninth century the Geonim of Babylonia, in Sura and Pumbedita, still held singular authority. Merchants asked the following question to Rav Naḥshon Bar Zadok, Gaon of Sura from 871–879:

> In our place people are used to buy slaves cheaply and there is no better trade than this. May we sell them at once without initiating them into Jewish rites, because only one out of a hundred abide in his newly accepted religion, and we get great profit from this trade?

Rav Naḥshon gave the following reply:

> Because they do not take the *mitzvot* onto themselves it is permitted to sell them to non-Jews. When the *Chachamim* said it is forbidden to sell Jewish slaves to non-Jews the slaves had taken on the *mitzvot*, but since these have not taken on the *mitzvot*, it is permitted.[21]

Thus Jews became the dominant slave traders during the ninth century and into the tenth. During the tenth century, the growth of anti-semitism, combined with Christians' refusal to leave slave-trade profits to Jews, served to end Jews' dominant position. But for nearly a hundred years Jews

---

[19] Another recognized exception took place when the former master sold a slave under the condition he not be circumcised. Mordechai Bar Hillel ha-Kohen, writing in the thirteenth century, stated that this exception could be used if the government prohibited slave conversions to Judaism. *Halakhot*, Yev. no. 41. Salo Baron has hypothesized that this sweeping evasion must have originated earlier when there was a more extensive slave trade. S.W. Baron, *A Social and Religious History of the Jews*, Vol. 4, 189. If this understanding had been widespread in the ninth century, however, there would have been no need for the ruling requested of Rav Naḥshon herein.

[20] *Giṭṭ.*, 44a.

[21] *Shaare Tzedek*, Book 3, Chap. 6, No. 27.

dominated this abhorrent practice: marching slaves chained in caravans from the place of their purchase, usually northern France, down across France to Spain, then to Morocco, and across the north coast of Africa, to be sold to Arabs, for whom they would likely become soldiers or concubines.[22] They did so because Europeans desired luxuries and, for a time, did not hate Jews. And, for the first time, they did it with rabbinic approval.

---

[22] See H. Beinart, supra n. 6, at 26.

4

"LEGISLATED SPIRITUAL DISCIPLINES:" JACOB AGUS' PHILOSOPHY OF JEWISH LAW

ELLIOT N. DORFF[*]

Jacob Agus was among the first to develop a philosophy of Jewish law distinctive to Conservative Judaism. Zacharias Frankel had long since argued for the legitimacy of change within Jewish law while still maintaining loyalty to it, and others like Alexander Kohut and Israel Friedlaender had subsequently continued and expanded that line of argumentation. Solomon Schechter had called attention to the role of "catholic Israel" in defining the content of the law, although not with much clarity or depth. Louis Ginzberg, Louis Finkelstein, and many others at the Jewish Theological Seminary of America had written essays and books about specific topics within Jewish law, but none had seriously and thoroughly tackled the philosophical questions inherent in the historical approach they were taking in their scholarship. Mordecai Kaplan was the sole exception, but his view of God in deistic terms as the power in nature that makes for salvation forced him to interpret Jewish ritual law as mere folkways, a view that was destined to split off from the Conservative Movement and become Reconstructionism.

In the late 1940s and the early 1950s, though, several factors made it imperative to formulate a distinctly Conservative philosophy of law. The Holocaust had just wiped out the eminent rabbinical seminaries of Europe. That meant that American Jews could no longer depend on, and were no longer constrained by, European rabbinic scholarship. On the contrary, American Jewry had suddenly become the largest Jewish community in the world, a place it occupies to this day. American rabbis, then, had to take on the responsibility of shaping Judaism in the last half of the twentieth century. Since the vast majority of America's Jews were affiliated with the Conservative Movement—still the largest religious movement in North America—that task was especially critical for Conservative rabbis. Boaz

---

[*] Rector and Professor of Philosophy, University of Judaism, 15600 Mulholland Drive, Los Angeles, CA 90077.

Cohen, Robert Gordis, and others leaped into the fray in what must have been an immensely exciting and heady time.[1]

It was precisely in this context that Jacob Agus wrote the philosophical essays which were to become the cornerstone of his later work in Jewish law. They were first published in the journal *Conservative Judaism* in close succession: "Torah M'Sinai" (February, 1947), "Law in Conservative Judaism" (February, 1948), and "Laws as Standards" (May, 1950). Those essays, together with his Seminary lecture, "Pluralism in Law" (Summer, 1953), subsequently appeared as Chapters 6, 7, 8, and 9 of his 1954 book, *Guideposts in Modern Judaism*.

In these writings Agus managed to develop what was arguably the most thoroughgoing philosophy of law for the Conservative Movement. More than anyone else (with the possible exception of Robert Gordis), Agus spelled out not only what the Conservative approach to Jewish law was and should be, but why one should adopt it. This required him to articulate not only an approach to Jewish law, but also a theory of revelation and, ultimately, a theology. On each of these topics Agus' arguments combine the latest in modern scientific theory with the knowledge we have gained through an historical approach to the Jewish tradition. As such, Agus quintessentially preserves all three of the characteristics which became the hallmarks of Conservative Judaism: a theistic, personal God who commands; an historical approach to understand the Jewish tradition, including its legal texts and practices; and a willingness to integrate those first two principles in concrete legal decisions.

A quarter-century later, Agus, who wrote on many other topics as well, returned to the subject of a Conservative philosophy of Jewish law. In his essay, "Halakhah in the Conservative Movement" (1975), he addressed the Rabbinical Assembly, the organization of Conservative rabbis, in very appreciative and hopeful terms. He understood the developments of the

---

[1] Mordecai Waxman collected and translated some of the relevant essays by Frankel, Kohut, Davidson, Schechter, Ginzberg, Kaplan, and Gordis in his book *Tradition and Change: The Development of the Conservative Movement* (New York: The Burning Bush Press, 1958). Boaz Cohen's essay on this topic, "Towards a Philosophy of Jewish Law," first published in 1949, has been reprinted in his book, *Law and Tradition in Judaism* (New York: KTAV, 1959), 1–38. Some of the early material (including one of Agus' essays) is reprinted along with some later essays in Seymour Siegel, ed., *Conservative Judaism and Jewish Law* (New York: The Rabbinical Assembly, 1977). In February, 1980, George Nudell wrote an unpublished, class paper entitled, "The Clearing House: A History of the Committee on Jewish Law and Standards." It describes the vicissitudes of the Committee to that point, together with the arguments which produced those vicissitudes. The paper is available through the Rabbinical Assembly office (3080 Broadway, New York, N.Y. 10027).

intervening years to be concrete indications of the accuracy and appropriateness of his own approach, and he suggested further plans for the future to embody this philosophy even more. As he put it then, "We must think of ourselves not merely as children of our forefathers, but also as ancestors of our children's children. We have to create fresh tradition."[2]

This essay, then, will concentrate on the essays listed above while noting relevant material in his other philosophical works which expanded on his vision of Jewish law. We will also see how Agus applied his perception of Jewish law to several concrete cases he addressed in responsa for the Conservative Movement's Committee on Jewish Law and Standards. In doing so, we hope to recapture an approach to Jewish law which, in this author's opinion, has much to teach us today.

The Sources of Authority for Jewish Law: Reason and Revelation

Following a long line of Jewish philosophers, Agus speaks of two "pillars" which form the foundation of Judaism: reason and revelation. He argues against those who would base Judaism on either one of those alone.

Revelation cannot be the exclusive source of Jewish law's authority, according to Agus, because "there can be no inner correspondence between our present feeling and the events of several thousand years ago."[3] That is, even if we want to believe that verbal revelation took place amidst thunder and lightning at Sinai, our own experience does not give us warrant for that belief, for we now do not experience such a revelation. The Passover liturgy wants us to identify with that event when it proclaims that "In every generation a person must see him/herself as if s/he left Egypt," but even that liturgy recognizes that the best it can hope for is that contemporary people **see** (that is, imagine) themselves **as if** they had left Egypt. Thus immediate experience will not provide the necessary ground for Judaism for contemporary Jews, even if it did for those who stood at Sinai.

Moreover, reason is necessary for faith if one "is to escape the manifold pitfalls of unbridled superstition and unmitigated fanaticism." The religious bent in people is that which recognizes human limitations and dependence on factors beyond human comprehension and/or control. Keen awareness of those elements in our experience makes for passivity, accep-

---

2 Jacob Agus, "Halakhah in the Conservative Movement," *Proceedings of the Rabbinical Assembly 1975* (New York: Rabbinical Assembly, 1976), 113. The entire essay appears at 102–117.

3 Jacob Agus, *Guideposts in Modern Judaism* (New York: Bloch Publishing Company, 1954), 279. Agus does not use the Passover liturgy to illustrate this point, as I do in the next several lines, but I think that it is in keeping with his meaning.

tance, and thankfulness. Religious people are therefore all too prone to accept superstitions as absolutely true and to acquiesce to fanatic and sometimes downright immoral actions based on blind faith in what is presented as religious truths, often on the basis of some interpretation of the religion's official revelation. Reason, then, is necessary to counteract these inclinations.

Reason is also necessary to balance another common religious tendency, namely, the emphasis on inwardness. In some forms of mysticism, for example, one turns inward to find God, either with the help of revelation or as a substitute for revelation. Often this is accompanied by a disdain for reason and a denial of the reality of the physical world. For Agus, though, genuine piety requires a dialectic from subjectivity to objectivity, and vice versa. One must balance inner perceptions and emotions with reason and experience focused on the world outside us. "For the life of the spirit is not a static reflection and crystallization of the Truth, but a dynamic apprehension of it from every changing angle, in the ceaseless change of perspective from subjectivity to objectivity, and back again. . . . To condemn objective piety [based on reason] on the grounds of inwardness is therefore to betray the marks of spiritual astigmatism."[4]

And finally, Agus notes, in our day revelation cannot justify propositions which are not supported by reason, even if there are no compelling proofs to the contrary and even if such propositions are deemed necessary for one's salvation. That is, revelation cannot fill in gaps left by reason. That is because "the dogma of 'Torah M'Sinai,' in its fundamentalist interpretation, is no longer a 'live' proposition to those who have made their own the spirit of Western culture and the modern methods of research in the history of religions."[5] In the past, Jews—perhaps even large numbers of them— may have believed that the manuscript of the Torah that we have in hand is the literal word of God at Sinai and therefore supersedes all other forms of knowledge in its authority and indeed sets the criteria for what will count as knowledge from any other source. In the modern world, however, that is no longer true. Western culture has all but totally triumphed among Jews, and therefore even religion must submit to the canons of intersubjective reason for its analysis and validation. In such a context, Agus asserts, basing the authority of Jewish law on a literalist interpretation of the Torah **in the absence** of rational grounds for believing what it says is no longer even what William James would call a "live" option for contemporary Jews. Where reason seems to **contradict** propositions affirmed on

---

4 Ibid. at 301, 302.
5 Ibid. at 280.

the basis of the Torah, revelation would lose even more credibility in the eyes of moderns.

On the other hand, Jewish law's claims to authority, according to Agus, should not be based on reason alone. When one does this, as many nineteenth-century Jewish thinkers did, "the Law is stripped of every vestige of authority, the whole range of tradition is denied any inherent truth-value, and worship becomes a mere human exercise in mnemonics."[6] For if reason is the sole source of authority, everything else—law, beliefs, story, revelation, poetry, custom, history—becomes a handmaiden in its service, demonstrating or reenforcing rational principles in some way. This strips Jewish law of its inherent authority, making whatever sanction it has a derivative of reason.

Reason, however, cannot sustain such a burden, and Agus provides four reasons to demonstrate why.[7] First,

> religious consciousness is a realm of unique values, *sui generis*, even as art and music, so that in it the concepts of ethics and esthetics acquire a special tone and substance. Beauty is transmuted into a feeling of the Divine, duty is viewed as self-orientation to the Divine Will and the measure of right and wrong is construed as the judgment of God.[8]

That is, even where reason can help us to understand phenomena like moral principles or aesthetic qualities, those phenomena, when viewed by reason, appear in its specific light. They take on a completely different coloration and meaning, however, when experienced in the context of religion. If one's view of these phenomena is going to be adequate to their substance, then,

---

[6] Ibid.

[7] In a later passage (at 301), Agus indicates why reason cannot be used exclusively to account for **any** area of life:

> The pole of reason or objectivity must be constantly replenished with subjective insights, if it is to keep from degenerating into a hollow mockery of itself. First, it must assimilate the subjective feeling of trust in reason itself. Second, it must operate with the subjective intuitive valuations of the sanctity of the human person, the validity of the goal of the Good or the validity of the moral law and the perception of beauty and harmony. Third, it renews itself and ascends to a higher level only thru (*sic*) periodic intuitive insights, that is, periodic reversions to the pole of subjectivity.

In religion, for Agus, revelation provides the pole of subjectivity, and hence with regard to religion he argues specifically for the need for revelation. As this passage indicates, though, Agus maintains that reason would need some such element of subjectivity in other areas of human experience as well for the reasons he mentions in this passage.

[8] Ibid. at 281. All citations in the next few paragraphs, in which I explain Agus' reasons for claiming that reason is not a sufficient ground for Jewish law, come from pp. 281–282 of *Guideposts*.

one must use both reason and other avenues of knowledge appropriate to the specific phenomena to know and understand them. In the case of Jewish law, the other appropriate approach is through revelation, as Jewish sources themselves attest.

Second, within religious consciousness all objects are seen as dependent and creaturely, functions of a higher power. That is, religious people view our finite world as limited in its power and dependent on that which goes beyond it. This perception is not a reasoned inference, but rather "an immediate intuition of the transcendent." One recognizes such a perception of our finite world as appropriate without creating a rational argument to claim so, but rather as soon as one experiences it. It is like the experience of trying on a pair of eyeglasses: one knows whether the view of the world they give you is right or not immediately. If asked to do so, one may be able to supply some arguments to demonstrate that a particular view of the world is suitable, but such arguments are not the basis of one's conviction that the eyeglasses give you a proper vision of the world; that comes from the experience itself. Reason is therefore not the sole ground of our religious knowledge.

Third, religion in general, and religious law in particular, develop organically. They are not the product of eternal, abstract truths applied in some ivory tower; they grow instead out of the continuing experiences of a community which affirms a religion's truths and lives by its laws. Because this is so, reason is really incapable of capturing much of the substance of Jewish law. Reason, after all, is universal in its nature, while Jewish law is peculiar to the Jewish people. Furthermore, a rational argument is, at least in theory, valid or invalid forever, while Jewish law is subject to changes over time. Jewish law may derive some of its authority from the rational and moral purposes it serves, but the particular and developing qualities of Jewish law prove that that cannot be the whole story.

And finally, fourth, "revelation is an actual phenomenon, not merely a euphemism, and Judaism is a revealed religion." In other words, any interpretation of Judaism which denies the revelational base of it in favor of reason alone is to that extent distorting Judaism.

Agus defines revelation as "the belief that truth and creative vision may come to man from God, thru [sic] channels other than the physical senses." He distinguishes three stages of revelation: (1) the intuition of the objective validity of ethical values; (2) experiencing the highest levels of religious feeling, designated "the feeling of the holy," "when the awareness of Divine mystery and majesty is the supreme note in man's consciousness," prompting one to dedicate oneself to God in the moral forms revealed in the first stage of revelation; and (3) "the covenant or destiny experience," when one acquires new insight and creative energy, such as the revelations which led to the appearance of Judaism in midst of the pagan world. All people are recipients of the first two levels of revelation if they open themselves to receiving it, but the third stage is the possession of only a privileged few.

Just as the second stage of revelation includes and fortifies the first, so too the third stage proves "its authenticity by the intensification it affords to the first two phases of revelation. . . . Religion, in the specific or Jewish meaning of the term, is thus seen to be inherently related to the ethical ideal, as the roots of the tree are to its fruits." Agus, in fact, takes it as a specific mark of "the Conservative conception of the authority of Jewish law" that the higher phases are to be judged for their authenticity by their effect on the lower levels,

> for whereas the higher states of revelation gain in inspiration and in creative power over the lower ones, they decrease correspondingly in the quality of objectivity. . . . Thus, concerning every form of piety, it is legitimate to inquire whether it conduces to the good life of ethics, and in regard to every claim of Divine inspiration, it is necessary to employ the yardsticks of genuine piety, as we know it.[9]

Deuteronomy, the fifth book of the Torah, suggests two criteria for determining whether a revelation is true. Chapter 13 says that if the prophet tells you to worship other gods, that proves that s/he is a false prophet. Chapter 18 makes prophetic authenticity depend upon whether the prophet's predictions come true. Agus' criterion of moral rectitude is neither of these, but it is closer to the first, for in both Deuteronomy 13 and in Agus' approach true prophets are to be recognized by the content of their words. Deuteronomy 13, though, makes the judgment depend upon the theological correctness of the prophet's words, while Agus focuses on their moral rectitude.

Laws as Standards

Agus is not simply restating the obvious when he makes the law depend upon the combination of reason and revelation. As we have seen, his commitment to reason forces him to deny an Orthodox, literalist understanding of the Torah which would locate the authority of Jewish law—ultimately, at least—in revelation alone. On the other hand, he also finds it necessary to

---

9 Ibid. at 282, 285, 288–289.

show why reason cannot be the exclusive source of authority for Jewish law either. Probably the hardest battle he had to fight within the Conservative Movement, however, was against three popular conceptions of Jewish law which base its authority on historical and/or sociological factors.

One such theory is that proposed by Mordecai M. Kaplan, to wit, that Jewish law consists of moral demands and of folkways. Agus points out that conceiving of many of the commandments as folkways robs them of legitimacy as commandments and of authority to command unto death. Folkways lack historical legitimacy to obligate, for Judaism from its very roots denied parental folkways in order to attain patterns of action which reflect divine truth:

> Is the nostalgic reverence for parental practice to be glorified as an absolute imperative? Such a consummation would indeed offer a strange climax to the great adventure of Judaism, which began with a revolt against established customs and parental mores, as expressed in the command given to Abraham, "go, thou, from thy land, the place where thou wast born and from the house of thy fathers."

Furthermore, philosophically folkways lack the power to bind, which, for Agus, can only come from a deep conviction that Jewish law articulates divine truth:

> Why should we strive with might and main to preserve folkways? . . . The motivation of Jewish piety was actually derived from a deep conviction in the truth of Israel's religious heritage, and the consequent common sense preference of eternal reward for temporary bliss. In this interpretation [of Jewish laws as folkways], however, the glory of Jewish martyrdom for the sake of Divine truth and the soberness of its mentality would be interpreted as the senseless stubbornness of a clannish people, fanatically isolating itself from the ways of the world, forebearing all mundane goods and spiritual values for the sake of mere tribal customs.

Interpreting Jewish laws as folkways, Agus is convinced, could only appeal to a transitional generation that lost the purpose but retained the sentiment of group survival for no good reason that it could give.[10]

A second conception of Jewish law, that of Ahad Ha'am, views it as a bulwark to preserve Jewish national identity in the Diaspora. This approach, Agus acknowledges, is widespread among the American rabbinate and

---

[10] Ibid. at 323–325; reprinted in Seymour Siegel, ed., *Conservative Judaism and Jewish Law* (New York: The Rabbinical Assembly, 1977), 30–31.

laity; it is invoked whenever there are appeals to preserving the "Jewish way of life." Historically, however, Jews obeyed Jewish law out of religious conviction; the survival of Jewish nationality was an effect rather than a cause. Indeed, it is not at all clear that the survival of every branch of a biological or historical group must be regarded as a supreme end in itself; the Nazi experience, at least, should call into question any philosophy which puts ultimate value in blood and folk. And finally, if preserving Jewish nationhood is the only reason to obey Jewish law, it should become obsolete now that the State of Israel has been established, at least for those who live there and even for those who choose to bask in its reflected national glory while living elsewhere.

A third understanding of Jewish law to which Agus objects goes to the very roots of the Conservative Movement, appearing as it does in the writings of Zechariah Frankel and Solomon Schechter. It is the idea propounded by the "historical school" and rooted in nineteenth-century romanticism that Jewish law is the product of the national psyche (soul) which developed over time and that it therefore must be maintained even if—perhaps especially if—it is irrational. Here again, though, "what is to prevent historic processes that functioned relatively well in the past to function poorly in the present, or even to cease functioning altogether?" Moreover, how can historical processes "be regarded as sources of absolute value, sufficient unto themselves?"[11]

These sociological/historical views, then, cannot provide a source of validity for Jewish law. They speak to the body of the law, not its soul. But if Conservative Jews are not, for reasons of historical accuracy, going to see the Torah, much less later Jewish law, as the direct transcription of God's word, how can they understand Jewish law in a way which preserves its authenticity and authority? Agus articulates his task in this remarkably candid way:

> Let us begin our analysis then with a frank and clear rejection of the literalist Orthodox position. We do not believe that God dictated the Torah to Moses, as a scribe to a pupil, and that He had transmitted to Moses all the comments, interpretations, and inferences relating to it that were later recorded in the Oral Law. Having taken this step, we find ourselves still profoundly convinced of the importance of the Law and its supreme significance. But if these vague sentiments of reverence are to serve as the enduring foundations for Judaism of the future, they must be envisaged in all clarity as proven true in terms of the contemporary situation and

---

[11] Ibid. at 329; in Siegel, ibid. at 35.

as rooted firmly in the eternal scheme of things. How then shall we think of Halachah?[12]

He outlines five elements of a viable answer to this challenge: It must acknowledge that (1) "the relationship of the Jew to God is the incontrovertible starting point" of any theory of Jewish law which preserves the self-understanding and motivation which Jews have had historically in obeying it. (2) The commandments historically have been authoritative not only because they were seen as the word of God, but also because they purified human beings morally and served as worthy instruments of piety. (3) The authority of the commandments traditionally has rested not only on the conviction that God commanded them, but also on their acceptance by the Jewish People. (Thus, according to Rabbinic legend, "the Torah was offered to the other nations, but it is not for them obligatory since they never accepted it.") (4) In addition to the moral-legal basis of Jewish law, the Jewish people's historical memory also played a major role in affording authority to Jewish law. We all were at Sinai, and we all, along with our ancestors and descendants, agreed to become part of the Covenant with God. Finally, (5) the precepts of the law constitute the minimal standards of the community; the good person must rise above its demands and act beyond the letter of the law.[13]

These tenets together, Agus maintains, leads to a conception of Jewish law as "standards," or "divinely imposed disciplines of the Jewish people." Agus stresses that the authority of Jewish law rests on both components of that formula, namely, God and the Jewish people.

In theological language, the authority of Jewish law derives from the love of God. Agus describes God as "the Pole of the Absolute, Ideal Personality;" using the language of physics, God is the ultimate point in the field of reality. In the love of God, then, "all moral and esthetic values are fused together into a new and creative unity." God thus functions dynamically as both the source and the goal of all human ideals, and the goal of all Jewish law "may be viewed as being motivated by the one sustained attempt to incorporate the love of God as a living reality in every phase of public and private experience." But it is not God alone who is the source of authority of the commandments, for love must be mutual. Therefore, Jewish law is both "Divinely inspired and self-imposed."[14]

---

[12] Ibid. at 322; in Siegel, ibid. at 29.
[13] Ibid. at 332–333; in Siegel, ibid. at 37.
[14] Ibid. at 333–335, 340–341; in Siegel, ibid. at 38–39, 42–43. Agus develops his point-field analysis of the meaning and existence of God in Chapters Four and Five of *Guideposts*.

Furthermore, it is multiple in character. Agus proposes that we think of Jewish law as a threefold ladder leading to God, corresponding to the three pillars of Jewish faith: Torah, worship, and good deeds. This model accurately describes both the accomplishments and the remaining challenges of those who climb high on one ladder while remaining on the lower rungs of the other ladders, and it also "permits us to regard all Jewish groups, seeking sincerely to elevate the level of spiritual life, as falling within the pattern of one common endeavor."[15] Thus, conceiving of Jewish law as three sets of standards enables us to understand and appreciate what we and others have done in striving for the divine goals of morality and piety, thereby engendering feelings of pluralism and cooperation within the Jewish community, while still depicting what we all have yet to do in seeking the ideal.

Tradition and Change

Legal expressions of piety are the body which enables the soul of piety—and, derivatively, of ethics—to become part of our lives. Without such concrete manifestations of ethics and piety, our claims of commitment to the latter would be empty.

> Religious seeing . . . is not only perception, but dedication and action as well. Thus, the original insight of Judaism was never simply Knowledge of the One God, but a consecration to the service of the One God. . . . Halachah is for us the way in which God's word is progressively being shaped into ways of life.[16]

Therefore, such legal forms must be preserved. Since they are easier to grasp than the abstract goals of morality and piety, though, laws tend to be conservative in nature, evidencing little room for changing the specific way in which they embody the moral and pious elements at their core. Therefore, while Agus is careful to say that legal forms must be maintained so that revelation in both its moral and religious aspects can enter our lives meaningfully, he also makes it clear that, in his opinion, laws are "identified as instruments" and must always be subject to evaluation according to the objective goals they are designed to advance. Put succinctly, morality and piety trump laws whenever the latter get in the way of the former or cease to further them.

---

15 Ibid. at 341–342; in Siegel at 44–45.
16 Ibid. at 295, 297.

... the revealed character of Jewish legislation refers to the general subconscious spiritual drive which underlies the whole body of Halachah, not to the details of the Law. The vital fluid of the Torah-tree derives from the numinous soil of the Divine, but the actual contours of the branches and the leaves are the product of a variety of climatic and accidental causes.[17]

At the same time, "it is necessary to beware of the kind of changes that destroy the spell of the Law." Even if a given law begs to be changed because it violates our sense of morality or piety, Agus says, rabbis must take care not to change a specific law in a way which undermines respect for the law as a whole. "The new must be so delicately grafted upon the old that the health of the tree as a whole will not be affected."[18]

This, of course, complicates matters. However difficult it may be to recognize when a given law sufficiently offends our sense of morality or piety to require change, it is even harder to balance such considerations against the need to preserve the integrity of the corpus of the law. Judging the law by the objective standards of morality and piety entices one to change the law, or at least to be ready to do so. Concern for preserving the integrity of the law, on the other hand, prompts one to be wary about any change. In Agus' terms, morality and piety, which are "objective" in that they are shared by everyone, come into conflict with the "subjective" ways individuals and groups have traditionally expressed them in practice.

But that is precisely Agus' point: a Conservative position must find a way to balance both of these impulses, just as it balances reason and revelation. In contrast to the Reform position, which focuses on reason and change at the expense of revelation and continuity, and in contrast to the Orthodox position, which does the reverse, the Conservative position affirms both elements of these two pairs equally: reason **and** revelation, tradition **and** change. Similarly, in his 1975 restatement of his position, he stresses the importance of law **and** spirit (*halakhah* and *aggadah*).[19] This inclusiveness subjects the Conservative Jew to the tension inherent in balancing parts of the tradition which do not sit well together; the simplicity, clarity, and confidence of those who embrace one or the other of the ex-

---

17 Ibid. at 298. See p. 292 for his statement on the need to preserve the law as an instrument of attaining morality and piety.

18 Ibid. at 299.

19 Supra n. 2 at 106–109. There he similarly objects to the "reductionism" of Orthodoxy and Reform in restricting Judaism to the codes or the Prophets and argues instead for "a holistic approach" which uses both those sources as well as all others which have developed within the Jewish tradition and constantly weighs how they should be used in ways appropriate to our times.

tremes of any spectrum are not available to the Conservative Jew. For Agus, though, the price is worth the gain, for the Conservative position is the only one which preserves both truth and Jewish authenticity:

> ... the life of the spirit is a ceaseless movement between the two poles of objectivity and subjectivity. He who would keep his soul turned to the rhythm of truth must forever be on the move. He cannot stop at either pole and embrace the whole truth in his bosom; back and forth, he must move between the subjective and objective poles of the spirit, if he is not to petrify in static, sterile self-admiration. For reason and faith imply and fructify each other....
>
> Coming now to the problems of Judaism proper, we maintain that our employment of a two-fold evaluation in the assaying of laws and ceremonies is true to the inward nature of piety. On the one hand, we accept the Halachah subjectively; on the other hand, we subject specific halachic precepts to criticism by means of the objective standards of piety and the good life that derive from the *yetzer tov* [good inclination] of modern thought and civilization. Both approaches are integral to the life of the spirit; we cannot afford to give up either one without forfeiting the soul of our faith.[20]

Legislation as a Method of Conservative Jewish Law

Agus, though, does not have the usual notions in mind when he affirms the necessity to preserve Jewish law. On the one hand, he thinks that much more must be done than "business as usual" to engender observance of the law; he envisions, in fact, a vigorous campaign to make it a priority for the Jewish masses. On the other hand, though, he thinks that the process of applying Jewish law in our day also cannot be "business as usual"; it must instead be done using much more aggressive legal techniques. What marks both of these contrary moves—the one toward tradition, the other toward change—is balance and vigor, two characteristics that pervade Agus' thought.

First, on the side of tradition, Agus asserts that Conservative Judaism must not be characterized exclusively by the ways it has broken away from Orthodoxy. That would be to cast it in a solely negative light, defining it according to what it does **not** do. Instead, the Conservative Movement must devote itself with enthusiasm and energy to stimulating knowledge, obser-

---

[20] Ibid. at 300, 303. Agus applies this analysis to **every** aspect of life, as the passage quoted in n. 7 above indicates. The objectivity represented by reason is necessary for, and must be balanced by, the subjectivity proper to the particular area of life in question.

vance, and piety among its adherents so that it is characterized by what Conservative Jews **do**. Toward that end, the movement "must undertake a campaign for the stimulation of a minimum of religious observances among our people, stressing in particular those precepts which contribute decisively and directly to the cultivation of the spirit of piety, such as the acceptance of regular weekly worship and study periods."[21]

Agus clearly would have liked more than "a minimum of religious observances," but he was enough of an educator to discern the difference between the ideal and the possible and the need to begin with something which could clearly be accomplished. Others of his colleagues apparently agreed with his assessment of the educational realities and with this aspect of his approach to Jewish law, for his idea of a campaign to engender observance was soon to be embedded in the responsum on the Sabbath, approved by the Law Committee, which he co-authored with two other rabbis. Whether or not one agrees with his strategy, it clearly indicates that Agus wanted to shift the momentum within the Conservative Movement from what it denied to what it affirmed, and his campaign to engender observance among the many Jews affiliated with the Conservative Movement was one aspect of Agus' understanding of a Jewishly serious movement.

While dedication to observance must be one mark of the Conservative Movement, another must be its readiness to modify its content to achieve its moral and religious goals. Agus maintains that the Conservative Movement's Law Committee, as constituted at the time, is "insufficient" to the task at hand. If the Conservative Movement sees itself authorized only to interpret and apply traditional law, it will never get beyond the claims of the Orthodox to be the only authentic form of Judaism, for that is precisely what they do. Even if Conservative responsa generally prefer the lenient option within the traditional materials, the movement will not be distinctive in character and, worse, will always feel itself undermined by the learning and zeal of the Orthodox. Moreover, such an approach is based on an exaggeration of the degree of freedom embedded in traditional Jewish law, and if the Conservative Movement does nothing else, it should not, as a movement dedicated to historical Judaism, misrepresent what the historical sources say.

The way out of this problem, according to Agus, is for the Conservative Movement to have the courage and creativity to act on its own principles. What Jewish history does reveal is that various Jewish communities over time went beyond the interpretive method and legislated laws (*takkanot*). Sometimes these represented changes in what had been traditional practice,

---

21 Ibid. at 304.

and sometimes they were simply positive law to address the community's needs not covered in the received law. In like manner, Agus asserts, "We need a law making body, not a law interpreting committee."[22]

Why have the Orthodox rejected such an approach? In large part, Agus avers, because they have an exaggerated sense of the deference which must be paid to earlier sources. They are, indeed, stymied by the authority they attribute to those of previous generations who, by that very fact, are, for the Orthodox, greater in wisdom and knowledge than any contemporary person or group could be. Such an approach, though, is not necessitated by the sources themselves, which demand that we have respect for previous generations but that judges in each generation decide matters "according to what their own eyes see." Therefore, the Orthodox methodology represents a **choice** as to how to read Jewish sources, and it is an arbitrary one at that, for it flies in the face of some of those very sources. Furthermore, the automatic Orthodox preference for the earliest decisions is "a mechanical principle of selection" of what should count in determining the law rather than one based on the merits of any particular case. As such, it does not hold much promise for wisdom in applying Judaism to modern circumstances.

> If we follow the principle that the rabbis of our own days are incompetents and that the rabbis of the past were all-knowing, we undermine the very basis for development and growth in religion, even while we presume to speak in the name of religious progress. Obviously, the past cannot of its own momentum effectively progress in the contemporary world. Again, if we deny Divine sanction to the "Rishonim" [rabbis of the tenth to the sixteenth centuries] and grant it to the masters of the Talmud [completed c. 500 C.E.], or if we deny it to the Amoraim and Tannaim [the rabbis of the first through the fifth centuries C.E.], reserving it for the prophets [who lived between the ninth and the fifth centuries B.C.E.], we should be operating with a mechanical principle of selection, for which there is no basis in our philosophy of Judaism. . . . From our viewpoint, then, the present is more determinative than the past, and the immediate past more authoritative than the remote past.[23]

Agus proposes, then, that the Conservative Movement make extensive use of the method of legislation (*takkanah*). He is careful to point out that

---

22 Ibid. at 309.
23 Ibid. at 311–312. I have embellished Agus' argument here, emphasizing the choice involved in the Orthodox interpretation of Jewish sources and adding the citation from B. Bava Batra 131a that a judge must decide according to what his own eyes see, but I think that this line of argumentation is very much in keeping with both the letter and the spirit of the arguments Agus himself makes.

that is a perfectly traditional way of doing Jewish law, evidenced in Jewish history from at least as early as the first century C.E. (indeed, arguably from the time of Ezra in the fifth century B.C.E.) and continuing throughout the Middle Ages and the modern period to contemporary times. The corpus of legislation includes measures which embodied far-reaching sociological change, as, for example, in the *takkanot* of Rabbenu Gershom (c. 1000 C.E.) which decreed monogamy and the need for a woman's consent to a divorce. Thus Agus thinks that there is ample precedent for using legislation as a legal method in our own time.

Moreover, that method is definitely needed now, for, as Agus asks rhetorically, "is not our time and circumstances so strikingly new as to justify the creation of new precedents?"[24] As we shall see, he has in mind not only the needs of contemporary Jewish society to make changes in the law, but also—and, perhaps, primarily—its need for legislation to reenforce practices which Jewish law already mandates.

In addition to these historical arguments, Agus supports the use of legislation on legal and philosophical grounds. Legally, as he points out, legislation was justified on the basis of Deuteronomy 17:11: "You shall act in accordance with the instructions they [the judges of your generation] give you and the ruling they hand down to you; you must not deviate from the verdict they announce to you either to the right or to the left." The "You must not deviate" (*lo tasur*) clause in the verse Agus calls "the magna carta of rabbinic legislation," and it is, indeed, the source of authority which the rabbis of the Talmud and thereafter used to stretch the law considerably in all directions.[25] If the Conservative Movement is not going to restrict itself to the legal method of interpretation, and if, on the other hand, it is not going to abandon Jewish law altogether, then, according to Agus, it must embrace the method of legislation "or else disappear from the scene, as a movement."[26]

Philosophically, says Agus, "this principle [of *takkanah*] is fully in accord with our dynamic conception of revelation."[27] He elaborates on his own concept of revelation at length in another essay included in his 1954 book, *Guideposts in Modern Judaism* and in a subsequent book (published in 1983) as well,[28] but in referring to "our dynamic conception of revelation"

---

[24] Ibid. at 316.

[25] See, for example, Elliot N. Dorff and Arthur Rosett, *A Living Tree: The Roots and Growth of Jewish Law* (Albany, New York: State University of New York Press, 1988), 402–420.

[26] Supra n. 4 at 317.

[27] Ibid. at 312.

[28] Ibid., Part II, Section 2; see also Jacob B. Agus, *The Jewish Quest: Essays on Basic Concepts of Jewish Theology* (New York: Ktav, 1983), 43–86.

here he undoubtedly has in mind any of the concepts of revelation within the Conservative Movement, many of which were stated explicitly only after Agus made his proposal. Even so, Agus clearly realized by 1949 that, by definition of "Conservative Judaism," all Conservative concepts of revelation would have to take into account the historical development of the Torah and would understand revelation as continuing in our day through the work of contemporary rabbis and thinkers.[29] That tenet of continuous revelation, Agus maintains, also argues for contemporary rabbis to use the legal vehicle of legislation as they discern the will of God in new ways, of which only some can be reasonably derived from interpreting previous elements of the tradition. As he put it in 1975:

3. The religious experience of revelation has taken in Judaism the form of a succession of covenants with God, of which Joshua 24 is the archetypical account.
4. *Takkanah*-legislation is in effect a periodic reenactment of the Covenant in regard to a specific problem. Continuous adaptation of the Law is therefore an expression of its vitality. The range of *takkanot* may be the world-fellowships of Israel, or the national communities, or the congregations, or *havurot*, or even families.

Every *takkanah* must be within the context of the overall Covenant made with all-Israel, as expounded in the "sacred tradition" of our people. But the various Jewish communities in different parts of the world are expected to enact *takkanot* for their own communities and on a temporary basis, *takkanot hakehillot*. Special *havurot* with their own *takkanot* were characteristic of the creative ages in Jewish history.[30]

Putting the Method of Legislation into Practice

Legislation, then, is one mode of applying Jewish law which the Conservative Movement must embrace. In the past, Jewish legislation has enjoyed two sanctions, "one deriving from the most sensitive conscience and the most creative scholarship of the age, the other deriving from the democratic principle of 'the consent of the governed.'" Accordingly, Agus proposes the establishment of two bodies: a "Jewish Academy," similar to the French

---

[29] For a survey of the varying doctrines of revelation within Conservative Judaism, Agus' included, see Elliot N. Dorff, *Conservative Judaism: Our Ancestors to Our Descendants* (New York: United Synagogue of America, 1977), 110–157.

[30] Supra n. 2 at 110.

Academy of Napoleon's time, consisting of selected rabbis, scholars, and laypeople; and periodic, joint special sessions of the United Synagogue and the Rabbinical Assembly empowered to accept or reject *takkanot* proposed by the Academy.

Agus deliberately calls the first body "the Jewish Academy" and **not** "the Sanhedrin" so as to rule out from the beginning any pretensions to the authority that the ancient Sanhedrin had (at least apparently) on its own: Agus' Academy would instead act like "the upper house" of a legislature whose actions would still need the confirmation of "the lower house," i.e., the special joint assemblies he describes. Unlike the British Parliament, however, the Academy would take the primary role in studying issues and initiating suggestions for legislation. As such,

> it should consist of the greatest men in our movement, those who have achieved distinction in the fields of scholarship, rabbinic leadership, Jewish education and social welfare. Like the [French] Academy, too, appointments should be made for life or for long terms—such appointments constituting the highest marks of recognition in our movement.[31]

The Academy would, in Agus' proposal, discuss not only matters of Jewish law, but also "principles and dogmas of faith, the latest developments in various fields of study bearing upon the philosophy of religion and ways and means of dealing with specific problems."[32] It thus, in his vision, would function not only in the role of the current Committee on Jewish Law and Standards, but also in place of the Commission on the Philosophy of Conservative Judaism, which produced the first Movement statement of Conservative ideology, and perhaps also in place of some of the other current committees or commissions dealing with specific problems within the Movement (like, for example, the Conservative Movement Council, which exists nationally, in the Pacific Southwest Region, and perhaps in some other regions, consisting of the presidents or their representatives of all the arms of the Movement and which is used for joint planning purposes). While Agus' proposal may be institutionally too cumbersome, demanding much too much of any one group of people, it has the theoretical advantage of making it clear at the outset that within Conservative Judaism, law, ideology, and social policy are not to be seen as disparate, independent entities, but rather as part of an integrated whole, each affecting the other. This certainly has been a distinctive mark of much of what the

---

[31] Supra n. 3 at 313.
[32] Ibid.

Conservative Movement has done in practice in the decades since Agus made his proposal.

Two points should be made about the membership of this body. First, in speaking of "the greatest **men** in our movement," Agus was probably simply using the language of 1948, when this was written, to refer to people of either gender. Female rabbis did not exist within the Conservative Movement until 1985, and so he could not have known of that possibility, but he certainly knew of other women leaders within the Movement, and he generally was supportive of expanding women's rights.

Second, it is interesting that Agus would include as members of the Academy not only scholars and rabbis, but also "laymen."[33] In practice, the Committee on Jewish Law and Standards did not begin to include lay representatives until 1990, and then only as non-voting members and only as the result of political pressure brought by the United Synagogue. Agus would have included lay leaders in his proposal forty years earlier, presumably as voting members. While he does not justify that suggestion specifically, he presumably thought that the primary group which was to be responsible for shaping the beliefs, practices, and policies of the Movement should include at least some representatives of the masses in whose name such pronouncements were being formulated. The Commission on the Philosophy of the Conservative Movement also had lay representatives—this time as full members—but there again they were added only after the rabbis and scholars had had time to begin the work on their own. As a member of both committees, I can attest that Agus was right long ago, for the lay members' contributions to the discussions of both groups have been both insightful and valuable.

Agus considers and answers several possible objections to the establishment of such an Academy. In response to the worry that using legislation as a legal tool will lead to antinomianism, especially in the context of the large gap between rabbinic and lay patterns of Jewish observance within the Conservative Movement, Agus points out that the initial *takkanot* need not be negative, that, indeed, "There is no need for 'takkanot' to sanction non-observance, but there is great need for 'takkanot' to raise the level of observance." Accordingly, the Academy's "first task shall be to lead and guide our movement in a nationwide, 'tshuvah' [return] effort, calculated to reestablish a minimum of observance among the members of our congregations . . . so that membership in a synagogue shall not be purely a financial transaction." It is only after that has been achieved that legislation would

---

33 Ibid.

be considered to correct certain abuses in Jewish life, like the refusal of a man to grant a writ of divorce (a *get*) when there is no good reason for his unwillingness.[34]

Furthermore, as Agus points out, the principle of "catholic Israel," embedded in the Conservative Movement by Solomon Schechter, would guard against any changes considered too radical by the Conservative community. Agus' proposal, in fact, gives that community a clear voice in the process of determining Jewish law, a voice laypeople lack when the law is established exclusively through rabbinic interpretation.

Another possible objection to such legislation is the dissension it might cause among the movements and within the Conservative Movement itself. Agus dismisses the first as a serious concern on both practical and theoretical grounds. Practically, "uniformity of observance among Jewish people today is out of the question," and to wait for such agreement "would be tantamount in practice to the utter bankruptcy of our religious leadership." Theoretically, there is no reason to expect such uniformity, for the ways in which the Reform, the Orthodox, and the indifferent understand Jewish law bespeak convictions radically at odds with each other and with that of Conservative Judaism.[35]

The possibility of conflict within, and even defection from, the Conservative Movement Agus takes much more seriously. The Academy he proposes, he says, should not dare try "to make up with one fell blow for a century of arrested progress." Caution and careful deliberation will be needed. On the other hand, though, he is convinced that the Conservative Movement must adopt the way of legislation if it is to live out its ideological roots and if it is to do what must be done in our time to make Judaism a dynamic, living religion rather than a "desperate holding action" or merely a "way-station" to assimilation.

> The question raised by this objection, therefore, is a very fundamental one—to wit, is there room on the American scene for a Conservative movement, as distinguished from a Conservative way-station? To phrase the question is to answer it. There is not only room, but crying need, for a Conservative movement. If there were no such steadily emerging movement, it would have had to be created. For our time calls for a bold constructive approach, which neither Reform nor Orthodoxy can give— the former thriving on the growing decay of tradition, the latter reduced to a desperate holding action.[36]

---

[34] Ibid. at 313–315.
[35] Ibid. at 316.
[36] Ibid. at 317–318.

In sum, then, the Academy's purpose would be to function in **both** capacities which Agus demands of a living Jewish legal system: seriousness of purpose on the part of both the institutions and the individual members of the Conservative Movement, as manifested by at least a minimum of observance of Jewish law, and, simultaneously, readiness to enact legislation to make the substance of Jewish law grow in appropriate ways to meet the needs of contemporary times.

Agus' Own Responsa

Agus wrote several responsa for the Conservative Movement's Committee on Jewish Law and Standards which illustrate his principles in concrete form. Undoubtedly the most famous of them is the responsum on the Sabbath, which he co-authored with Rabbis Morris Adler and Theodore Friedman. It secured the support of a majority of the Law Committee in 1950, and it has been the subject of much debate within the Conservative Movement ever since.

One immediately sees Agus' theory at work in the responsum's call for a program for the revitalization of the Sabbath. The campaign does not demand total observance, but rather has "as its immediate goal the acceptance on the part of the people of . . . basic indispensable elements of Sabbath," which the responsum articulates in detail. The emphasis is on creating Agus' "minimal standards." These include elements of traditional Jewish Sabbath observance, such as preparation for the Sabbath and the traditional Friday night home rituals. The responsum does not demand all things required by Jewish law, however, and even those it includes are stated with room for individual adjustments. So, for example, attendance at public worship should happen "at least once on the Sabbath;" "One should refrain from all such activities that are not made absolutely necessary by the unavoidable pressure of life and that are not in keeping with the Sabbath spirit, such as shopping, household work, sewing, strenuous physical exercise, etc."; and "The type of recreation engaged in on the Sabbath should be such as is calculated to enhance one's spiritual personality in its intellectual, social, and esthetic aspects." The tone is clearly one of encouragement rather than one of obligation, and the content is explicitly directed at achieving the Sabbath's spiritual goals rather than asking for a blind obedience to the law as law.

The most controversial parts of the responsum, however, concerned riding to the synagogue and the use of electricity. The authors urged people not to use a motor vehicle on the Sabbath as an aid to both one's own repose and to keeping the family together, but they also said that "where a family resides beyond reasonable walking distance from the synagogue, the use of a motor vehicle for the purpose of synagogue attendance shall in no wise be construed as a violation of the Sabbath but, on the contrary, such attendance shall be deemed an expression of loyalty to our faith." The authors assert this because most Jews no longer know how to pray at home or to study Torah on their own, that "were it not for synagogue attendance on the Sabbath, there would be no prayer for most of our people" and no Torah study either. Furthermore, "in the spirit of a living and developing Halachah responsive to the changing needs of our people, we declare it to be permitted to use electric lights on the Sabbath for the purpose of enhancing the enjoyment of the Sabbath, or reducing personal discomfort or of helping in the performance of a mitzvah."[37]

The responsum itself announces three principles "implied in this program," principles in which Agus' philosophy is clearly evident: (1) Despite the "cynical skepticism" which some may have about such a program of reconsecration, there have been many such efforts in the past, so that what we learn from history is that "The Jewish religion does not favor the emotional excesses of the Christian 'revivalist' movements, but it fosters the principle of voluntary acceptance of a pattern of life." At the same time, the authors say, rabbis must be realistic in their demands of their community, for, as the classical Rabbis said, "To overreach is to court failure" (*tafasta m'rubah lo tafasta*), "it is better to build a fence of ten handbreadths that is likely to stand than one of a hundred handbreadths that is liable to fall" (*tov assarah t'fahim v'omed mimeah t'fahim v'nofel*), and "it is better not to say a thing which will not be heeded" (*mutav shelo lomar davar sheaino nishma*). All of these features of this principle are vintage Agus: creating a positive program for rededication; rooting one's approach in what Judaism has been historically; basing the authority of Jewish law, at least in part, on the voluntary acceptance of the people; and creating minimal standards which have a reasonable chance of being accepted rather than adopting an "all or nothing" attitude.

(2) The community power to enact ordinances is "virtually unlimited, provided its ordinances are made with consent of the resident scholars and provided further that they be inspired by the purpose of 'strengthening the faith,'" and such enactments should be made jointly "through their spiritual leaders and lay representatives." This is clearly Agus' program for using the legal vehicle of legislation (*takkanot*) to accomplish desired ends.

---

[37] Morris Adler, Jacob Agus, and Theodore Friedman, "A Responsum on the Sabbath," *Proceedings of the Rabbinical Assembly* (New York: Rabbinical Assembly, 1950), 122–123, 130. Reprinted in Mordecai Waxman, ed., *Tradition and Change* (New York: The Burning Bush Press, 1958), 361–362, 368; and, in part, in Dorff, supra n. 29 at 168–169.

Here the authors apply it to riding to the synagogue on the Sabbath and the use of electric lights, both of which they justify in this responsum not only on narrow, legal grounds, but also on principled grounds of enhancing the joy of the Sabbath (*oneg shabbat*) and, primarily, of enabling Jews who would otherwise be unable to observe the Sabbath to do so.

(3) "The power of communities to make special enactments in behalf of the faith, through their spiritual leaders and lay representatives, is in turn a corollary of the principle of development in Jewish Law." This development has historically included creating new practices and repudiating old ones. As the authors demonstrate through reference to a number of talmudic and medieval sources, the authority for that development is based, at least in part, on the necessity for the community to accept the law voluntarily for it to be valid; God's command is not enough.[38] As we have seen, these principles are deeply rooted in Agus' view of Jewish law.

These decisions were not, however, grounded only in considerations of morality, aesthetics, or piety; they also follow upon an extensive analysis of the specific legal issues involved in riding and using electricity. Thus, the theory used by the three authors was **not** to replace legal reasoning, but rather to weave it into a broader consideration of how to accomplish the goals of the law in a contemporary setting. Since most Conservative congregants drove and used electricity in any case, though, skeptics commonly interpreted the responsum as simply a way of giving retroactive sanction to the laity's practice and prospective sanction to those rabbis who wanted to do these things as well, rather than part of a concerted effort to revitalize Sabbath observance based on a serious reading of Jewish sources.

Agus himself complained bitterly about the fate of the responsum within the Movement when it was again discussed by the Law Committee eleven years later (1961). Any rabbi by himself, he points out, and even the rabbis together as a group could not possibly launch the revitalization effort on their own; from the very beginning it was to be a movement-wide effort.

> Our central agencies [by which he apparently means the lay organizations of the Conservative Movement] ignored this effort altogether, with the result that the Sabbath Revitalization effort remained merely an intra-Rabbinical Assembly project. . . . It would have been far better for the movement if the Sabbath Responsum had been directly endorsed by the Rabbinical Assembly [and not merely by the majority of the Law Committee] and freely accepted by the United Synagogue and its affiliates. We should then have had truly autonomous legislation, bearing potent ethical-spiritual influence.

---

[38] Ibid., in *Proceedings* at 124–128; in Waxman at 362–366; in Dorff at 169–171.

Agus notes that some rabbis objected to the self-declared status of the responsum as a *takkanah*, preferring that the Conservative Movement restrict itself to the more common method of interpretation. He thanks the leadership of the Rabbinical Assembly for preventing a vote from being taken on the floor of the Rabbinical Assembly convention intended to nullify its classification as a *takkanah*, and he argues that, in our time, legislation is, in fact, the **preferred** way of achieving united action because it prevents the anarchy inherent in individual opinions:

> Actually, the sole difference between a *takkanah* and an interpretation is that the former is a **communal** enactment and the latter is a private opinion. It is clear that a conscious policy of limitless commentary, allowing free interpretation by individual rabbis, borders on anarchy. On the other hand, a communal enactment is likely to restrain arbitrary and extremist policies and to frame new enactments in the spirit of the tradition as a whole and of previous precedents.

There is still plenty of room for individual rabbis to make legal decisions based on their authority as the local rabbi (*mara d'atra*, literally, "teacher of the place"), Agus maintains, but that is properly restricted to whether **this** bottle of wine is kosher, not whether, as a community, we are going to declare a principle which governs such decisions invalid in our day. That is, he draws the line "between **general** rules and **individual** applications," holding that in the former the way of legislation is the only one which prevents anarchy.

Agus says, however, that the Committee on Jewish Law and Standards should get involved in setting **policy** for individual applications of the law, especially when the issues at hand occur on a regular and frequent basis. So, for example, it is proper that the Committee discuss whether this Sabbath responsum permits driving to a synagogue other than one's own to attend a Bar or Bat Mitzvah (which Agus thinks is perfectly proper) or to visit the sick (which Agus thinks should be done only in an emergency). Given this, one wonders whether Agus has in effect vacated the status of the communal rabbi to make decisions; he certainly has limited it considerably.

Agus argues against those who object to the responsum on the grounds that it widened the rift between the Conservative and Orthodox. If ecumenicism within Judaism is the issue, he points out, then relationships with the Reform Movement should occupy the attention of Conservative leadership at least as much as ties with the Orthodox. Moreover,

> Unity is neither desirable nor attainable by way of squeezing all of Jewish life back into "the four ells of Halachah," as it took form in the

Shulḥan Arukh; nor is it either desirable or attainable by way of fostering a rank anarchy of individual interpretations behind a facade of official loyalty to the Halachah; nor is it either desirable or attainable by way of negotiations between "spiritual statesmen on the summit" on a quid pro quo basis....

To me, the only kind of religious unity which is salutary is the one that derives from the recognition of the distinction between the ethical-spiritual core of faith and the ritualistic-historical expressions of it. Hence, it is only in the growth of the liberal spirit that we can eventually attain the goal of creative unity.[39]

When Agus addressed the problem of "the chained woman" (*agunah*) in another responsum, his belief in the preferability of using legislation as a legal technique prompted him to object to the proposal put forward by Rabbi David Aronson that the rabbinic court, based on the talmudic principle that the rabbis have the right to annul marriages, should issue a writ of divorce if the husband refuses to grant one for reasons which the court finds insufficient or is missing. Agus claims that that approach requires rabbis to issue a writ which says the opposite of what is in fact the case (namely, that the husband voluntarily divorces his wife) and it misunderstands the talmudic principle in the first place to be a condition of marriage instead of what it really is, namely, an assertion of the rabbinic prerogative to govern marriage law and to institute new procedures when necessary. "On this view, we have the right to analyze the problem of divorce and the 'agunah' in basic terms." Agus does precisely that in suggesting a number of measures to deal with the various kinds of "chained women," including some suggestions openly based on the desire to equalize the status of men and women in marital law. In saying these things, Agus was objecting to a bold proposal on the part of another liberal Conservative rabbi on the grounds that there are clear limits to our ability to interpret precedents responsibly to achieve the results we need and want and that legislation is a much more honest and desirable method for doing so.[40]

Finally, it is interesting to note that Agus maintained his principles to the very end of his life. In his responsum entitled "The Mitzvah of Keruv" (1982), dealing with how the Conservative Movement should balance its

---

[39] The above description of Agus' 1961 reevaluation of the Sabbath responsum comes from his paper, "Reevaluation of the Responsum on the Sabbath," which is stored in the Rabbinical Assembly Archives as an unofficial paper submitted to the Committee—that is, a paper on which the Committee did not take a vote. I want to thank Rabbi Gail Labovitz, Administrative Assistant of the Committee on Jewish Law and Standards in 1991–1992, for making this responsum and the one cited in the next footnote available to me.

[40] Jacob Agus, "*Re Agunah*," an undated and unofficial responsum in the Rabbinical Assembly Archives.

objections to intermarriage with its desire to attract the non-Jewish spouse to convert to Judaism, he advocates communal action to assert the firmness required to resist intermarriage, for in a democratic country, people will not accept the authority of an individual rabbi but will understand and respect communal standards:

> ... So long as the spirit of anarchy is kept within bounds, legal adjustments, even if far-reaching in character, may be enacted, without damaging the structure of authority within the movement.
>
> We live in a democratic age, where the supreme authority of a *mara d'atra* [local rabbi] is likely to be disregarded, if not resented, while the collective authority of a national or world-wide body of representative rabbis, scholars and laymen is generally acceptable. A people, so religiously mature that it could glory in Rabbi Joshua's triumph over the mystical *bat kol* [voice from heaven] with the slogan, *lo bashamayim hi* ["The law is not in heaven"], can certainly be trusted in our day to understand that laws can be divine, when they are man-made. But, they are not likely to tolerate the arbitrary tyranny of the resident rabbi or scholar, acting on his own judgment.[41]

Agus' 1975 Retrospect and Prospect

In addressing the Rabbinical Assembly convention in 1975, Agus was enthusiastic about the developments of the intervening quarter-century and eager to undertake the next important steps in putting his approach into practice. He pointed out, first, that "the Conservative tendency" from its earliest stages represented an integration of German and Russian Jewish expressions mixed with a heavy dose of American individualism and pragmatism, and that Solomon Schechter and Louis Ginzberg were already moving in the same direction as he was proposing, thus giving his approach deep roots in the history of the movement.

There have historically been, in Agus's description, three ways in which Jewish law has changed, and those three ways have occurred in the experience of the Conservative movement as well. First, "a more or less unconscious process of selective neglect and selective emphasis" has produced, in Agus' understanding, aspects of Jews' personal behavior, such as adopting current American styles of dress rather than wearing *arbah kanfot*, *sheitels*, or a *kippah* at all times; the non-use of *tevillah* by women and the neglect of the niceties of *niddah* laws; the neglect of ancient laws such as *tevillat*

---

41 Jacob B. Agus, "The Mitzvah of Keruv," *Proceedings of the Committee on Jewish Law and Standards of the Conservative Movement, 1980–1985* (New York: Rabbinical Assembly, 1988), 147.

kelim, afiat akum, bishul akum and *chalav akum;* the disregard of halakhic condemnation of those who are *mechal'lei shabbat;* and the eating of fish in restaurants.[42]

Second, through a conscious and deliberate interpretation of the law on the part of rabbis acting individually or jointly through a national institution or committee, the Conservative movement has, among other things, permitted the use of grape juice for Kiddush during the Prohibition era (and presumably for those who medically cannot drink wine), the use of the "Lieberman *ketubbah*," the non-enforcement of the laws of illegitimacy (*mamzerut*), the permission to turn electric lights on and off on the Sabbath, the decision to allow the Rabbinical Assembly's national Beth Din to solve the *agunah* problem through annulment, and "perhaps the most important decision of this category," the appointment of scholars who invoke the historical approach in the study of sacred Jewish texts, for that implied the rejection of the authority of those scholars who did not use such methods and thus created the Conservative movement's own cadre of halakhic authorities.

Third, Agus sees several developments of the third quarter-century as embodiments of the legislative approach he himself advocates. Specifically, the *takkanot* "which resulted from the concurrent action of rabbis and laymen in formulating and carrying out congregational innovations" include gender-mixed pews, gender-mixed choirs, synagogue architecture directed forward with rabbis and cantors facing the congregation, abbreviated reading of the weekly Torah section, the elimination of some prayers and the reciting of other prayers in English, the use of an organ in services, *aliyot* for women, introduction of the *Bat Mitzvah* program and rite, riding to services on the Sabbath, and the late Friday night service. "A major *takkanah*," in Agus' view, "was the adoption of the *Sabbath and Festival Prayerbook*, with the changes regarding sacrifices and the change in the wording of two *berakhot* (which had read *shelo asani ishah* and *shelo asani goy*)." Although Agus admits that in some cases (e.g., mixed pews and the use of the organ in services) the rabbis were not consulted before the practice was initiated, "the acceptance of this action by local rabbis and their congregations renders it a *takkanah*." He therefore joyfully proclaims that

> I believe that we now have virtually completed the first chapter in the adjustment of Jewish law to American conditions . . . By and large, we are no longer plagued by the abyss between theory and practice which nullified our credibility in the past.[43]

---

[42] Supra n. 2 at 111.
[43] Ibid. at 111–113.

In line with his assessment of what had occurred by 1975, Agus proposed that the process be taken further in a new, serious way. "We can now proceed to undertake the truly challenging task of developing new standards for personal and public life, through the application of the ethical principles of our tradition."

The one problem in accomplishing this was the absence of a clear cadre of laypeople with whom the rabbis can collaborate in applying the moral principles and insights of the tradition to new circumstances, for true standards must come out of the combined knowledge and deliberations of rabbis with laypeople who are both learned in a variety of disciplines and committed to Judaism. He therefore proposes the reestablishment of the *kallot* of talmudic times so that lay Jews who take Judaism seriously in their lives may consult with rabbis on applying the tradition to new moral circumstances, ultimately producing wise *takkanot* which would have the authority of both the rabbinate and catholic Israel. In this way we would be doing nothing less than creating a new Talmud:

> The Talmud was not simply a folk-creation, nor yet a neat edition of academic learning. It stood between the two levels of culture, balancing the one against the other. It was made possible by the existence of a religious middle class: the *haverim* of tannaitic times and the *kallah*-sessions in Babylonia. This mediating group balanced the dialectic of the Torah-scholars by the pressures and ideals of the market-place. They made the difference between an organized community and a faceless mob....
>
> Our greatest lack today is not so much the paucity of scholars as it is the loose and protean character of the laity in our movement. On the other hand, we have many religiously oriented attorneys, sociologists and political scientists whose expertise in their respective fields is quite as important as the rabbinic knowledge of our tradition. Any meaningful discussion of social issues must include their participation. I suggest that we begin to consolidate a firm core of men and women, consisting of those who undertake to attend institutes of learning on a regular basis—modern *kallahs*.[44]

Agus' idea is, at least to this author, downright exhilarating. It envisions giving Judaism new life and meaning in the lives of contemporary Jews by applying classical sources in an intelligent way to the problems—especially the moral problems—which confront us now. One can only do this, as he says, if one is fully cognizant of the previous development Jewish law has undergone and therefore convinced that an historically authentic

---

[44] Ibid. at 115–116.

approach can and should use all of the methods built into Jewish law for change and development. Moreover, just as one must be rooted in the past, one must recognize one's duty to the future, and that balance should guard against overzealous preservation of the past as it simultaneously keeps us from rash decisions which uproot us from that past. To strike the balance which will preserve Jewish continuity and yet speak meaningfully to contemporary circumstances, rabbis must take advantage of the general knowledge and the moral and Jewish sentiments of committed Jewish laypeople so that the resulting *takkanot* will be as wise an expression of the tradition and of the will of God as contemporary Jews can discern and formulate. The collaboration between rabbinic and lay leaders will also ensure that the *takkanot* will have authority as the product and practice of catholic Israel.

The progress which Agus claims the Conservative Movement had made in adopting his approach by 1975, however, is, I think not as clear as he would like to believe. All of the modifications in Jewish practice which he mentions did, indeed, occur, but many of them only gradually made their way into most Conservative synagogues (e.g., roles for women in synagogue liturgy) and some have been reversed (e.g., enthusiasm for the late Friday night service and for the "cathedral style" architecture of Conservative synagogues of mid-century).

Moreover, Agus' classification of the changes into his three legal categories is highly debatable. So, for example, the responsum on the Sabbath, of which he himself was a co-author, is, despite its title as a "responsum," classified by Agus in this article as a *takkanah*, and I frankly doubt that many of the rabbis who voted for it saw it as that. They saw it instead, as the title suggests, simply as a responsum using the usual legal methods for writing responsa. One might agree or disagree with the reasoning, but it does not present itself, and was surely not understood, as new legislation but rather as a rabbinic response to a question. A *takkanah* would not need the careful description included in the responsum of what goes on in the gas chamber of an automobile to demonstrate that starting up a car is not a violation of a biblical command but, at most, of a rabbinic ordinance which contemporary rabbis may therefore weigh against other considerations. Agus' misclassification of legal developments such as that is important to note because it demonstrates that the movement as a whole had not consciously accepted Agus' philosophy of law, even if it had acted in many instances in accordance with it. The conscious reasons held by many of those who supported the new measures were consonant with many other philosophies of law as well, and I would guess that few people consciously embraced the approach and the program which Agus espoused.

That, of course, does not mean that his philosophy was faulty. It may just be that he was a man ahead of his time, that even if the Conservative movement did not adopt his philosophy of Jewish law then, it should now. It certainly has much to recommend it. At the same time, I frankly doubt that the Conservative movement in its present frame of mind is ready to make Agus' approach its own. Agus' philosophy of Jewish law fits squarely within Conservative Judaism as one possible option, but many within the contemporary movement are not ready for measures labeled emendations (*takkanot*). On the contrary, the move to the right which has characterized all streams of Judaism has had its effects on Conservative Judaism as well, and so even those who support changes in the law prefer to package them as normal, rabbinic rulings rather than as new legislation. The need for a strong sense of rootedness is greater than Agus' need to clean house legally and to face the future exuberantly.

Afterward

Rabbi Jacob Agus, arguably more than any other Conservative rabbi of his generation, clearly and thoroughly articulated a philosophy of law appropriate for the Conservative Movement, rooted in both reason and revelation, reflecting the developing history of Jewish law and its inherent values, and embracing both tradition and modernity in a conscious and serious way. One cannot help but admire the honesty and erudition of his approach as well as its concern for preserving tradition while making it vital for contemporary Jews. He himself, however, wrote very few responsa for the Law Committee, and his proposal to use the legal technique of legislation has not been widely adopted by the Conservative Movement. If anything, the Movement has shied away from taking such steps, preferring instead to justify its actions within the more commonly used legal technique of interpretation.

In our own time, though, some of Agus' proposals have effectively been adopted, although without citing him as their ideological progenitor. The decision to ordain women, a major point of conflict within the Movement, was not handled by the Committee on Jewish Law and Standards alone, but was rather entrusted to a Movement-wide commission which took testimony from Conservative Jews in a number of cities. That commission ultimately reported to the Rabbinical Assembly convention, which directed its Membership Committee to accept applications regardless of gender once the Jewish Theological Seminary of America ordained its first woman rabbi, and the faculty of the Seminary had to vote to do so before either the actions of either the commission or the Rabbinical Assembly took effect. Even though this was not the procedure that Agus had proposed, his suggestion that such significant actions be taken by the Movement as a whole found expression in this rather convoluted process. His insistence that both laypeople and rabbis be involved was also evident in the process by which the Conservative Movement framed its first ideological platform, *Emet Ve-Emunah: Statement of Principles of Conservative Judaism*, for that was written by the Commission on the Philosophy of Conservative Judaism with representatives from all arms of the Movement. This was actually closer to Agus' model, for the commission did not have to gain independent approval of any of the Movement's arms for its document. And finally, although I proposed in a responsum for the Committee of Jewish Law and Standards that there be a Movement-wide commission to study areas of human sexuality, including, but not restricted to, the issues raised by homosexuality, with its recommendations reported to all of the arms of the Movement, only the Rabbinical Assembly chose to take up the idea, creating a Commission on Human Sexuality with a mandate to study such issues and to report its findings to the Law Committee.[45] None of these is quite what Agus wanted, but they all have elements of his proposals. He, however, laid the ideological groundwork for such an approach much more clearly than any of the initiators of these actions, and he did it thirty years before they happened! We may yet see the Conservative Movement develop much more aggressively in ways he foresaw long ago.

---

[45] My responsum, entitled "Jewish Norms for Sexual Behavior," was validated by eight members of the Committee on Jewish Law and Standards at its meeting on March 25, 1992; it will be published in the collection of Law Committee responsa for 1990–1995, and, in the meantime, it is available from the Rabbinical Assembly office, 3080 Broadway, New York, New York 10027. The Rabbinical Assembly, meeting in convention in May, 1992, passed a resolution directing its officers to establish such a commission which would report its findings to the Law Committee within two years. See *Proceedings of the Rabbinical Assembly 1992* (New York: Rabbinical Assembly, 1993), pp. 317–318. The Commission produced an educational document on human sexuality (Elliot N. Dorff, *"This Is My Beloved, This Is My Friend:" A Rabbinic Letter on Intimate Relations* [New York: Rabbinical Assembly, 1996]) and a report to the Law Committee indicating the aspects of human sexuality which, in the opinion of the Commission, must be addressed anew or reconsidered by the Law Committee. It is currently doing that through its subcommittee on Marriage and Sexuality. The Chancellor of the Seminary and the President of the United Synagogue of Conservative Judaism both refused to get involved in the Commission's work on the grounds that these legal matters should be decided solely by rabbis. Agus would forcefully disagree!

5

THE TOSEFTA IN LIGHT OF THE LAW AGAINST USURY

HILLEL GAMORAN[*]

In the course of studying the Bava'ot, with concentration on the usury laws, we faced a number of questions regarding the Tosefta. 1) Is the Tosefta a collection of statements which originated in the Tannaitic academies or could it be a pseudepigraphic work? 2) Is the Tosefta essentially a commentary on the Mishnah, as has been asserted by a number of scholars? 3) Were the Tosefta statements added to a completed Mishnah, or were they, rather, statements available to R. Judah Hanasi, but not selected by him for inclusion in the Mishnah? and, finally, 4) When were these statements collected and published in the form of our present day Tosefta? Since our studies encompass but a small portion of the literature, it goes without saying that our conclusions are subject to modification as further research brings new data to light.

Pseudepigrapha?

Let us begin by refuting a suggestion made by Jacob Neusner that the Tosefta may be a work of pseudepigrapha. "It is difficult," he says, "to establish criteria for evaluating whether the Tosefta is a pseudepigraphic document, written by later figures but claiming the authority of earlier ones, or a collection of statements, external to those preserved in the Mishnah, deriving from the Mishnah's framers themselves. At this point nothing is to be taken for granted. We may assume neither the authentic, nor the pseudepigraphic character of the Tosefta's attributions of its materials, and, with them, of the Tosefta's origin."[1]

We are convinced that the suggestion that the Tosefta may be pseudepigraphic is untenable. There are a number of reasons why we believe that

---

[*] Jackson School of International Studies, University of Washington, 2023 43 Ave. E. #B, Seattle, WA 98112, e-mail: hillgam@u.washington.edu

[1] Neusner, *The Tosefta, An Introduction*, (Atlanta: Scholars Press, 1992), xxii.

the Tosefta does indeed derive from Tannaitic times and is not a document composed by later authorities to look as if it were Tannaitic.

1) Appearance

The Tosefta looks like the Mishnah. It deals with the same subject matter as the Mishnah. It cites the same authorities as does the Mishnah. Furthermore, the language of the Tosefta is similar to that of the Mishnah.[2] In every way the Tosefta looks as if it comes from the same circles that produced the Mishnah.

2) Frequency of Attributions

Of the named authorities in the three Mishnah Bava'ot, the name of R. Judah (bar Ilai) appears 23.4 percent of the time. In the Tosefta Bava'ot his name appears 20.7 percent of the time. Are we to imagine that the Tosefta authorship counted the frequency of R. Judah's name in the Mishnah (as we did), noted that his name appeared more than once in five of the named sages and then replicated this frequency in the Tosefta in order to convince readers of its Tannaitic provenance? The four other most frequently named sages in the Mishnah's Bava'ot, R. Simeon ben Gamaliel, R. Meir, R. Simeon (bar Yohai) and R. Yose, appear 36.5 percent of the time. The parallel in the Tosefta is 29.6 percent, again remarkably similar.

If we delete the names of the 4th and 5th generation Tannaim, which appear in the Tosefta Bava'ot but almost never in the Mishnah, then the names of the foremost authorities are repeated in the Tosefta Bava'ot in almost exactly the same proportion as in the Mishnah Bava'ot. The five most prominent students of R. Akiba appear as 61.1 percent of the named sages in the Mishnah and as 61.9 percent of them in the Tosefta. It stretches the imagination beyond credulity to think that someone in post-Tannaitic times, seeking to give the Tosefta a Mishnah-like appearance, would have attached names of Tannaitic sages to texts in precisely the same proportions as they appear in the Mishnah.

---

[2] Kutscher and Moreshet have designated the language of both the Mishnah and the Tosefta as mh¹, the Hebrew of the Tannaim, as distinct from mh², the Hebrew of the Amoraim. E. Y. Kutscher, *A History of the Hebrew Language*, (Jerusalem and Leiden: The Magnes Press and E. J. Brill, 1982), 116. Menahem Moreshet, "The Language of the Baraytot in the Babylonian Talmud Is Not MH¹" (Hebrew), in E. Y. Kutscher, *Sefer Zikaron Le-Hanokh Yalon*, (Ramat Gan: Bar Ilan University, 1974), 275.

Prominent Sages in the Bava'ot
A Comparison of their Frequency in the Mishnah and the Tosefta

	Bava Kamma		Bava Metzia		Bava Batra		All 3 Bava'ot	
Sage	Mish.	Tos.	Mish.	Tos.	Mish.	Tos.	Mish.	Tos.
Judah	28.60%	18.60%	25.40%	27.30%	19.00%	15.90%	23.40%	20.70%
Sim.b.Gam.	4.80%	3.60%	12.70%	11.80%	16.50%	9.10%	12.50%	7.70%
Meir	16.70%	10.00%	11.30%	10.90%	2.50%	3.40%	8.90%	8.60%
Simeon	11.90%	5.00%	8.50%	9.10%	6.30%	6.80%	8.30%	6.80%
Yose	2.40%	2.10%	7.00%	12.70%	8.90%	5.70%	6.80%	6.50%
Total	64.40%	39.30%	64.90%	71.80%	53.20%	40.90%	59.90%	50.3%

Same Table as Above
But without the 4th and 5th Generation Tannaim

	Bava Kamma		Bava Metzia		Bava Batra		All 3 Bava'ot	
Sage	Mish.	Tos.	Mish.	Tos.	Mish.	Tos.	Mish.	Tos.
Judah	29.30%	22.80%	26.50%	31.90%	19.00%	23.00%	23.90%	25.50%
Sim.b.Gam.	4.90%	4.40%	13.20%	13.80%	16.50%	13.10%	12.80%	9.50%
Meir	17.10%	12.30%	11.80%	12.80%	2.50%	4.90%	9.00%	10.50%
Simeon	12.20%	6.10%	8.80%	10.60%	6.30%	9.80%	8.50%	8.40%
Yose	2.40%	2.60%	7.40%	14.90%	8.90%	8.20%	6.90%	8.00%
Total	65.90%	48.20%	67.70%	84.00%	53.20%	59.00%	61.10%	61.90%

3) Amoraic Viewpoint

The most convincing argument against considering the Tosefta to be pseudepigraphic is that its statements[3] (usually worded a little differently in the Gemara) were accepted by the Amoraim in the Talmudim as genuinely Tannaitic. For example:

a. R. Yohanan, R. Eleazar, and R. Hoshaya seek to explain R. Judah's statement (T. BM 4:2) allowing a mortgagee to take the usufruct of a field

---

[3] In referring to Tosefta statements in the Gemara (the baraitot), we are not suggesting that the Amoraim took these statements from the work which we now know as the Tosefta, only that the content of these statements was known by the Amoraim and accepted by them as coming from the Tannaitic schools.

during the loan period. Their discussion clearly shows that they believed in the authenticity of his ruling (Y. BM 5:3, 10b).

b. A statement in the Tosefta (T. BM 4:8) allows ass-drivers, who receive advance payment for goods, to grant householders a bargain price, and not be in violation of the law against usury. R. Judah b. Pazzi limits to a one day journey the distance that an ass-driver may travel. R. Huna requires the householder to accept liability for any loss to the goods until they are delivered. Both sages view the Toseftan statement as a reliable Tannaitic ruling requiring their input (Y. BM 5:3, 10b).

c. Abaye (along with Rabbah and Rava) seeks to explain why, when a merchant has no wine in his possession, the Mishnah declares the transfer of a wine debt for a wheat debt to be usurious (B. BM 62b). To answer the question Abaye cites a Toseftan passage (T. BM 4:3). It is clear that he and his colleagues accepted his citation as genuinely Tannaitic.

d. The Mishnah requires that when an investor and a storekeeper establish a partnership, agreeing to divide the profits evenly, the storekeeper must be paid for his labor lest his labor be construed as usury. The Mishnah, however, does not say how large the storekeeper's salary should be. A Toseftan statement (T. BM 4:11) provides the opinions of three Tannaitic sages ranging from a token payment to a full payment. After some discussion in the Gemara (B. BM 68b) of the conflicting opinions, R. Nahman rules in favor of allowing a token payment. Again there is no doubt that the Amora viewed the Tannaitic statement as authentic.

e. A Tosefta pericope (T. BM 5:13) declares that after borrowing from his landlord, a tenant may pay a higher rent for the land and it need not be considered usury. The assumption is that the tenant uses the loan to improve the field and, thus, he is paying a higher rent for a better field. The passage points out, however, that this permission does not apply to one who rents a store or a ship. Such a person may not pay a higher rent after receiving a loan. R. Nahman, in the name of Rabbah b. Avuha (B. BM 69b), accepts the authority of this statement and elaborates, explaining that were the store renter or the ship renter to use the loan to improve the store or the ship, then, in their cases too, an increase in rent would be allowed.

f. The Mishnah gives the law about when a landowner may lend wheat to his tenant without violating the law against usury. In the Tosefta's statement of the law (T. BM 6:8), a distinction is made between a case where the loan is made before the tenant has begun his work in the field and one where the work in the field has already begun. Rava, in the name of R. Idi (B. BM 74b), explains the reason for this distinction. Since these Amoraim accepted the Tosefta's statement as authentic, they needed to reconcile it with the Mishnah.

The six above examples, two from the Jerusalem Talmud and four from the Babylonian Talmud, contain the names of sages ranging from the 1st through the 4th generation of Amoraim. We can conclude, even from this small sample, that the Amoraim believed that the Toseftan statements were indeed Tannaitic. They taught lessons based on those statements; they interpreted the Mishnah in light of the Toseftan additions to the Mishnah and they felt obligated to reconcile apparent contradictions between Mishnaic and Toseftan rulings. It is hard to imagine that the Amoraim could have been deceived and would have accepted the Toseftan statements as authentic were they not so.

4) Consistency of Viewpoints

One more piece of evidence showing that the Tosefta is not pseudepigraphic deals with viewpoints of individual Tannaim (or their schools). Though the number of passages attributed to named authorities in one chapter of Mishnah (M. BM 5) and three chapters of Tosefta (T. BM 4-6) is small, even this small sample may be helpful. The names of R. Judah and R. Simeon are mentioned only once each in the Mishnah's chapter on usury. R. Judah is quoted as saying that one who contracts for the purchase of produce to be delivered at some time in the future should expect to receive the lowest (not the average) market price for his money. In this case R. Judah is apparently not concerned that the buyer might receive some special benefit because he paid in advance. Can we deduce from this single quotation that R. Judah does not believe in interpreting the usury ban in its strictest form? R. Simeon's one mention in our Mishnah cites him as condemning even usury through words. Does this single quote suggest that he believes in a stringent interpretation of the prohibition against usury?

Let us turn our attention to the Tosefta to see if the point of view of these two Tannaim (or their schools) as reflected in these single Mishnah references is reflected in the Tosefta. The Tosefta speaks of two laws where R. Judah and R. Simeon are at odds. One has to do with how much an investor needs to pay a storekeeper in a 50/50 arrangement in order to avoid the usury ban. R. Judah says that it is enough if the investor allows him to dip his bread in his brine or give him two dried figs. R. Simeon, on the other hand, requires that he be given a full wage. The other dispute deals with the case of two women who engage in a partnership to raise eggs. R. Judah allows the arrangement without concern about paying the working partner for her labor; R. Simeon forbids. In both cases, R. Simeon assumes a stringent attitude while R. Judah takes the softer position.

There are two further mentions of R. Judah in the Tosefta.[4] In one (T. BM 4:2), he says that even if the lender takes the usufruct of a mortgaged field, there is no violation of the usury law. In the other case (T. BM 6:15), R. Judah is identified as the sage who says that all the days of the dry season are considered equivalent and all the days of the rainy season are considered equivalent (and it is not considered usury if one labors in exchange for another's labor as long as it is in the same season of the year).

R. Simeon is quoted (T. BM 6:18) in the Tosefta in one additional instance, providing Scriptural support for praising those who do not lend on interest and declaring that those who lend on interest will pass away from the world.

Thus we have seven occasions in which the names of R. Judah or R. Simeon are mentioned in the Tosefta. All four times that R. Judah is quoted, it is to mitigate the harsh restrictions of the law against usury; all three times that R. Simeon is mentioned, it is to reinforce the strict observance of the law. These seven mentions all conform with the positions taken by these two sages in the single mention of each in the Mishnah. Is it coincidence? Is it a result of a Tosefta editor placing words in the mouths of sages in such a way as to outwit future scholars? Neither seems plausible. What seems reasonable is that both the Mishnah and the Tosefta reflect an authentic divergence of views between two sages (or two schools).

For all these reasons, then, we believe that the Tosefta is not a work of pseudepigrapha; it is a collection of genuine Tannaitic statements.

A Commentary?

We will now turn to the question of whether the Tosefta is a commentary on the Mishnah. Several scholars have designated the Tosefta a commentary on the Mishnah. Baruch Bokser writes:

> Various scholars have . . . noticed how Tosefta contains teachings which gloss, explain, and otherwise relate to Mishnah. Albeck, Epstein, Melammed, and others have tried to delineate and differentiate the ways in which this occurs. . . . Lieberman throughout his commentary on Tosefta, *Tosefta Ki-fshutah,* shows how Tosefta contains lemmata of Mishnah which are then glossed, as well as clauses which directly refer to and depend upon the text of the Mishnah. . . . Tosefta thus provides an example of a commentary.[5]

Abraham Goldberg holds that each layer of Tosefta explains a layer in the Mishnah at least one generation earlier. The Tosefta, then, is "the prime

---

[4] In T. BM 4:18, R. Judah would make it easier than the sages to dissolve a partnership. We have not considered it here because it does not relate to the issue of usury.

[5] Baruch Bokser, *Post Mishnaic Judaism in Transition,* (Chico: Scholars Press, 1980), 444–5.

commentary . . . to the Mishna."[6] And Jacob Neusner says that "the Tosefta's materials . . . cogent . . . only in relationship to the Mishnah, serve as the Mishnah's first commentary, first amplification, and first extension—that is, the initial Talmud."[7]

Looking at an outline of the usury laws (Mishnah Bava Metzia, chapter 5 and Tosefta Bava Metzia, chapters 4-6) one might imagine that the Tosefta, indeed, serves as a commentary on the Mishnah.

Topic	Mishnah	Tosefta
Introduction	5:1	4:1
Debtor/Landlord Dealing with Creditor/Tenant	5:2a	4:5
Debtor Selling Field to Creditor	5:2b	4:2a
Mortgages	5:3	4:2b
Half-Profit Investment of Money or Produce	5:4a	4:11–22
Half-Profit Investment of Livestock	5:4b–5	4:24–5:12
Usurious Transactions with Non-Jews	5:6	5:14–21
Purchase of Futures	5:7	6:1–7, 10a, 11–13, 16a
Landlord Lending to his Tenant/Farmer	5:8	6:8–9
Lending Produce for Produce	5:9	6:10b
Lending Labor for Labor	5:10a	6:14b–15
Conclusion	5:10b–11	6:16b–18

---

[6] Abraham Goldberg, "The Tosefta—Companion to the Mishna" in Shmuel Safrai, ed. *The Literature of the Sages, First Part*, (Assen/Maastricht and Philadelphia: Van Gorcum and Fortress Press, 1987), 283.

[7] Jacob Neusner, *The Tosefta, An Introduction,* supra n. 1 at xvii. Judith Hauptman and Lawrence Schiffman also speak of the Tosefta as a commentary on the Mishnah. "In their very essence the Tosefta, BT, and PT each contain a Tannaitic commentary on the Mishnah," Judith Hauptman, *Development of the Talmudic Sugya,* (New York: University Press of America, 1988), 73. "The Tosefta was the earliest commentary on the Mishnah." Lawrence Schiffman, *From Text to Tradition, A History of Second Temple and Rabbinic Judaism,* (Hoboken: Ktav Publishing House,

The Mishnah and Tosefta material are closely related to each other. With only minor variations, the Mishnah and the Tosefta follow the same order in discussing the various topics. Nonetheless, we believe that there is reason to reject the suggestion that the Tosefta should be considered a commentary on the Mishnah.

Absence of Comments

For one thing, if the Tosefta were primarily a commentary on the Mishnah, it would comment on Mishnah statements which are difficult to understand or which raise obvious questions. For example, the first mishnah in chapter five of Bava Metzia introduces the subject of usury. It opens with a clear explanation of stipulated usury and follows with an example of usury resulting from a business transaction. This illustration is a bit complicated. A man pays for wheat at a price of 25 dinars per kor. When its price rises to 30 dinars per kor, he requests delivery of his wheat, telling the vendor that he intends to buy wine with the proceeds. The vendor replies that he will credit him with an amount of wine that can be purchased with the proceeds of the wheat sold at 30. The mishnah ends by explaining that the vendor has no wine.

This mishnah raises a number of questions which beg for answers. Is a person allowed to pay in advance for produce and profit from a rise in the market price? Isn't this usury? Is a vendor allowed to promise future delivery of wine for the wheat which he owes? And finally, what difference does it make whether or not the vendor possesses wine at the time that he makes the promise? The Tosefta, however, doesn't answer any of the questions raised by the Mishnah. (The Gemara takes up these questions in B. BM 62b.)

The second mishnah of chapter five says that one may increase a rental charge but not a sale price. The Mishnah then explains what this means. If one who rents out property says that he will accept 10 selas for the annual rental if paid now, but one per month if paid monthly, this is allowed; but if one selling property says that he will accept 1000 zuz if paid now, but 1200 if paid later, this is forbidden. The Mishnah does not explain why the increased rental is permitted and the increased sale price is forbidden. Now, if an author were composing a commentary on the Mishnah, this would be

---

1991), 10. Alan Avery-Peck also designates the Tosefta as a commentary on the Mishnah, "The Mishnah, Tosefta, and the Talmuds," in Jacob Neusner, ed., *Judaism in Late Antiquity*, (Leiden: E. J. Brill, 1995), 191.

the question that he would need to answer. (This is, in fact, the question first answered in the Bavli when this mishnah is examined.) But the Tosefta's author does not do so.

The first part of the third mishnah provides one more example of the Tosefta not commenting on a Mishnah passage that would appear to require commentary. The Mishnah tells of a person who makes a partial payment toward the purchase of a field and the seller declares, "Whenever you wish, bring me the balance due and take your field." This, the Mishnah declares, is forbidden. But the Mishnah doesn't tell why it is forbidden. If we look to the Tosefta for an explanation, we will be disappointed. (The Gemara deals with the matter in B. BM 65b.) The Tosefta is silent, again suggesting that it is something other than a commentary.

If the Tosefta is not a commentary on the Mishnah, how then shall we characterize it? In examining the usury laws, we found, broadly speaking, three types of pericopae, those which supplement the Mishnah, those which explain the Mishnah and those which are independent of the Mishnah.

Statements Which Supplement the Mishnah

By far the largest proportion of the Tosefta pericopae dealing with usury serve to supplement Mishnah's statements. Let us look, for example, at how the Tosefta relates to the fourth pericope of chapter five of the Mishnah. The Mishnah declares that an investor may not give money to a storekeeper with an agreement to share the profits or the losses equally unless he pays the storekeeper for his labor. The Tosefta does not explain **why** this payment had to be made as would be expected in a commentary, but it does supplement the Mishnah with a large number of pericopae on the subject raised in the Mishnah. The Tosefta is interested in the question of how much the storekeeper should be paid. It furnishes the opinions of three Tannaim, R. Meir, R. Judah and R. Simeon, with differing views as to whether the working partner should be paid a token wage, a minimum wage or a full wage. The Tosefta then continues with twelve additional pericopae on the subject of half-profit investments. They explain that the working partner may not practice his craft during the time he is supposed to be working for the partnership, nor may he buy and sell his own goods during that time. They give rules for arrangements other than a 50/50 split. They take up the case of when the investor shares some of the work. They discuss proper accounting methods. They deal with a situation in which the working partner buys the wrong produce. They discuss how the partnership may be dissolved. All these are subjects of interest. They are matters which surely came up in the course of business dealings and, hence, in the academies. But they cannot be considered a commentary on the Mishnah; they are a *Tosefta*, a **supplement** to the Mishnah.

One of the principles of the usury law was that it did not apply to non-Jews. In one paragraph (M. BM 5:6), the Mishnah provides the basic information: 1) One may borrow from and lend to non-Jews on interest. 2) The law which forbids a Jew from accepting an investment from another Jew in which the return of the investment is guaranteed, does not apply to a non-Jew. 3) As far as usury is concerned, the resident alien is in the same category as the non-Jew. 4) A Jew may lend a non-Jew's money on interest to another Jew only if the non-Jew is aware of the transaction.

The Tosefta includes eight pericopae (T. BM 5:14–21) on the subject of loans involving non-Jews. They cover a variety of situations where intermediaries play a role in making a loan. In each case the Tosefta rules on what is allowed and what isn't. They are statements which supplement the teachings of the Mishnah.

Statements Which Comment on the Mishnah

As previously stated, we believe that it is misleading to generalize by calling the Tosefta a commentary on the Mishnah. We do agree, however, that there are individual Tosefta pericopae which function as a commentary and explain the meaning of the Mishnah. The second part of Mishnah 5:3 is a good example. It explains that one is allowed to lend money, accept the debtor's field as collateral for the loan and stipulate that if the debt is not repaid within three years, the field will be forfeited. The Mishnah adds that Boethus b. Zonin followed this practice with the approval of the sages. The information which the Mishnah does not supply, is who possesses the field and enjoys the usufruct during the mortgage period. Here the Tosefta (4:2) provides the necessary information, explaining that this arrangement is permitted only if the mortgagor continues to take the usufruct. As for Boethus b. Zonin, according to the Tosefta, when he lent money, the mortgagor did take the usufruct. Furthermore, the Tosefta informs us that R. Judah disagrees with the anonymous opinion. In his view, it does not matter who takes the usufruct. Clearly, then, this pericope provides an example of where the Tosefta serves as a commentary on the Mishnah.

Tosefta material most looks like a commentary when quotations from the Mishnah are interspersed throughout the Tosefta, when a line from the Mishnah is followed by Tosefta material, and then another line of Mishnah is followed by more from the Tosefta. We find this in the usury laws in the section that deals with the purchase of futures. The Mishnah (M. BM 5:7) provides the basic principles of the law explaining what procedures need to be followed in order that payment for future delivery of produce not violate the ban on usury. The Tosefta follows a format of quotation and explanation in three pericopae (T. BM 6:1–3). We should note, however, that even though the Tosefta, when laid out in this way, has the appearance of a commentary, it does not mean that the Tosefta was **originally** composed as a commentary. The Tosefta pericopae may have been composed independently of the Mishnah and the Mishnah quotations may have been inserted by a later Tosefta editor in order to provide a reference point and to help clarify the Tosefta statement.[8]

Independent Statements

It has long been noted that the Tosefta includes passages which are independent of the Mishnah. This is true for the chapters on usury as well. For example, the Tosefta explains (T. BM 5:15) that, from a legal point of view, there is no objection to a man borrowing from his wife and children on interest, but it should not be done because it gets them into the habit of practicing usury. In another instance (T. BM 5:22) the Tosefta quotes R. Meir as saying that the court fines someone who lends on interest by ruling that he may collect neither the principal nor the interest. In yet another ruling (T. BM 5:25–6) the Tosefta states that one who lends on interest and then repents must repay the interest he collected. If he died, his children do not have to return the interest which their father gained unless it was in the form of a specific object. In that case they would have to return it for the sake of their father's honor. These are but three examples of Tosefta pericopae on the subject of usury, which, being independent of the Mishnah, are not by any measure a commentary on the Mishnah.

Designating a Tosefta statement as 1) explaining the Mishnah, 2) supplementing the Mishnah or 3) being independent of the Mishnah is not an exact science. Some passages are questionable regarding into which category they fit. In any case, we have made an effort to place each Tosefta statement from the chapters on usury into its proper place. As can be seen in the table below, the overwhelming majority of pericopae serve to supplement the Mishnah.

---

[8] "The editors at times deleted and at times added passages from the Mishnah that are in the Tosefta." Saul Lieberman, *Tosefta Ki-Fshutah 3*, (New York: Jewish Theological Seminary of America, 1962), 14 (Hebrew numbering).

Tosefta Bava Metzia Chapters 4–6

Type of Statement	Statement	Total
Explains the Mishnah	4:2b, 5:13–14, 6:1–3	5 1/2
Supplements the Mishnah	4:4–6, 4:10–25, 5:1–12, 5:16–21, 6:4–18	52
Is Independent of the Mishnah	4:1–2a, 4:3, 4:7–9, 5:15, 5:22–26	11 1/2

It seems to us, then, that one should avoid calling the Tosefta a commentary on the Mishnah for it may give the misleading impression that the authors of the Tosefta composed their material to explain the Mishnah. Though it is true that, in many respects, the Tosefta's final editors crafted their work to look like a commentary on the Mishnah, it is, essentially, a collection of statements from the time of the Mishnah. Some of those statements were, in fact, composed before their Mishnah parallels.[9] In our view, then, it would be more accurate to call the Tosefta a collection of statements dealing with the same topics as covered in the Mishnah and arranged in, more or less, the same order as the Mishnah, or, a **supplement** to the Mishnah.

Which Came First?

We now turn to the question: which came first, the Mishnah material or the Tosefta material? Those scholars who have called the Tosefta a commentary on the Mishnah, clearly, are of the opinion that the Tosefta was composed after the Mishnah. We have argued, however, that it is wrong to call the Tosefta a commentary on the Mishnah and that we must examine the evidence to determine which document preceded the other. We can agree that many Tosefta pericopae were, indeed, composed after their Mishnah par-

---

[9] See below nn. 11–13.

allels. Logic would dictate that many of the Tosefta's rulings about 50/50 investments were composed after the single Mishnah statement which gives only the general principle. The same may be said regarding the laws about lending to non-Jews and the laws about purchasing futures. The supplementary material provided by the Tosefta was surely composed after the basic rules delineated in the Mishnah. Nevertheless, there is no doubt that some Tosefta pericopae preceded their Mishnah parallels. For example, the Tosefta (T. BM 6:3) tells that one may contract for the purchase of manure all year long even if the seller does not have any at the time that the deal is struck because manure is always available somewhere. The Mishnah parallel (M. BM 5:7) appears to have followed the Tosefta for, in addition to providing the same ruling, it adds that R. Yose objects. R. Yose allows such a transaction only if the seller possesses the manure at the time the deal is struck. Another example deals with a landlord who lends grain to his tenant. The Tosefta (T. BM 6:9) allows it as long as the grain is used for planting and not for consumption. The Mishnah parallel (M. BM 5:8) appears to come after the Tosefta for, after stating the law, it includes a reference telling how R. Simeon b. Gamaliel carried on this practice.

What we have concluded from our studies with Bava Metzia has been reached by others dealing with other tractates. Meyer Feldblum's study of tractate Gitin[10] and Dineke Houtmann's work in tractate Shevi'it[11] both show that it is more likely that the Mishnah pericopae were selected from an already existing body of Tannaitic material rather than that the Tosefta statements were later additions to the Mishnah. Furthermore, support for the idea that Tosefta pericopae preceded the Mishnah's comes from Shamma Friedman. He shows that where parallel passages appear in the Mishnah and the Tosefta, the Tosefta generally contains the older source.[12] It is clear, then, that some Tosefta statements preceded their Mishnah paral-

---

10 Meyer Feldblum, *Perushim Umehkarim Batalmud,* (New York: Yeshiva University Press, 1969), 17–20 and English section, 8–9.

11 Dineke Houtmann, "The Interdependence of Mishnah and Tosefta of Tractate Shevi'it," in *Proceedings of the Eleventh World Congress of Jewish Studies,* Div. C, Vol. 1, (Jerusalem: The World Union of Jewish Studies, 1994), 17–24.

12 Shamma Friedman, "Mishnah and Tosefta Parallels," in *Proceedings of the Eleventh World Congress of Jewish Studies,* Div. C, Vol. 1, (Hebrew Section), (Jerusalem: The World Union of Jewish Studies, 1994, 15–22 and "Mishnah-Tosefta Parallels," (Hebrew) in *Bar Ilan Annual,* 26–27 (1995), 277–288. Friedman also develops this theme in "Tosefta Atika: L'yahas Makbilot Hamishnah V'hatosefta," in *Tarbiz,* 62/3 (1993), 313–338. There (p. 314) he writes, "Investigation shows that the relationship between the Mishnah and Tosefta parallels is not always, as is commonly held, that the law in the Mishnah is the primary source, and that the Tosefta is the later one. On the contrary, we have frequently found that the opposite is so, and that the parallel which is in the Tosefta is the older tradition in comparison with the one in the Mishnah."

lels and some followed them. It would be accurate to describe the Tosefta material generally as being contemporaneous with the Mishnah.[13]

How then did the Mishnah and the Tosefta become two separate books? The evidence suggests that it came about as a result of the decision of Rabbi Judah Hanasi and his associates to publish the Mishnah. Rabbi Akiba's students, although they taught according to their mentor, did not always teach in the same way. They sometimes heard different versions of the law; they sometimes emphasized different legal principles or arrived at decisions based on differing viewpoints. Rabbi had before him a mass of diverse, unedited (or not highly edited) legal statements. He undertook to organize those statements and work them into a (more or less) uniform document.

We have said earlier that the language of the Mishnah is similar to that of the Tosefta,[14] and this is so. But the editorial work of Rabbi left its mark. Hayim Lapin's study of Bava Metzia, produces evidence of the editorial process.[15] Shamma Friedman, after comparing the style of the Mishnah with that of the Tosefta, describes the Mishnah as "edited and cultivated."[16] And Natan Braverman says that whereas "the Tosefta was compiled by bringing together the sources as they were," the Mishnah was edited with an aim for "linguistic unity."[17]

One of the most significant challenges that lay before the Mishnah's editors was the task of selection. They not only had to edit the material that lay before them; they had to leave out much of that material altogether. There were too many statements in existence to include them all in their work.[18] Let us remember that the study of the law in the academies was an oral exercise.[19]Even if we believe that the Mishnah was composed in written

---

[13] Of course, the Tosefta does include material from the generation of R. Judah Hanasi which post-dates the Mishnah.

[14] Supra n. 2.

[15] Hayim Lapin, *Early Rabbinic Civil Law and the Social History of Roman Galilee* (Atlanta: Scholars Press, 1995), 35–117.

[16] Friedman, "Tosefta Atika," supra n. 12 at 314.

[17] Braverman, "Bein Leshon Ha-Mishnah Li-Leshon Ha-Tosefta, "*Divrei Ha-Qongres Ha-Teshi'i Le-Mada'ei Ha-Yahadut*, Div. D, vol. 1, Jerusalem (1986), 36–7.

[18] "If Rabbi were to have tried to write down and compose (in the Mishnah) everything that had been taught in his day, it would have been too long and would have been lost." *Iggeret R. Sherira Gaon*, B. M. Lewin (ed.) (Haifa, 1921), 36.

[19] Though Lieberman's thesis, in "The Publication of the Mishnah", in *Hellenism in Jewish Palestine* (New York: Jewish Theological Seminary of America, 1962), 83–99, that the Mishnah's publication was strictly oral, has been challenged, there can be little doubt that written documents were not utilized in the academies. See Martin Jaffee, "How Much 'Orality' in Oral Torah?" *Shofar*, 10 (1992), 53–72.

form, there is no question that its compilers intended that it be used for oral study in the academies. The text was "so formulated as to be relatively easy to memorize."[20] If so, there had to be limits to its size.[21] If the Mishnah was to be memorized and discussed orally in the academies, then its allowable bulk became one of the prime considerations of the editors. Rabbi had before him the teachings of Rabbi Meir, of Rabbi Judah, of Rabbi Simeon, of Rabbi Yose and others (or their academies), and he picked those rulings which he believed were the most authentic expression of Rabbi Akiba's teachings. At times, he felt that alternative rulings were worth noting, so he included them in the Mishnah with the names of the authorities responsible for them. But more often, rather than be inclusive, he was exclusive. He excluded more material than he included. He included only what he felt were the major points and omitted much of the detailed elaboration of the law. He included the law that required paying a working partner for his labor but left out the rules governing how much he was to be paid, what activities he could undertake and how the accounts should be figured. He included the general principle that allowed usurious transactions with non-Jews but excluded various cases in which loans with non-Jews could result in usury among Jews. He placed inside the Mishnah the rule controlling the purchase of futures but left outside the canon the multitude of questions about market conditions which might affect the sale.[22] In each instance, he inserted into the Mishnah what he considered to be the essence of the law and omitted details which he felt would make his work too lengthy.[23]

---

20 Jacob Neusner, *Oral Tradition in Judaism: The Case of the Mishnah*, (New York and London: Garland Publishing, 1987), 74.

21 "A good textbook, of necessity, needs to be selective in the presentation of the material, in order to offer the student a maximum of information in a minimum of text." Goldberg, supra n. 6 at 223.

22 In reference to the usury laws, Benjamin De Vries says, "We can surmise that the editor of the Mishnah condensed his chapter from a collection, similar to the Tosefta, which was comprised of several chapters." *Mehkarim Be-sifrut Hatalmud*, (Jerusalem: Mossad Harav Kook, 1968), 98.

23 As Louis Jacobs put it, Rabbi Judah Hanasi formed "a digest of the Oral Law." Louis Jacobs, *Structure and Form in the Babylonian Talmud*, (Cambridge: Cambridge University Press, 1991), 1. See Lapin, *Early Rabbinic Civil Law*, supra n. 15. In the body of his work, especially pp. 35–59, the author shows that the Mishnah's redactors used and edited a variety of sources, but he does not point out the important role played by the redactors in **selecting** which sources to include. However, in his appendix, p. 318, Lapin admits to their task of picking and choosing among the sources by speaking of "the likelihood that there was more material available to the redactors of the Mishnah (at least of Mishnah Bava Metzia) than that which appears in the Mishnah alone."

Baraitot

The final question with which we will deal is how the Tosefta, as we know it today, came to be. Rabbi succeeded in his enterprise because of the power and influence of his position and because his work was a compendium of legal headlines which could serve as a unifying canon for the Jewish people. But the pericopae which Rabbi had omitted were preserved. After all, not everyone was happy with his accomplishment.[24] Some felt that he had assumed too much authority in selecting certain statements of the law and in leaving out others. Collections of baraitot, statements not included in the Mishnah, began to be assembled. Some of the best known collections of baraitot were made by R. Hiyya, R. Hoshaya and Bar Kappara who lived at the end of the Tannaitic period.[25] There were others as well. From the very start of Mishnah exegesis, baraitot were cited to explain or to challenge Mishnaic statements. Much of the texts of the Talmudim consists of exercises in harmonizing the Mishnah with the baraitot.

The Jerusalem Talmud's section on the usury laws is a collection of 36 baraitot with some commentary and analysis by early Amoraim and by the anonymous Gemara. For the most part, the baraitot are close in wording to the Tosefta. All of them are found in the Tosefta in one form or another.

The Babylonian Talmud's usury chapter contains 57 baraitot, 34 of which are found in the Tosefta; they are not as close in wording to the Tosefta as are the baraitot in the Yerushalmi. Also, the Bavli, unlike the Yerushalmi, uses the baraitot for a sustained examination of the Mishnah. For example, the Gemara inquires (B. BM 62b regarding M. BM 5:1) why it matters whether or not a merchant selling wine futures actually possesses the wine. The Gemara offers three different solutions to the problem, each one depending on a baraita. Rabbah cites an anonymous baraita. Abaye cites a baraita from the collection of R. Hiyya and Rava provides a baraita of R. Hoshaya (a variation of Rabbah's). The baraitot, which, with variations, are found in the Tosefta, are the focal point of the Amoraic treatment of the Mishnah.

Another example deals with the question of paying wages to the working partner of a partnership. The Mishnah (M. BM 5:4) simply says that he must be paid. The Gemara's discussion (B. BM 68b), which centers around four baraitot (all, with variations, being in the Tosefta), treats the issue of

---

[24] David Halivni, "The Reception Accorded to Rabbi Judah's Mishnah," in E. P. Sanders et al. (eds.), *Jewish and Christian Self-Definition*, Vol. 2 (London: S. C. M. Press, 1980), 204–12, 379–82.

[25] Boaz Cohen, *Mishnah and Tosefta*, (New York: Jewish Theological Seminary of America, 1935), 26–30.

how much he should be paid. Once again, it is evident that the material omitted from the Mishnah was preserved by the sages. Coming, as it did, from Tannaitic times, it was invested with authority and became the focal point for discussion of the law in the academies in the ensuing generations.

Though the baraitot were authoritative, they were not equal in sanctity to the Mishnah. They were preserved because of their authority, but they were not codified as part of the Mishnah. They remained part of various collections. At some point, many of them were gathered together and published as a work called the Tosefta.

Redaction of the Tosefta

Though the Tosefta's statements derive from Tannaitic times, the question still remains as to when these statements were assembled and published in the form that we know them today? That the Tosefta was published after the time of the Mishnah is beyond dispute since the Tosefta contains statements of sages who lived a generation later than the last mentioned sages in the Mishnah. (In the three Bava'ot, sages of Rabbi's generation are mentioned 69 times in the Tosefta and but 4 times in the Mishnah.) If we date the publication of the Mishnah at about 200 C.E., then the Tosefta may be dated, **at the earliest**, at about 225 C.E. This is, indeed, when Goldberg believes it was completed. He says that the Tosefta, "is so close to the Mishna and so natural a continuation of it, that its editing cannot have been much later. All signs point to a difference of, largely, one generation, i.e. to a date around 220–30 C.E."[26]

Neusner's date for the redaction of the Tosefta is not as early as Goldberg's. He believes that the Tosefta was redacted about 300 C.E.[27] For him, then, the Tosefta was completed at a point after the publication of the Mishnah, but before the redaction of the Jerusalem Talmud.[28]

---

[26] Goldberg, supra n. 6 at 284.

[27] There is some question about this date because of confusion in *The Tosefta, An Introduction*, supra n. 1. On p. xvii, Neusner says that the Tosefta "is a work of the third century, 200–300." But on p. xx, he states that we can rely on M. D. Herr for when the work reached its present form who says "that the Tosefta in its present form was not edited before the end of the fourth century C.E." Then, on p. xxi, he offers, as a guess, a date of 360 for when the Tosefta reached its present shape. Still, in the same work, on p. xxii, he writes, "The Tosefta came to a closure about two centuries after the Mishnah, one may guess at about 300 [We must assume that this sentence contains a misprint]." We rely on ca. 300 as the date Neusner prefers because that is the date he assigns to the Tosefta in *Formative Judaism, Religious, Historical, and Literary Studies, Seventh Series*, (Atlanta: Scholars Press, 1993), 85 and in his *Introduction to Rabbinic Literature*, (New York: Doubleday, 1994), 129.

[28] This time frame is significant because Neusner teaches that to understand the history of an idea, one can rely only on the date of a document's final redaction, not on the dates of the

Other scholars have suggested later dates for the publication of the Tosefta.[29] Chanoch Albeck has argued that the editors of the Babylonian Talmud did not have the Tosefta at their disposal.[30] He has offered many examples of differences between passages in the Tosefta and their parallels in the Bavli to show that the Bavli editors must have had a source other than the Tosefta for their baraitot.[31] Furthermore, he has provided numerous instances of when the Talmud's editors failed to cite statements from the Tosefta and would surely have done so had they been aware of them.[32] "It is clear," he says, "that the editor [of the Tosefta] lived at the end of the period of the Amoraim."[33]

Yaakov Elman generally accepts Albeck's arguments and adds to the weight of evidence. He shows, through his study of Pesaḥim, that the Babylonian Amoraim worked "in the absence of an easily available and accessible compilation of sources, . . . in other words, . . . in the absence of a commonly available Tosefta."[34] "Toseftan baraitot," he says, "came to the Bavli's redactors as individual baraitot, perhaps loosely connected, and not part of a Tosefta-like composition."[35]

---

persons to whom statements within a document are attributed. "Sayings," he says, "attest to the viewpoint of the framers of the documents who collected the sayings . . . and gave them a position of authority in the compilations they produced . . . These books represent views held by the authorship behind them, at the point at which a document reached conclusion and redaction." Neusner, *Introduction to Rabbinic Literature,* supra n. 27 at 17.

The Tosefta fits into Neusner's "document by document" system for the development of ideas (first the Mishnah, then the Tosefta, then the Yerushalmi and finally, the Bavli, *The Tosefta, An Introduction,* supra n. 1 at xxii) as long as it is agreed that it was compiled after the Mishnah and before the completion of the Jerusalem Talmud. But, if the evidence continues to accumulate in support of a post-Amoraic redaction (in accordance with the position of Albeck and Elman), then the "document by document" system doesn't apply to the Tosefta. It would make no sense to place the Tosefta after the Bavli in studying the history of ideas. The order should be Mishnah/Tosefta, then Yerushalmi, and then Bavli because the **contents** of the Tosefta are contemporary with the Mishnah. It simply cannot be said of the Tosefta that it represents the viewpoint of those who collected and published the sayings. Its language, its style, its authorities and its concerns all argue for designating it a Tannaitic document.

29 M. D.. Herr says that it is "obvious that the Tosefta in its present form was not edited before the end of the fourth century C.E." "Tosefta," *Encyclopedia Judaica*, 15, 1284.

30 Chanoch Albeck, *Mehqarim Ba-Baraita Ve-Tosefta Ve-Yahasan La-Talmud*, (Jerusalem: Mossad Harav Kook, 1969), 93.

31 Chanoch Albeck, *Mavo Latalmudim* (Tel Aviv: D'vir, 1969), 58–72.

32 Albeck, *Mehqarim,* supra n. 30 at 94–138.

33 Albeck, *Mehqarim,* supra n. 30 at 88.

34 Yaakov Elman, *Authority and Tradition: Toseftan Baraitot in Talmudic Babylonia*, (New York: Ktav Publishing House, 1994), 137.

35 Elman, supra n. 34 at 278.

In spite of the similarity in appearance between the Mishnah and the Tosefta, studies by Menahem Moreshet[36] and Natan Braverman[37] have pointed to differences in language usage and in editorial practice between the two documents. These differences could be the result of a much later completion date for the Tosefta. Saul Lieberman has written of the Babylonian influence on the Tosefta[38] and Elman has discovered this influence in his studies.[39] Elman says, "The existence of Babylonian material in the Tosefta . . . indicates that the process of the formation of our Tosefta was more extended and complicated than an early date would allow."[40]

Our examination of the baraitot in the chapters on usury (BM 5 in both Talmudim) supports the Albeck/Elman thesis. Of the 36 baraitot in the Yerushalmi and the 34 in the Bavli which have parallels in the Tosefta, not a single one is the same as its Tosefta parallel. Some of the differences among the texts are minor. For example, a dispute between R. Meir and the sages is recorded in the Tosefta (T. BM 5:22) and in both Talmudim (J. BM 5:1, 10a and B. BM 72a). All three texts state that R. Meir holds that a note which includes interest is invalid and that the creditor may not collect either the interest or the principal, whereas the sages maintain that though the interest is not collectable, the principal is. The viewpoint of the sages is expressed in almost exactly the same words in all three texts, but R. Meir's opinion (without altering the basic meaning) is worded differently in each version. The Tosefta says, "If one lends his neighbor on interest and comes before the court, they fine him and he does not collect either the principal or the interest. These are the words of R. Meir." The Yerushalmi says, "If a Jew lends on interest to a Jew, he does not collect the principal or the interest. These are the words of R. Meir." Finally, the Bavli, in its version says, "If a note has interest recorded in it, they fine him and he does not collect the principal or the interest. These are the words of R. Meir." The fact that the wording dif-

---

36 Moreshet, "Ha-Nasu Ha-Qodem Li-Shenei Nose'im Bi-Leshon Hazal," in M. Bar Asher, A. Dotan, G. B. Sarfatti and D. Tene, *Mehqarei Lashon Mugashim le-Ze'ev Ben-Haim,* (Jerusalem: The Magnes Press and the Hebrew University, 1983), 363–6.

37 Braverman, "Bein Leshon Ha-Mishnah Li-Leshon Ha-Tosefta," in *Divrei Ha-Qongres Ha-Teshi'i Le-Mada'ei Ha-Yahadut,* Div. D, vol. 1 (Jerusalem: World Union of Jewish Studies, 1986), 31–38.

38 "The Tosefta was put into its fixed form in the academies of the Babylonian Geonim . . . and it is almost certain that it was at times edited according to the Babylonian tradition." Lieberman, *Tosefta Ki-Fshutah 3,* (New York: Jewish Theological Seminary of America, 1962), 14 (Hebrew numbering).

39 Elman, "Babylonian Baraitot in the Tosefta and the 'Dialectology' of Middle Hebrew," *AJS Review,* XVI/1–2 (1991), 1–29.

40 Elman, *Authority and Tradition,* supra n. 34 at 279.

fers in each case suggests that the Talmudic authors did not have a redacted Tosefta text in their hands. But the fact that the sense of all three passages is the same, leads to the conclusion that they knew the meaning of the baraita from an oral tradition[41] and were able accurately to record its meaning in both Talmudim.

This is the pattern found in most of the seventy parallel baraitot which we examined. The Talmudic selections are similar to their Tosefta counterparts, but the differences in wording indicate an oral transmission rather than a recording from a written text. Furthermore, some of the differences between Talmudic baraitot (especially in the Bavli) and their Tosefta parallels are not so minor. For example, the Tosefta (T. BM 4:2) says, "If a person owed someone money and wrote him a note selling him his field (to cover the debt), as long as the seller consumes the produce, it is permitted, but if the buyer does, it is forbidden. R. Judah says, 'In either case it is permitted.' Said R. Judah, 'Thus did Boethus b. Zonin do in accordance with the ruling of R. Eleazar b. Azariah.' They said to him, 'Is there proof from that? (In that case) the seller consumed the produce.'"

The Jerusalem Talmud (J. BM 5:3, 10b) recounts the baraita accurately with minor variations in wording. But the Bavli's version (B. BM 63a) is not only worded with substantial differences from the Tosefta/Yerushalmi version, but it also reverses the role of Boethus b. Zonin. In the Tosefta/Yerushalmi text we are led to believe that Boethus b. Zonin was a man of wealth who was in the habit of lending money and accepting land as collateral. But the baraita in the Bavli describes Boethus b. Zonin as a person who once mortgaged his field. The change in the role of Boethus b. Zonin can be explained if we understand that the editors of the Bavli were not in possession of a completed Tosefta text.

One more example deals with the matter of lending on interest within a family.[42] The Tosefta (T. BM 5:15) says, "A person could borrow from his wife or children on interest except that it would teach them to engage in usury." A baraita in the Yerushalmi (J. BM 5:7, 10c) uses almost the same words. It reads, "A person could borrow from his sons and daughters on interest except that it would teach them to engage in usury." But the Bavli

---

[41] The differences between the language of the Tannaim and that of the Babylonian Amoraim in their baraitot is a reflection of "the separation of time and place . . . and especially because they [the baraitot] were taught orally." Menahem Moreshet, "New and Revived Verbs in the Baraytot of the Babylonian Talmud," in E. Y. Kutscher, ed., *Archive of the New Dictionary of Rabbinical Literature*, (Ramat Gan, Bar Ilan University, 1972), 158–9. See also Elman, "Babylonian Baraitot," supra n. 40 at 18 where he states, "A close examination of tPisha and bPes supports this contention of oral transmission."

[42] Albeck cites this example in *Mehqarim*, supra n. 30 at 120.

(B. BM 75a) quotes R. Judah in the name of Rav as saying, "A person could lend his children and the members of his household on interest in order to give them a taste of interest, but it is not right because they might come to be attached to it." It is clear that the editors of the Gemara were aware of the teaching inherent in the Tosefta/Yerushalmi statement, but its text was not available to them.

Albeck's research revealed many instances of the Gemara being unaware of Tosefta material altogether. Our study of the usury laws found examples of this same phenomenon. The Tosefta (T. BM 4:4) states, "If one sells a field to his neighbor, and says to him . . . , 'Whenever I want, I will come and pay you for it and take it back,' it is permitted." The Yerushalmi (J. BM 5:3, 10b) repeats the baraita in almost the same words, but it is not found in the Bavli. In fact, the Bavli (B. BM 65b) discusses this very issue and concludes that such an arrangement is forbidden unless the **buyer** voluntarily makes this offer. Surely the Gemara would have dealt with the Tosefta statement, which allows the **seller** to make the stipulation, had it been aware of it.[43]

One more example of a Tosefta statement unknown to the Bavli editors deals with a person who guarantees a loan. The Tosefta (T. BM 5:20) reads, "If a Jew borrows from a non-Jew, or a non-Jew borrows from a Jew, another person may become his guarantor and need not fear (that he is violating the ban against usury)." The Yerushalmi (J. BM 5:7, 10c) includes this baraita with minor variations, but the Bavli is unaware of its existence. The Bavli (B. BM 71a–b) cites a baraita (found in the Sifra, Behar 5:2 but not in the Tosefta) which says, "'Do not take from him interest or increase,' but you may become a guarantor for him." The Bavli understands this to mean that when a Jew borrows from a non-Jew, another Jew is allowed to serve as the guarantor of the loan. But the Bavli does not consider the case of a non-Jew borrowing from a Jew. Clearly, the Gemara editor did not know of the Tosefta passage, for if he had, he would have included such a relevant statement in the discussion.

Our studies of the baraitot in chapters five in the Yerushalmi and the Bavli thus confirm what Albeck concluded from his wide-ranging investigation and what Elman learned from his research in Pesaḥim, that the editors of the Babylonian Talmud, although aware of individual baraitot and perhaps clusters of baraitot, did not have available to them the Tosefta as we know it today.

---

43 See Hillel Gamoran, "The Talmudic Law of Mortgages in View of the Prohibition Against Lending on Interest," *Hebrew Union College Annual*, LII (1981), 155–6.

Conclusion

To summarize, based on our studies: 1) The Tosefta is, as it appears to be, a work which originated in Tannaitic times. 2) Because it comes from the same time period as the Mishnah, and most of its material supplements the Mishnah rather than explains the Mishnah, it is inappropriate to call the Tosefta a commentary on the Mishnah. 3) The Tosefta consists largely of material which existed at the time of the Mishnah but was not selected for inclusion in the Mishnah. 4) The Tosefta was not redacted until after the close of the Babylonian Talmud. This places its publication in the period of the Saboraim or the Geonim.[44]

---

[44] I am indebted to Martin Jaffee for his careful reading of an earlier draft of this paper and for his valuable suggestions.

6

Mental Capacity and the Deathbed Will

Ben Tzion Greenberger[*]

בימים ההם חלה חזקיהו למות ויבא אליו ישעיהו בן אמוץ הנביא
ויאמר אליו כה אמר ה' צו לביתך כי מת אתה ולא תחיה.[1]

The human drama of the deathbed will is indeed compelling. The testator, in contemplation of his imminent death, expresses his final wishes regarding the disposition of his property, often without being able to reduce these wishes to writing. The sanctity of this moment leads us to the instinctive conclusion that the words of the dying testator be given greater legal effect than those similarly spoken by a healthy person, whose testament will be recognized as valid only if it complies with certain rigorously defined legal formalities.

Nevertheless, the attitude of most modern legal systems to the phenomenon of the deathbed will has been on the whole a negative one. Ever since the English Statute of Frauds imposed clear rules regarding the necessity of a signed and witnessed writing for valid wills, the evidentiary function of this requirement for the prevention of fraud has been deemed to be of such overriding importance that even in deathbed situations, and perhaps **particularly** in deathbed situations, the law has insisted on a valid writing as a prerequisite for a valid will. In the final analysis, the law has generally preferred to rely upon the general dispositive patterns of the intestacy laws rather than risk the potential of fraudulent testimony regarding the final wishes of a dying testator that he is of course himself no longer able to corroborate.

Ḥazal, on the other hand, have clearly ruled in favor of validity for oral deathbed wills: "*Divrei shchiv me'rah ke'ketuvim ve'he'messurin dammi*"[2]—

---

[*] Judge of the Magistrate's Court, Jerusalem and Rabbi of Congregation Mitzpe Nevo, Ma'aleh Adumim.

[1] *Kings* II, 20:1.

[2] *Gittin* 15a; *Baba Batra* 151a, 156a; M.T. *Zehiyah U'Mattanah*, 8:2; Tur, *Ḥoshen Mishpat*, 250. Cf. *Talmud Yerushalmi*: דברי שכיב מרע כבריא שכתב ונתן, Y. *Peah* 3:7, Y. *Ketubot* 11:1; Y. *Gittin* 1:5; Y. *Baba Batra* 9:6. See, *Talmudic Encyclopedia*, vol. 7, p. 115.

"The oral declarations of the *shchiv me'rah*—the terminally ill testator—are to be legally recognized as if written and delivered." Setting aside, for the moment, the difference between the more general term *shchiv me'rah*, the terminally ill, and the deathbed patient, clearly a much narrower term which is but a subset of the former, it should first be stressed that there exists a fundamental difference between the will of the *shchiv me'rah* (hereinafter referred to by its traditional name, the "*matnat shchiv me'rah*") and the conventional will, regarding the legal basis of the testamentary power conferred:

> For wills, testamentary power is general, deriving from the very nature of ownership, which is recognized as including the legal power to dispose of property upon death.

In Jewish law, testamentary power per se does not exist;[3] the order of succession is fixed by Torah law,[4] and the property owner is generally powerless to cause his property to pass by inheritance in some other fashion.[5] The *matnat shchiv me'rah* is an exception to this general rule; the consensus of the authorities is that the validity of the *matnat shchiv me'rah* is of rabbinic origin, and derives from the concern of *ḥazal*, "*shemah titaref da'ato*," literally, that the mind of the *shchiv me'rah* might otherwise become unbalanced.[6] The emphasis in the recognition of the *matnat shchiv me'rah* is thus entirely outside the scope of property and inheritance law. Testamentary power is here not an attribute of property ownership; it is a function of the concern of *ḥazal* for the dying person's fragile mental and physical state, which could be adversely affected if the dying person harbored any doubt as to whether his final wishes would be carried out. This rabbinic enactment attests to the unavoidable legal recognition by *ḥazal* of the universal psychological need to express one's final wishes as to the disposition of one's property when one fears imminent death, a need so powerful that to deny its legally binding nature was deemed by *ḥazal* to risk causing *tiruf hada'at*.[7]

---

[3] M. *Baba Batra*, 8:5–6.

[4] Num. 27:8–11.

[5] M.T. *Naḥalot* 6:1.

[6] *Baba Batra* 147a; M.T. *Zehiyah U'Mattanah*, 8:2; Shulḥan Aruch, ibid.

[7] Having recognized this danger of *tiruf ha'daat*, furthermore, the implications thereof may be deemed relevant not only regarding the legal validity of the gift dictated by the testator, but also in matters of *issura*, such as the laws of *shabbat*. Professor Avraham, for example, in his *Nishmat Avraham* (*Ḥoshen Mishpat*, 250) cites a ruling of Rav Shlomo Zalman Auerbach that permits the violation of *shabbat* laws, even of biblical origin, where deemed necessary to appease the *shchiv me'rah*, such as where he insists that his son be brought to him to finalize his will with him, and this can be accomplished only by the son's driving an automobile.

Thus, while most legal systems relate to the question of the mental status of the testator as a peripheral issue that is raised only where an attempt is made to deny the testator the testamentary capacity he would otherwise possess by virtue of his inherent right as a property owner, Jewish law considers this question to be central to the issue of testamentary power, **since it is the testator's perception of impending death that creates this testamentary power.**

In order for such a gift to qualify, therefore, there must objectively exist those factors which would justify *ḥazal*'s concern that *shema titaref da'ato*: first, the testator must be in some state that objectively justifies his perception of impending death, and second, there must be some evidence that the gift in fact is a result of this perception. We therefore find three distinct categories of such gifts:

a. The basic *matnat shchiv me'rah* is one where the testator is described by Rambam and the Shulḥan Aruch as: ". . . someone ill whose entire body is weak, whose strength has failed due to the illness, to the point where he is unable to walk and he is bed-ridden."[8] Here it is not the **medical** assessment of impending death that governs; the circumstances described make no mention of the type of illness, the objective severity of the patient's condition and the existence, or the lack thereof, of a terminal prognosis. What is relevant is the effect of such a physical state upon the perceptions of the testator and upon the possibility that denial of his desire to "put his affairs in order" might cause the testator psychological distress that could serve to worsen his physical state. For that purpose, it is the **perception** that matters, not the reality, and the above-described physical facts—bed-ridden, general weakness, inability to walk—are deemed sufficient to justify the conclusion that a perception of death could exist in the testator's mind.

This in and of itself is insufficient, however, since the mere existence of physical factors does not prove that the testator was in fact motivated by such a fear of imminent death. If the testator makes no explicit declaration in that regard, a legal presumption that the gift was death-motivated will be created only where the testator disposes of his **entire** estate,[9] since it may then be assumed that the testator would not have disposed of all his assets, leaving himself penniless, unless he expected never to recover from his current condition. A partial gift of specific assets, on the other hand, would not qualify as a *matnat shchiv me'rah*, and would not be recognized as valid in the absence of the normally required acts of *kinyan* appropriate for the type of asset involved.

---

8 *Baba Batra* 146b; M.T. id., 8:2; Shulḥan Aruch, id., 250:5.
9 Shulḥan Aruch, id., 250:4.

b. The second type of valid testament is that of the *"metzaveh maḥamat mittah"*[10]—this phrase, strikingly parallel to the Latin *"gift causa mortis,"* reflects a situation involving the same physical circumstances described above which justify a perception of death, but here the testator explicitly declares that his gift is death-motivated, or the circumstances are of such clarity that no explicit declaration is necessary, such as where the testator is overheard bemoaning his imminent death, or even where we hear nothing explicit in this regard but more than three days have passed since he took ill.[11] Here the gift may be valid even if only partial, and it is this detail which distinguishes the *"metzaveh maḥamat mittah"* from the more general *matnat shchiv me'rah*; since the testator expressly declares the motivation for his gift, or the circumstances clearly indicate that this is his most probable motive, the presumption created by the disposition of the testator's entire estate is unnecessary. In the case of the *"metzaveh maḥamat mittah,"* as opposed to the general *matnat shchiv me'rah*, the mere fact that the gift is partial is not in and of itself inconsistent with our conclusion that the gift is death-motivated, since it could very well be the case that the testator is willing to rely upon the general pattern of distribution of the intestacy laws, and his partial gift is limited only to those dispositions he wishes to make that deviate from the statutory pattern. [12]

c. The third type of death-motivated gift validated by *ḥazal* is a subset of the *metzaveh maḥamat mittah*, and involves situations where the perception of imminent death is not the result of illness or physical infirmity, but rather of external circumstances which objectively justify such a perception. The classic talmudic formulation included four categories of individuals: המפרש בים, היוצא בשיירא, היוצא בקולר and the מסוכן; that is to say, one setting out on a sea voyage, one joining a caravan, a prisoner facing execution and the dangerously ill who was taken ill suddenly and is in grievous condition.[13] This category is problematic when compared to the previous categories; while a death motive may be objectively justified in the case of a condemned prisoner, no such compelling argument exists for one who is about to embark on a sea voyage or caravan trek across the desert. Clearly we must take into account the perceived danger of such journeys in talmudic times, and adjust as necessary for the perceived dangers faced by the testator in his own milieu.

---

10 *Giṭṭin* 66a; *Baba Batra* 151b; M.T. id., 8:23–24; Shulḥan Aruch, id., 250:7.

11 Shulḥan Aruch, id.; Remah, id., 250:5; S'ma, id., 242:11.

12 E.g., S'ma, id., 250:21. An interesting application of these guidelines is to be found in the suggestion of Professor Avraham (*Nishmat Avraham,* id.), that a testator who is about to undergo surgery under general anesthetic would similarly qualify as a *"metzaveh maḥamat mittah."*

13 M.T. id., 8:24; Shulḥan Aruch, id., 250:8.

It should be added that since the above-described testaments are entirely the result of the perception of impending death, if the testator should recover from his illness, or survive the dangers of his journey, it is presumed that the testator had no intention of disposing of his property in such circumstances and the gift is therefore automatically voided.[14]

We have thus seen that the testator's mental state is the key factor contributing to the legal recognition of his last will and testament. This does not mean to say that *hazal* ignored the more traditional concern that this very same perception of imminent death might in fact impair the testator's legal capacity in cases of imminent death; to the contrary, the unique rule of validity of *matnat shchiv me'rah* is in fact superimposed upon the more general provisions of Jewish law regarding the minimum mental capacity required for valid legal transactions[15]. These general rules regarding capacity are in fact particularly relevant to deathbed situations, in light of the testator's precarious physical and mental condition. Deathbed status therefore simultaneously serves to create testamentary power but also to place it in question, because of those very same factors which served to create it. Validity will thus be attained for testator's gifts if, on the one hand, he is found to be aware of, and motivated by, circumstances justifying an apprehension of imminent death sufficiently powerful to warrant concern for his continued mental well-being, but, on the other hand, only if his mental capacity to perform such a legal act is not impaired by that very same apprehension.

While other systems have attributed decisive weight to their concern that the testator's capacity may be weakened in such circumstances, thereby creating doubt as to whether he possesses a sufficient level of capacity to make a reasoned disposition, and also as to whether his weakened state might invite abuses, fraudulent testimonies and the like, *hazal* have clearly come down on the side of concern for the testator's *lifetime* well-being, evidencing relatively little concern for those factors which have been so decisive in other legal systems.

While not ignoring the problem, the issues of mental capacity, fraud, and undue influence, which occupy such a central role in Anglo-Saxon textbooks on Wills and Inheritance law, have not been overly stressed in the halachic sources. Thus, in an influential responsum of the Ritvah, cited by Karo in his *Beit Yosef* commentary to the *Tur* and by Remah in his gloss to Shulḥan Aruch,[16] it was held that a will of a *shchiv me'rah* will be deemed valid even if it contains no reference to any examination of testator's com-

---

[14] Shulḥan Aruch, id.
[15] Shulḥan Aruch, id., 250:6; Aruch Hashulḥan, id., 250:27.
[16] 250:6.

petence on the part of the attesting witnesses.[17] Ritvah rules that the requirement that an examination of the competence of a *shchiv me'rah* be performed where he has given instructions for the writing and delivery to his wife of a bill of divorce,[18] is only relevant where he is known to have been suffering from an affliction that had impaired his mental capacity in the past. In other circumstances, on the other hand, Ritvah lays down the general principle that "the usual *schiv me'rah* is of sound mind and his instructions are binding without any examination [of his mental status]."[19]

There may, of course, be specific circumstances, such as a particular mental condition known to be suffered by the testator, which force us to raise the issue of mental competence; every developed legal system has recognized and dealt with the problems of the mentally incompetent individual, known in Jewish law as the "*shoteh*."[20] However, the issue of mental capacity in such situations is not a function of the individual's deathbed status but of his *pre-existing* mental condition, and the legal treatment of such issues is therefore not of particular interest in formulating a comprehensive understanding of the legal treatment of the *matnat shchiv me'rah* per se.

The critical issue here is the extent to which deathbed status **itself** creates doubt as to the mental capacity of the testator. This in turn would appear to require the formulation of precise criteria for a finding of sufficient mental capacity. Medical criteria may be of supportive utility in this regard, but it is clear that legal standards of capacity are definitely not parallel, but are *sui generis* to the law itself.

As stated above, the *shchiv me'rah* status does not in and of itself raise any question as to competence of the testator, and the issue of standards to be examined therefore does not arise. However, as illustrated above, this status as a *shchiv me'rah* is attributable to a variety of circumstances which range across a broad spectrum of possible mental states, from the relatively benign, healthy testator departing upon a dangerous voyage, to the testator who is bedridden with a physically debilitating illness but who is obviously in full control of his faculties by any imaginable standard of measurement, to the testator who cannot speak but appears to be fully aware and responsive, to the testator who may be deemed a "*goses*," whose death is imminent. In such relatively acute conditions reflected at the latter edge of this spectrum, we do find expressions of concern for testator's mental status, and we

---

[17] *Resp. Ritvah*, 123.
[18] *Giṭṭin* 67b; Shulḥan Aruch, *Even Ha'ezer*, 121.
[19] Ritvah, id.
[20] See, e.g., *Hagigah* 3b–4a; M.T. *Edut* 9:9.

therefore encounter the requirement of *"bedikot,"* of particular examinations designed to test the testator's mental capacity.

Based on the principle found in a baraita cited in tractate *Gittin*, "כשם שבודקין אותו לגיטין כך בודקין אותו למשאות ולמתנות ולעדויות ולירושות",[21] ("Just as we must examine him for *gittin* so must we examine him for commercial transactions, the giving of testimony and the making of testaments"), we find that just as where a *shchiv me'rah* requesting that a *get* be written and delivered to his wife, must be examined as to capacity where he is no longer able to speak, so too would the *shchiv me'rah* testator have to undergo an examination as to capacity if he could not speak but communicates via gestures, nodding his head in response to questions posed to him, and the like.[22] This examination is deemed necessary because the very fact that the testator has lost his ability to speak may either be an **indication** that his mental capacity is impaired, or the loss of speech due to the progression of his illness may itself have depressed or shocked the testator to the point where his capacity may thereby have been impaired.

Even in the case of the *goses*, while several *Rishonim* are of the opinion that his very status deprives the *goses* of the ability to perform legal acts of any kind,[23] the consensus of halachic authorities has established that the principle "*Hagoses harei hu ke'hai lekol davar,*"[24] "The *goses* is deemed to be alive for all purposes," is applicable with regard to legal capacity, and the possibility of validly declaring his last wishes is therefore not precluded by the mere fact of his physically extreme condition.[25] Some authorities do hold that the *goses* can only do so if he is capable of speaking;[26] others recognize the capacity of the *goses* even where he can no longer speak, so long as he can convey his wishes via gestures[27] (and there is some evidence that even the more stringent opinions restrict themselves specifically to *get*, where the consequences of an invalid bill of divorce would be far more serious than the possibly inappropriate transfer of an inheritance from an intestate heir to the named legatee).

In formulating the required examination regarding capacity, we find an interestingly different approach in Jewish law as compared to that of

---

21 *Gittin* 71a.

22 Shulḥan Aruch, id., 121:5.

23 E.g., Tosafot *Kiddushin* 78b, *d'h lo tzriha*; opinion of R. Yonah as cited in Rashba, Ran, and Mordehai to *Gittin* 70b; Rosh, *Kiddushin*, 4:15; Ṭur *Even Ha'ezer* 121.

24 *S'maḥot* 1:1; M.T. *Evel* 4:5; Ṭur Shulḥan Aruch *Yoreh De'ah* 339:1.

25 Tosafot, id. (second opinion); Ri, as cited by Rosh, id., Rashba, Ran, and Mordehai to *Gittin*, id; Shulḥan Aruch *Even Ha'ezer*, 121:7.

26 Mordehai, *Gittin*, id.; Remah, *Even Ha'ezer*, id.

27 Bet Yosef, *Even Ha'ezer*, 121; Shulḥan Aruch, id.

Anglo-American law. A typical statement of the Anglo-American test is that of Atkinson on Wills,[28] who bases his remarks on the classic English case on the subject of capacity, *Banks v. Goodfellow*:[29] "One is of sound mind for testamentary purposes only when he can understand and carry in his mind in a general way: (1) the nature and extent of his property; (2) the persons who are the natural objects of his bounty; and (3) the disposition which he is making of his property."

We thus find that in English and American law, there exists a clear differentiation regarding the relative degrees of cognitive functioning required in various capacities. Thus, the degree of competence required for wills is specific to wills: evaluation of capacity is transaction-oriented; it is determined by questions relating to the nature and situation of the testator's property and the identity of the "natural objects of the testator's bounty."

In Jewish law, on the other hand, the questions to be asked are totally general in nature—the Babylonian Talmud formulates questions such as whether the testator would like to have the witnesses pick fruits for him that are known to be out of season and the like,[30] thereby indicating that capacity, in whatever context, is a function of common sense and general awareness.

It should be noted that the *Yerushalmi*, as opposed to the *Bavli*, actually does require questions specific to the testamentary dispositions being made,[31] and Karo, in his *Bet Yosef*,[32] cites the *Yerushalmi* together with the *Bavli* without noting the radical difference between these two approaches. In his Shulḥan Aruch,[33] on the other hand, Karo rules, in the context of competence examinations for the giving of a *get*, that questions should be asked "*bedavar aḥer*" (lit., "on some other thing"), clearly indicating that he had adopted the *Bavli* approach.

In this regard, it is of interest to note that there is some support for the position that, while examination is not required of a *goses* so long as he can speak, his instructions will be granted legal validity without an examination so long as these instructions are in and of themselves coherent and rational; if they are not, an examination of competence would then be required. A classic example of this approach is to be found in the oft-cited responsum of the great 16th century Turkish halachic authority, Mahari ben Lev.[34] Thus, the requirement that the testator recognize the natural objects

---

[28] (1953), at p. 232.
[29] Court of Queens Bench, L.R. 5 Q.B. 549 (1870).
[30] *Giṭṭin* 70b–71a; Remah, Shulḥan Aruch, id.
[31] *Giṭṭin* 7:1.
[32] *Even Ha'ezer* 121:1.
[33] Id.
[34] *Resp. Mahari ben Lev*, 2:81.

of his bounty does play some role in the halachic rules as well: the failure of the testator to fulfill this standard would not, however, result in Jewish law in a determination of incompetence, but would merely create a requirement that a competence examination be performed where one would otherwise not be required. The examination itself, however, would focus on generalities of the kind described above, so as to test the testator's general rather than transaction-specific mental competence.

It should be evident from the above that in the overall equation of those concerns deemed relevant in determining whether the oral deathbed will should be recognized as valid, we find that the halachic approach uniquely favors recognition, based on its overriding concern for the testator's well-being so long as he is still alive. That this concern is paramount is clearly evident both from the rabbinic enactment itself, which grants legally binding force to the testator's instructions although not reduced to writing, and from the relatively lenient attitude exhibited by *ḥazal* toward the issues of mental competence which may arise in specific deathbed-related circumstances. It is only in the most extreme cases that a competence examination is required at all, and its content, being totally general in nature, poses little if any impediment to many testators who might not have faired as well if interrogated according to the Anglo-American model.

One further point in this regard. The concern of modern legal systems with the possible abuses of the deathbed testament are clearly not misplaced. The weakened mental state of the testator, which sometimes lasts for a considerable period of time, provides fertile ground for a determined party to take advantage of his closeness to the testator, either blatantly to defraud by lying as to what was said by the testator before his death, or at least to exert influence upon the testator intended to produce a will that reflects the wishes of the influencing party more than the true wishes that the testator might have expressed if left on his own. It is therefore somewhat surprising, at first glance, to find that the early halachic sources displayed very little concern for these issues. A typical example of this phenomenon is found in a responsum of Tashbetz,[35] in which the surviving brothers of a young decedent challenged the validity of his deathbed gift to his mother, which deprived them of the inheritance to which they would have been entitled by intestacy. Their challenge was based on the argument that the mother had unduly influenced the boy to make the gift to her while she cared for him during the period of his final illness. Tashbetz refused to consider such an argument, claiming that it could not form the basis for a valid claim of duress:

---

[35] *Resp. Tashbetz*, 4:*Ṭur bet*, 3. See, also, *Resp. Beit Yehuda, Ḥoshen Mishpat*, 13.

אין ההסתה וההדחה נקראים אונס,
שההסתה אינה אלא בדברי פיוס ותחנונים מהמסית
עד שהמוסת גומר בלבו ודעתו לעשות מה
שאומר לו המוסת. ואם היה באמת בעל כורחו,
אז יש לקבל טענה זו רק ע"פ עדים שמסר
להם מודעה, כי אדרבה - אנו אומרים, אילו לא
עבדה ליה אימיה נייחא, לא הוי יהיב לה מידי.

This case may be limited to its specific facts, in that apparently there was significant evidence that the son indeed wanted to benefit his mother in gratitude for her devoted service in caring for him. However, there is no indication in the responsum that Tashbetz was at all receptive to the kind of argument represented by modern undue influence cases, which are willing to probe beneath the surface in order to determine whether the testator's apparently independent expression of his final wishes might not be merely as a mouthpiece for the wishes of someone else who had succeeded in replacing the testator's will with his own.

Other *Poskim*[36] take a more expansive attitude toward the parameters of *oness*, or duress, holding that any form of evidence that proves that a gift was made against the true wishes of the donor may invalidate the gift, and the undue influence argument would therefore appear to be available according to this approach.

Furthermore, several 20th century *Poskim* have explicitly taken note of the potential abuses of the deathbed will; whereas the entire construct of this body of law has been demonstrated to reflect the overriding concern of *ḥazal* to grant validity to the deathbed will in order to provide for the testator's piece of mind, the modern approach has begun to shift in the direction of creating safeguards against fraud and other abuse, even at the expense of denying validity to deathbed wills otherwise valid according to traditional halacha.[37]

The following observations of the late Chief Rabbi of the State of Israel, Rabbi Yitzhak Isaac Halevi Herzog, warrant special mention in this regard. In his monumental work, "Constitution and Law in the Jewish State According to the Halacha,"[38] Rabbi Herzog proposes the enactment of a *takkanah* that would do away completely with the oral deathbed will. He states as follows:

---

[36] Such as the 17th century Egyptian Posek, Rabbi Avraham ben Mordechai Halevi in his responsa *Ginnat Veradim, Ḥoshen Mishpat, klal* 5, 1, and S'ma, *Ḥoshen Mishpat*, 242:1.

[37] See comments of Rabbi Herzog, infra.

[38] *Teḥukah leyisrael al pi hatorah* (Jerusalem: Mossad Harav Kook, 1989).

The deathbed will is not at all a complicated matter, and there would appear to be no need to legislate. From my experience, however, I have come to realize that there is room for consideration of some form of *takkanah*, "because the generation is not worthy," and there are sometimes those who conspire to defraud the heirs by presenting witnesses who are prepared to testify [falsely] that the decedent in fact made a deathbed will before his death. In cases that have come before us, we have concluded, after a thorough examination of the facts, that the petition was fraudulent, and we refused to accept the testimony. It therefore appears that there is justification for a *takkanah* that would require that oral wills, although valid, be subjected to additional investigation.... If I had the ability to do so, I would in fact go further than this and, in order to close the door before those who would defraud, I would ordain that oral wills be null and void entirely.... [I]n our times... there is almost no one who cannot write or at least sign his name, and we therefore needn't be concerned lest the testator's peace of mind be affected. Proof of this may be derived from the fact that in all the years that I have sat on the Rabbinical Court of Appeals there has been presented testimony concerning an oral will on only two occasions, and in both cases we found the testimony to be false.[39]

It is indeed unfortunate that the enlightened respect of *ḥazal* for the wishes of the testator must give way to the protective devices necessary to prevent fraud and abuse. While the *takkanah* proposed by Rabbi Herzog was never in fact enacted, his remarks are rather indicative of the probable directions that this body of law will take as it evolves in the future. The almost universal recognition of the testator's expressed wishes as genuine and competent will invariably give way to greater suspicion and doubt, accompanied by greater stringency in requiring examinations of competence as well as greater openness to attack on grounds of undue influence and duress.

---

[39] Id., as translated in Greenberger, Ben Tzion, "Rabbi Herzog's Proposals for *Takkanot* in Matters of Inheritance," *Jewish Law Association Studies*, Vol. 5, pp. 49–112, at p. 104–105.

7

THE PROBLEM OF *IGGUN* AND ITS SOLUTIONS

MOSHE ISH-HOROWICZ[*]

Introduction

Iggun is the status of a woman "anchored" to her husband or *levir* (Latin for brother-in-law) who is either unable or unwilling to release her to remarry.

The following three categories of such women, *agunot*, are distinguished:

i. When the husband is asked but refuses to give his wife a divorce.

ii. When the husband deserts his wife without giving her a *get*. He either absconded to an unknown address deliberately or was separated unintentionally, as happened in wars or during the Holocaust. Then, neither can he be persuaded to divorce her nor can his death be established, for his or a *levir's* death frees the *agunah* to remarry.

iii. When she is a childless widow, a *yevamah*, who cannot remarry because the *levir (yavam)* refuses to release her by submitting to the ritual of "ḥalitsah."

Such prevention of remarriage is no longer tolerable. It is unjust and cruel, contrary to the ethically and theistically righteous spirit of Jewish law. Denial of a divorce ensues from women's inequality. The traditional marriage ceremony does not signify a union of two equals. It is the man who symbolically, by his ring, buys the wife—who becomes his possession—and "consecrates her to himself" as his wife. Consequently in a broken marriage the wife is unable to divorce her husband. He also can release her without coercion or compulsion by handing over to her a *get*, i.e., a bill of divorcement. With it he relinquishes his possession, the wife, and "expels" her which renders her a *gerushah*. He finally declares that she is free to remarry. His refusal to grant the *get* leads to *iggun*.

---

[*] Ph.D.
1, Tarlton Court, Broadlands Avenue, London SW 16 1ND, UK
(for long spells also address: 8 Hankin Street, Apt. 15, Tel Aviv, Israel 62506).

Iggun and Righteousness

The gravity of the plight of *agunot* and an outcry for an immediate solution emerge, for instance, from the past Chief Rabbi, Lord Jacobovits' article in the *Jewish Chronicle* (9 Sept. 1988, p.45). In it he quoted his late father (*z"l*) on the last day of his life when he was partly in delirium: "I could not sleep at night . . . because the *agunot* appeared before me, the women I could not help . . . And if I became grey it was because of the *agunot*, not because of the Nazis." Because of their intolerable plight in breach of the principles of *tzedek*, righteousness, their situation cries for compassion and justice. As the prophet Malachi said, "To you who revere God, the sun of righteousness shall arise with healing in its wings"[1]—healing all the ills, social, *halakhic* and other including those of *agunot*.

Women Refused a Divorce

To ease the plight of such *agunot*, the rabbis permitted the pressuring of such husbands to grant the *get* to their wives, even through an agent. They decreed that such a *get* cannot be corrected or rescinded, even though this is contrary to the Written Torah.[2]

Levirate Marriage

Iggun ensuing from levirate marriage, "*yibbum*," presents a most conspicuous case of lack of logic and morality. The opening phrase from Deuteronomy 25:5–6 sets the background: "If brothers dwell together"—and only then, in the same clan, as was customary in antiquity—and if one of them dies without issue, his brother must marry the widow. It was a compassionate law. It was his duty to care for all her needs, including conjugal rights, a home, and motherhood, that she need not marry "a stranger." The firstborn shall succeed to the name (and inheritance) of the deceased brother that his name be not blotted out of Israel."[3]

Ḥalitsah

Deuteronomy 7–10 incorporates the humiliating and offensive declarations and rites of *ḥalitsah*, a punishment directed against a recalcitrant brother-in-law who refused to do his duty and marry the *yevamah*. Nowadays the

---

[1] Malachi 3:20.
[2] *Giṭṭin*, 33a.
[3] Deut. 25:5–6; *Yev.* 24a; *Yad Hilkhot Naḥalot* 3:4.

brothers may live continents apart; they may not even know their sisters-in-law. Scripture does not impose any restrictions on the women's remarriage, but tries to prevent the *levir's* rejection of the widow. Nor does Scripture envisage *halitsah* if she refuses to marry a willing *levir*, in which case he should not be punished. In fact, partly because of prohibition of bigamy in Christian countries, and mainly because of extortions by greedy or malicious brothers-in-law who refused to submit to *halitsah* unless rewarded, levirate marriage has been by now totally forbidden. Yet, strangely, the punishment of *halitsah* has not been abolished and blackmail is allowed to continue. Moreover, even if a righteous *levir* wants to marry the widow, he may not, but must submit himself to the indignities of *halitsah* and utter the lie that he refuses to marry the *yevamah*, in breach of the biblical prohibition of lying, in Leviticus 19:11. The decent man then submits to spitting and insults designated for a rogue defaulting on his duties.

This is not only wrong and unjust, but contrary to the ruling, "whoever is subject to the obligation of levirate marriage is also subject to *halitsah*, and whoever is not subject to levirate marriage is not subject to *halitsah*."[4] This is acknowledged also by Isaac Alfasi, Rambam and Joseph Caro.[5]

Nevertheless, contrary to the above sources, luminaries and others, one 13th century rabbi, Rabbenu Tam, reversed the above ruling and decided that *halitsah* took precedence over *yibbum*. It is obvious that in our generation it is imperative to revert to the biblical, talmudic and rabbinic origins, that *halitsah* is the *levir's* punishment if he refuses to perform his duty towards his sister-in-law. However, since he is now prohibited from marrying his sister-in-law, he must not be punished.

In the Talmud, Abba Saul gave preference to *halitsah* only if the *levir* wanted to marry the widow because of her beauty or another ulterior motive and not for the sake of performing the *mitzvah* of levirate marriage. But even then he was overruled by the sages and also by Rabbi Caro, in the sixteenth century.[6] The *levir* also should be exempted from the humiliating *halitsah* when the late brother was married to his wife's sister, whom he is forbidden to marry because it would be incestuous,[7] or when he is an apostate, or is infected by a dangerous disease, or is mentally retarded, etc. When the *levir* is a minor, he cannot be subjected to *halitsah* until he becomes *bar mitzvah* and the widow has to wait for up to thirteen years and a day or longer.[8]

---

[4] *Yev.* 3a.
[5] *Yev.* 3b; *Yad Hilkhot Yibbum* 1:2; *Sh. Ar. EH* 165:1.
[6] *Yev.* 39b; *Sh. Ar. EH* 165:1.
[7] Lev. 18:18.
[8] Mishnah in *Yev.* 104b; *Sh. Ar. EH* 172:12.

At the end of the *ḥalitsah* ceremony, the rabbis of the *Beth Din* recite the prayer: "May it be the Divine will that the daughters of Israel have no need to resort to either *ḥalitsah* or *yibbum*." This borders on hypocrisy because also today the Torah is not in heaven and neither a heavenly voice nor visions nor prophets are allowed by the rabbis to establish the *halakhah*.[9] Thus they and their courts alone have taken over the exclusive authority and duty to legislate and implement righteousness.[10] This implies abandoning *ḥalitsah* and *iggun* with their blackmail, injustices, and misfortunes, as the Chief Rabbinate of Israel have similarly abolished levirate marriage in 1944 and 1950 for the sake of righteousness, without waiting for Elijah, the Messiah, or even a Sanhedrin.

Concessions to Prevent Iggun

In some countries, civil courts can provide partial help to prevent *iggun*. However, through the ages, our own sages and rabbis did find solutions which were based on our own righteous laws and traditions. They ruled that "concessions should be made" to allow a woman to remarry so as to avoid "the danger of her becoming an *agunah*."[11] They permitted *agunot* to remarry even on the testimony of incompetent witnesses such as a child, a slave, or by hearsay, attesting to the death of an absconded husband or *levir*.[12] This is in breach of biblical law, which demands at least two or three legally qualified witnesses.[13] This concession to free *agunot* to remarry conforms with Rabbi Judah the Prince's saying in Mishnah Avot 2, 1 that in a dilemma like the above the consequences matter, and prevention of the plight of *iggun* is a prevailing mandatory mitzvah for the sake of compassion and justice. On the same grounds *ḥalitsah* too should be abolished. Moreover, in accordance with Rambam's *Hilkhot Mamrim* 2:4, that even biblical laws may be changed if necessary—the more so rabbinical rules, "in order to strengthen religion . . . to bring many back to religion, or to save many (Israelites) from grief in other matters . . . according to the call of the hour." Furthermore, according to *Yad Mamrim* 2:1, an old law established by even a great Beth Din may be changed by a **contemporary** Beth Din for a different reason; this judge you should obey, as it is written in Deuteronomy 7:9: "You shall come to the judge who shall be in those days."

---

9 *BM* 59b; ibid.; *Eruvin* 13b; *Sifra beḥukkotay* 13, 7 on Lev. 27:34.
10 Deut. 17:9; infra n. 20.
11 *Giṭṭin* 3a, *Yev.* 88a and *Tosafot*; *Rosh* 51, 2; Rambam's Responsa *Pe'er Ha-dor* 86; et al.
12 *Mishnah Yev.* 16, 5–7.
13 Deut. 17:5.

Conditional Marriage and Divorce

To prevent *iggun*, sages and rabbis also introduced various forms of pre-nuptial and post-nuptial conditional marriages and divorces.[14] The sages introduced them by applying very considerate rabbinic rules, such as: "Go easy with Israel; let them transgress inadvertently rather than deliberately."[15] Rabbi Prof. E. Berkovits followed Mahari of Brun and proposed conditions, especially "retroactive marriage annulment," as a matter of utmost urgency.[16] "For the problem of *agunot* has almost ceased to exist." Instead, "they were finding partners without obtaining a divorce, thus causing the problem of *mamzerut*.[17] "The time has come to act for the Lord, for the sake of the sanctity of the people of Israel."[18] The above suggestion would thus prevent *ḥillul ha-am*, apart from the *ḥillul ha-Shem* inherent in the injustices of *iggun* and the plight of *agunot*. The Conservative/Masorti movement has adopted Rabbi Berkovits' solutions, while the British Reform *Beth Din* has abolished both *ḥalitsah* and *iggun* and ultimately releases an *agunah* by retro-active marriage annulment and issuing a certificate that Mrs. X is free to remarry in a Reform Synagogue.

Contemporary Orthodox rabbis like David Bleich and Shlomo Riskin submitted their own proposals, but Orthodoxy in the United Kingdom refused to yield until Chief Rabbi Sacks and five Orthodox rabbinates ultimately succeeded in agreeing on a formula for a Pre-Nuptial Agreement (PNA) to be signed by the bridegroom and the bridge before the marriage ceremony in order to prevent *iggun* in the future. The text of the PNA appears in the Appendix. The significance and ramifications of this breakthrough are enormous. For the first time a Chief Rabbi and five contemporary right-wing Orthodox Rabbinates broke their bar on conditional marriages. The PNA was achieved mainly by women's efforts although strict Orthodoxy did not allow them to quote any rabbinic sources in support of their just cause. This breakthrough established a precedent and shows that changes in the *halakhah* and practices are possible without a Sanhedrin or worldwide consensus. It also shows that they have been made for the sake of compassion and justice and other facets of righteousness such as the equality of women and the will and voice of the community. As Rabbi Ishmael B. Elisha said, "We do not lay a hardship on the community unless the majority can endure it."[19] Where there is a will there is a way, because the

---

14 *Shab.* 56a; Mishnah *Giṭṭin* 7, 3; *Ketubot* 2b; 3a; 9b.
15 *Bava Batra* 60b.
16 Rabbi Prof. E. Berkovits, *Conditional Marriage and Divorce* (H), 1966.
17 Ibid., pp. 161–2.
18 Ibid., p. 164, applying *Mishnah Ber.* 9,5, on Psalms 119:126.
19 *BB* 60b.

rabbis are not only administrators of law, but also makers of laws by majority vote in a Sanhedrin or in qualified *Bathei Din*.[20]

Flaws in the new PNA charter

Chief Rabbi Sacks' PNA Charter (see Appendix) is not flawless: it deals only with a bride and a bridegroom; it does not refer at all to an *agunah* refused *ḥalitsah*. Also, the PNA is only preventive; it may help in the future but cannot free either existing *agunot* or women already married who may still become *agunot*. Even now, many do not want to sign a PNA, resenting the thought of a divorce at the time of their marriage. Also doubtful is the efficacy of the suggested inadequate sanctions, social and congregational, envisaged for a reluctant spouse who signs the PNA and subsequently refuses to honor it. They are insignificant in comparison with the severe fine, alimony, prison, even ban imposed in Israel on the recalcitrant husbands and *levirs* who nevertheless persisted in their defiance.

Actually, in *Hilkhot Gerushin* 2:20 Maimonides ordains that if a *Beth Din* decrees that if the husband must divorce his wife but refuses to do so, then he could be beaten until he concedes and gives the *get*. Today, flogging is inconceivable, but the "annulment of marriage" which follows can resolve the problem, bearing also in mind that the husband has obviously reneged on his commitment to take proper care of his wife.

The Retroactive Marriage Annulment

An apparently faultless solution to the plight of *agunot* is already envisaged in the Talmud. It is *hafka'at ḳiddushin*: a retroactive marriage annulment by a *Beth Din*. It is founded on the absolute principle that "a man marries a woman on conditions laid down by the rabbis:"[21] namely, "according to the law of Moses and Israel." As they had the authority to sanctify the marriage, the rabbis have equally the authority to annul the marriage retroactively in circumstances which necessitate it and on terms which objective experts on such family settlements can evaluate.[22] Both spouses are then free as if they had never married. If the woman remarries and bears children, they are not *mamzerim*, even if the first husband returns. The freedom and return to normal life will help both partners to forget the recriminations and the traumas which led to the broken marriage and its

---

[20] Deut. 17:8–9; 32:7; *Bava Metsia* 59b; *Eruvin* 13b; *Tanḥuma Noaḥ* (Zundel) 3; *Pesikta Rabbati* 3,1; 21,6; *J. San.* 4, 2, with *Pnei Moshe*; *Song of Songs Rabbah* 2,4, par. 1; et al.
[21] *Ketubot* 3a; *Giṭṭin* 33a; *Yev.* 19b; et al.
[22] Judge Myrella Cohen, QC, *Jewish Chronicle*, 28 June 1996.

cancellation.

In practice, retroactive marriage annulments were recorded in various localities and at various times. One is even recorded in the *Mappah Perusah* on the *Shulḥan Arukh*, sanctioned by Rema in the special case of the marriage of a bridegroom whose brother was an apostate.[23] Rema authorized the insertion of the pre-nuptial condition that, if he dies without issue, his wife should be considered as having never married, in order to exempt her from levirate marriage and from *ḥalitsah* by the apostate brother (Mahari of Brun). This is a retroactive annulment; otherwise she would remain an *agunah* forever. Such tragic *iggun* would arise if the brother became an apostate after the marriage, before which the imposition of a conditional dissolution of marriage could not have been envisaged. To prevent the hopeless *iggun*, the dissolution should be effected retroactively in the compassionate spirit of the law (*lifnim mishurat ha-din*).[24] Alternatively, Rabbi Jacob ben Yehuda Weil permits a childless widow to remarry if the *levir*, although an apostate, submits to *ḥalitsah*.[25]

Recently, D. Pearlman, too,[26] recognized the full authority of the *Beth Din* and suggested its use, not for annulling the marriage, but for issuing a *get* to the wife in spite of the husband's objection. This is a serious flaw from the Orthodox point of view. In contrast, the retroactive marriage annulment does not need the husband's presence and consent. Nor does it make the wife a divorcee, forbidden to a *kohen* and unjustly stigmatized in many circles. The problem of *ḥalitsah* is not considered in Perlman's proposal. It is, however, disposed of by *hafḳa'at ḳiddushin*; for, if the deceased man was never married, the brother is not a *yavam*, and the ex-sister-in-law is not a widow.

Thus *hafḳa'at ḳiddushin* is different in concept and character from a *get* and involves a different procedure. Once the *Beth Din* establishes that the marriage has irrevocably broken down, the husband is involved only in the negotiation of the terms of the family settlement.

Tragedy would also strike a woman who remarries on the grounds of a mistaken testimony about the death of her first husband. If he were later to turn up alive, then according to the *Halakhah*, she has to divorce both husbands and the children from the second husband are *mamzerim* (*rot*). Retroactive annulment of the first marriage especially before remarriage would resolve the problem because it would release her to remarry without

---

[23] *Sh. Ar. EH* 157:4.
[24] *Berakhot* 7a. Apply also supra n. 11 and n. 15.
[25] Responsum no. 54 on *Sh. Ar. EH* 157:4.
[26] Jewish Chronicle, 31 May 96.

the above tragic consequences.

Hafka'at kiddushin avoids or disposes of the limitations, inflexibility, one-sidedness and other difficulties in implementation which are inherent in pre-nuptial conditions. For instance, after years of marriage, the birth of children, and likely changes in their financial situation, some of the old marriage conditions would become irrelevant. Instead, and rightly so, before the annulment of a broken marriage, the *Beth Din* would take into consideration all the then prevailing circumstances.

Other Solutions

As shown, *hafka'at kiddushin* may be used as a condition in a PNA as well as independently in the case of a broken marriage. However, apart from receiving an ordinary divorce from her husband or a *get* from the *Beth Din* according to Mr. Pearlman's suggestion, the problem of *iggun* could also be resolved as follows:

a. On the basis of equality of sexes, a wife should be able to approach a rabbinical court for divorcing her husband against his will, as the husband does in divorcing her. A range of circumstances should also be established in which a divorce may be imposed on a recalcitrant spouse.

b. A "deserted wife" should be allowed to remarry after a certain time and under specific conditions and circumstances.

c. A man should write a conditional divorce before a long journey and before he commences his military service, especially in times of war, to prevent her becoming an *agunah* when her husband or *levir* may disappear, perhaps killed or taken prisoner.[27]

d. A signed conditional marriage[28] or a signed conditional *get*,[29] which becomes valid in specified circumstances, in all eventualities, is left by the husband for the *Beth Din*, to use at its discretion.

e. Apply all the considerate and righteous rules for avoiding or alleviating the fate of *agunot* as discussed above.

f. A husband who beats his wife is duty-bound to give her a divorce if she asks for it.[30]

---

27 *Ket.* 9b; *Shab.* 56a.
28 *Sh. Ar. EH* 38.
29 *Ket.* 2b; 3a; 9b; *Sh. Ar. EH* 144, 1–7.
30 Sh. Y. Cohen and Sh. Luria, in A. Strikovski, ed. *Daf Letarbut Yehudit*, No. 213, *Sivan* 5155, pp. 3–4, Minister of Education and Culture, Jerusalem.

Objections to Hafka'at Kiddushin

Some objections raised against *hafka'at kiddushin* concern its ease and simplicity. However, in principle, "ease" and "concessions" for helping *agunot* are mandatory facilities universally ordained by all sages and rabbis to prevent *iggun*. The *Beth Din*, however, retains the authority to decide first whether the marriage has broken down irrevocably and whether a *get* or *halitsah* can be achieved without blackmail or coercion, or whether the husband or *levir* cannot be traced or his death cannot be established.

Untenable and inconceivable is an argument that the hardships of *iggun* are a burden that *agunot* should bear as a price for being Jewish. Such opinion is contrary to the fundamentals of righteousness and tradition in Judaism. As invariably quoted in this essay, we are commanded to make every possible concession even in biblical laws of testimony in order to prevent a woman from becoming an *agunah*.[31] The recent PNA in the United Kingdom refutes this argument. At this conference Michael Broyde told us that a rebellious wife who even committed adultery and forfeited her *ketubah* should nevertheless be given a *get* by the husband. For ours is a religion of compassion, justice and peace; and *iggun* is evil and denigrated throughout the ages, in the Bible, the Talmud, and all rabbinic writings.[32]

Another untenable argument rejects the retroactive marriage annulment under the pretext that it is "antiquated." Since when can righteousness and a solution to the most painful problem in Judaism be considered "out of date?" The annulment has been used and recommended throughout generations since the Talmud. Rabbi Prof. Berkovits refuted the above argument in 1966 by his important references to *hafka'at kiddushin* and its powerful recommendations.[33]

Epilogue

Thus *hafka'at kiddushin*, the retroactive cancellation of marriage, avoids and resolves all the above problems in the spirit of righteousness, primarily ethics, which is the foundation of Jewish faith, law and practice. As Maimonides affirms: "The decisions (of the Torah) are not vengeance on the people, but mercy, kindness and peace in the community."[34] Rabbi

---

31 Supra n. 11 and 12.
32 The episode of Tamar and Judah; Ruth 1:13; E. Berkovits supra n. 16; A.H. Freiman *Seder Kiddushin ve-Nissuin* 1945; et al.
33 Supra n. 16 throughout the book and n. 32.
34 *Yad Hilkhot Shabbat* 2:3.

Prof. E. Berkovits asserts: "God forbid that there should be anything in the application of the Torah to the actual life situation that is contrary to the spirit of ethics."[35] Like levirate marriage in the past, ancient *ḥalitsah* and the one-sided *get*, both leading to *iggun*, became so unethical and intolerable that their abolition, too, became imperative. As the celebrated Kotzker Rabbi asserts with reference to the second of the Ten Commandments, "The prohibition against the making of idols includes within itself the prohibition of making idols out of mitzvot." The chief purpose of a *mitzvah* is its **inward meaning, not its outward form**.[36] Obsolete *ḥalitsah* and the one-sided *get*, and the one-sided marriage (*ḳiddushin*), in which the husband's ring (a token payment) bought him the wife, all became such idols which led to the intolerable *iggun*. Nowadays the ring is not seen to represent the purchase of a wife, as the officiating rabbi is at pains to explain. It rather signifies the mutual commitment to love, devotion, and loyalty, sanctioned in the union of two equals, the bride and the bridegroom. This is expressed in the traditional seven blessings, much more than in the *ketubah* contract signed by the bridegroom.

And those extremists who still refuse to relent and to break the chains of injustice and hardship of *iggun*, let them take heed to the warning of the Sephardi Chief Rabbi of Israel, Rabbi Ben-Zion Meir Hai Uziel, z"l, who quoted (in a different context) the divine words from the Book of Ezekiel:[37] "Woe unto the shepherds of Israel ... Should not the shepherds care for the flocks? ... Neither have you bandaged the hurt, nor have you brought back those who were lost, but with force have you ruled over them and with ruthlessness."

Not one of our shepherds—Orthodox, Reform or Conservative—disputes the evil of *iggun*. The process of liberating *agunot* must not be stopped.

Appendix

The text below is an amended version of the PNA of the *Beth Din* of Chief Rabbi, Dr. Jonathan Sacks, the London *Beth Din*. An alternative version, without the arbitration clause 2, is also available.

---

35 E. Berkovits, *Not in Heaven*, 1983, p. 19.
36 Newman, *Hasidic Anthology*, p. 193.
37 *Piske Ouziel, Bishe'elot Ha-zeman, Mosad ha-Rav Kook*, Jerusalem, 1977, par. 63a; Ezekiel 34:2, 4.

Pre-Nuptial Agreement

1. The bride and bridegroom agree that, in the event of any matrimonial dispute, they will both attend the Court of the Chief Rabbi, the London *Beth Din* (or such other *Beth Din* as that *Beth Din* shall direct) when required to do so and that they will comply with the instructions of that *Beth Din*, including co-operation in any mediation recommended, in seeking to resolve all problems arising out of or in connection with their Jewish marriage.
2. The bride and bridegroom further agree that if the problems concerning their Jewish marriage are not resolved, under Paragraph 1 above, any dispute arising out of or in connection with that marriage shall be referred to and finally resolved by arbitration by the London *Beth Din* (or such other *Beth Din* as that *Beth Din* shall direct), in accordance with *Halachah* under the Arbitration Acts, 1950, 1975 and 1979 (or any amendment, consolidation or replacement thereof) and in accordance with the procedural rules of the relevant *Beth Din*.
3. The bridegroom further undertakes that, irrespective of civil proceedings being instituted in respect of the marriage, he will fulfil all his financial obligations to his wife as determined by the London *Beth Din* (or such other *Beth Din* as that *Beth Din* shall direct). This obligation shall not affect the authority of the civil court under the Matrimonial Causes Act, 1973 or any amendment or replacement thereof, or the authority of any civil court to whose jurisdiction the bride and/or the bridegroom may be subject, and shall be subject to obtaining the approval of the court where required or appropriate.
4. Neither the bride nor the bridegroom shall apply in any civil proceedings without prior approval in writing of the *Beth Din* for an order to enforce an award of the *Beth Din*, or for an order in relation to non-compliance with this agreement.
5. The bride and bridegroom confirm that they have made this agreement freely and in the full knowledge and understanding of the meaning of its terms.

8

INSOLVENCY IN JEWISH LAW

JONATHAN M. LEWIS[*]

> Whatever we receive from this world—and indeed the entire Universe makes countless contributions to every breath we take on earth—is only a loan granted us to help us strive for and bring about those goals by means of which we advance the welfare of G-d's world in accordance with His Will as revealed to us in His Law. No one exists solely for himself and the greater the loan he has been granted, the greater his obligation and the sum total of achievement that may be expected of him in return.
>
> Rabbi Samson Raphael Hirsch[1]

Introduction

In the continuing wake of global recession, insolvency is as topical a subject as any. Yet very little appears to have been written in English on insolvency in Halacha. This seems strange.

Does Halacha simply leave the subject to civil legal systems? Insolvency relates primarily to property rather than status; so perhaps the principle of *dina d'malkhuta dina*—that, in matters of property, Halacha recognises and applies those laws which exist for the benefit of the state and its people, provided that this does not involve infringement of the Torah—is all that there is to say on the subject.

---

[*] The writer is a practising English lawyer specialising in matters of insolvency and business law. In the preparation of this essay, his warm appreciation is gratefully recorded to Rabbi Yaakov Grunewald of Pinner, London for his assistance with texts and generally; to Dr. Meir Tamari and Dayan Isaac Berger for the opportunity of discussion with each of them; to Professor Bernard Jackson of the University of Liverpool for assistance with the provision of material; to Paul Baris and Kim Trieger of Yigal Arnon & Co. for their assistance in relation to developments within the Israeli legal system; and to Mr. Ezra Kahn, the Librarian of Jews' College, London, for his assistance with the resources of the library. Naturally, errors are the responsibility of the writer alone.

[1] Samson Raphael Hirsch, *Chapters of the Fathers*. Philip Feldheim Inc. Jerusalem—New York, 5727—1967, pp. 32–33.

But this cannot be right. A moment's thought of the centuries of history of at least the great Ashkenazi communities of Western and particularly Eastern Europe will confirm that, sadly, coping with poverty was a way of life. More often than not, communities were largely autonomous and there was no effective *dina d'malkhuta* to speak of. So Halacha must have something to say on the issue.

In the modern world, insolvency systems have two principal functions: to distribute the available assets of the debtor between his creditors, and to provide a means of discharging the debtor from his debts, hopefully to enable him to make a "fresh start." What does Jewish Law have to say on these questions?

This essay attempts to address this subject. It considers the ethics of insolvency; the emphasis placed upon the prevention of insolvency; the rules which were developed for distributing insolvent estates amongst creditors; conflicts of laws issues; limitations upon the taking and the enforcement of security; the position of the insolvent debtor; procedures for the enforcement of debt; imprisonment for debt; the way in which Jewish Law on imprisonment for debt has come to influence the Law of Israel; attitudes towards interest on debts; and the absence from Jewish Law of anything analogous to the modern concept of a procedure for releasing the bankrupt from his liabilities to enable him to make a "fresh start."

The Ethics of Insolvency

Perhaps a succinct statement of the traditional Jewish philosophy of solvency and insolvency may be found in the Psalms. "The wicked man borrows and does not repay, but the righteous man deals graciously and gives" (Psalms 37:21).

Rabbi Simeon took up the theme, and the citation from the Psalms, in *Pirke Aboth*, 2:14.[2] His teacher posed the negative test question of ethics: "Go and see which is that evil way which a man should shun." He received various replies. Rabbi Eleazer said "An evil eye." Rabbi Jehoshua said "An evil associate." Rabbi Jose said "An evil neighbour." Rabbi Simeon said "He who borrows and does not pay. He who borrows from man is as he who borrows from the Omnipresent, as it is said (in Psalms 37:21) 'The wicked man borrows and does not repay, but the righteous man deals graciously and gives.'" Rabbi Eleazar said "An evil heart."

The teacher preferred Rabbi Eleazar's answer—an evil heart—on the logical basis that it subsumed all of the others, not that it displaced them.

---

2 Babylonian Talmud, *Aboth D'Rabbi Nathan*, Chapter XIV, Page 24 (a).

The interesting point about Rabbi Simeon's answer is that it is a very specific response—much more specific than the other responses—to as broad a negative question of practical ethics as can be posed. An explanation lies in the immediately preceding positive question posed by his teacher in 2:13—"Go and see which is that good way to which a man should cleave." Rabbi Simeon's reply to this question is "he who foresees the event." Simeon has in mind the virtues of foreseeing consequences and learning by experience, and the corresponding vices of presuming on the future without considering the consequences, acting without thought that one's action might lead to sin and, in business terms, taking risks and being unable to meet consequent liabilities.[3]

Samson Raphael Hirsch[4] interprets Simeon's answer in terms of a social compact between man and the Almighty. The greater the loan of the world's riches which a man receives, the greater is he its debtor. "The greater the pleasures he has borrowed, the greater will be the bankruptcy of his life which will be charged against him."[5]

Bunim[6] develops the thought. The Torah[7] commands us: "If there is a needy man amongst you . . . do not harden your heart and shut your hand against your needy kinsman. Rather open your hand wide, and lend him sufficient for the needs which he lacks." Says Bunim, "If the Almighty orders us to lend to the needy, it is only just to regard Him, as it were, as the endorser and guarantor of every such loan, that is made in obedience to the Torah's decree."[8]

---

[3] *Pirke Aboth*. The Tractate "Fathers" from the Mishnah, commonly called "Sayings of the Fathers." Ed. R. Travers Herford. New York, The Jewish Institute Press, 1925, pp. 53–55.

[4] Note 1, supra, expressed in the passage quoted at the outset of this article.

[5] Edward Zipperstein, *Business Ethics in Jewish Law*. Ktav Publishing House Inc., New York, 1983, p. 78.

[6] Irving M. Bunim, *Ethics from Sinai*. Philip Feldheim, Inc., New York, 1964. Volume 1, pp. 180–181.

[7] Deuteronomy 15:7–8.

[8] Bunim illustrates the thought, in a characteristically Jewish way, by recounting the story of the man who asked for a loan of $1,000 (perhaps not the authentic currency!) from Baron Rothschild. The Baron replied that he would be willing to grant the loan, providing the borrower would produce an endorser, someone who would sign with him, to guarantee payment. The man thought for a while, and finally admitted that he could not think of anyone who would sign for him. "In fact," concluded the man sadly if not bitterly, "the only one who probably trusts me is the Almighty Himself." Rothschild gave the man a penetrating stare. "Very well," he said, "that name will be fine." Before the startled man he drew up the promissory note and wrote on it "Endorsed by the Ruler of the World." And the man received the money.

Six months later the borrower reappeared to pay the loan. Rothschild refused to take the money. Utterly astounded, the borrower asked for an explanation; and the Baron smilingly replied, "The loan has already been repaid by the endorser!"

There is also the idea of divine justice, operating in the economic sphere as in all others. Wealth is a reward for observing the commandments, and poverty a punishment. "There will not be then any more poor people among you, for the Lord will bless you in the land which the Lord your G-d is giving you to occupy as an inheritance to possess it. But this will only be so if you hearken diligently to the voice of the Lord your G-d, to observe all of this commandment which I command you this day."[9]

So Polonius' paternal counsel to Laertes "Neither a borrower nor a lender be"[10] might be re-cast in Jewish Law "neither an irresponsible borrower nor a non-repayer be." A society which neither condemns wealth nor sanctifies poverty rapidly realises that the institution of credit is essential, and desirable, to even the most rudimentary economy. A man may borrow, responsibly. And he must repay his debts. A point may come at which he is unable to do so. But he still remains a debtor to the Almighty. If he does not repay, he is considered a "rasha"—an evil person.[11]

To what extent this concept of ultimate personal responsibility is applicable in the economic circumstances of the present day is really a matter of the individual's personal philosophy. To term an insolvent individual, or the proprietor of an insolvent business, or a redundant employee who cannot meet his financial commitments, an inevitable "rasha" is a harsh judgement. This cannot be the meaning of Rabbi Simeon's answer.

The writer ventures this interpretation. "He who borrows and does not repay" is in fact in the Hebrew future tense. It is the person who, when he borrows money, contemplates not repaying, or at least does not sufficiently consider whether there is a real likelihood that he will be able to repay. If he proves unable to repay it, he will view this as a "business risk." He will not work overtime just to repay his creditors. If his business is failing, he will seek more money from the bank, and threaten them that, if they close the business down, they will receive little, whilst he will start a new business financed by a new bank. If he recovers from a business failure, and prospers again, he will not make any contributions to the creditors of the failed business. Such conduct we all see every day, in a business world which views debt as a matter of collectability rather than morality. Nobody would term the man overwhelmed by force of circumstances a "rasha." But perhaps

---

The story does not relate whether the debtor repaid his guarantor by paying the loan to charity; hopefully he did!

9 Deuteronomy 15:4–5.
10 Shakespeare, *Hamlet*, I 3, 75.
11 See supra, n. 2.

this is not so unfair a judgement on some of the irresponsible borrowers who bring such anguish in their wake.

For centuries English Law, for example, with its roots deep in Christian thought, regarded insolvency not only as culpable but as quasi-criminal. Imprisonment for debt was commonplace. The more lenient attitudes of today are comparatively recent in origin. Perhaps this is another key to understanding Halachic attitudes to insolvency. If to contemporary eyes they seem harsh, in their own times they would probably have seemed enlightened when set alongside the norms of non-Jewish society. For Jewish debtors not to repay their Jewish creditors undermined the structure of a Jewish community; for them not to repay their non-Jewish creditors might place the entire Jewish community in danger. In modern times debt and insolvency have fallen to be dealt with by civil, not by Jewish, law; so the modern attitudes which have caused civil legal systems to come to treat insolvency as a matter of economics rather than of ethics have had less occasion to influence Halacha.

The Prevention of Insolvency

Jewish Law has much less to say about the treatment of insolvency than about its prevention. Prevention is better than cure. Thus much of the regulation which Jewish Law imposes upon commerce and business is clearly aimed at preventing insolvency. Man must pursue justice; and he must do so in every area of his endeavour, including the economic. A just economic system will allow the wealthy to flourish without impoverishing the poor. All wealth derives from the Almighty, who loans it to man to satisfy his needs and to discharge his obligations, which include helping the weak and the poor. The standard works on business law are replete with examples.[12] The law on competition in trade, control of prices and profits, limitations on private property, charity and communal taxation are a few obvious instances of restraints upon economic activity. So a society in which men deal justly, do not undertake obligations which they cannot discharge and do ultimately discharge their debts ought not in principle to need an insolvency system.

---

[12] See, for example, Meir Tamari, *With All Your Possessions: Jewish Ethics and Economic Life*, The Free Press (a division of Macmillan, Inc.) New York and London, 1987, esp. Ch. 3, "The Challenge of Wealth," and Edward Zipperstein, *Business Ethics in Jewish Law*, Ktav Publishing House Inc., New York, 1983, esp. Ch. X, "Judaic Outlook on Wealth," to both of which the writer is generally indebted in the preparation of this essay.

The Torah speaks about the thief who is unable to repay his victims.[13] Perhaps this is its only reference to the **state** of insolvency. But the concept of the **prevention** of insolvency is rooted in Torah. "If" (or, perhaps, "when" connoting an obligation) you lend money to [any of] My People, to the poor who are with you, you are not to be to him as a creditor, and you are not to lay interest upon him."[14] There is a positive duty to lend money to a fellow Jew who needs it. This is an act not of *tzedakah*—charity—which is directed at the poor, but of *chesed*—lovingkindness—which is directed at rich and poor alike. "To the poor person the interest-free loan represents a chance to establish himself in a craft or business, thus breaking the cycle of poverty. In the case of the rich, the interest-free loan represents a form of assistance during periods of extreme liquidity problems, thus preventing bankruptcy." Interest-free loans have indeed always been an important part of Jewish communal structures.[15]

Torah also speaks about the septennial release of debts. "At the end of seven years you are to make a release. And this is the manner of the release: every creditor is to release from his hand the demand for payment which he has the right to demand from his neighbour, he is not to exact payment from his neighbour and his brother, for it is pronounced a release to the Lord."[16] At the end of each seventh—Shemittah—year all financial obligations between Israelites are to be annulled, the creditor being legally barred from making any attempt to collect his debt. "The law of the Sabbatical year acts also as a statute of limitation on the bankruptcy law for the poor debtor, in discharging his liability for debts contracted, and in enabling him to start life anew on an equal footing with his neighbour, without the fear that his future earnings will be seized by his former creditors."[17]

By contrast with the Shemittah of the land (*Shemittah Karka'ot*), which was held applicable only to the land of Israel, the Shemittah of debts (*Shemittah Kesafim*) was extended by the Rabbis to every land.

An unfortunate and predicted consequence of this benign legislation was that, contrary to the prohibition in Deuteronomy 15:9–11, people were reluctant to make loans to each other as the Sabbatical year approached. The proper functioning of an economic monetary system was itself a neces-

---

[13] Exodus 22:1–2. Discussed in Bernard S. Jackson, *Theft in Early Jewish Law*, Oxford University Press, 1972, pp. 139–144.

[14] Exodus 22:24.

[15] Tamari, op. cit., pp. 169–172.

[16] Deuteronomy 15:1–2.

[17] *The Jewish Encyclopedia*, Funk and Wagnalls Company, New York and London, 1901, Volume X, "Sabbatical Year and Jubilee," p. 605.

sary condition for the protection of the poor. Hence Hillel introduced the daring and controversial legal procedure of the Prosbul.

The Prosbul was a declaration whereby the creditor transferred to the court the right to collect his debt.[18] It represented a dramatic example of a solution to a Halachic problem. In the words of Eliezer Berkovits:

> A very famous case of a halachic problem and its solution is Hillel's prosbul. To put it concisely and perhaps not quite accurately, it was the transformation of private debts into public debts. Otherwise, in accordance with the written law of the Bible, these debts would have been forfeited in the shemittah year. This was a bold innovation, which Samuel, of a later generation, would have liked to abolish. How and why was it instituted by the great Hillel? He was committed to the law of the shemittah. But in his time, this law came into conflict with other valid concerns of Judaism. On the one hand, there was a Torah obligation to protect the interests of the poor who, as the seventh year was approaching, could not obtain any loans for fear that in the shemittah year the money would be lost. On the other hand, there was also the important practical consideration for the effective functioning of the economic process within society, which is also a valid concern of Judaism. Rab Hisda expressed the meaning of the term prosbul with an etymologically monstrous, yet essentially correct interpretation: *pros bulee ubetee*, an ordinance in the interest of the poor and the rich. Where did Hillel find the authority for his innovation? Where was it written in the Torah? It was, of course, not found in any text, in any code. He found it within himself. There was a clash between equally valid laws, principles and concerns of the Torah. He had to find a resolution to the conflict. There was no text, no *Torah SheBikhetav* to tell him which course to follow. He could find the solution to the problem within his own understanding of the comprehensive ethos of Judaism as he was able to gather it in his own heart and his own conscience from the totality of the Torah— teaching and the Torah-way of life.[19]

On similar principles, other categories of debt were also exempted from the operation of Shemittah: wages, merchandise on credit, loans on pledges, a note guaranteed by mortgage, a debt handed to the Beth Din for collection (this being the theory of the Prosbul), and a note stipulating that the debtor waives the defence of Shemittah in relation to that particular note.[20]

---

18 *The Jewish Encyclopedia*, op. cit., Volume X, "Prosbul," p. 219; Zipperstein, op. cit., pp. 43–44.

19 Eliezer Berkovits, *Crisis and Faith*, New York, Sanhedrin Press, 1976, pp. 86–87.

20 *The Jewish Encyclopedia*, op. cit., Vol. X, "Sabbatical Year and Jubilee," p. 606, and the talmudic references there cited.

Priorities Between Creditors

The subject of priorities between creditors is complex[21] and beyond the scope of this essay. What follows is intended only as a brief background to the topic of the distribution of insolvent estates.

In common law legal systems, the essential distinction is between secured and unsecured loans. Secured loans are generally characterised by, amongst other features, a publicly accessible registration system. Halacha never developed such a system. It has been suggested[22] that, before the age of printing, the formality associated with a written and witnessed document—a *shetar*—served to publicise the existence of the security interest created by the document.

In Halacha, the distinction is between written loans (*shetarot*) and oral loans. A creditor by *shetar* takes precedence in levying payment on the debtor's land, whether the land is still in the debtor's possession (the debtor's "free" property) or whether the debtor has disposed of it to a third party (his "encumbered and alienated" property). This reflects a principle of Jewish Law which gives the creditor a lien—a right "in rem"—over the debtor's land, as well as a right of recourse "in personam" against the debtor himself. This lien over the debtor's land takes priority over any similar right acquired by a subsequent creditor.[23]

As between creditors by *shetar*, priority is determined by the sequence in which the obligations were created. So where the debtor's property includes land, creditors by *shetar* have recourse to that land in the sequence in which their liens were created. This concept is similar to the order of priorities which exists in modern legal systems in relation to specifically charged assets.[24]

By contrast, obligations contracted by *shetar* over moveables do not give rise to a creditor's lien. Nor do obligations contracted only orally (rather than by *shetar*) create any priority rights between creditors, over moveables nor even over land (although there are minority opinions in relation to land).[25]

---

[21] See, for example, George Horovitz, *The Spirit of Jewish Law*, Central Book Company, New York, 1963, Sections 239, 257, 379; Elon, op. cit., 629–630.

[22] Larry Rabinovich, "Introduction to Secured Transactions in Halakha and Common Law," *Tradition* 27:3/1993, page 36, Rabbinical Council of America.

[23] Menachem Elon, *The Principles of Jewish Law*, Keter Publishing House, Jerusalem, 1975, p. 629.

[24] Elon, op. cit., 630.

[25] Elon, op. cit., 630.

Two other categories of creditors have the same status as creditors by *shetar*. These are the victim of a tort committed by the debtor or his property, and a divorced wife or a widow claiming under her *ketuba*. Their claims are enforceable against the property of the debtor in the same way as those of a creditor by *shetar*.[26]

In common law systems, secured claims generally take precedence over unsecured ones. In Halacha, it is not entirely clear whether written loans take precedence over oral ones. This issue is the subject of a major controversy between most of the Halachic authorities of the Middle Ages, and remains unresolved.[27]

The Distribution of Insolvent Estates

When priorities have been determined, the issue which remains is how to divide an inadequate amount of assets between a category of creditors as between whom there are no priority rights. Modern western legal systems essentially find the answer to this question in the principle of proportionality. The estate is divided between creditors of the same class in proportion to their claims, so that all receive the same calculated percentage of their debts. Jewish Law adopted a different approach.

The line of thinking began in a talmudic discussion.[28] A man dies leaving three wives. Their *ketuboth* entitle them to different sums—in the examples 100, 200 and 300 *zuzim* respectively. The claims against the estate thus total 600 *zuzim*. The estate is insufficient to meet their claims—in successive examples the estate comprises 100, 200 and 300 *zuzim*. The debate turns not so much upon issues of insolvency as such as upon the question of the proportions of the estate to which each wife is entitled to lay claim and the effect of renunciations by a wife of her right to claim a proportion of the estate. The significance of the discussion in the present context is that underlying it is a presumption not of proportionality in the treatment of creditors but of equality, in the sense that each receives the same amount. Where the estate is 100 *zuzim*, the Mishnah rules that it is divided equally between the three claimants, despite the disproportion of their claims. The Gemara, though discussing possible alternative solutions to the cases where the estate is 200 and 300 *zuzim* respectively, does not question this ruling in relation to the 100 *zuzim* estate at all. And at the end of a complex discussion of the distribution of the 200 and 300 *zuzim* estates, Rabbi Judah

---

[26] Rabinovich, op. cit., 43–44 and the authorities cited at note 61.
[27] Rabinovich, op. cit., 45, and the authorities there cited.
[28] Babylonian Talmud Ketuboth, Chapter X, 4, 93a, 93b.

the Prince says that he does not agree with the result—which is one of inequality between the three wives—and that, quite simply, the three wives should take equal shares. He clearly regards this as so obvious as not to need any explanatory reasoning. So he goes so far as to disregard issues of legal entitlement and renunciation in favour of the principle of equality.

As it happens, none of the examples in the discussion involves any of the three claims being for less than one third of the estate. Had this been the case, one may safely surmise that a claimant would not have been entitled to recover more than her entitlement.

The argument is developed, into the area of insolvency per se, by Maimonides (1135–1204) in the Mishneh Torah[29] and by Joseph Caro (1488–1575) in the Shulkhan Arukh.[30]

The Shulkhan Arukh gives two examples:

1. The fund is 300 *dinars*, and there are three creditors with claims for 300, 200 and 100 *dinars* respectively. Each receives one third of the fund, i.e., 100 *dinars*. This is effectively the talmudic example above.
2. The fund is between 500 and 600 *dinars*, and there are the same three creditors for 300, 200 and 100 *dinars* respectively. Each claimant first receives an amount which is equal to the smallest claim (i.e. 100 x 3 = 300). Of the balance (between 200 and 300 *dinars*), each of the two remaining creditors receives an amount equal to the smallest claim (i.e. 100 x 2 = 200). The remainder (up to 100 *dinars*) goes to the highest claimant.

The Mishneh Torah gives an almost identical set of examples. "And in this manner," concludes the Rambam, "the division is made between the creditors when they all come at the same time to obtain satisfaction, even if they be one hundred in number."[31]

Why does the Rambam express himself in this way? If the system of priorities between creditors operates as it should, many of a man's creditors should take their place in a sequence of priorities, rather than compete with each other. Perhaps the answer lies in commercial realities. People who become insolvent often prove to have a plethora of creditors, often for un-

---

[29] Mishneh Torah. Volume 13 (Sefer Mishpatim). Treatise 3 (Hilchot Maalveh Ve-loveh), Chapter 20, Halacha 4. Translated in "The Code of Maimonides," Book Thirteen, by Jacob J. Rabinovitz, New Haven, Yale University Press, 1949, pp. 152–153.

[30] Shulkhan Arukh. Ḥoshen Mishpat, civ, 10. Ṭur, Ḥoshen Mishpat civ. Bet Yosef civ. Discussed in *The Jewish Encyclopedia*, op. cit., Volume II, "Bankruptcy," p. 494.

[31] See supra, n. 29.

certain amounts and often with little or no evidence of their claims. People in business deal with their regular suppliers and customers on an on-going trading basis. The net balance owed, one way or the other, is constantly fluctuating. When a businessman becomes insolvent, it is often not possible to say when a given debt arose, because it is in reality the adjusted result of numerous separate transactions. So the only feasible answer is to treat such creditors as ranking equally between themselves.

So the principle is one of simple equality in the amount received by equally ranking creditors. All equally ranking creditors receive an equal share of the fund, irrespective of the amount of their claim. The only qualification is that, self-evidently, a creditor cannot receive more than the amount of his debt.

Mathematically, this calculation can be made in two ways. Let us assume that:

The fund is:	810	and that
The creditors are:		
A	50	
B	100	
C	150	
D	200	
E	500	
F	600	
	1600	

Method A: Equally ranking creditors whose claim is for less than a proportionate share of the fund are paid in full. This process is repeated on the diminishing fund. Once the claims of all remaining creditors exceed a proportionate share of the diminishing fund, those creditors share in the fund equally.

So in the example:

The fund is	810
There are six creditors. One sixth of the fund is 810/6 = 135.	
A's claim, at 50 is less than the average of 135.	
So A is paid in full.	50
This diminishes the fund to	760
There are now 5 remaining creditors.	
One fifth of the diminished fund is 760/5 = 152.	

B's claim, at 100, is less than the average of 152.
So B is paid in full.   100
This diminishes the fund to   660
There are now 4 remaining creditors.
One quarter of the diminished fund is 660/4 = 165.

C's claim, at 150, is less than the average of 165.
So C is paid in full.   150
This diminishes the fund to   510
There are now 3 remaining creditors.
One third of the diminished fund is 510/3 = 170.

The claims of D, E and F, at 200, 500 and 600 respectively, all exceed the average of 170. So the diminished fund is shared equally between them so that

D receives   170
E receives   170
F receives   170

<u>Method B</u>: Each equally ranking creditor receives an allocation equal to the amount of the smallest claim, until his debt has been paid. This process is repeated until the fund is exhausted. In the final allocation, the balance of the fund is allocated equally between the remaining creditors.

So, in the example:

	1st Allocation	2nd Allocation	3rd Allocation	Final Allocation	Total Payments
Fund: 810	810	510	260	60	
Balance of fund remaining after previous allocation					
Creditor Claim					
A 50	50				= 50
B 100	50+	50			= 100
C 150	50+	50+	50		= 150
D 200	50+	50+	50+	20	= 170
E 500	50+	50+	50+	20+	= 170
F 600	50+	50+	50+	20+	= 170
1600	300+	250+	200+	60	= 810

Amongst legal systems, this method of distribution is unusual, and perhaps unique. It treats creditors equitably, not in the sense of proportionately, but in the sense that they take equal shares of the estate. Interestingly, Maimonides ends his discussion with the comment: "But some of the Geonim have taught that division of available property is made among the creditors in a ratio equal to that of their respective debts." But this principle of proportionality, to us more familiar, seemingly remained a minority view, although the authorities were divided on the issue.[32] It has been suggested that the principle of proportionality has been followed only in recent times, doubtless under the influence of modern legal systems.[33]

The assumption underlying this system may simply be the fairness of absolute equality. Alternatively it may be that the smaller is a man's claim, the more significant it is to his finances, and conversely, that the larger is his claim, the better able is he to absorb the loss of a larger proportion of it. The method of distribution emphasises both the Jewish concept of social justice—that society should be so structured as to protect its economically weaker members—and the desirability of prudence in lending—that a man should "see the event" and should not lend to a borrower who may not be a good risk more than he can afford to lose.

To modern Western thinking, this method of distribution is strange, in the sense not only of unfamiliar but also of peculiar. But it bears thoughtful consideration. As a practising insolvency lawyer, the writer may perhaps venture to confirm the accuracy of the generalisation that "small" creditors are greatly disadvantaged by even a "small" bad debt, for which, say, a 10% distribution in an insolvency is little economic compensation, whilst "large" creditors find the same, say, 10% distribution of correspondingly little economic value. Obviously, the higher the percentage distribution, the less true is the generalisation. But, a priori, distributions in insolvencies are generally rather closer to the 0% end of the scale than the 100%! So this strange system of distribution may in fact tend to protect the "small" creditors without correspondingly prejudicing their "larger" counterparts.

Nor should the distribution be regarded as final; rather, as provisional. A debtor must repay his creditors the balance of their debt if and when he can. People dissipate small sums; and the 10% distribution is equally insignificant to "small" and to "large" creditors. Under the Halachic system, the small creditor receives a proportion of his debt sufficient to be significant, with the hope of recovering the balance one day. The larger creditor

---

[32] Elon, op. cit., 630.
[33] Berger, "Jewish Insolvency Law: An Ethical Approach," *Le'ela*, Jews' College, London, April 1993, page 5, penultimate paragraph, and the authority cited in note 13, being Teshuvot Shem Aryeh-Ḥoshen Mishpat, no. 66.

receives the same absolute amount, with the same hope of recovering the balance one day; and because he may choose to do business with the debtor again, and perhaps again on a large scale, he may have the economic strength to influence the debtor to honour his past obligations.

Later Developments

During the Middle Ages, the law developed through the introduction of further rules, some of which sought to protect the creditors as a whole. So it was enacted that, in cases where the law afforded no preferential rights, a proportional share of the debtor's estate had to be reserved for those creditors who had not yet claimed repayment and even for "future" creditors whose claims had not yet become due for payment. It became customary to announce publicly that any creditor failing to lodge his claim against the debtor within a specified period of time would lose his right to do so.[34]

The Responsa literature deals with all aspects of life, including, inevitably, matters commercial. Within communities, local business customs sometimes developed; and yet transactions were sometimes agreed to and documented in ways which did not entirely follow these customs. One such situation was addressed by Rabbi Asher Ben Yehiel (the "Rosh"), writing in Spain in the early part of the fourteenth century.[35] A creditor held the debtor's house as security on the documented contractual basis that he could enforce his claim against the security without the debtor being entitled to have the value of the property assessed by a Beth Din and established by auction, as was otherwise the local custom. The Rosh found that in Sephardic Spain—perhaps by contrast with his native Germany—contractual documents were regarded as giving way to the custom of the city, unless that custom itself conflicted with traditional sources. He therefore ruled that, despite the terms of the contract, the value of the property must be evaluated, and the property auctioned, in order to protect the debtor from its sale at an undervalue. However he ruled that this must be done immediately, even though the value of the property might rise over time, in order not to deny the creditor the immediate recourse to the debtor's assets for which he had bargained and thus not to discourage lenders from making loans to people who needed them. As to the order of application of the debtor's assets, he held that recourse must be had firstly, if it was available,

---

[34] Elon, op. cit., 630.
[35] Responsa Rosh, 80: 8.

to money; then to moveables; and only then to real property, or at least to as much of it as was necessary to satisfy the debt, even though the value of the property might at that particular time have fallen.

At various periods, and in various places, economic crises led to an increase in cases of insolvency, and of communal enactments—"*takkanot*"—to deal with them. *Takkanot* are one of the legal sources for the development of Jewish Law. They are rulings enacted to supplement the Law, often within a given community. Over time, some acquired widespread application (a famous example being Rabbi Gershom's ban on polygamy); others lapsed with the passage of time, or disappeared with the community itself.

Takkanot were mostly instituted by the Halachic scholars, but, particularly from the tenth century, many derive from enactments by the community through its leaders. Many of these enactments addressed issues of insolvency and, specifically, the issue of imprisonment for debt, because of their close connection with the social and economic conditions of the community.[36]

In relation to insolvency, *takkanot* sometimes provided for the appointment of a trustee ("*ne'eman*") over the property of an insolvent (a "*bore'ah*," or fugitive, as he is referred to in the *takkanot* of Poland, Germany and Lithuania in the 17th and 18th centuries). The debtor's property became vested in the trustee, whose task it was to take possession of it, sell it and distribute the proceeds amongst the creditors. *Takkanot* prescribed a punishment of a year's imprisonment for a debtor who wilfully squandered his property and could not then pay his debts.[37]

Questions arose as to the extent to which the *takkanot* of one community or jurisdiction should be followed elsewhere. Writing in Hungary in 1836,[38] the Ḥatam Sopher was asked to rule whether a supplier who had sold merchandise on credit to a person who had died was entitled to recover his merchandise in priority to the deceased's other creditors. The Council of the Four Lands (which were Greater Poland, Lesser Poland, Russia and Lithuania, and did not include Hungary) had issued a *takkanah* directed against fraudsters who obtained goods on credit and then disappeared with them, to the effect that the supplier was entitled to recover his goods in priority to the claims of other creditors. The Ḥatam Sopher held that this *takkanah* should not be followed, both because the circumstances which it envisaged were quite different to those in the present case (an argument obviously not confined to *takkanot*) and specifically because Hungary was

---

[36] Elon, op. cit., 637.
[37] Elon, op. cit., 630–631.
[38] Responsa Ḥatam Sopher, Ḥoshen Mishpat, no. 55.

beyond the jurisdiction of the Council of the Four Lands (even though, interestingly, the Council had itself been dissolved in 1764).

Conflicts of Laws

Nowadays, of course, most business transactions are entered into in reliance upon national law rather than upon Halacha. In areas of life over which national law may make no claim—family relationships, religious obligations and testamentary freedom are examples—Halacha will generally be applicable. In those over which it does—including the conduct of an insolvency and the treatment of creditors—Halacha will recognise national law.

Such a situation was presented to Rabbi Moshe Feinstein in 1978.[39] A creditor of a Swiss company had received partial repayment at around the time that the company became insolvent. Rabbi Feinstein held that if the repayment was made by the directors after the commencement of the insolvency, the directors would have exceeded their authority. A Beth Din must then require the recipient to restore the payment to the receivers, in accordance with national law, so that it could be included in the legally mandated system of distribution to all creditors. If however the repayment was lawfully made by the directors, even shortly before the commencement of the insolvency, a Beth Din need not then require the recipient to restore it. The parties had entered into their transactions in reliance upon national law, and Halacha would therefore give effect to that choice.

Limitations upon Taking and Enforcing Security

Jewish Law limits the security which a lender may accept from his borrower. He may not accept the means of a man's livelihood: "no man shall take the mill or the upper millstone to pledge, for he takes a man's life to pledge;"[40] "a team of plough oxen" may not be taken.[41] Nor may "utensils which are used in the preparation of food, such as a mill, a wooden kneading trough, a kettle used for cooking, a slaughterer's knife, and the like."[42] Security may not be taken from a widow, whether she be poor or rich; if

---

[39] Rabbi Moshe Feinstein, *Iggot Moshe*, Ḥoshen Mishpat, Vol. 2, Responsum no. 62, published 1985.

[40] Deuteronomy 24:6.

[41] Mishneh Torah, Volume 13 (Sefer Mishpatim), Treatise 3 (Hilchot Maalveh Ve-loveh), Chapter 3, Halacha 3. Translated in "The Code of Maimonides," Book Thirteen, by Jacob J. Ravinovitz, New Haven, Yale University Press, 1949, p. 85.

[42] Ibid., Halacha 2.

taken, it must be returned.[43] The debtor's garments must be returned to him at sunset.[44]

There is a symmetry in Halacha, providing rights for the weaker members of society but imposing corresponding obligations upon them. So the recipient of a loan—which will, of course, be free of interest, because of the prohibition upon interest—is obligated to repay the debt and not to waste the loan.[45] Even if the lender is wealthy and the borrower poor, the borrower must if necessary surrender the whole of his property to repay the debt.[46] Any other principle would burden the lender with responsibility for the borrower and blur the distinction between mercy and justice.

At the same time, Jewish Law imposes strict limits upon the action which an unpaid creditor may take to recover his debt. He may not press the debtor when he knows that the debtor is unable to pay.[47] He may distrain upon the property of his debtor only through the court.[48] He must "return the pledge to the debtor at the time when he needs it, if the debtor is an indigent man in need of things taken as a pledge. The creditor must return to the debtor the pillow at night that he may sleep on it, and the plough during the day that he may do his work with it."[49] "The creditor must return to the debtor in the daytime articles that are used during the day and at night articles that are used during the night. If there are two utensils in his hands he keeps one and returns the other."[50] He must return a "night garment" and "articles which the debtor uses in the course of his work, or wears during the day."[51] As compensation to the creditor, the pledged articles are exempt from the operation of the Shemittah year, and become available to the creditor upon the debtor's death.[52] If the pledged article is something which is needed by the debtor, the creditor's obligation to return it subsists indefinitely.[53]

Similar restrictions apply to a court representative—a bailiff—who makes distraint upon a debtor. He "must not take things that a man could not give as a pledge, such as the garment he is wearing, the utensils with

---

[43] Ibid., Halacha 1.
[44] Exodus 22:25–26; Deuteronomy 24:12–13.
[45] Tamari, *With All Your Possessions*, op. cit., pp. 54, 173–176.
[46] Mishneh Torah, ibid., Chapter 1, Halacha 4.
[47] Mishneh Torah, ibid., Halacha 2.
[48] Deuteronomy 24:10–11. Mishneh Torah, ibid., Chapter 3, Halacha 4.
[49] Mishneh Torah, ibid., Halacha 5; translation, ibid., pp. 86–87.
[50] Ibid., Halacha 6.
[51] Ibid., Halacha 5.
[52] Ibid.
[53] Ibid., Halacha 6.

which he eats, and the like. He must leave a bed and a mattress for the rich and a bed and a mat of reeds for the indigent, and everything else that is found in the hands of the debtor he may take in distraint."[54]

Entering the debtor's home, in order to distrain on his assets in satisfaction of a debt, is prohibited. The creditor must stand outside, and wait for the debtor to bring the property out to him.[55] This concern for the self-respect of the debtor impeded the effective recovery of debts if the debtor claimed that he had no assets and if none were found outside his home. So, over time and conflicting scholastic opinions, it was decided that the prohibition upon entering the debtor's home applied only to debts arising from loans and not to debts otherwise incurred, and that a court officer—a bailiff—could enter the debtor's home in order to seek assets upon which to levy execution. If there was a choice of assets upon which to levy execution, the bailiff should remove those of intermediate value—not those of higher value, as the creditor would wish, nor those of lower value, as the debtor would wish. If it is clear that the debtor is impoverished and has no property, entering his home remains prohibited, since "this can only cause him shame and suffering."[56]

The problem also arose of levying execution in the absence of the debtor. Execution could not be levied if the debtor could be notified by an agent of the court in a return journey lasting not more than thirty days. As to whether execution could then be levied, opinions differed. The majority opinion was that execution could be levied in the debtor's absence once the creditor had presented his bond of indebtedness, taken an oath that the debt had not been paid, proved that the debtor was abroad and proved that the debtor was still the owner of the assets upon which execution was to be levied.[57]

The Position of the Insolvent Debtor

A man is obliged to repay his debts. So, if he claims that he cannot fulfil this obligation, the Beth Din is required to value and sell all of his assets, including expensive personal belongings and those of his wife and family. The debtor is left with the minimum requirements of a person who is just above the poverty line.[58] The debtor must bring all of his moveable property

---

54 Ibid.
55 Supra, n. 48.
56 Elon, op. cit., 622–623.
57 Elon, op. cit., 631.
58 *Jewish Studies*—Pub. Jerusalem Academy of Jewish Studies, Yeshivot Dvar Yerushalayim, No. 34, Spring 5750—1990, p. 30, "Ethical Issues in Bankruptcy: a Jewish Perspective." Dr. Meir Tamari, at p. 32, and the authorities there cited (although the citations at reference 7 appear to have been mistranscribed).

"without leaving even a single needle." He is allowed food for thirty days, suitable clothing which will last him for twelve months, bedding, shoes and religious objects. If he is a craftsman, he may retain his basic tools.[59] Some authorities permit a scholar to retain his books. At the beginning of the 19th century, Moses Sofer permitted a shopkeeper to retain his stock, in order to preserve his livelihood. The concept is an "arrangement" for the benefit of poor debtors ("*siddur le-va'al ḥov*"), under which an exclusion of certain property from the reach of creditors ("*mesaderin le-va'al ḥov*") ensures that the debtor is left with a "shred" ("shareyd") or "remnant" of his property.[60]

But the responsibility for supporting the debtor then becomes that of the whole community.[61] The care of the poor and needy is financed through communal taxation. Every member of the community must bear his share, including the bankrupt's creditors. So, ironically, a wealthy man who is owed only a modest sum by his debtor may find, if he is instrumental in bringing about the debtor's insolvency, that, quite apart from recovering little or nothing of his debt, he actually has to bear a tax liability to support his debtor which is far greater than the debt itself.

Normally there are strict limits on the amount of charity that a poor man may be given from the community purse: "two meals a day, a pallet to sleep on and some sort of housing."[62] But, in the case of the failed businessman, Jewish Law recognises that his problems will be not only financial but also social and psychological. So it holds that, where a rich man becomes poor, the community is required to provide him with everything to which his lifestyle had accustomed him. "Even if it had been his wont to ride a horse, with a manservant running in front of him, and he has now become poor and has lost his possessions, one must buy him a horse to ride and a manservant to run before him, as it is said, "Sufficient for his need in that which he wanteth" (Deut. 15:8). You are thus obligated to fill his want; you are not, however, obligated to restore his wealth."[63]

Nevertheless, the debtor remains under a moral obligation to repay his debts, from the assets which he hopes to acquire once he has re-established himself, in order to be "clean before G-d and men."[64]

---

[59] Mishneh Torah, ibid., Chapter 1, Halacha 7.
[60] Elon, op. cit., 628–629; Rabinovich, op. cit., 45–46, and the authorities there cited.
[61] Tamari, "Ethical Issues in Bankruptcy," op. cit., p. 33, citing Shulkhan Aruch, Yoreh Deah, Section 248, Sub-section 1.
[62] Tamari, op. cit., p. 31.
[63] Mishneh Torah, Vol. 7 (Sefer Zeraim). Treatise 2 (Hilchot Matnot Aniyim). Chapter 7, Halacha 3. Translated in "The Code of Maimonides," Book Seven, by Isaac Klein, New Haven and London, Yale University Press, 1979, p. 77.
[64] Tamari, op. cit., p. 32.

Debt Enforcement Procedures

Debt collection procedures have to strike a balance between providing an effective remedy for creditors, so as not, in a talmudic phrase, "to bolt the door before a borrower," and violating the personal freedom and dignity of the debtor. Over the centuries, different procedures were introduced in an attempt, in Maimonides' phrase, "to deal with swindlers and not with those generally accepted to be paupers." One procedure, which obtained in certain periods and places but was not generally accepted into Jewish Law, was to place a debtor (other than a known pauper) who pleaded a lack of means under communal sanctions for a fixed period, at the end of which he was required to take an oath that he had no means. Another procedure was to require debtors who pleaded a lack of means to take an oath of *"ein li"*—"I have no means"—to the effect that he has no undisclosed means and that everything that he earns or receives (beyond the amount required for his minimum sustenance) he will pay to his creditors, until his debts have been discharged.[65] The sanction lay in the very fact of oath-taking, because of the solemnity with which vows have always been viewed.

Debt enforcement procedures exist to protect the debtor. They involve a stay of execution, to allow the debtor an opportunity of raising money to repay the debt; compliance with various procedural steps, including the issue of warnings; the issue of an authority to the creditor to pursue (*"adrakhta"*) uncharged property or to seize (*"tirpa"*) charged property; independent appraisal (*"shuma"*) of the value of the property which is to be sold; public announcement or advertising (*"hakhrazah"*) of the property, in order to find the highest bidder; and sale of the property to the highest bidder, or at least to a person paying the appraised value.[66]

The creditor has a preferential right to acquire the property for himself if nobody offers more than the appraised value, or if he matches any other offers.[67]

If the debtor has both cash and other property, he must discharge the debt in cash if he can. If he cannot, he rather than the creditor may select the assets from which to discharge the debt. But the creditor cannot demand land if the debtor offers chattels; and the creditor can decline land, and wait until the debtor can pay him in cash.[68]

To avoid the delays and inconvenience to creditors which these procedures and rules could involve, it became customary in many places to

---

[65] Elon, op. cit., 632–633.
[66] Elon, op. cit., 624–626.
[67] Elon, op. cit., 626.
[68] Elon, op. cit., 627. See also the Responsum of the Rosh referred to at n. 35 above.

stipulate in bond agreements that the debtor had to pay his debt in cash, without putting the creditor to the trouble of taking execution proceedings; and, to that end, that the debtor was obliged to deal personally with the sale of his property and to pay the creditor in cash.[69]

If land owned by the debtor had been transferred to his creditor in satisfaction of a debt, the creditor was not strictly obliged to return it if the debtor subsequently acquired the means to repay the debt in cash. But it was enacted in a *Takkanah* referred to in the Talmud as "*shuma hadar*" that the debtor should be allowed to repurchase his land (although not his moveable property) if it was still in the possession of the creditor. The reason was to "do what is right and good in the eyes of the Lord."[70]

These problems have had to be addressed by Israel's legal system, as by all others. The Execution Law of 1967 sets out in detail the law in regard to matters such as execution procedures, the order of distribution of a debtor's property, attachment of chattels and land, property exempted from execution, ascertaining the debtor's financial position, imprisonment for debt, etc. The general trend of this law follows the rules of Jewish Law.[71] This is further discussed below.

Imprisonment for Debt

Imprisonment for debt was commonplace in non-Jewish society in medieval Europe. So Jewish debtors were amongst those imprisoned by non-Jewish creditors. Hence it was held that if a person or his children were seized or imprisoned by non-Jews for debt, the Jewish community was under an obligation to ransom them, by paying the debt, on the first and indeed on a second occasion that this occurred. However there was no such obligation on a subsequent occasion unless the captors threatened to kill the debtor. If a debtor died in captivity, his children had to be ransomed.[72] A woman took precedence over a man as far as feeding, clothing and redemption from captivity were concerned, unless both were exposed in captivity to forcible sin, in which case the man took precedence.[73]

---

[69] Elon, op. cit., 628.

[70] Deuteronomy 6:18; *The Humanity of Jewish Law*, Dayan Dr. M.S. Lew, Soncino Press, London, 1985, p. 35, citing *Baba Metzia* 108b (although this citation appears to have been mistranscribed); Elon, op. cit., 627.

[71] Elon, op. cit., 633.

[72] Mishneh Torah, Volume 7 (Sefer Zeraim), Treatise 2 (Hilchot Matnot Aniyim), Chapter 8, Halacha 13.

[73] Ibid., Halacha 15.

As to Jewish Law, imprisonment for debt is generally prohibited. The Torah permits it only in the case of a male thief, who is sold in order to repay his debt to his victim[74] and of a person who sold himself as a slave because of his utter poverty, including, presumably, the inability to pay his debts.[75] The Shulkhan Arukh rules that imprisonment for debt is not permitted.[76]

The history of imprisonment for debt, and of the *takkanot* dealing with it, is a subject in itself.[77] For a debtor able but simply unwilling to pay, imprisonment was a real sanction. Imprisonment for debt was in fact sanctioned by Jewish communities at various periods: during the biblical era, in talmudic times, in medieval times in Spain and in the seventeenth and eighteenth centuries in Poland, Lithuania and Germany. Whilst some authorities spoke forcibly against this practice, it came about through a combination of fraudulent commercial practices, pressure from creditors and absorption—either less consciously or by virtue of the principle of *dina d'malkhuta dina*—of the often axiomatic acceptance in the non-Jewish societies amongst which Jews lived of the rightness of the concept of imprisonment for debt. Indeed, contractual provisions for imprisonment for debt were sometimes upheld. Conditions in Jewish prisons were at least generally more humane than those in non-Jewish prisons.[78]

The dilemma posed by the defaulting debtor gave rise to many *takkanot* on the issue of imprisonment for debt. The period from the end of the sixteenth century to the middle of the seventeenth century was a period of severe economic crisis for the Jews of Poland, Lithuania and Germany, giving rise to an increase in cases of non-payment of debt and of insolvency. Numerous communal *takkanot* from this period deal with "*boreḥim*" (a term originally applied to runaway debtors or bankrupts and later to all defaulting debtors), and with the issue of imprisoning them. These *takkanot* often permitted imprisonment of the debtor, at least for a short period, even though he might be a pauper without means of payment.[79]

Imprisonment for debt continued to be permitted in a series of communal *takkanot* from the seventeenth and eighteenth centuries. Such *takkanot* were enacted by the Council of the Four Lands of 1624; the Council of

---

[74] See supra, n. 13.
[75] Leviticus 25:39.
[76] Shulkhan Arukh, Ḥoshen Mishpat, 97, 15, citing rabbinic responsa.
[77] Aaron M. Shreiber, *Jewish Law and Decision Making, a Study through Time*, Temple University Press, Philadelphia, 1979, pp. 314, 414–417 and the copious authorities there cited; Elon, op. cit., 633–639.
[78] Shreiber, ibid.
[79] Elon, op. cit., 637–639.

Lithuania (1623–1652); the Council of Moravia (1650–1659); and the communities of Posen (1642), Nikolsburg and Tiktin (in the first half of the 18th century).

An interesting example is a *takkanah* of 1637 by the Council of Lithuania, which obliged a creditor who demanded a debtor's imprisonment to provide for the debtor's sustenance as determined by the Court, but gave the creditor the right to recover the cost of this together with the debt.

These *takkanot* nevertheless evoked strong criticism from halachic scholars for deviating from the fundamental principle of Jewish Law against prejudicing an impoverished debtor in any way. The authority which Jewish Law confers on communal leaders to enact *takkanot*, even though they may be contrary to a particular rule of Jewish Law, is confined to matters of civil and criminal law, and does not extend to matters of ritual law; and some authorities viewed the issue of imprisonment for debt as a matter of ritual law, by which it was forbidden. Eventually, the trend of these *takkanot* came to be rejected by the Jewish legal system as being in direct conflict with the principle of Jewish Law that imprisonment was to be permitted only as a means of recovering a debt when the debtor is able to pay but conceals his assets and evades payment, not as a means of punishment for debt.[80]

One compromise between imprisonment and enslavement for debt and satisfaction of the debt was to compel the debtor to work off the debt: compulsory labour. This was recognised by various legal systems during the Middle Ages. So, under those influences, it came to be considered by Jewish scholars during that period. Jewish Law had always leaned against labour-hire, as a restriction upon the personal freedom of the worker. Compulsory labour was therefore generally rejected, although some exceptions were allowed by some authorities.[81]

Imprisonment for Debt in Israel

Although this essay has to do with Jewish Law rather than the Law of Israel, the former has had an interesting and recent influence on the latter in relation to imprisonment for debt.

Israel, too, was confronted by the problem of imprisonment for debt. A bill introduced to the Knesset in 1957, proposing the complete abolition of imprisonment for debt, failed. The subject was debated a number of times by the Knesset over the next decade until the enactment in 1967 of the Execution Law. This provided (in sections 67–74) that an enquiry is to be made

---

[80] Ibid.
[81] Elon, op. cit., 623–624.

by the Chief Execution Officer ("CEO")into a debtor's financial position, in order to ascertain his ability to comply with the judgement; the debtor may then be ordered to pay the debt in one sum or by instalments; if he fails to do so within the period prescribed by the chief execution officer, he may be imprisoned for a period of up to 21 days if there is no other way of compelling him to comply with the judgement (section 70); and having once served a term of imprisonment, a debtor may not be imprisoned again in respect of the same debt or instalment. In respect of a debt deriving from maintenance for a wife, children or parents, however, an order for imprisonment may be issued without a prior enquiry into the debtor's means.[82]

The issue of imprisonment for debt under the Execution Law of 1967 came to be considered by the Supreme Court of Israel, sitting as the High Court of Justice, on 31st August 1993 in the case of *Perach 1992 for a New Israel—Aid to Victims of Laws and Regulations (non-profit) vs. Minister of Justice and Police Commissioner* (High Court of Justice Petition 5304/92). The opinion of the Court was given by Justice Menachem Elon, with Justices Barak and Matza concurring.

Section 70 of the Execution Law provides (as stated above) that where the CEO has ascertained that the debtor has not paid the judgment debt and that there is no other way of compelling him to do so, the CEO may issue an imprisonment order against him for up to 21 days. Regulation 114 of the Regulations made pursuant to the Execution Law provides that the CEO may issue such an order if the debtor has not then shown other means of implementing the judgment. The Court found that such prison orders were routinely issued, and that the holding of a hearing to enquire into the means of the debtor had effectively become optional.

The Court reviewed the history of Jewish Law on imprisonment for debt, from the times of the Bible and of the Talmud through the rulings of authorities from the twelfth through to the eighteenth centuries, and up to the history of legislation in Israel. The Court interpreted the Execution Law of 1967 on the basis of considerations of Jewish Law, and found that the routine manner in which prison orders for imprisonment were issued pursuant to Regulation 114 was contrary to these considerations. It ruled that the imposition of a prison term by the CEO is a judicial rather than an administrative act and requires a clear judicial investigation in the presence of the debtor. The Court held that the injury to the efficiency of debt collection is less weighty than the injury to the debtor's liberty and honour where imprisonment is ordered routinely and without the debtor having an opportunity to be heard.

---

[82] Elon, op. cit., 639–640.

The Court accordingly held Regulation 114 to be invalid, and laid down a procedure which effectively requires the CEO to hold a hearing into the means of the debtor, in which the debtor appears before him. Only if the debtor fails to appear, and only if it is clear to the CEO that he has the means to pay and that there is no other way of compelling him to do so, may the CEO then issue an order of imprisonment. A debtor who is so imprisoned is then to be brought before the CEO within 30 days.

The case is a most interesting example of the way in which the Court in Israel, perhaps particularly under the influence of Justice Menachem Elon and others, is applying the principles of Jewish Law in order to guide it in the development of the Law of Israel.

Following the decision in *Perach*, the Knesset enacted Amendment No. 15 to the Execution Law, which came into effect on 15th November 1994. Many of its provisions relate to imprisonment for debt. Their effect is to make it much more difficult for a debtor to be imprisoned for debt, and to encourage instead the attachment and sale of property.

The Knesset has also recently enacted the Basic Law: Dignity and Liberty of Man. The Basic Law provides that it is not to be used to invalidate any law preceding it. Nevertheless, the Court ruled in *Perach* that prior laws must be interpreted in the spirit of the Basic Law, and interpreted the Execution Law accordingly.

Section 180 of the Bankruptcy Ordinance (New Version) 1980 provides that, if a creditor requests an imprisonment order against a debtor under Section 70 of the Execution Law, the Court can, with the consent of the creditor, issue a receivership order rather than an imprisonment order against the debtor, who will thereby be deemed to have undertaken an act of bankruptcy. Indeed the interaction between the remedies of bankruptcy and of execution proceedings was considered by the Supreme Court in the case of *Ashkenazi v Official Receiver, Civil Appeal* (4892/91, 38(i), 45), which was decided in November 1993.

Interest on Debts

Inevitably, interest on borrowed money raises particular problems. If a debt bears interest, the debtor may claim protection from paying interest forbidden by the Torah, but cannot escape paying the debt itself.[83]

The Shulkhan Aruch discusses the case of two Jews who hold bonds from a non-Jew whose assets are insufficient to pay both in full. The proceeds come to a Jewish court for distribution. The interest is held to rank for

---

[83] See supra, n. 64.

distribution with the principal. An objection from the holder of the later bond, that the interest arose after the date of the earlier bond, will not be upheld.[84] But Rabbi Moses Isserlis considers[85] that the later creditor may redeem by paying interest up to date.

The Absence of Bankruptcy Procedures

In modern secular legal systems, insolvency procedures have two principal functions: to distribute the available assets of the debtor between his creditors, and to provide a means of discharging the debtor from his debts.

The distribution of assets in Jewish Law has been discussed above. As to the release of the debtor from his debts, Jewish Law has no such procedure "in bankruptcy." In biblical times, and subsequently, the septennial release of debts effectively achieved this object. From talmudic times there developed too the concept of *"siddur le-va'al ḥov"*—an arrangement for the benefit of poor debtors. This was a less formal arrangement, falling short of what would today be termed bankruptcy.[86]

As times and circumstances changed and the septennial release of debts ceased to be available, some accommodation with governing civil legal systems—*dina d'malkhuta*—became necessary. In medieval Spain, for example, a practice developed, in accordance with the principle of *dina d'malkhuta dina*, of giving effect to governmental ordinances which stayed collection of a debt until other creditors had an opportunity to present themselves and their claims. The custom was to proclaim publicly that all creditors who failed to present their claims by a certain day would lose their rights.[87] Generally, too, the Rabbis recognised that civil legal systems were obliged to provide a mechanism—a bankruptcy procedure—to enable insolvent debtors to be released from their obligations to their creditors, and accepted this, under the principle of *dina d'malkhuta dina*.[88]

In the final analysis, though, debtors remained under a moral obligation to repay their debts one day if they could, "in order to be clean before G-d and men."[89] In the end, "The wicked man borrows and does not repay."[90]

---

[84] Shulkhan Arukh, Ḥoshen Mishpat, civ, 15. Discussed in *The Jewish Encyclopedia*, op. cit., Vol. II, "Bankruptcy," p. 494.

[85] Shulkhan Arukh, Ḥoshen Mishpat, lxxxvi, 1. Discussed in *The Jewish Encyclopedia*, op. cit., Vol. II, "Bankruptcy," p. 494.

[86] See supra, n. 60.

[87] George Horovitz, *The Spirit of Jewish Law*, op. cit., Section 257 and the authorities there cited.

[88] See supra, n. 5

[89] See supra, n. 64.

[90] Psalms 37:21.

Enough has been said in this essay to explain why Jewish Law does not know the concept of bankruptcy proceedings, and indeed why it approaches the subject of insolvency through eyes different from those of modern Western legal systems.

9

Parental Rights in the Marriage of a Minor

David Novak[*]

Halakhah: Practical and Theoretical

Practical questions of Jewish law cannot be practically resolved without personal contact between the questioner (*sho'el*) and the respondent (*meshiv*). For there is the ancient admonition to "be deliberate (*metunim*) in judgment,"[1] which means that the particularities of each case must be thoroughly investigated in all their detail before actual legal judgement (*pesak din*) can be responsibly rendered. That investigation cannot be conducted abstractly. There is a fundamental difference between practical questions (*sh'elot*) and theoretical ones (*kushiyot*).[2] To take it upon oneself to answer a practical halakhic question that has not been personally submitted to him or her is also the impropriety of usurping the authority of an actual rabbi or group of rabbis to whom practical questions ought to be submitted by those who accept their halakhic authority.[3] Nevertheless, there are times when issues arise that involve such intense public discussion of questions vital for Jewish law and theology, that Judaic scholars committed to the tradition (*talmidei hakhamim*) might well have an obligation to discuss them in order to generally educate the public rather than to literally adjudicate a real case.[4] Sometimes such issues arise because of public policy discussions in society

---

[*] Maimonides Professor of Jewish Studies and Director of Programme of Jewish Studies, University of Toronto, University College, 15 King's College Circle, Toronto, Ontario M5S 3H7, Canada.

[1] *M. Av.* 1.1. See *San.* 7b; Maim., *Mishneh Torah: Sanhedrin*, 20.7.

[2] See, e.g., *Ned.* 60a for the most literal meaning of *sh'elah*, i.e., a practical question requiring the particular answer of a rabbinic sage. Cf., e.g., *B.K.* 117a for the academic character of a *kushya*.

[3] See *Shabb.* 19b; *Eruv.* 94a; *Pes.* 30a; *Ḥul.* 53b.

[4] For the obligation to answer any question pertaining to Jewish teaching on any subject, see *Kidd.* 30a–b re *Prov.* 7:3 and *Tos.*, s.v. "*al tegamgem*;" *B.M.* 23b and *Tos.*, s.v. "*bemasekhet*." Cf. *A.Z.* 19a and *Rashi*, s.v. "*mimakom*."

at large, such as the issues of abortion, the treatment of AIDS patients, and euthanasia. Sometimes such issues arise because of public policy discussions in the larger Jewish community, such as the role of women in Jewish religious life. And sometimes such public policy issues are keenly highlighted by notorious cases that receive wide publicity. This paper is in response to intense discussion in the larger Jewish community (so much so that it was also widely reported in the general press) about a particular case involving basic issues pertaining to the traditional Jewish family. Here again, without presuming to actually adjudicate a case involving persons who do not look to me for halakhic answers, I feel it is not inappropriate to offer some comments and some general suggestions about a situation that has generated much confusion. Hence my remarks are theoretical (*talmud*), not practical (*hora'ah*)—although theory and practice are closely related in Judaism.[5]

As reported in the press, the case whose general issues I want to explore here involves a halakhicly observant Jewish man who initiated a marriage (*ḳidushin*) for his daughter, who is a small child and thus a minor (*ḳetanah*). The questions connected with this case are: (1) By what right could he initiate such a marriage?; (2) Do the sources of Halakhah approve such an act?; (3) Is there any remedy for this act, which is reported to have been done in order to prevent the man's estranged wife from taking custody of his daughter? It must be added that there seems to be virtually unanimous revulsion in the entire Jewish community for this most unusual act.

The Right to Initiate Marriage for a Minor Girl

One of the dogmas of Judaism is that we are ruled by a two faceted Torah: the Pentateuch (*torah shebikhtav*), especially in its self-evident prescriptions (*gezerot hakatuv*), and the Oral Tradition (*torah sheb`al peh*).[6] The Oral Tradition consists of three main parts: (1) undisputed traditions attributed all the way back to Moses (*halakhot*); (2) rabbinic interpretations of Scripture (*derashot*); (3) rabbinic decrees (*gezerot*) and enactments (*taḳanot*).[7] All subsequent codes and responsa are built upon these primary sources. In order to understand any institution of Jewish law, one must see its development in the two faceted Torah.

---

[5] For the difference between *talmud* and *hora'ah*, see B.B. 130b and Meiri, *Bet Habeḥirah* thereon; Ber. 33b and *Rashi*, s.v. "halakhah;" Ket. 56a. For the close relation of theory and practice, theory (*talmud*) being the proper generator of practice (*ma`aseh*), see *Sifre: Devarim*, no. 41; Ḳidd. 40b.

[6] See Ber. 5a re Exod. 24:12; Maim., *Mishneh Torah*: Introduction.

[7] See Maim., *Mishneh Torah: Mamrim*, chap. 1.

Based on the scriptural verse, "my daughter I have given to this man" (*Deut.* 22:16), the Rabbis interpret that a father has the right to initiate a marriage for his minor daughter, who herself has no inherent legal right to initiate one for herself.[8] Furthermore, a father is to be believed *prima facie* when he simply declares that he has initiated such a marriage.[9] From this scripturally based right several issues arise: (1) concern about a marriage conducted without the consent of one of the partners; (2) concern about the possibility of legally sanctioned intercourse with a prepubescent girl, which many people have long regarded as *de facto* rape. These are especially volatile issues when more and more incidents of the sexual abuse of both women and children are receiving greater and greater public scrutiny and condemnation.

Although child marriages were quite common in biblical and early rabbinic times for whatever reasons, already in the late tannaitic period (2nd century C.E.) there was growing disapproval of this practice.[10] By the early amoraic period (3rd century C.E.), an actual rabbinic decree was issued either in the name of the Babylonian authority Rav or the Palestinian authority R. Eleazar: "It is forbidden (*asur*) for one to contract a marriage for his daughter when she is still a minor (*ketanah*) until she is mature and can say 'it is X whom I want.'"[11] It is assumed by some commentators that the problem this decree intends to eliminate is the strong possibility that once a woman who was married by her father's act when she was a minor, upon becoming an adult she will subsequently reject the husband who, in effect, was forced upon her.[12] This seems to follow from the general rabbinic assumption that marriages should be initiated with the intention of permanence.[13] However, one can very well interpret reason for the rabbinic prohi-

---

8 M. Ket. 4.4; Ket. 46b; M. Ḳidd. 2.1; *Sifre: Devarim*, no. 235. On Ḳidd. 64b and *Rashi*, s.v. "*umashnay*" re *Jer.* 29:6, it is stated that this is not only a father's right (*zekhut*) but his duty (*mitzvah*). Cf. B.B. 141a, Tos., s.v. "*bat;*" *Bereshit Rabbah* 60.12 re *Gen.* 24:57, ed. Theodor-Albeck, 653 and n. 3 thereon; *Rashi, Commentary on the Torah: Gen.* 24:57. However, none of the codes treats this text as legally binding. Hence the use of the word *mitzvah* there is best translated as "meritorious" rather than "obligatory." Accordingly, there is no legal violation (*averah*) if a father does not contract a marriage for his minor daughter. For this use of the term *mitzvah*, see, e.g., Zev. 48a; Y. Pes. 2.4/29b. Cf. Yev. 20a and parallels.

9 Ket. 22a.

10 See Louis Ginzberg, *Perushim Veḥidushim Beyerushalmi: Berakhot* 1 (New York, 1941), 369; Ephraim E. Urbach, *Halakhah* (Jerusalem, 1984), 243–244, nn. 12–13.

11 Ḳidd. 41a. See Maim., *Mishneh Torah: Ishut*, 3.19; R. Jacob ben Asher, *Ṭur: Even Ha`Ezer*, 37; R. Joseph Karo, *Shulhan Arukh: Even Ha`Ezer*, 37.8 (cf. R. Samuel Phoebus, *Bet Shmu'el* thereon, n. 11).

12 Ḳidd. 41a, Tos., s.v. "*asur;*" Rabbenu Nissim (*Ran*) on *Alfasi: Ḳidd.*, chap. 2, ed. Vilna, 16b, s.v. "*keshehi na`arah*."

13 See Giṭṭ. 90b re *Mal.* 2:14. Cf. Yom. 18b and Tos., s.v. "*yiḥuday*."

bition being a rejection of *de facto* rape. Indeed, the medieval commentator, R. Menahem Meiri, sees the whole development of the institution of Jewish marriage as resulting in the elimination of the coercion of women, that is, what we now would call "marital rape." As he puts it in his commentary on the Talmud tractate devoted primarily to the institution of Jewish marriage, Kiddushin,

> What emerges from this in terms of actual law (*pesak*) is that a marriage is not initiated for a woman without her consent (*b`al korhah*). And that is the law even though the language of Scripture does not indicate it . . . Nevertheless, it is a matter not requiring a scriptural statement (*ayn zeh tsarikh kera*). For if so [namely, if we were to only follow Scripture], there would not be one daughter of Abraham left [namely, wanting to remain in Judaism]. Indeed, in almost every other matter, no transaction initiated under duress (*ones*) is valid.[14]

Nevertheless, if such a marriage prohibited by rabbinic decree was in fact contracted, it is valid *ex post facto*, and its termination would require nothing less than a full Jewish divorce (*get*). I shall return to this point later.

Earlier rabbinic sources, which predate the actual enactment of this prohibition, are more concerned with the issue of sexual intercourse between an adult man and a female child. Thus it is reported that R. Eliezer, at the insistence of his mother, married his niece when she was a minor, but he did not actually consummate the marriage until his wife reached maturity.[15] This seems to be based on the notion that the primary purpose of marital intercourse is procreation, something that would not result from intercourse with a child.[16]

The common thread that runs through most of the rabbinic discussions of this issue seems to be concern for the welfare of the bride. Either we are to be concerned with her being forced to have intercourse without her consent, or her being forced into a union wherefrom she will not derive the mutual benefit of parenthood, or her being forced into a union likely to be impermanent.

---

[14] *Bet Habehirah: Kidd.*, ed. Sofer, 8 quoting *Ket.* 72b, 82b. See Louis M. Epstein, *Sex Laws and Customs in Judaism* (New York, 1948), 179ff. For the legal disapproval of agreements made under duress, see, e.g., *B.B.* 40a–b. For the theological disapproval of such agreements, see *Shabb.* 88a re *Est.* 9:27. For the natural law implications of the phrase "not requiring a scriptural statement," see Nahmanides, *Commentary on the Torah: Gen.* 6:2, 13; also, D. Novak, *The Theology of Nahmanides—Systematically Presented* (Atlanta, 1992), 107ff.

[15] Y. *Yev.* 13.2/13c. See *Avot Derabi Nathan* B, chap. 48, ed. Schechter, 66a; *Nidd.* 13b.

[16] For the development of the notion that marital intimacy per se is also an end of marriage, see David M. Feldman, *Birth Control in Jewish Law* (New York, 1968), 60ff.

The Reasons for the Rules

What we finally have is a rabbinic revocation of a right granted by Scripture. We must now see how scriptural and rabbinic law are both differentiated from each other and related to each other.

There are two essential differences between a scriptural norm and a rabbinic norm. In terms of their respective authority, any specific rabbinic norm is justified **because** of a general authorization derived from Scripture. Hence it is "mandatory (*mitzvah*) to heed the rulings of the rabbinic sages (*divray ḥakhamim*)" because "you may not deviate (*lo tasur*) from the ruling (*davar*) they declare to you" (*Deut.* 17:11).[17] But Scripture as the word of God is its own authorization.[18] Conversely, in terms of their formulation, specific rabbinic norms require that there be explicit reasons for their enactment.[19] These reasons are to form the basis of the rational arguments of the human sages engaged in formulating the law for other humans over whom they have legal authority.[20] These reasons are then to be a matter of publicly persuasive knowledge.[21] Whether scriptural norms have specific reasons or not is a matter of long theological dispute.[22] However, even if all of them do have reasons, God being the solitary lawgiver need not reveal them when formulating the law. He has no colleagues whom He need persuade during the process of legal formulation.[23] And since God's authority is not con-

---

17 *Yev.* 20a and parallels; *Shabb.* 23a; *Y. Sukk.* 3.4/53d; also, R. Nissim Gerondi, *Derashot Haran*, no. 5, ed. Feldman, pp. 87–88.

18 See, e.g., *Sifra: Vayikra*, ed. Weiss, 15b re *Lev.* 4:2 and note of Ra'avad thereon.

19 See *Giṭṭ.* 14a and *Tos.*, s.v. "*kehilkhata*." For the difference between rabbinic authority and rabbinic ratiocination (*sevara*) leading to the exercise of that authority, see *Ḳidd.* 74a and Rashi and *Tos.*, s.v. "*shuda dedayanay.*" It would seem that both Rashi and Rabbenu Tam (whose view is contrasted with his) recognize the indispensability of both elements of rabbinic jurisprudence, the only difference between them being which aspect of it is denoted by the term *shuda dedayanay* ("judicial discretion"). See, also, Z. W. Falk, *Arkhay Mishpat Veyahadut* (Jerusalem, 1980), 28.

20 See *Eruv.* 13b; Maim., *Commentary on the Mishnah: Sot.* 3.3.

21 See *A.Z.* 35a; *B.B.* 31b–32a and 173b; *Eruv.* 68b; *San.* 31b; *Ker.* 20a; also, Urbach, *Halakhah*, 108. Cf. R. Ovadia Yosef, *Yabi`a Omer*, 4 (Jerusalem, 1986), *Oraḥ Ḥayim*, no. 21, p. 84. For the importance of knowing the correct reason for a rabbinic enactment in order that it be properly applied, see *Ḳidd.* 46b.

22 For what might be termed the "fideistic" view, see, e.g., *Sifra: Kedoshim*, ed. Weiss, 93d; *Bereshit Rabbah* 44.1; *Bemidbar Rabbah* 19.1. For what might be termed the "rationalist" view, see, e.g., Maim., *Guide of the Perplexed*, 3.26; Nahmanides, *Commentary on the Torah:Lev.* 19:19; *Deut.* 4:3. Of course, the authority of any law, whether scriptural or even rabbinic, is valid whether or not the reason for it is understood or not by those to whom it is addressed. See, e.g., Maim., *Mishneh Torah: Teshuvah*, 3.4; *Sifre: Devarim*, no. 154 re *Deut.* 17:11.

23 See, esp., *San.* 21b. As for the application of even scriptural law, i.e., subsequent to its formulation, it is a major point of rabbinic theology that the decisions of the rabbinic authorities about **God's** law are accepted by God Himself (see *Shemot Rabbah* 15.3 re *Exod.* 12:2 and *Lev.* 23:2; *B.M.* 59b) in the sense that God obeys His own law (see *Y. R.H.* 1.3/57a–b).

tingent on popular consent, unlike human political authority, He need not reveal the reasons for His laws to His subjects.[24] Thus they will have to speculate as best they can whatever reasons they can think of for these scriptural laws—after the fact. And, indeed, scriptural law can at times appear to be absurd.[25] But where scriptural law applies to interhuman relationships (*bayn adam leḥavero*), such speculation is easier than when it only pertains to the human relationship with God.[26]

The essential reason for a rabbinic norm is its ground, and if the reason no longer applies, the rule itself is subject to possible repeal, or radical reinterpretation.[27] But a scriptural norm may not be repealed, whether or not the reason for it we have inferred still applies.[28] At most, one can only interpret a scriptural norm so that it does not apply except under rare circumstances.[29] Nevertheless, a rabbinic norm that limits a scriptural norm can be better understood and better applied if we can see a common reason for both norms in their interrelation. In some ways each type of law is compared with the other, especially when a rabbinic law is directly related to a scriptural law.[30]

This point comes out in the rabbinic treatment of the initiation of the marriage of a minor child by either her mother or her brothers when her father is dead and she is legally an orphan (*yetomah*). Since this is not a scriptural right, the reason for this rabbinic entitlement is more explicit and more determining in the practical application of the law.[31] Under these circumstances, the girl so married has the right to annul her marriage when she reaches her majority.[32] According to Maimonides, if the marriage was contracted before her sixth birthday, then even if she was extraordinarily in-

---

[24] See *A.Z.* 36a–b.

[25] See, e.g., *Bemidbar Rabbah* 19.4. Cf. *Eruv.* 68b; *B.B.* 31b and *Rashbam*, s.v. "lezeluta debay dina."

[26] See D. Novak, "Jewish Ethics and Natural Law," *Journal of Jewish Thought and Philosophy* 5 (1996), 205ff.

[27] Because of the general consensus among halakhists not to explicitly repeal any talmudic decree, based on *M. Eduy.* 1.5, reinterpretation has often been the method of effecting change when needed. See *A.Z.* 36a and *Rashi*, s.v. "lo pashat." Cf. Maim., *Mishneh Torah: Mamrim*, 2.7 and R. Joseph Karo, *Kesef Mishneh* thereon; also, Rabbenu Asher, *Teshuvot Haro'sh*, 2.8.

[28] See *Kidd.* 29a re *Num.* 15:23.

[29] See, e.g., *T. Sot.* 14.2 and Saul Lieberman, *Tosefta Kifshuta: Nashim* (New York, 1973), 751; *Sot.* 48b re *Num.* 5:31; *Makk.* 7a.

[30] See *Yev.* 11a and parallels.

[31] The reason given for this right (*Yev.* 112b) is that it enables the mother or brothers of a fatherless girl, who is without a male protector who is socially significant, to benefit her with such a male protector (i.e., a husband). Without such a male protector, it is feared that she might be sexually abused by strangers.

[32] *M. Yev.* 13.1–2.

telligent, we assume that there was no consent at all and that the annulment of the marriage requires no formal proceeding at all. If the marriage was contracted between her sixth and tenth birthdays, then even if she was extraordinarily unintelligent, we investigate as to whether she is discerning enough to understand the meaning of her marriage and thus have been able to give her consent (*venitkadeshah leda`atah*). If that was indeed the case, then the annulment of the marriage requires a formal procedure called *mi'un*, which the newly matured woman institutes herself. Maimonides concludes by stating that such a marriage is valid in the full scriptural sense (*kidushin gemurin min hatorah*) if she simply remains with her husband (without complaint) after reaching her majority.[33] Clearly, the purpose of the Rabbis permitting such a marriage was to benefit a fatherless girl, who was usually quite vulnerable, socially and economically. Early marriage was thus considered to be a form of social and economic protection for her. But as we have seen, consummation of the marriage before the maturity of the girl was frowned upon.

It is a halakhic principle that one may benefit someone else without his or her consent.[34] However, if someone acted on behalf of someone else assuming that this other person would have wanted this benefit (*zekhut*), yet that other person subsequently reveals that he or she actually regarded the "benefit" as a detriment (*hovah*), then the "beneficial" act is null and void retroactively.[35] This is especially so when the object of any such beneficance is a child, being a most vulnerable person in need of the most beneficial action from others. Thus, for example, if a gentile child was converted to Judaism, then that child upon reaching his or her majority has the right to retroactively annul what was done on his or her behalf if he or she subsequently believes otherwise.[36] Furthermore, the Rabbis decreed that in the event of marital breakup a child is better off with his or her mother at one age and better off with his or her father at another age.[37] Nevertheless, the

---

[33] *Mishneh Torah: Ishut*, 4.7–8; *Gerushin*, 11.7. See his *Commentary on the Mishnah: Yev.*, 13.2, ed. Kafih, 36; *T. Yev.* 13.1; *Yev.* 108a. Cf. *Y. Yev.* 13.2/13c; R. Joseph ibn Habib, *Nimukkay Yosef* on *Alfasi: Yev.*, chap. 13, ed. Vilna, 36a. For Maimonides' generally lenient attitude towards situations where women are unwilling to continue living with their husbands, see *Mishneh Torah: Ishut*, 14.8 re *Ket.* 63b. There he states, "a woman is not to be like a captive (*keshevuyah*) to have to have intercourse with a man she hates." Cf. *Ket.* 63b, *Tos.*, s.v. "*aval;*" R. Jacob ben Asher, *Tur: Even Ha`Ezer*, 77 and R. Joseph Karo, *Bet Yosef* thereon.

[34] *M. Eruv.* 7.11 and parallels. See Maim., *Mishneh Torah: Zekhiyah Umatanah*, 4.2.

[35] See *Kidd.* 23a and Nahmanides, *Hidushay Haramban* thereon; also, *B.M.* 19a.

[36] *Ket.* 11a. See D. Novak, "the Legal Question of the Investigation of Converts," *Jewish Law Association Studies* 3 (Atlanta, GA., 1987), 167ff.

[37] *Eruv.* 82a–b.

16th century Egyptian authority, R. David ibn Abi Zimra (*Radbaz*) ruled that judges have the duty to do what is most beneficial for each individual child, thus acting more on the intent of the earlier rabbinic rules rather than on their literal formulation.[38]

The issue of benefit comes out in medieval treatments of the institution of child marriage. Thus in one gloss on the talmudic text where the prohibition of child marriage is stated, the following poignant remark is found:

> But now it is our practice to initiate marriages (*lekadesh*) for our daughters, even when they are minors (*ketanot*). This is because the exile weighs more and more heavily upon us, so that if a man now has the means to provide his daughter with a dowery (*nedunia*), then [he should initiate her marriage now] lest at a later time [when she has reached her majority] he will not have the means to do so and his daughter will remain unmarried (*agunah*) permanently.[39]

This seems to imply that the reason for **both** the original scriptural right and the later rabbinic revocation of the initial exercise *ab initio* of that right (although, as we have seen, not its effect *ex post facto*) is the same, namely, to benefit the girl.[40]

This comes out in another medieval gloss on a related talmudic text. There the Talmud states that in the event of a minor girl married without the consent of her father, Rav ruled that "either the father or the daughter has the right to prevent (*l`akev*) the marriage from being considered valid."[41] The gloss notes that if the father has the right to contract a marriage for his daughter without her consent, why should her opinion have any legal force at all. One answer suggested is that it is a benefit (*zekhut*) for him because it is normally assumed that it is a benefit for his daughter. But if she indicates (as a minor) that this is not what she wants, then it would be a detriment (*hov*) for the father as well because he would not want something for his daughter that she herself would not want for herself.[42] Here it should be noted that the same recognition of the force of intent even regarding a minor, which Maimonides saw in the rabbinic institution of the marriage of an orphaned minor by either her mother or her brother, is now seen in the

---

38 *Teshuvot Haradbaz*, 1, no. 123. See ibid., no. 429.

39 *Kidd.* 41a, Tos., s.v. "*asur.*"

40 For the assumption that a girl should always accept the marital choice made by her father for her because her father always intends her benefit, see *Teshuvot Hage'onim*, ed. Harkavy, no. 212.

41 *Kidd.* 46a.

42 Ibid., Tos., s.v. "*bein.*"

scriptural institution of the marriage of a minor at the initiation of her father.

However, another medieval commentator, R. Israel Isserlein, notes that there is a difference between acting on somebody else's behalf, even if she does not object in his presence, and her acting on her own behalf independently. The difference is between the right of a father to allow his minor daughter to initiate her own marriage, mentioned in the Talmud and codified by the early post-talmudic authorities (*ge'onim*), and holding her hand at the wedding ceremony (which it is reported that R. Meir of Rothenburg actually did with his own daughter) and having the girl utter her consent. For the latter act is in effect the father's consent.[43] In other words, consent is essentially an individual matter. It cannot be cogently performed for one by someone else, however well intentioned that other person might be.

Possible Legal Remedies

Since the act of initiating a marriage for one's minor daughter runs contrary to the general trend of Jewish tradition, involving as it does the issues of coercion and possible rape, what can the authorities of the particular traditional Jewish community of which this man is a member do to remedy this act, one which has become a public scandal (*ḥilul hashem*), namely, when Jewish law appears to be morally odious by standards common to Judaism and the surrounding gentile culture?[44] Here again, let me emphasize that I am not presuming to actually adjudicate this notorious case. That would be neither my right nor my duty. Instead, I am simply offering a suggestion (*etsah tovah*) to any authorities who might be asked for a legal ruling (which they could accept, reject, or ignore) as to what they might do.[45] And, more importantly, I do regard it to be my duty to inform the larger Jewish community about the issues of Jewish family law this notorious case raises.

Some scholars have suggested that this man be punished as a violator of the rabbinic norm prohibiting a father from initiating a marriage for his minor daughter. When Jewish communities had more political autonomy than they do at present in our secular societies, the usual penalty for such a violation of rabbinic law was corporal punishment (*makat mardut*).[46] So, for

---

[43] *Terumat Hadeshen*, 1, no. 213; see Ibid., 2, no. 33.

[44] See *Ber.* 19b and parallels; *Yev.* 79a; *B.K.* 113b; also, *Sefer Ḥasidim*, ed. Bologna, no. 1101; R. Ḥayyim Yair Bachrach, *Ḥavot Ya'ir*, no. 31.

[45] For the notion that one without legal authority can advise those having it, see *B.M.* 119a; *Nidd.* 50a, Tos., s.v. "kol."

[46] See R. Isaac Lampronti, *Paḥad Yitshak*, s.v. "*makat mardut.*" Cf. B. M. Lewin, *Otsar Hage'onim: Ḳidd.* (Jerusalem, 1939), 111, no. 245 re *Ḳidd.* 41a.

example, even though one has the scriptural right to initiate marriage by an act of intercourse, the 3rd century Babylonian authority, Rav, prescribed lashes for anyone who actually exercised that right. The Talmud points out that he did so to prevent public lewdness (*pritsuta*).[47] When that type of coercion is impossible, already by the time of the Mishnah (2nd century C.E.) it was recognized that a Jewish court could, in effect, deputize non-Jewish authorities to exercise coercion on its behalf.[48] In the case at hand, this could be accomplished by appeal to secular laws prohibiting child marriages. Nevertheless, even if such action would be successful, it publicly declares the impotence of traditional Jewish communities to themselves effect justice for their own members, especially when those oppressed are female rather than male.[49]

Some scholars have suggested the less drastic measure of social ostracism, for example, denying this man certain privileges in the synagogue and in other communal settings.[50] Of course, the effect of such ostracism depends to a large extent on how subordinate this man is to the authorities of his own community, let alone whether these authorities are actually willing to do anything in this case. However, recent experience with the growing scandal of traditional Jewish men who refuse give their wives the divorces that by rabbinic decree these women are entitled to has shown, alas, that such men are often impervious to anything less than actual physical coercion.[51] Their personal interests in the morally odious acts of extortion or revenge, more often than not overrride whatever respect one would assume they have for religious authorities. And, even though such measures are more matters of inner Jewish publicity, they, nevertheless, declare the same impotence of traditional Jewish communities to morally clean their own houses.

There is, however, a solution to this scandalous situation this man's act has created, which is less radical since it does not rely on secular authorities,

---

[47] Ḳidd. 12b; Maim., *Mishneh Torah: Ishut*, 3.21. See Y. Yev. 5.2/6d; also, Ḳidd. 21b–22a and Rashi and Tos., s.v. "shelo." For the initial scriptural right to initiate marriage by an act of intercourse, see M. Ḳidd. 1.1; Ḳidd. 9b; Maim., *Mishneh Torah: Ishut*, 3.5.

[48] M. Giṭṭ. 9.8; Giṭṭ. 88b.

[49] Thus Maimonides insists that one is to only rely on non-Jewish authorities when there is no remedy available from the Jewish authorities (see *Mishneh Torah: Sanhedrin*, 26.6). However, in this case, as we shall presently see, there is a remedy available to Jewish authorities.

[50] E.g., one could declare this man unfit to be a witness in a Jewish legal proceeding. See M. San. 3.2 and Maim., *Commentary on the Mishnah* thereon, ed. Kafih, 109; San. 26b; Maim., *Mishneh Torah: Edut*, 11.6. For the use of ostracism, even for offenders against moral rather than strictly legal norms, see B. M. 48b; Y. Ḳidd. 3.1/63c.

[51] See Maim., *Mishneh Torah: Gerushin*, 2.20.

but more radical as an inner Jewish procedure. I suggest that the rabbinical court (*bet din*) of the traditional Jewish community of which this man is a member take it upon itself to annul this marriage.[52] Such legal action is considered radical to be sure, but it has sound talmudic basis, and in rare cases when great human suffering could only be eliminated by its invocation it has actually been invoked.[53]

Of course, it could be countered that when this procedure was invoked, it was for the benefit of a large number of Jewish women. To this we can only answer that to allow this situation to continue is in many ways to permit this evil man to ruin the life of his daughter. Less radical solutions to her predicament could only leave her sexually tainted for the rest of her life.[54] Only annulment (*afka`at ḳidushin*) removes any taint at all from her. Only this procedure truly frees her to live a normal Jewish life. Any time when we can eliminate undeserved suffering caused by the sins of others we must do so. As the prophet put it, "The fathers have eaten sour grapes, and the teeth of the children are set on edge!" (Jeremiah 31:28) And to those who would say that this involves only one Jewish girl, we would remind them of the teaching of our Sages, namely, "one who saves even one Jewish life, it is as if he has saved an entire world."[55] Whether it is one life or many lives, surely the Torah's command, "Justice Justice you shall pursue" (Deuteronomy 16:20) applies here and now. There are, of course, many cases of injustice in this world which human beings cannot rectify, and which we can only hope that God will rectify, either in this world or in the world-to-come.[56] But when we do have the power to rectify any injustice and do not do so, either because of inertia, timidity, prejudice, or erroneous piety, then we ourselves must answer to God as to why we did nothing when we could have done something effective for justice.[57]

The justice being sought here is not being sought because of non-Jewish criteria. It is not a matter of feminism or egalitarianism that have so clearly

---

52 See *Giṭṭ*. 33a and parallels; R. Isaac bar Sheshet Parfat, *Teshuvot Harivash*, no. 399; also, D. Novak, "Annulment in Lieu of Divorce in Jewish Law," *Jewish Law Annual* 4 (1981), 188ff. [reprinted in D. Novak, *Halakhah in a Theological Dimension* (Chico, Calif., 1985), 29ff.].

53 See R. Moses Isserles, *Darkhay Mosheh* on *Ṭur: Even Ha`Ezer*, 7, n. 13.

54 See *Yev.* 59a; Maim., *Mishneh Torah: Isuray Bi'ah*, 17.18.

55 *San.* 37a. From the context of the *Mishnah* quoted there (*San.* 4.5), it is clear that the correct text is *nefesh ahat*, i.e., any human life. In the case of literal life, that is no doubt the case. However, the reading of most Mss. of *Talmud Bavli* can be applied to various forms of social "death," wherein Jews have special obligations for each other (see Maim., *Mishneh Torah: Matnot Aniyim*, 10.2). For the allusion to social difficulties as "death," see. e.g., *Ned.* 7b re *Exod.* 4:19 and Rabbenu Nissim (*Ran*), s.v. "*shene'emar*."

56 See, e.g., *Ḳidd.* 39a and *Tos.*, s.v. "*matnitin*;" *T. San.* 8.3; *San.* 37b; *Ḥul.* 142a.

57 See *Bereshit Rabbah* 60.3; also, *Vayikra Rabbah* 32.8.

entered into so much contemporary Jewish discussion of moral and political issues. One could well argue that, especially in the area of Jewish marriage, such ideologies are non-Jewish or even anti-Jewish.[58] Instead, we have here a case where **Jewish** criteria of justice, which we have seen are evident in the development of the normative Jewish tradition on this question and others related to it, are the basis for the justice to be sought here. To refuse to employ these criteria and to conservatively plead for legal caution I think is, in the words of one of our greatest jurists, Nahmanides, to be "a scoundral within the letter of the law" (*naval birshut hatorah*).[59] Surely, all of us are duty bound to plead for justice to those humanly capable of exercising it, and if they are deaf to such pleas, then we are duty bound to plead the case of this innocent child to God.[60] Those guilty in the case are both the father who committed this proscribed act, and the rabbinical leaders of his community who, it was reported, allowed him to do so with impunity.[61]

---

[58] See, e.g., *Y. Kidd.* 1.1/58c; Maim., *Mishneh Torah: Ishut*, 1.1, 4.
[59] *Commentary on the Torah: Lev.* 19:2.
[60] See *B.K.* 93a re *Gen.* 16:5 and *Rashi* and *Tos.*, s.v. "ehad" re *Exod.* 22:22–23.
[61] See *Shev.* 39a–b re *Lev.* 27:37; *San.* 44a; Maim., *Mishneh Torah: Melakhim*, 9.14.

10

REMARKS ON *PESQUISA* IN MEDIEVAL JEWISH LEGAL PROCEDURE

STEPHEN M. PASSAMANECK[*]

The old Castilian word *pesquisa* means judicial inquiry, or inquest, or even inquisition. It was a well-known feature of medieval Spanish law, well attested and documented; and the word appears once in medieval Spanish-Jewish legal literature, responsum no. 58 of Judah b. Asher's responsa, *Zichron Yehudah*, ed. Berlin, 1846.

Yitzhak Baer in his extensive examination of Jewish life in medieval Christian Spain discusses the *pesquisa* as it appears in Judah b. Asher's collection of cases.[1] The context of Baer's citation is refutation of the atrocious proposition, advanced by some Spanish scholars, that the procedures of the Spanish ecclesiastical Inquisition somehow sprouted from Jewish legal roots. He notes the currency of *pesquisa* in the Castilian legal practice of the 13th and 14th centuries, briefly describes how it operated, and then cites the crucial passage from Judah b. Asher's responsum.

Baer's citation of the responsum, however, clearly raises two questions which require some comment before the task of closer examination of *pesquisa* itself and its implicit or explicit existence in medieval Jewish legal procedure can fairly begin.

First the citation in Baer reads as follows: "And one is not to pronounce the ban: anyone who knows anything reflecting upon the acceptability of one of the witnesses, whether he is suspect of any crime, let him come forth and testify—since such procedure would be *pesquisa*, which it is forbidden to make against anyone, *according to the laws of the land* . . ." (emphasis added). It is certain beyond any doubt, however, that *pesquisa* was not forbidden under the "laws of the land." Moreover, the emphasized phrase does not appear in the standard edition of the responsum, nor is there any

---

[*] Professor of Rabbinics, Hebrew Union College, Los Angeles.
[1] Yitzhak Baer, *History of the Jews in Christian Spain*, 2 vols., Jewish Publication Society of America (Philadelphia: 1961), vol. 2, p. 453.

notation *ad loc.* of any manuscript containing this rather important bit of information. On any plain reading of the statement, Baer appears in error. We shall revisit Baer's opinion later in this paper.

Second, Baer characterizes the notion of *pesquisa* as an illegal form of "inquisition" and as foreign to Jewish law. He does not explain in what sense it is illegal and foreign. Is the *pesquisa* a foreign element which Jewish law, or Jewish lawyers, reject outright as inconsistent with Jewish law or contrary to it? Or is it a foreign idea which may appear implicitly in Jewish legal texts despite its gentile origin and which is perhaps illegal in this form in gentile law, but licit in some other form? (Can Jews use that legal form of it?) Baer seems to suggest the former idea: *pesquisa* is a foreign idea, in some manner inconsistent with Jewish law, and thus R. Judah b. Asher rejects it. These matters bring us to the point of these remarks.

To put the proposition of this present investigation simply, indications of a procedure strongly akin to *pesquisa*, if not *pesquisa* itself, do appear in late 13th and early 14th century Spanish Jewish legal texts, despite Judah b. Asher's apparent rejection of it and despite Baer's characterization of it as illegal and foreign, even though the term *pesquisa* does not explicitly appear in other texts. Indeed, Judah b. Asher himself suggests something very like *pesquisa* even in the context of his apparent categorical rejection of it.

One point must be kept firmly in mind. The *pesquisa*, or inquisitorial procedure, discussed here is distinct from an inquisitorial procedure based upon taking a confession from the accused. Aragonese law in the later 14th century forbade such process founded on confession, and Jewish authorities knew they had to step carefully when trying a criminal defendant in order not to violate any rules against inquisitorial confessions, since, after all, their criminal jurisdiction rested on a royal grant of such power as we shall have occasion to observe.[2]

We shall proceed to study *pesquisa* by first reviewing the concept and its context as given in Spanish law of the latter 13th and early 14th centuries, and then review the procedures reflected in two rabbinic responsa of that period, one case of a wife's permissibility to remain married to her husband when adultery by the wife is suspected, and one case of complaint alleging serious procedural flaws in a matter of criminal punishment. In both cases a rabbinic jurist is functioning as a sort of appellate judge, reviewing the law as it was applied in other tribunals.

---

2 *Responsa* of Isaac b. Sheshet, ed. Constantinople, 1547, no. 234; see also Baer, op. cit., vol. 2, pp. 444–456, who discusses the Aragonese rule against cases built on confession.

Three major Spanish law codes from the period in question provide major sources for the complex Spanish legal situation in the relevant period, the *Fuero Real*, the *Siete Partidas*, and the *Espéculo*.[3]

The law code that was in force throughout this period was the *Fuero Real*, the Royal Charter. The king granted charters to particular institutions and groups.[4] They were statutes that had the essential nature of a contract which granted certain rights, privileges, and exceptions to more general statutes or usages.[5] The royal charters gave jurisdiction to these groups or institutions to superintend certain specified legal matters. The great Spanish royal jurist, Alfonso X "The Learned" (ruled 1221–1284) supervised and guided the codification of the Royal Charter, the most traditional of Spanish law codes, which was completed in 1255.[6] From then onwards, the sovereign granted the Royal Charter from time to time to various towns, etc., either to supplant or modify existing charters of rights and privileges. Scholarly opinion proposes that Alfonso wished to achieve a measure of unity in the legal system in which the several towns and cities all had their particular local, municipal charters granting jurisdiction.[7] Obviously royal judges appointed by the king were always bound by the Royal Charter, while municipal judges enforced their local charters as modified by The Royal Charter.

It is a commonplace that Spanish Jewish communities of the period received royal charters of rights and privileges, bestowing upon them various degrees of autonomy in both civil and criminal matters.[8] Although these charters granted the Jews the privilege of enforcing their own law, there could be no doubt that the Jews became quite familiar with royal law and its provisions.[9] Moreover, in addition to the rabbinical courts of the period, Jewish communities established other courts, whose members were known by the title *berurim*, selectmen, or *mukdamim*, and by other titles, whose duty it was to seek out and punish evildoers, and enforce local Jewish ordi-

---

[3] Evelyn S. Procter, *Curia and Cortes in Léon and Castile 1072–1295*, Cambridge University Press (Cambridge: 1980), p. 121.

[4] E.N. Van Kleffens, *Hispanic Law Until the End of the Middle Ages*, Edinburgh University Press (Edinburgh: 1968), pp. 124f, and p. 130.

[5] Ibid.

[6] Procter, *op. cit.*, p. 121.

[7] Ibid.

[8] Abraham Neuman, *The Jews in Spain*, 2 vols. Jewish Publication Society of America (Philadelphia: 1942), vol. I, pp. 23f. See also S. M. Passamaneck, "The *Berure Averot* and the Administration of Justice in XIII and XIV Century Spain," *Jewish Law Association Studies*, ed. B. S. Jackson (IV: 1990), pp. 135–146.

[9] Baer, *op. cit.*, vol. I, p. 212, pp. 224–233; Neuman, *op. cit.*, vol. I, pp. 19–41.

nances, according to their chartered commissions and Jewish law insofar as they were competent in it.[10]

With respect to *pesquisa* itself, as a feature of royal law, studies in medieval Spanish law disclose that *pesquisa* was the most frequently used method of proof for various proceedings in Castile.[11] The *Fuero Real* ordered the use of indictment *ex officio* if there were no private accusation of wrongdoing.[12] Presumably, once the indictment was issued, investigation of the matter, *pesquisa*, followed directly. *Pesquisa* is characterized as a form of inquiry, inquisition, in which specially appointed persons of probity and integrity took testimony on matters of fact.[13] Although *pesquisa* was particularly apt in certain types of land claims, it was applied in many types of cases.[14]

The fullest description of *pesquisa* comes from studies of the second major Spanish law code, the *Siete Partidas*, also the work of Alfonso X, promulgated around the year 1265, or ten years after the *Fuero Real*.[15] The *Siete Partidas* did not itself become law until promulgated in the *Ordenamiento de Alcalá* of 1348, which is the end of the period under notice here, about 88 years after Alfonso completed it.[16] Powerful elements of Spanish society, namely the nobility, the clergy, and the towns, strongly objected to the *Partidas* because it abrogated their ancient privileges.[17] Further, it was a blend of old Spanish law and Roman legal materials, which those groups considered a distasteful engrafting of alien law onto the ancient Spanish law that traced back to Visigothic roots.[18] The work remained alive, however, because lawyers studied it and discussed its provisions.[19] The *Partidas* had the further merit of an excellent structure and organization in addition to its integration of Spanish law and Roman jurisprudence.[20] At any rate the *Siete Partidas*, though not the law of the land, was apparently very well known in legal circles, and there is no reason to believe that its explication of *pesquisa* is not an accurate reflection of the institution as it was known and under-

---

10 Ibid.
11 Procter, op. cit., p. 90.
12 Ibid., p. 248.
13 Ibid., p. 40.
14 Cp. n. 10.
15 Van Kleffens, op. cit., p. 188, p. 207; Baer, op. cit., vol. 2, pp. 445f.
16 Procter, op. cit., p. 122.
17 Van Kleffens, op. cit., p. 207.
18 *Ibid.*, p. 168; cp. also A. Esmein, *History of Continental Legal Procedure*, Little Brown and Co. (Boston: 1913), pp. 295ff. (Vol. V, Continental Legal History Series.)
19 Van Kleffens, op. cit., p. 211.
20 Ibid.

stood in the period under notice, and as it was practiced under the Royal Charter.

Part III, title XVII, laws 1–12 inclusive describes *pesquisa* in detail.[21] The introduction to the specific laws sounds the tone and sets the general purpose for them: ". . . improper acts are so concealed that the truth cannot be ascertained regarding them from witnesses . . . it became necessary for kings to seek another method of proof called an investigation (*pesquisa*) by means of which the truth of matters could not be concealed from them through want of testimony . . . examiners have power to take testimony themselves by reason of their office, although the parties may not produce it before them." Thus, we see that *pesquisa* is an *ex officio* search for truth in matters where the old Germanic procedure of accusation, provided in ancient Spanish law, proved to be inadequate.

The second law in the series of twelve provides that inquiry be made "of the deeds of certain persons who are of bad reputation; or of certain particular acts where it is not known who was responsible for them; or of certain acts performed by well known men. . . ."

The third law provides that investigations are to "look into evil deeds committed secretly: night homicides, violent felonies at night . . . evil things done in secret by day or by night." These investigations occurred when no individuals brought complaints. When there was a specific, individual complainant, apparently no *pesquisa* was instituted.

The fourth law provides that examiners should be "moral men who fear God and are of good reputation, since as a result of their investigations many persons must die, and suffer other corporal penalties or loss of property . . . (they are to) be diligent to establish the truth as rapidly as possible—be prudent and zealous." Certainly when we consider the personnel of the lay courts in contemporary Jewish communities, the standards for judges would have been no less than those prescribed by this statute.

The ninth law provides that the examiners shall take an oath to discharge their office faithfully and not act "through love or fear nor for bribes taken or promised." The clerks of the court of inquiry are also to be sworn, as are the parties appearing before the court. Each sworn witness is to be questioned separately. Those questioned under oath are not to reveal what they declared under oath.

The eleventh law provides "that a transcript of the investigation, including the names of witnesses and their statements, is to be given to the

---

[21] *Las Siete Partidas*, tr. Samuel P. Scott, Commerce Clearing House, Inc. (Chicago: 1931), pp. 685–691; cp. Esmein, op. cit., p. 299. For the recapitulation of the procedure under Jewish authority, cp. Baer, op. cit., vol. 2, pp. 66f.

parties interested in the investigation, that they might defend their rights by testifying against the statements or evidence of said witnesses, and make use of all the defenses . . . against witnesses. . . ."

The *Partidas* go on to amplify the matter of *pesquisa* in language that is quite chilling to modern western sensitivities, but apparently quite reasonable in Spain in the mid-13th century. Part VII, title I, laws 28 and 29 declare in part that the king and the judge can "by virtue of their office, punish crimes even though no one may give information of them, or any accusation be made concerning them." The law establishes five instances in which *pesquisa* is in order. The third instance calls for the investigation," where a malefactor goes about committing illegal acts, either stealing or committing other offenses openly in such a way that the men of the neighborhood know it, and it is notorious and the acts are of such a character that they cannot be concealed . . . in any of the cases aforesaid a judge who has jurisdiction can, by virtue of his office, punish such malefactors for the above mentioned offenses committed by them although they have been neither accused or denounced nor any other proof adduced against them." This appears to place an enormous and sweeping power in the hands of the judges. If they can impose severe penalties on the basis of sworn testimony as the only proof of wrongdoing against the accused, they had better be persons of the highest moral sensitivity. The powers of the Jewish courts of selectmen were no less broad.[22]

Law 29 takes up the matter of impeached witnesses. They may be liable to civil or criminal penalties if the impeachment is proven correct. The judge, however, is not to punish such witnesses. The shame of having one's testimony rejected and the fact that the impeached witness becomes infamous thereby are deemed sufficient punishment.

The picture of the *pesquisa* necessary for comparison with Jewish cases emerges from these passages of the *Partidas* in detail. There were investigating magistrates clothed with enormous power. Sworn testimony was taken. Accusation and denunciation were absent. The misdeeds were serious. Records and transcripts were kept and provided to the accused to aid in any defense he might attempt. And, of course, the judges had to be persons of the highest moral character.

The *Siete Partidas* appears to the later and more complete version of Alfonso's *Libro de los Fueros* or *Libro de las leyes*.[23] The earlier form of Alfonso's law code, the third of the codes of the period, goes by the name of the *Es-*

---

22 Baer, Ibid.; cp. n. 8, Passamaneck, "The *Berure Averot* and the Administration of Justice in XIII and XIV Century Spain; and, e.g., Baer, op. cit., vol. I, pp. 212–236.

23 Procter, op. cit., pp. 121f.

péculo,[24] a portion of which is incorporated in a sentence handed down by Alfonso in 1261. Scholarship on these two works makes it clear that neither work was promulgated in any of Alfonso's *cortes* yet the Espéculo may well have been recognized as the operative code in Alfonso's court in the early part of the reign.[25] The inclusion of the part of the *Espéculo* in a sentence of the royal court bespeaks its currency and significance.

The use of the *Espéculo* brought about changes in legal procedure, according to the scholarly assessment of the work and its place in Spanish legal history.[26] Ancient procedure by accusation was retained in royal courts for some purposes, but *pesquisa* became part of criminal procedure under the provisions of the *Espéculo*. Cases were not brought by a complaining party, or by a dead man's relatives in the event of homicide, but rather by the king or royal official.[27] This constituted an indictment that was followed by the *pesquisa* on oath. Penalties upon conviction obtained through *pesquisa* included death, mutilation, or confiscation of property.[28] The more thorough and precise *Siete Partidas* provides us with the details of *pesquisa*, but there is no reason to believe that the *pesquisa* noted in *Espéculo* differed from it in any substantial fashion, any more than *pesquisa* in *Fuero Real* would have been something other than we have noted.

The Espéculo as a law code was rescinded in 1272.[29] The condition of Spanish law after the withdrawal of the *Espéculo* returned to its previous complexity of ancient custom and local charter, but the *Fuero Real*, as has been noted, gave some measure of unity to the system since it was used as a municipal charter in some locales and in cases of appeal from those towns to the king's court.[30] We can be absolutely sure of one point: no matter what law code did or did not obtain, *pesquisa*, judicial *ex officio* investigation, formed part of Spanish law.

With this rather extensive review of *pesquisa* in the principal Spanish legal sources of the period in mind, we turn to two Jewish legal cases of that period, preserved in the responsa literature. Granted that the explicit term *pesquisa* does not appear in them, does their description of the nature of the cases under review and of the court's procedure suggest that *pesquisa* became the model for what was done? The responsa primarily relate a set

---

24 Ibid.
25 Ibid., pp. 121–123.
26 Ibid., p. 248.
27 Ibid.
28 Ibid.
29 Ibid.
30 Ibid., p. 249.

of facts and then analyze the Jewish law that relates to those facts in order to achieve some resolution to a question of Jewish law. But when the facts to be analyzed come themselves from a lay court, a court of *berurim*, we need not expect those facts to comport precisely to the processes of traditional Jewish legal procedure. Indeed in some situations, such as serious criminal cases, the sources clearly inform us that classical Jewish procedure in such matters was no longer followed.[31]

The first case for comparison comes from R. Solomon b. Adret (Rashba, 1235–1310, Barcelona). The case is no. 1187 in volume one of his responsa (Ed. Lemberg, 1811; ed. B'nai Brak, 1958).

The matter concerns the decision of *berure kahal*, the selectmen of the community, who demanded that a man divorce his wife as an unfit spouse by reason of her adultery with a gentile. The facts presented were these. Reuben came home one night. He had a lamp in his hand. He noticed his wife asleep on the bed. He found a naked gentile lurking under the bed, clad only in a cloak and shoes. The gentile dashed out Reuben's lamp and they grappled and shouted. The noise alerted the people in the building who searched for the gentile (who had apparently fled in the confusion) with no success. They did find his jacket and trousers. The woman cried out because of what her husband said. (His words are not given, but one can imagine several possible speeches for him.) She claimed that the jacket and trousers had been given her to mend because she was a seamstress. The man said afterward to the Jews of the place that Heaven forbid he should suspect his wife of wrongdoing. Perhaps the gentile had entered to rob her or rape her . . . They resumed normal married life. Sometime later the couple took up residence in Lerida. (Apparently the Lerida community sent the inquiry to *Rashba*.) Because there were in Lerida community selectmen who investigated (matters) in order to remove transgressors from among them, the matter of the man and his wife was disclosed to them.

They asked the man to declare the truth of the matter to them. They put him in the most profound fear—to tell the absolute truth, and enemies of his wife's relatives made him stand up (and defend himself). Afterwards, he repeated the incident (to the selectmen). They said to him, "At that time did you believe that your wife had committed adultery with that gentile?"

---

31 See, e.g. *Responsa* of R. Asher b. Yehiel, ed. Venice, 1552, nos. 17:1, 8; R. Judah b. Asher, *Zichron Yehudah*, ed. Berlin, 1846, nos. 58 and 63; R. Isaac b. Sheshet, *Responsa*, ed. Constantinople, 1547, no. 234; Stephen M. Passamaneck, "R. Judah b. Asher on Capital Penalties," *Jewish Law Association Studies*, ed. S. M. Passamaneck and M. Finley (VII: 1994), pp. 153–172, see also M. Elon, *Jewish Law: History, Sources, Principles*, 4 vols., trans. B. Auerbach and M.J. Sykes, Jewish Publication Society (Philadelphia, Jerusalem: 1994), vol. 2, pp. 692–698.

He said, "Possibly that was the truth and I believed it at the time." They immediately said to him, "If so, she is forever prohibited to you in marriage!" And they made him swear an oath that (he would divorce her) and never take her back.

That very day, he publicly recanted (his testimony) in the presence of the community. He said his wife was fit (to be his wife) in his view. As for what he had said (to the selectmen), enemies had incited and misled him to say what he had said and he swore an oath on this assertion. . . .

In the event, *Rashba* argued that there was in fact no solid case in Jewish law for the divorce. He saved the marriage and rejected the decision of the selectmen.

Our concern, however, is not the appellate decision of *Rashba*, as such, but what the selectmen did, how they went about handling the case of this couple.

Without very much imagination, one can discern the looming presence of the *pesquisa* in the origin of the case and the selectmen's procedure. First, there was a local magistracy commissioned to investigate and remove wrongdoers from the community. Next, the husband should have been the aggrieved and complaining party in such a case, if any aggrieved party were found at all. Obviously, the husband did not, in the long run, believe his wife guilty of any infidelity or breach of proper marital conduct that would have prompted him to sue for divorce. Third, the nature of the alleged offense is reasonably well covered under the *Siete Partidas*, Part III, title XVIII, law 3, requiring that *pesquisa* applies to evil deeds committed secretly. While the alleged offense in Jewish law is a violation of the laws of proper marital conduct, and conceivably results in mandatory divorce, as *Rashba* argues in his responsum, such a finding would require far more evidence and far better evidence than the selectmen had to go on. Fourth, the information that the selectmen received came from parties who, their motives of enmity toward the woman's relatives aside, could only relate rather old hearsay. At worst the information constituted a rumor that at one time something untoward had perhaps occurred. Since the case involved a most delicate matter, we can be quite sure the selectmen questioned their informants closely. They were after all charged to investigate allegations of evil.

Siete Partidas, Part III, title XVII, law four admonishes the examiners in *pesquisa* to be zealous, and these selectmen certainly exhibited plenty of zeal; the same law demands prudence, yet a powerfully negative attitude toward adultery, or anything that suggested it, which is strongly supported by traditional Jewish law at every turn, could easily account for an abundance of zeal and a modicum of prudence in this case.

The selectmen brought the husband in to tell the truth. Although the text does not declare he was formally put under oath, it does say that they put him in the most profound fear—which in practice may easily amount to the same thing: one way or the other the man was suitably impressed with the need for honesty.

Of course, the inquiry directed to *Rashba* gives only enough facts to prepare the way for the authority's answer. There is no intention to give a full recounting of the selectmen's procedures; only their decision is important for *Rashba*. The few facts we can glean amount to this: there was a rumor or a denunciation, alleging adultery, that came to the attention of the selectmen-investigators of Lerida. The event had not occurred in their community; it had occurred elsewhere some time in the past. But the possibility that a man was unlawfully maintaining a marital relationship was just the sort of evil they were in office to eradicate. Upon hearing the allegation (and no doubt questioning the informers), they called in the accused husband. After having been put in fear of any dishonesty, he related the past incident. He was asked if at that time he had possibly harbored the notion that adultery had occurred. He said that it was possible. That was quite enough for the selectmen. They swore him to put her away forever—this was obviously his punishment. In the *pesquisa* procedure, the accused is called in to testify after the testimony against him been taken while he is not present.

The points of correspondence with judicial inquiry, *pesquisa*, are sufficiently clear: a special court charged with rooting out evil; a rumor or an incipient scandal concerning a possible egregious evil; doubtless an examination of the informers and then of the accused who is made to fear consequences of dishonesty, if not actually sworn. The accused tries to answer the charges. The case was, however, conclusive against him because of his admission of a possibility; punishment was pronounced.

One element at least of *pesquisa* does not seem to be present. There is no mention of a transcript of the testimony furnished to him. Yet in the event the husband surely knew why he had been summoned and he knew apparently who the informants were and, of course, what they had said. It is not clear whether or not the interrogation of the husband occurred in the presence of the informants, but there is no reason to believe that the selectmen did not question them and him in separate interviews. The absence of a full catalogue of procedural details should not surprise us, in the brief rehearsal of facts presented to *Rashba*. And similarly, absence of any mention of an actual transcript does not necessarily constitute a fatal flaw in the general picture of *pesquisa*.

The points of general similarity to *pesquisa* are enough to indicate that even if the selectmen did not undertake *pesquisa* exactly after the fashion of royal Spanish *pesquisadores*, they were at least not so very far away from the basic pattern of Spanish judicial inquiry.

There is clearly no evidence in the responsum that the selectmen followed any sort of classic Jewish legal procedure: the testimony of competent witnesses before a court of three competent judges, etc.

The next responsum comes from a slightly later period. R. Yom Tob b. Abraham Ashbili (*Ritba*, first half of the 14th century) was a pupil of Solomon b. Adret. The responsum is no. 131 in the Jerusalem, Mosad Harav Kook edition, 1959, of *Ritba's* responsa. The compiler of the work, Joseph Kapah, notes that this responsum indicates that *Ritba* was held in especially high esteem by the Spanish crown because Saul, the complainant, had appealed his case to the king, who in turn submitted the matter to *Ritba* for a Jewish legal opinion.[32] In this text we may be certain that the Jewish authority had a fairly good idea of how the Spanish legal system operated; and how Jewish law functioned under chartered privileges of jurisdiction and authority. Moreover, one is very much aware when reading the text that the charges against Saul were criminal and may have brought criminal punishment upon him, *inter alia*, amputation of a hand. Jewish jurisdiction in such cases depended upon a Royal Charter's granting it,[33] and Saul's appeal was to king's bench, where the *Fuero Real* was the law, not the *Talmud* and not the *Mishneh Torah*, royal consultation with an eminent rabbi notwithstanding.

Our present interest, however, remains with the procedure, and possible *pesquisa*, in the case. Fortunately, Saul's appeal rests on allegations that the court of original jurisdiction had proceeded improperly, and *pesquisa* is a matter of procedure. Saul alleges eight improprieties of which four are germane here.

He first says that judgment was rendered against him even though the complainants did not personally come to court and make their claims against him in his presence. His second point is that the court did not read to him the testimony that was produced against him so that he might

---

[32] Perhaps the most important section of this responsum is *Ritba's* memorialization to the king himself, either Ferdinand IV, who ruled from 1295–1311 or Alfonso XI, who ruled from 1311–1350. See Baer, op. cit. vol. 2, p. 452; Baer asserts that *Ritba's* opinions reflect "contemporary views," not those of the traditional Jewish law. The rabbi's statement, however represents the Jewish law of his time and place and is no less authentic for its non-traditional tone.

[33] See, e.g., Baer, op. cit., vol. 1, pp. 225–232; and S. M. Passamaneck, "The Berure Averot and the Administration of Justice in XIII and XIV Century Spain," cp. n. 8, above.

answer the allegations and contest their validity. His third point raises the issue that the witnesses were related to each other and thus their testimony was invalid in Jewish law. The eighth point was that he had asked the judge, after the case went against him, to give him an opportunity to appeal to king's bench or to the Rabbi Don Astruc, but the judge did not wish to do so.

Ritba had consulted the judge in the case and brought that judge's point-by-point response to the allegations to the royal attention. The judge's statement combined the answers to the first and second points. The complaints were in the nature of "community complaints;" that is, one gathers that a number of people contributed to the charges against Saul. And in the case of community complaint, the complainants are not required to leave their community to appear before a judge in another town. It was, moreover, apparently sufficient under the prevailing rules of procedure that the complainants showed their charges to R. Don Astruc, perhaps to certify their legal form.[34] Don Astruc had then asked Saul if he had any answer to make to the charges, but Saul did not wish to respond. Further, the judge said to Saul prior to the verdict, when they read the complaints in Saul's presence, that if Saul had any arguments concerning them, that he should prepare them and he, the judge, would consider them. But Saul did not wish to respond at all until the complainants themselves came before him. We have already noted that this was not necessary and certainly was not going to happen. Since Saul remained adamant, how then should the testimony be read in his presence? It was not.

Furthermore, the judge declares he showed (Saul?) the seals of the witnesses who gave testimony against him because prior to the hearing he had tried to get Saul to allow a delay before the commencement of hearing, until the return of a certain document from the king (king's court?), but Saul did not choose to delay matters and sought an immediate hearing. Saul, however, says that he was under the impression that the judge only wanted to proceed on the murder charge for which he had been arrested. This part of the judge's response is somewhat confusing. What seems to have happened was that Saul had been arrested for murder, but the case was rather more complicated. The reference to showing the seals of the witnesses probably

---

34 The text is not at all clear on the matter of "sufficiency." The judge merely asserts, *"w'dai ki hir'u taromotehem l'rav Don Astruc . . ."* It seems possible that Don Astruc might have been consulted as to the legal form of the testimony. That idea is at least reasonable in the context of showing a communal complaint of witnesses who would not themselves appear at the hearing. No data allowing a clear identification of Don Astruc are present in this responsum. The surname Astruc appears in several contexts in Iberian-Jewish history.

indicates that the judge assured Saul that the testimony taken was in proper form and that those witnesses were not required to be present and would not be present at trial. With the authenticated testimony in hand, a continuance was necessary in order to allow some royal document to arrive. Saul would have none of it; he wanted to get on with the murder charge. One may speculate that Saul believed the authenticated testimony was insufficient or improper for the murder charge, but the royal document would have sealed his fate and that was why he would not agree to wait. Perhaps. Like defendants before and after Saul, he apparently reasoned he could eventually successfully counter the witnesses' statements one way or another.

Saul's third point of complaint asserts that the testimony was improper because witnesses were related to each other. The judge's response to that point answers this particular challenge squarely. He writes that the community where the testimony was taken had a local ordinance providing that the testimony of the *mukdamin* bearing their seals, whether those persons were related to each other or not, was deemed lawful testimony and not subject to impeachment on the ground of their relationship to each other, which is a basis for impeachment of witnesses in classic Jewish procedure. But before the judge made that point, he inserted some instructive detail. He says that he, the judge, ordered the *mukdamin* to issue a ban (*ḥerem*) and to take testimony according to law. They did so and sent him the testimony thus produced. The ban was obviously for the purpose of requiring anyone with knowledge in the matter to step forward and speak. The procedure amounts to a type of *ex officio* investigation, a *pesquisa*.

Jewish legal procedure allows a litigant to have a ban issued for the purpose of bringing forward potential witnesses for him.[35] The process is available to a litigant; it is not the Court's place to initiate this ban on its own behalf—nor is the ban for the purpose of discovering persons to impeach witnesses. But the basic idea—a ban to summon witnesses—exists in the *halakhah*. In the case under notice, however, we are not strictly in the realm of Jewish procedure because the case was a homicide, which apparently involved other misdeeds as well, in which case Jewish courts tried the case under extraordinary procedural rules. Therefore, we should simply take it in

---

[35] E.g., *Shulhan Arukh*, "Hoshen Mishpat" 28:2, on the basis of a responsum of Solomon b. Adret and a responsum of Asher b. Yehiel, etc. See also *Responsa* of Simon b. Zemah Duran, *Tashbez*, part 2 no. 19. Scripture adumbrates the matter of an oath—a solemn curse—instituted for the purpose of requiring witnesses to come forward and testify, though they might not wish to become involved in the lawsuit, Leviticus 5:1; cp. B. Sotah 33a, B. Sanhedrin 37b, Mishnah, B. Shebuoth 35a.

stride that a Jewish judge could and did issue a lawful order to a lay court to impose the ban and summon witnesses under it even though the lay court, or some of its members, may not have been themselves the complaining parties under Jewish law. The ban is at best a variation on a Jewish theme; at worst, an adaptation of a gentile procedure for use in an unusual Jewish case.

Alternatively, one may suspect that the lay court of the community indeed felt itself to be complainants of a sort since the unlawful act or acts presumably occurred in their jurisdiction. On this theory we approach the generally held notion of a criminal complaint as involving "the people" versus the accused. In fact, *Ritba* goes on to memorialize the king on a similar point. He declares that if testimony in a community complaint like this, which was issued because of general misfortune, could be invalidated because complainants were, e.g., related to each other, no community could punish an informer or other troubler of the community. Thus, general communal complaints and the consequent testimony from community members, even if related, are upheld.

On the eighth point, the judge simply replies that he indeed did allow an appeal and showed the attested document to prove that fact.

Ritba's task in this matter was to convince the king that the Jewish court had acted properly and Saul's complaints were groundless. Clearly, one of the best approaches in such a matter was to assure the sovereign that what had happened among his Jewish subjects comported very well with the requirements of the *Fuero Real*, which of course provided for *pesquisa*. This is arguably exactly what happened.

The king certainly knew that the *Siete Partidas* (Part III, title XVII, law one), and doubtless the *Fuero Real*, provided for *pesquisa* to be conducted over a large area or in regard to an entire town, with reference to all or some of its inhabitants. The results of the *ex officio* investigation then go to the court of competent jurisdiction and the judge can impose sentence on the basis of the investigatory findings (Part VII, title I, law 28). This is precisely what did happen. The king would have understood the process as *pesquisa*, or something so close to it that the details did not matter.

The testimony was, moreover, taken on pain of the excommunicatory ban. In context that would have served well enough as an oath, if indeed the witnesses were not actually sworn. The witnesses may very well have been sworn, but we are told only that testimony was to be taken *kadin*, in the lawful manner. Saul's opportunity to answer the charges against him was also familiar to anyone conversant with royal law. The process of *pesquisa* clearly requires this to be done (Part III, title XVII, law eleven).

Toward the end of *Ritba's* rehearsal of the judge's point-by-point refutation of Saul's allegations, he says that in everything the judge did he relied upon the advice of sages (perhaps Don Astruc for one) and the custom of the Rabbis.[36] *Ritba* knew very well that classic Jewish criminal procedure did not apply here. What did apply was the customary procedure developed by the rabbinate to deal with such persons as Saul. That customary procedure, in this case at least, strongly resembles the *pesquisa*, something the king would have known, understood, and very likely approved.

Rashba's case gives us the bare outlines of *pesquisa* procedure, and his pupil *Ritba's* responsum reflects *pesquisa* in significant detail. Yitzhak Baer, in his thorough work on the Jews in Christian Spain, asserts that the procedural methods adopted by Jewish courts clearly bear the imprint of the procedures current in the surrounding gentile culture.[37] This is particularly the case, he says, with respect to *inquisitio*; and *inquisitio* is none other than *pesquisa*.

What then are we to make of Judah b. Asher's clear rejection of *pesquisa*? His case involves another Saul, or was it the same one, who struck one Isaac a mortal blow. Judah b. Asher addresses his response to the honored and learned elders of Cordova, which is not too far from Seville, where his contemporary *Ritba* passed much of his career. The Saul in this case complained about the testimony and the witnesses against him. There is mention of exculpatory information on other charges against Saul. R. Judah suggests that the reason the elders inquired of him was to get his opinion on possible punishment for Saul, should the testimony prove true, his opinion on their duty to investigate the truth of Saul's written statement against the witnesses and their testimony, and if that statement proved true—whether or not the testimony was therefore invalid. The Saul in *Ritba's* case filed complaints against the proceeding that found him guilty, specifically raising questions about the witnesses and their testimony. But there is no mention of Don Astruc, or the judge, or the *mukdamim,* or Saul's behavior at the trial in Judah b. Asher's text. Both texts mention amputation of a hand as punishment, but in *Ritba's* case the punishment seems to have already occurred. While such considerations prompt some lively speculation, they do not affect the present inquiry at all. We return then to *pesquisa*.

Baer cited only the sentence in which *pesquisa* actually appeared with only the briefest context for it. The fuller context gives the Rabbi's opinion in richer detail:

"First of all we are to investigate whether or not Saul's statements with respect to the witnesses are true. But you are not to institute a ban (requiring, on pain thereof, that) anyone who knows (anything) about any of the witnesses—that such witness may be suspected of some wrongdoing—

---

[36] The text: *Ki kol mah she`asa be`atzat ḥakhamin k'minhag harabbanim . . . hu alehem samakh.*
[37] Baer, op. cit., vol. 2, pp. 448, 450f, 454.

shall come and testify, because this is a *pesquisa* and one is not to do this against anyone. If, however, people of repute come before you, (people) who shall testify against any of them (the original witnesses), you shall institute a ban in their presence that they shall testify truthfully; and you shall take their testimony. If any testimony appears against any of them (the original witnesses) that he transgressed one of the well-known negative commandments of the Torah, (that original witness) is thereby unfit and you are not to take notice of his testimony. If (there is testimony that) the (original) witness transgressed in a matter which renders him unfit to testify by reason of rabbinical ordinance, he becomes unfit to testify (further). Testimony already given is valid. . . ."

The full context presents us with a puzzle. One is not to institute a ban in order to bring in persons who may impeach witnesses. That is *pesquisa*, and it is not to be done. Yet if people come forward on their own, they are to be put under a ban to testify truthfully. There is nothing apparently improper with a call for impeaching witnesses without a ban to force them to court. The second, and acceptable, method is, however, as much a *pesquisa* as the unacceptable procedure. The *Sieta Partidas*, for example, provides that the parties who come to testify are sworn, not that some penalty to force them to appear is pronounced (Part III, title XVII, law nine). Even though Judah b. Asher's text does not mention testimony under oath *per se*, the use of the ban would serve the purpose of insuring honesty well enough.

On balance, Judah b. Asher really could not be definitively rejecting *pesquisa*, or some variant of it, as reasonable and lawful procedure. Testimony gathered *per inquisitio* after all seems to be part of the *minhag rabbanim* mentioned by *Ritba*. Moreover, we have noted that Baer's scholarship explicitly notices the influence of gentile procedure on Jewish procedure in the late 13th and early 14th centuries.[38]

What Judah b. Asher may be saying is this: a *pesquisa* for the purpose of impeaching witnesses who testified at the original trial is acceptable, but the court must not use the threat of excommunication to cast too broad a net and force the issue. In other words, it is procedurally acceptable to call for witnesses and then place them under threat of ban for dishonesty, but do not exercise the enormous power of the ban just on the presumption that it will summon testimony to impeach witnesses. That is too radical a step—it is not to be done to anyone. That is an improper approach to *pesquisa*.

There appears to be sufficient evidence to conclude that *pesquisa* became a normal and normative legal procedure in Jewish courts of me-

---

[38] Ibid.

dieval Spain, notwithstanding the negative mention of *pesquisa* by R. Judah b. Asher. The *pesquisa*, the judicial inquiry under oath, was the Spanish method of going against malefactors when no accuser could or would come forward. It is not at all surprising that Jewish lay courts, created by royal charter to begin with, would adopt *pesquisa* or some variation of it to discharge their commission to expose and punish evildoers in their several communities. Nor should we wonder that rabbinical courts, when given the jurisdiction by Royal Charter to hear and decide serious felony cases, would adopt or adapt the *pesquisa* as a means of pursuing and procuring justice against those who sorely troubled their communities.

Finally, the Jewish legal system early developed and retained the idea of *malkin al lo tovah hashemuah* in matters of alleged sexual impropriety.[39] Can a system which maintains such a notion find much wrong with the concept of *pesquisa*, when men of piety and integrity undertake the inquiry?

If these remarks on *pesquisa* throw any light at all upon the history and development of Jewish law, the illumination may amount to this: when Jewish law operates as a living, functioning system of law by reason of the charter or legislation of a host government, with its own functioning system of law, one should not find it strange, unusual, or even contrary to Jewish practice, if some of the host system, at least in terms of policy or procedure, finds its way over time into some areas of the Jewish system, notwithstanding its unique religious character.

---

[39] B. Kiddushin 81a.

11

THE LAW OF THE PURSUER AND THE ASSASSINATION OF PRIME MINISTER RABIN

CHAIM POVARSKY*

Introduction

In November 1995, the Israeli Prime Minister, Mr. Itzhak Rabin, was assassinated at a rally supporting the peace process with the Palestinians. In March 1996, the assassin, Yigal Amir, a right-wing nationalist, was convicted by the District Court in Tel Aviv and sentenced to life imprisonment.[1] In his defense, the defendant claimed that Mr. Rabin's peace plan with the Palestinians, under which Israel was to surrender most of the territories of Judea and Samaria (the "West Bank"), would have seriously jeopardized the lives of the Jewish people in Israel. Therefore, according to the defendant, Mr. Rabin was a *rodef*, or a "pursuer" (one who is about to commit homicide or a serious injury[2]), whose killing is permissible under Jewish law.

Even before the assassination, some of the right-wing rabbis in Israel argued (theoretically, rather than for practical purposes), that Mr. Rabin was a pursuer. The vast majority of authorities rejected this idea and considered it repugnant. Because of the sensitivity of the issue and the tremendous tension it generated, the issue has not been adequately discussed and analyzed. The discussion of the *rodef* principle, in connection with Rabin's assassination, infuriated many people in Israel and abroad.[3] On the other hand, there

---

* LL.B., 1966, The Hebrew University in Jerusalem; LL.M., *magna cum laude*, 1977, Tel Aviv University; J.S.D., 1986, Tel Aviv University. Professor of Law, Director of the Institute of Jewish Law, Touro College, Jacob D. Fuchsberg Law Center. Chairman of the Jewish Law Association.

1 The State of Israel v. Amir, T.P.H. 498\95 in the District Court in Tel Aviv (unpublished as yet).

2 See infra notes 29–34 and accompanying text (describing in more detail the *rodef* principle).

3 The assassination of Prime Minister Rabin was not the first political murder in Israel. Political assassinations took place not only in ancient Israel as recounted in II Kings, but also in modern-day Israel, in the 30's and 70's of this century. Rabin's assassination, however, was the first assassination—and hopefully the last—in modern Israel of a prime minister. Except for

have been complaints about the lack of knowledge of the Jewish legal perspective on this issue.[4]

The question is two-fold, one factual and the other legal. The factual question as to whether Mr. Rabin's peace plan would have indeed jeopardized the lives of Jewish people in Israel, involves political and military considerations and will not be addressed here. The legal question as to whether the law of the pursuer may apply to Rabin's assassination, which is the focus of this article, is based on an assumption, which might very well prove to be wrong, that Mr. Rabin's peace plan was a tragic mistake and would have inevitably undermined the security of Israel and resulted in the loss of many Jewish lives. Under these circumstances, would a Jewish leader, who sincerely believes that his policy would benefit the Jewish people, and perhaps is the only way for securing their future, as Mr. Rabin believed, be regarded as a *rodef*?

Justice Edmond A. Levi, who presided over Amir's trial and delivered the court's opinion, believes that the pursuer principle does not apply today because of the absence of the Sanhedrin, the Jewish Supreme Court.[5] This suggestion is undoubtedly based on the talmudic statement that since the removal of the Sanhedrin from its location in the Holy Temple in the first

---

some small marginal groups, the vast majority of the Jewish people, proponents and opponents alike, were shocked by this assassination. One of Israel's powerful strongholds, from a secular perspective, is its democracy. In addition to the loss of a great leader, people feared that Rabin's assassination might reflect a general breakdown in Israeli democracy and the rule of law. An analysis of Rabin's assassination from a legal perspective must ignore the social, political and emotional aspects of this episode and concentrate solely on its legal aspects, even though the legal language might sometimes sound cold, indifferent, emotionless and even cynical.

4 In a recently published extract of an opening address, made by Justice Hadassa Ben-Itto, in December 1995 in Israel, during the Tenth International Congress of The International Association of Lawyers and Jurists, Justice Ben-Itto, the President of the Association, was quoted as saying the following:

> [H]ere is an assassin (Mr. Amir) who uses religious codes; he and his comrades quote opinions from which they purport to have drawn spiritual guidance in their act of conspiracy and subversion. As Jews we must confront this abhorrent phenomenon lest our spiritual heritage be presented both to our young generation and to the world at large, in a perverted light. We as jurists and lawyers have a particular role to play in this respect. We are all experts in the laws of our respective countries, but sadly, most of us have to confess to complete ignorance of the laws which compromise such a large part of our national heritage.... A public discussion is suddenly taking place concerning the true interpretation of *dinim*, laws, like *din rodef* and *din moser*, and although these particular laws do not deal with religious but rather with secular matters, like the right to self-defense of an individual and a community, we cannot participate in this argument due to our collective ignorance.

See The Use of Jewish Law as an Alibi for Murder is an Insult to our Tradition, 8 JUSTICE 7–8 (March 1996).

5 The State of Israel v. Amir, supra note 1, at ¶36.

century, capital punishments are not applied any more.[6] However, this ruling does not apply to pursuer cases, because the purpose of the law of the pursuer is not punishment but the preservation of life. As Rabbi Asher, one of the great halachic authorities in the 13th and 14th centuries, stated:[7]

> [A]lthough the four types of capital punishment were abolished when the Sanhedrin moved from its location [in the Holy Temple], the significance of this rule is that one cannot be sentenced to death in a court of law for committing a capital crime. . . . The killing of a pursuer, however, in the cases discussed in the Mishnah, is not a punishment for committing a crime, but rather a measure for saving the pursued from death or injury [and was not abolished].

This article will focus on the pursuer principle under Jewish law. Amir's allegation that his dastardly act finds support in Jewish law will be examined thoroughly.

The Necessity Defense under Israeli and Western Law

The court in Amir's case did not discuss the pursuer defense under Israeli law. The court, apparently, felt that under the circumstances of the case the defense lacks any merits and there is no need to address it. Instead, the court focused on the various elements of first degree murder, such as criminal intention, pre-meditation and determination to kill.[8] The court also rejected the argument that the defendant was mentally incapable of considering different alternatives and other reactions for expressing his opposition to Rabin's peace plan, and, therefore, could not resist the commission of the crime.[9]

In Israeli and Western law terminology, the pursuer defense could be defined either as a "defensive force defense" or "necessity defense." Both defenses are considered justifications. While the defensive force defense justifies an otherwise illegal act against an aggressor or one who unlawfully threatens to cause harm to others, the necessity defense justifies the violation of the law for the purpose of avoiding a greater evil which might otherwise take place. The necessity defense is sometimes referred to as the "lesser evils defense" or "choice of evils."[10]

---

[6] See B. Talmud Sanhedrin 41a; Maimonides, *Mishneh Torah*, The Book of Judges, The Laws of Sanhedrin 14:13.
[7] See Responsa Rabbi Asher (Rosh) ch. 17. See also Responsa Rivash ch. 238.
[8] See The State of Israel v. Amir, supra note 1, at ¶34–35.
[9] Id. at ¶24.
[10] See, e.g., 2 Paul H. Robinson, *Criminal Law Defenses* 45 (1984).

In a sense, the defensive force defense is part of the necessity defense, because both defenses require the balancing of evils. The only difference is the culpability of the victim (the aggressor) in defensive force cases, which might justify the defendant's action against him, even where the evil prevented by the action is less than the evil caused by it. Some scholars,[11] however, believe that the culpability involved in defensive force cases does not necessarily prevent the application of the "lesser evils" principle. Rather, the victim's culpability is one of the factors which might determine which of the two evils is the lesser one. Because of the victim's culpability, causing him harm is less of an evil, and consequently, the action may be justified based on the lesser evils principle.[12]

In Amir's case, the defendant did not argue that Rabin was an aggressor. Rather, he argued that Rabin's policy would have jeopardized the people's lives and posited a danger to Jewish lives. It would, therefore, be appropriate to regard the defendant's argument, in Western law terminology, as a necessity defense rather than a defensive force defense. The necessity defense, however, under Israeli and Western law, is subject to some restrictions, and might not apply in Amir's case.

One of the restrictions of the necessity defense concerns the relationship between the defendant and the saved person. Under Israeli law, the necessity defense, when applied to a homicide committed to save the life or honor of a third party, is available only where the defendant had a duty to protect the third party. Section 22 of the Israeli Penal Law 5737–1977, entitled "Necessity," provides:

> [A] person may be exempted from criminal responsibility for any act or omission if he can show that it was only done or made in order to avoid consequences which could not otherwise be avoided, and which would (have) inflicted harm or injury on a person, honor or property or on the person or honor of another *whom he was to protect* or on property placed in his charge ... (emphasis added).[13]

In a recent case discussed by the Supreme Court of Israel,[14] the defendant shot and wounded two girls in a car. One of the defendant's arguments

---

11 Id. at 69–70.

12 Killing an armed robber to prevent a robbery would be justified, even if nobody resisted the robbery and there was no danger that anyone might get hurt. The armed robbery would apparently be considered a greater evil than the killing of an armed robber. Likewise, killing three murderers to save the life of one victim would be justified, according to the choice of evils principle, because killing one innocent person is a greater evil then killing three murderers. Id.

13 *Sefer Ha-Chukkim of 5737*—LSI Special Volume: Penal Law, 5737–1977, §22.

14 Mak v. The State of Israel, C.A. 3984\92, 47 P.D. (3) 135.

was that he sincerely believed that the car carried Arab terrorists who were on their way to commit a terrorist act against Israelis. The Supreme Court rejected this defense, stating, *inter alia*, that the necessity defense does not apply in this case because the defendant had no obligation to defend the people who might have been killed as a result of the assumed terrorist act.[15] The same argument could be raised against the application of the necessity defense in Amir's case. The defendant had no legal obligation to protect the people who might have been killed or injured as a result of Rabin's policies. Although the defendant himself or his family might have been the victims of those policies, this is a remote possibility and would not justify the application of the necessity defense.

The necessity defense's requirement of a special relationship between the actor and the person to be protected has been abandoned by many Western legal systems. For instance, the American Model Penal Code §3.02, entitled "Choice of Evils," provides:

> Conduct which the actor believes to be necessary to avoid a harm or evil to himself or to another is justifiable. . . .[16]

Likewise, Model Penal Code §3.05, entitled "Use of Force for the Protection of Other Person," provides in part:

> (1) Subject to the provisions of this Section and of Section 3.09, the use of force upon or toward the person of another is justifiable to protect a third person when: (a) the actor would be justified under Section 3.04 in using such force to protect himself against the injury he believes to be threatened to the person whom he seeks to protect. . . .[17]

The commentators of the Model Penal Code noted that some of the old common law authorities believed that the defense of necessity does not apply to a defendant who used force to defend others with whom he had no special relationship. This position, however, was not adopted in England. Under current English law this defense also applies to strangers. In the United States, some jurisdictions require a relationship between the defendant and the third party for the application of the necessity defense. Others justify the protection of a stranger to avoid a felonious attack or to avoid an attack in a habitation. The commentators concluded that "[t]he

---

[15] Id. at 140. See infra note 30 (discussing the Jewish law view on this issue).
[16] Model Penal Act §3.02 (1) (1985) (adopted 1962).
[17] Model Penal Code §3.05(1)(a) (1985) (adopted 1962).

simple solution to the whole problem is to assimilate the defense of strangers to the defense of oneself," as provided in Section 3.05, which has been adopted by several states.[18]

The necessity defense may also not apply where the defendant's action was directed against governmental policies. The necessity defense is based on a recognition that where two evils are competing one should be allowed to select the lesser evil.[19] The necessity defense is a special license provided by the legislature to violate the law in order to avoid a harmful situation.[20] The necessity defense will, therefore, not apply where the legislature sets forth special procedures for removing the evil or avoiding its harmful effects. To remove an evil which might arise from wrong governmental policies, the legislature provides parliamentary measures, such as a non-confidence vote, legislation annulling the government's decisions and new elections. By laying down these procedures the legislature implicitly indicated that the dangerous governmental policies cannot be modified by violation of the law, and that the necessity defense should not apply in this case.[21]

Furthermore, by laying down procedures for changing harmful governmental policies the legislature implicitly indicates that any governmental policy cannot be considered evil as long as it was not lawfully reversed.[22]

---

[18] See Model Penal Code §3.05, Commentary at 1 (1985) (adopted 1962). See also Arnold N. Enker, *Duress And Necessity In the Civil Law*, ch. 4 (Bar-Ilan University, 1977) (discussing the necessity defense according to Israeli law and other Western legal systems).

[19] See, e.g., Robinson, supra note 10, at 46; 1 Wayne R. LaFave, *Substantive Criminal Law* 629 (1986).

[20] See, e.g., United States v. Schoon, 971 F.2d 193, 196–97 (9th Cir. 1991), *cert. denied*, 504 U.S. 990 (1992):

> [I]n some sense, the necessity defense allows us to act as individual legislatures, amending a particular criminal provision or crafting a one-time exception to it, subject to court review, when a real legislature would formally do the same under those circumstances. For example, by allowing prisoners who escape a burning jail to claim the justification of necessity, we assume the lawmaker, confronting this problem, would have allowed for an exception to the law proscribing prison escapes.

[21] Id. See, e.g., United States v. Kabat, 797 F.2d 580, 591 (8th Cir.1986), *cert. denied*, 481 U.S. 1030 (1987) (noting that the necessity defense was never intended to excuse criminal activity by those who disagree with the decisions and policies of the lawmaking branches of government); United States v. Dorrell, 758 F.2d 427 (9th Cir. 1985) (holding that the defendant could express his concern over nuclear war through a political process, but cannot raise the necessity defense to criminal charges of trespass and destruction of property, allegedly committed to protest against the production of nuclear weapons).

[22] *Schoon*, 971 F.2d at 198 (stating that a policy or law validly enacted by Congress cannot constitute a cognizable harm). Also, by approving a certain policy, the legislature implicitly indicates that the policy is correct, and consequently the necessity defense would not justify committing an illegal act in an attempt to change that policy. See, e.g., State v. Dorsey, 395 A.2d

Violating the law in order to obstruct the implementation of a wrong and harmful governmental policy would, therefore, not be justified, even where political measures would have no effect.[23] On the contrary, a failure to change the policy through ordinary procedures might reaffirm the rightness and validity of the policy. Because the Israeli legislature set forth procedures for reversing allegedly wrong and harmful policies of a legitimate government (that is, through a non-confidence vote, legislation or election), the necessity defense would not apply in Amir's case.[24]

Another restriction of the necessity defense concerns the imminence of the threat. One of the questions discussed with respect to the necessity defense is whether the application of this defense requires that the evil the offender sought to prevent was imminent. Different legal systems offer various solutions.[25] It has been argued that this restriction is merely a modification of the necessity requirement. That is, in the absence of an imminent threat the action taken may not be necessary. If the threat is real and certain, the necessity defense would apply even where the threat is not imminent.[26]

Israeli law as well as many other legal systems do not require imminence for the application of the necessity defense.[27] But even if imminence is not required, in the absence of an immediate danger it would be very difficult for a defendant to prove that his action was necessary to avoid a

---

855 (1978) (dismissing the defense based upon an allegation that nuclear power plants pose a serious life threat by generating atomic energy, the court stated that the legislature's determination that the plants were safe forecloses the necessity defense).

23 See, e.g., In re Weller, 210 Cal. Rptr. 130 (1st Dist. 1985). A defense of necessity raised by trespassers who protested on the premises of a defense contractor the development of certain missiles, was barred by the court. The defendants' belief that their protest was required to eliminate a threat of a nuclear holocaust was not sufficient to constitute a necessity defense, even though other legitimate actions they tried, such as political campaigning and leafleting, were not successful. The court ruled that in a free society a remedy for an unwise policy decision must be sought through the ballot box or by court action. Id.

24 Justice Edmond A. Levi, who delivered the court's decision in Amir's case, believes that Jewish law would not allow the killing of a prime minister based on the pursuer principle because "[t]here are democratic proceedings available in the State of Israel by which a government can be changed (a non-confidence vote or election)." The State of Israel v. Amir, supra note 1, at ¶36. As discussed below, however, this argument which was originally raised against a necessity defense, may not apply against a defense based on the pursuer principle under Jewish law. See infra notes 78–95 and accompanying text.

25 See Robinson, supra note 10, n.16, at 76–77 (1984); LaFave, supra note 19, n. 58, at 639.

26 Id.

27 Prior to 1977, Israeli law required an immediate threat for the application of the necessity defense. See Criminal Law Ordinance, §17 (1936). This section, however, has been replaced by Israeli Penal Law, §22 (5737–1977). See supra note 13 and accompanying text (discussing the current Israeli law of the necessity defense).

greater evil. In Amir's case, since the threat to Jewish lives allegedly generated by Rabin's peace plan was not immediate, but rather contingent upon future political and military developments, a necessity defense would not be applicable. However, to apply the necessity defense the defendant may not be required to show that a threat indeed existed, but rather that he reasonably believed in the existence of a real threat.[28]

The Pursuer Principle under Jewish Law

The principle of the pursuer under Jewish law[29] generally applies where a person is about to commit a murder or another capital crime, which would inflict a serious injury or shame on another person. Any bystander, including a stranger,[30] is allowed and even required to kill the pursuer,

---

[28] See, e.g., Nelson v. State, 597 P.2d 977, 979–80 (Alaska 1979) (stating that a person's action should be weighed against the harm reasonably foreseeable at the time, rather than the harm that actually occurs). Thus, even if Amir was mistaken about the fatal consequences of Rabin's peace plan, he could still have raised the necessity defense by showing that his fears were reasonable, provided that all other requirements for the necessity defense were satisfied. In other cases, however, the court arrived at a different conclusion. Likewise, modern codes in the U.S. took different positions on this issue. See LaFave, supra note 19, n. 42, at 635 (citing conflicting codes and cases on this issue).

[29] The principle of the pursuer under Jewish law may be defined as a necessity defense. The necessity defense under Jewish law, however, which is based on the preservation of life principle, is not limited to pursuer cases. It includes cases which do not involve a pursuer, such as saving the life of a sick person or one who was badly injured in an accident.

Classical Jewish legal sources do not use the term necessity in the context of criminal defenses, rather they use the term *pikuaḥ nefesh* or preservation of life. This is so, apparently, because generally the permission to violate biblical law in order to avoid an evil is limited to actions committed for the purpose of saving life. It is true that one may kill a pursuer even to save another from an injury or shame. In this case, however, the defense is based not only on the need to prevent the injury but also on the need to prevent the commission of a capital crime. See infra notes 35–39 and accompanying text. See also infra notes 74–95 and accompanying text (discussing the differences between Jewish and Western law regarding the necessity defense).

[30] Under Jewish law, the *rodef* (pursuer) defense is not limited to defendants who have either a family relationship with the pursuer's victim or a special duty to protect him. Any defendant may raise this defense. It may be argued that under Jewish law strangers have a duty to rescue, based upon the biblical commandment, "Neither shalt thou stand aside while mischief befalls thy neighbor" (Leviticus 19:16). This commandment, however, does not apply in certain cases; for instance, when the intervenor's life would be jeopardized by the attempt to rescue his neighbor. See, e.g., B. Talmud Bava Metzia 62a (stating that if two people are lost in the desert facing dehydration, and one has a pitcher with water which may keep alive only one of them, he has no duty to share his water with the other because his life comes first). If the intervenor decides to risk his life and save the victim by killing the pursuer, the intervenor will nevertheless be acquitted based on the pursuer principle, even though he had no duty to do so. See supra notes 13–18 and accompanying text (discussing Israeli and Western law on this issue).

if other means for preventing the crime are not available.[31] The Mishnah states:[32]

> The following must be saved even at the cost of their lives: He who pursues his neighbor to slay him, [or] a male [for pederasty],[33] [or] a betrothed woman [to rape her].[34]

The Mishnah does not indicate who is to be saved in these cases. One would assume that it is the victim who is to be saved. Rashi, however, interpreted the Mishnah to mean that it is the pursuer who is to be saved from committing the sin.[35] Tosafot[36] finds support for this interpretation in the second paragraph in the Mishnah:

---

[31] See, e.g., B. Talmud Sanhedrin 74a. Citing Rabbi Yonathan Ben Shaul the Talmud states that if the bystander could prevent the crime by injuring the pursuer, and instead the bystander killed the pursuer, the former is subject to capital punishment. Later authorities debated the meaning of capital punishment in this case. According to Maimonides it refers to divine punishment. See Maimonides, *Mishneh Torah*, The Book of Torts, The Laws of Murderer and Preservation of Life 1:13. Rabbi Y. Karo reasons that because the bystander's intention is to save one's life and well-being, a warning would have no effect on him. In the absence of an effective warning one must not be executed by a court. See Rabbi Y. Karo, *Kesef Mishneh*, commenting on Maimonides, ibid. Other authorities disagree. See, e.g., Rabbi Yehuda Rozanis, *Mishneh Le'Melech*, commenting on Maimonides ibid. (citing Tur).

[32] Mishnah Sanhedrin 8:7.

[33] Homosexuality is a capital crime under Jewish law. See Leviticus 20:13; B. Talmud Sanhedrin 54a; Maimonides, *Mishneh Torah*, The Book of Holiness, The Laws of Forbidden Intercourse 1:4. Thus, one who pursues a male for forced homosexual contacts is about to commit a capital crime, which is a requisite element for the application of the pursuer principle, as discussed below.

[34] Under Jewish law, betrothal is not engagement, but rather part of the marriage ceremony. A marriage ceremony include two parts: Betrothal (in Hebrew *eirusin* or *ḳiddushin*) and nuptials (in Hebrew *nesu'im*). Betrothal (which is performed today by the delivery of the ring to the bride under the canopy) establishes the family relationship between the spouses and between each one of them and the relatives of the other. The significance of this family relationship is that the parties may not remarry without first obtaining a divorce, and none of them may marry certain relatives of the other, even after the couple is divorced or one of them dies. See, e.g., Maimonides, *Mishneh Torah*, The Book of Women, The Laws of Forbidden Intercourse 2:1. The nuptials (which are performed by standing under the canopy or the seclusion of the couple in a room) establish the rights and duties of the parties. See Maimonides, ibid., The Laws of Marriage 12:1–3. Intercourse between a betrothed woman and a man other than her husband would constitute adultery which is a capital crime. Id. at 1:3. Because the pursuer of the betrothed woman is about to commit a capital crime, causing enormous shame and embarrassment to the victim, he may be killed by any bystander.

[35] Rashi, commenting on Sanhedrin 73a, s.v. *ve'eilu*.

[36] Tosafot, commenting on Sanhedrin 73a, s.v. *lehatzilo*.

But he who pursues after an animal [for bestiality] or would desecrate the Sabbath, or commit idolatry, must not be saved at the cost of his life.[37]

In these cases there is no victim to be saved. The phrase "must not be saved" in these cases necessarily refers to the pursuer, that is, the pursuer is not to be saved from sinning at the cost of his life. By analogy, it may be concluded that also the term "must be saved" in the first paragraph refers to the pursuer, as interpreted by Rashi. Tosafot, however, points out that this interpretation is inconsistent with the language used in the Talmud in connection with the rape case. The Talmud states that the *betrothed woman* is to be saved at the cost of the pursuer's life.[38]

Contemporary scholars[39] have concluded that both interpretations are correct. The law of the pursuer was intended to achieve two goals: saving the victim and preventing the pursuer from committing the crime. Thus, the killing of the pursuer is not justified unless both conditions were satisfied, that is, the pursuer is about to commit a crime that would seriously harm another person. Moreover, the killing of the pursuer is justified only where

---

37 Mishnah, supra note 32.

38 B. Talmud Sanhedrin 73a (drawing an analogy between rape and murder the Talmud states that just as in the rape case it is "permissible *to save the betrothed woman* by killing the pursuer" (emphasis added), so too in an attempted murder case it is permissible to save the victim by killing the murderer).

39 See, e.g., 2 Rabbi C.O. Grudzinski, *Achiezer*, ch. 18 (1922). Rabbi Grudzinski is discussing the case of a pursuer who was damaging property in the course of the pursuit. According to the Talmud, the pursuer is not responsible for the damage of the property based on the principle of *kim lei be'derabah minei*, or "apply to the offender the greater punishment." Under this principle, one who is subject to two punishments simultaneously receives only the greater punishment of the two. This implies that the killing of a pursuer is considered punishment. Rabbi Grudzinski explains the talmudic rule by pointing out that according to Rashi, the killing of the pursuer has two objectives: saving the victim and punishing the pursuer for his attempted crime. Because of the punitive aspect of the pursuer's killing the *kim lei be'derabah minei* principle would apply, and his estate will not be charged for the damages he caused while he was pursuing. Id. See also Rabbi M. di'Trani, Kiryat Sefer, The Laws of Murderer and Preservation of Life, ch. 1 (indicating that the concerns in the case of the rape of the betrothed woman are both the prevention of a crime and the saving of the victim); Rabbi M. Hevroni, *Masa'at Moshe*, commenting on Sanhedrin ch. 26; Enker, supra note 18, at 212–18 (discussing the salvation and punitive aspects of the pursuer principle).

Other authorities, however, seem to disagree with the interpretation of Rashi and Tosafot. For instance, according to Rabbi Nissim (*Ran*), the phrase "it is permissible to save the betrothed woman," used by the Talmud in the context of the rape case, clearly indicates that the purpose of the killing of the pursuer is to save the victim. The phrase "must not be saved" which the Mishnah used in the context of the attempt to desecrate the Sabbath or commit idolatry, argues Ran, is inaccurate. The Mishnah simply followed the language it used in the first paragraph ("must be saved"). See *Ran*, commenting on Sanhedrin 73a.

the pursuer is about to commit a capital crime. Any lesser offense would not justify the killing of the pursuer.[40] Quoting the Tosefta the Talmud states:

> [H]e who pursues his neighbor to slay him, he who pursues a male [for sexual abuse] or a betrothed maiden, a woman forbidden him on pain of death at the hand of the court or one forbidden on pain of extirpation[41]— these are saved at the cost of their own lives. But a high priest in pursuit of a widow and an ordinary priest in pursuit of a divorcee or a *halutza*[42] [which are forbidden but are not capital sins] may not be saved at the cost of their lives.[43]

The above analysis may indicate that the culpability of the pursuer is one of the requirements for applying the pursuer defense. Such a conclusion, however, would be inconsistent with the law applying the pursuer principle to a pursuer who is a minor. The Talmud discussed the question whether a minor who is going to commit homicide could be killed by a bystander based on the pursuer principle.[44] Most authorities decided that the law of the pursuer also applies to a minor.[45] But since one of the aims of the pursuer principle is the prevention of a crime[46] and since a minor is not legally responsible for his actions, why is it permissible to kill the minor in order to save him from committing a crime for which he is not held legally responsible?[47]

---

40 Under most Western legal systems, including Israeli law, the necessity defense generally applies even where the victim was entirely innocent. See, e.g., supra notes 13–17 (defining the necessity defense under Israeli and American law). Generally, under Jewish law, one may not kill, or even maim an innocent person to save the lives of others. See infra note 112 and accompanying text.

41 Extirpation (in halachic literature *karet*) is a form of heavenly execution.

42 A *halutza* is widow of a childless husband who participated in the *halitza* ceremony to enable her to remarry. See Deuteronomy 25:5–10; Maimonides, *Mishneh Torah*, The Book of Women, The Laws of Levirate Marriage 15:19–20.

43 B. Talmud Sanhedrin 73a.

44 B. Talmud Sanhedrin 72b.

45 See, e.g., Maimonides, *Mishneh Torah*, The Book of Torts, The Laws of Murder and Preservation of Life 1:6; *Shulchan Aruch, Choshen Mishpat* 425:1.

46 See supra note 39 and accompanying text.

47 Indeed, based upon the minor-pursuer case some authorities have concluded that the purpose of the law of the pursuer is not the punishment of the pursuer, but rather the saving of the victim. See 2 Rabbi Y. Landau, *Responsa Nodah Be'Yehudah, Choshen Mishpat* 60. See also supra note 39 (citing Ran). Rashi and Tosafot, however, are of the opinion that at least one purpose of the pursuer principle is saving the pursuer from committing a crime, and according to the Talmud only the prevention of a capital crime justifies the application of the pursuer principle. See supra notes 40–43 and accompanying text. The question then remains as to why is it permissible to kill the minor pursuer who is not responsible for his actions.

It would appear that the primary purpose of the law of the pursuer is the saving of the victim. This concern alone, however, would not justify the killing of the pursuer, because one may not set aside one life to save another. The killing of the pursuer is justified when the pursuer is about to commit a capital crime. Although a minor is not responsible for his actions, nevertheless, because he is about to commit an act which usually constitutes a capital crime, his killing is justified in order to save the victim's life.[48]

The Biblical Source for the Pursuer Principle

The Talmud finds the source for the law of the pursuer in the biblical passage discussing the rape of a betrothed woman. Scripture states:

> [I]f a girl that is a virgin be betrothed to a husband, and a man finds her in the city and lies with her, then you shall bring them both out of the gate of that city, and you shall stone them with stones that they die; the girl because she cried not, being in the city, and the man because he has humbled his neighbor's wife. So shalt thou put away evil from among you. But if a man finds a betrothed girl in the field and the man force her and lie with her, then only the man that lay with her shall die, but to the girl thou shalt do nothing. There is in the girl no sin worthy of death, for as when a man rises against his neighbor and slays him even so is this matter. For he found her in the field, and the betrothed maiden cried out, but there was none to save her.[49]

Citing Rabbi Yishmael's school, the Talmud interpreted the phrase "[b]ut there was none to save her" to imply that if there is a bystander he

---

[48] See, e.g., Rabbi Grudzinski, supra note 39, at ch. 19 (discussing the case of a minor who is a pursuer, Rabbi Grudzinski argues that because of the gravity of the minor's action it is permissible to kill the minor to save the victim's life, even though the minor is not responsible for his action). It should be noted that although the primary objective of the law of the pursuer is saving the victim, the Mishnah emphasizes the need to prevent the pursuer from committing a crime, according to the interpretation of Rashi and Tosafot. See supra notes 35–36 and accompanying text. The Mishnah focusses on the crime prevention rather than on the saving of the victim, apparently, in order to highlight the distinction between the two sets of cases discussed in the Mishnah. See supra notes 34, 37 and accompanying texts. The Mishnah indicates that although the concern over the prevention of a crime may also exist in the second set of cases (*i.e.*, the attempt to commit bestiality, desecrate the Sabbath or commit idolatry), one is not allowed to prevent these offenses by killing the offender because there is no victim to be saved in these cases. The prevention of a crime is a good cause for the application of the law of the pursuer only if the crime involves a serious threat to one's life, health or reputation, as illustrated in the first set of cases (i.e., the attempt to commit homicide, or a forced incestuous or homosexual relationship).

[49] Deuteronomy 22:23–27.

must save her by all means (including the killing of the pursuer).⁵⁰ By way of analogy the law of the pursuer was also applied to homicide cases.⁵¹

---

50 B. Talmud Sanhedrin 73a.

51 Discussing the rape case, Scripture states: "There is in the girl no sin worthy of death, for as when a man rises against his neighbor and slays him so is this matter." See supra note 49 and accompanying text. This analogy (in halachic terminology—*hekesh*) between rape and homicide serves not only for the acquittal of the betrothed woman from a charge of adultery, but also for other purposes, such as the application of the pursuer principle in homicide cases.

Under Jewish law, the defense of the intervenor is not based on the self-defense principle, which allows one to defend himself against a deadly attack by killing or injuring the assailant. These two defenses derive from different sources and may be subject to different rules. The self-defense principle was mentioned in the Talmud in the context of the burglary case (B. Talmud Sanhedrin 72a. See infra notes 54–57 and accompanying text) and the informer case (B. Talmud Berachot 58a. See infra note 53). Rashi indicates that the biblical source for the self-defense principle is the burglary case where the homeowner was allowed to kill the burglar to save his life. See Rashi, commenting on Sanhedrin 72a, s.v. *Ḥazakah*, and Berachot 58a, s.v. *Hatorah amra*). Another early authority, Rabbi Menachem HaMeiri, cites *Midrash Tanḥuma* (Numbers, *Parashat Pinḥas* ch. 3), according to which the self defense rule has been deduced from G-d's commandment to the Israelites to wage a war against the Midianites: "And the Lord spoke to Moses, saying: Vex the Midianites and smite them, for they vex you with their wiles, with which they have beguiled you. . . . " (Numbers 25:16). *Midrash Tanḥuma* comments: "Based on this passage our sages [concluded that] If someone comes to kill you, rise up and kill him first." See Meiri, *Beth Habechirah*, commenting on Sanhedrin 72a. See also Rabbi Chaim D. HaLevi, "Law of Self Defense in Our Communal Life" (Hebrew), 1 *Techumin* 343, 344–45 (1980).

As to the *rodef* principle, its source is the rape case and the analogy between the rape and the murder cases, discussed previously. No attempt has been made to link the defense of protecting others to the self-defense rule. Furthermore, as pointed out previously, different rules may apply to each of these defenses. For instance, if the intervenor could stop the pursuer by injuring or maiming him, the intervenor is not allowed to kill the pursuer. Killing the pursuer under these circumstances is a capital crime. See supra note 31. The pursued person himself, however, according to some authorities, would not be punished if he killed the assailant in self defense, even if the later could have been stopped by a non-lethal injury. See, e.g., Rabbi Eliyahu Mizrachi (*Re'eim*), commenting on Genesis 32:8; Rabbi Mordechai Yaffe, *Levush Ha'oreh*, commenting on Genesis 32:8; Rabbi Y. Rosanis, *Mishneh Le'Melech*, The Laws of Wounding and Injuring 8:10. Other authorities, however, do not distinguish between the two cases, holding that the pursued person as well is not allowed to kill the pursuer if the latter can be stopped otherwise. See, e.g., Rashi, commenting on Sanhedrin 74a, s.v. *veyachol*, and Sanhedrin 57a s.v. *veyachol*; Rabbi Meir Abulafia, *Yad Rama*, commenting on Sanhedrin 57a.

Another distinction between the pursuer and the self-defense principles concerns the requirement of a forewarning. In self-defense the assailant need not be forewarned to desist. The victim may kill the assailant even without any prior warning. In the case of the pursuer, however, the pursuer must be warned (if time permits) before aggressive action may be taken against him. See Rivash ch. 328 (citing *Re'ah*); Rabbi Rosanis, ibid.; Rabbi Y.M. Epshtein, *Aruch Hashulchan*, *Choshen Mishpat* 425:5. See also 4 Rabbi Ovadia Yosef, *Yabia Omer*, *Choshen Mishpat* ch. 5 (2d ed. 1986) (discussing the distinctions between the pursuer and the self-defense principles).

Until recently many Western authorities based the defense of protecting others on the self-defense principle. The intervenor was regarded as the alter ego of the victim. The self-defense

Obviously, the ordinary law of the pursuer, discussed previously, which requires that the pursuer is about to commit a capital crime, would not apply to Mr. Rabin. Even assuming that Mr. Rabin's peace plan was illusory and would have eventually endangered many Israeli lives, he was not about to commit a capital crime.[52] Mr. Rabin's actions could at most be considered an indirect and unintentional threat to Jewish life.

The Application of the Pursuer Principle in Non-capital Crimes

The law of the pursuer, however, has also been applied in cases which do not involve a capital crime. Here are some examples.

---

principle was expanded to include those who "stepped into the shoes" of the victim and were allowed to exercise the victim's right of self-defense. See, e.g., State v. Chiarello, 174 A.2d 506, 511 (N.J. Super. Ct. App. Div. 1961), *cert. denied*, 177 A.2d 343 (NJ. 1962), quoting the trial court: "In other words, you must treat the defendant [the intervenor] as William Edward's [the attacked person's] alter ego, and this includes imputing to the defendant all of William Edward's knowledge of the situation, what the defendant saw and how he interpreted what he saw" (Id. at 509). The court, however, subsequently pointed out that "[t]he American Law Institute rejects the 'alter ego' rule as repugnant to the fundamental principle of Anglo-American criminal jurisprudence that the defendant must be shown to have *mens rea*, or guilty intent. Model Penal Code §3.05(1) (1962);" Griffin v. State, 158 So. 316, 317 (noting that it is well settled by the decisions of this court that he who invokes self defense in protection of a third person is placed in the shoes of him whom he seeks to protect). The alter ego theory resulted in denying the intervenor the defense of protecting the victim in case the victim was at fault (e.g., the victim initiated the first attack against the person who was later killed by the intervenor), even though the intervenor was not aware of it; or where the intervenor mistakenly but sincerely believed that the "victim" was under attack (by the person who was later killed by the intervenor).

In the early 1980's many authorities believed this consequence to be unsatisfactory, because it may deter potential intervenors from coming to the rescue of victims. See, e.g., Alexander v. State, 447 A.2d 880 (Md. Ct. Spec. App.), *aff'd*, 451 A.2d 664 (Md. 1982). The court stated that:

> [o]ne goes to the aid of another at his peril, his protection from criminal charges depends not on what appears to him when he intervenes, but rather upon the rights of the person whom he has succored. As Perkin points out, it has been common but quite unfortunate to say that the defender 'stands in the shoes' of the one defended with exactly the same privilege or lack of privilege as possessed by the latter.

(Id. at 882–83). See also Marco F. Bendinelli & James T. Edsall, "Defense of Others: Origins, Requirements, Limitations and Ramifications," 5 *Regents U. L. Rev.* 153, 169–70 (1995) (concluding that today, all American jurisdictions, except one, have abandoned the alter ego theory and replaced it by standards which extend the intervenor's defense to cases where he reasonably believed that his action was required).

Under Jewish law, the intervenor's mistaken belief that the "victim" was under threat would apparently be treated as any mistake of facts in criminal cases. If the intervenor killed the "pursuer," he will be regarded as committing an inadvertent homicide.

[52] See, e.g., B. Talmud Bava Kamma 77a (stating that if a person ties up someone and the later dies out of starvation, the former is not subject to capital punishment). See also Maimonides, *Mishneh Torah*, The Book of Torts, The Laws of Murderer and Preservation of Life 3:10.

(1) *The Informer Case.* An informer is one who divulges information about Jewish property to a corrupt regime, thereby risking the life of the innocent property owner. The assumption is that the corrupt ruler would torture and eventually kill the owner to get hold of his property. The law of the pursuer has sanctioned the killing of the informer, even though he was not committing a capital crime.[53]

(2) *The Burglary Case.* Scripture provides: "[I]f a thief be found breaking in, and be smitten and dies, there shall be no blood shed on his account."[54] This verse was interpreted in the Talmud[55] to mean that a burglar may be killed by the homeowner or any other person.[56] Although the burglar's purpose is to steal property, the homeowner's life is at stake, because of the presumption that the homeowner would confront the burglar to protect his property, and to defend himself the burglar would kill the homeowner. Therefore, Scripture allowed the killing of the burglar to save the homeowner's life, even though the killing of the homeowner may not have been contemplated by the burglar.

Moreover, according to early authorities, there is no presumption that the burglar would kill the owner if confronted by the latter. On the contrary, it is assumed that in this case the burglar would leave the stolen property behind and escape. The homeowner, however, might block the burglar's way and try to kill him, and in self-defense the burglar would kill the homeowner. According to this interpretation, if the burglar indeed killed the homeowner, the former would most probably not be guilty of homicide, based on the self-defense principle. Nevertheless, because the burglar is aware of the possibility that he might be attacked by the homeowner, and as a result he will have to kill the homeowner to protect himself, he is considered a pursuer whose killing is permissible.[57]

---

[53] See, e.g., B. Talmud Bava Kamma 117a; Maimonides, *Mishneh Torah,* The Book of Torts, The Laws of Wounding and Damaging 8:10; *Shulchan Aruch, Choshen Mishpat* 388:10. See supra note 52 (citing sources which discuss the case of indirect homicide).

[54] Exodus 22:1.

[55] B. Talmud Sanhedrin 72a–b. See also Maimonides, *Mishneh Torah,* The Book of Torts, The Laws of Theft 9:7–9; *Shulchan Aruch, Choshen Mishpat* 425:1.

[56] B. Talmud Sanhedrin 72b. See also Maimonides, *Mishneh Torah,* The Book of Torts, The Laws of Murder and Preservation of Life 1:13; *Shulchan Aruch, Choshen Mishpat,* ibid.

[57] See Rabbi Nissim (Ran), *Ḥidushei Haran,* commenting on Sanhedrin 72a (stating that thieves are not coming to kill, and if the homeowner would confront the thief, the latter would not kill him. However, the homeowner might attempt to kill the thief if the latter did not return the stolen property, and in the ensuing fight the homeowner might get killed. Because the thief knows all this and he is the one who started the fight and broke in, he is considered a pursuer whose killing is permissible). See also Rabbi Meir Abulafia, *Yad Rama,* commenting on Sanhedrin 72a.

(3) The Abortion Case. The Mishnah states that if a woman has difficulty giving birth, and the only way to save her life is to abort the fetus, the abortion is permissible. However, if most of the fetus[58] has already emerged from its mother's womb, the newborn may not be touched because one may not set aside the life of one person to save another.[59] The Talmud raises the question:[60] Since the newborn is jeopardizing the mother's life, why is it not permissible to kill the newborn, based upon the law of pursuer? The Talmud answers that the mother in this case is not being pursued by the fetus but rather "by heaven." This argument was also proffered by Maimonides.[61]

But why then is it permissible to abort the fetus when it is still in its mother's womb? According to Rashi, the fetus may be aborted because it is not considered a person.[62] Maimonides suggests that the fetus may be aborted because it is jeopardizing its mother's life and is considered a pursuer.[63] On the face of it, Maimonides' interpretation is problematic, as many commentators pointed out,[64] because it seems to contradict the Talmud's argument (adopted by Maimonides), according to which the mother is not pursued by the fetus but rather by heaven. Furthermore, since the threat to the mother's life is a result of a heavenly act, the fetus is not committing any act and certainly not a capital crime. The application of the law of the pursuer to the fetus seems to indicate that an innocent person may be regarded as a pursuer merely by passively endangering the life of another.

(4) The Fugitive Case. The Jerusalem Talmud[65] discusses a case of a person who escaped from a gang of outlaws and found refuge among a group of Jewish people. The outlaws threatened to kill the entire group unless the

---

[58] Likewise, if only the head of the fetus came out, it is considered a newborn and may not be touched. See Rabbi Shimson of Senz and Rabbenu Asher, commenting on Mishnah Ohalot 7:6.

[59] Mishnah Ohalot 7:6.

[60] B. Talmud Sanhedrin 72b.

[61] Maimonides, *Mishneh Torah*, The Book of Torts, The Laws of Murder and Preservation of Life 1:9. Discussing the abortion case, Maimonides concludes that "once its head has appeared it must not be touched, for we may not set aside one human life to save another human life, and what is happening is the course of nature." Id.

[62] Rashi, Sanhedrin 72b, s.v. *Yatza Rosho*.

[63] Maimonides, supra note 61 (discussing the law of pursuer Maimonides states that "[c]onsequently, the sages have ruled that if a woman with child is having difficulty in giving birth, the child inside her may be taken out by drugs or by surgery, because it is regarded *as one pursuing her* and trying to kill her" (emphasis added)).

[64] See, e.g., Rabbi Ch. Soloveichick, *Ḥidushei Rabbenu Chaim Halevi*, commenting on Maimonides, The Laws of Murderer and Preservation of Life 1:9; Rabbi M. Feinstein, *Iggrot Moshe*, 2 *Choshen Mishpat* 69:2.

[65] J. Talmud Terumot 8:4.

individual is handed over to them for execution. According to Rabbi Yohanan, because the individual was singled out by the outlaws, he may be handed over even if he is totally innocent. According to Resh Lakish, however, the individual may not be handed over unless he is guilty of a capital crime.[66] Some authorities believe that the fugitive may be surrendered, based upon the law of the pursuer.[67] Although the fugitive does not commit any crime, but is only hiding from the outlaws,[68] nevertheless, because he is the cause of the threat to the lives of the others, based upon the law of the pursuer his surrender is justified.

(5) The Bunker Case. During the Holocaust a group of Jews were hiding from the Gestapo in a bunker. A baby began crying, putting the entire group under an immediate threat of being discovered and slain. One of the group covered the baby's face with a pillow, resulting in the baby's suffocation. After the war, rabbinical authorities justified the act based upon the principle of the pursuer,[69] even though the baby obviously was not committing any crime. The mere fact that the baby was jeopardizing the life of the group justified the application of the law of the pursuer.

(6) The Counterfeiter Case. Discussing the law of the pursuer, Rabbi Moshe Isserles (Rema) stated: "One who is endangering the public, as for example where one is engaged in counterfeiting which is prohibited by the authorities, is considered a pursuer and could be handed over to the

---

[66] Id. To illustrate his view, Resh Lakish mentioned the case of Sheva Ben Bichri, who was killed to prevent the destruction of a city. See II Samuel 20:14–22; infra note 89. See also Maimonides, *Mishneh Torah*, The Book of Science, The Foundation of the Law 5:5 (deciding the law according to Resh Lakish's view); Rabbi Menachem Hameiri, *Beth Habechirah*, Sanhedrin 72b (following Rabbi Yohanan's view); Rema, *Yoreh Deah* 157:1 (citing authorities who differ on whether the law follows Rabbi Yohanan or Resh Lakish's view); Rabbi Yoel Sirkes, *Baith Chadash (Bach), Yoreh Deah* 157, and Rabbi David Ben Shmuel, *Turei Za'av (Taz), Yoreh Deah* 157:8 (arguing that according to Resh Lakish, whose view is to be followed, the fugitive may be surrendered even if he is guilty only under the rules of the outlaws, but not under Jewish law). See also Rabbi A.Y. Karelitz, infra note 67.

[67] See, e.g., Rabbi A.Y. Karelitz, *Chazon Ish*, Sanhedrin ch. 25 (noting that the one who was singled out is regarded as a pursuer, because by taking refuge in a community he put the members' lives at stake). See also Rabbi David Ben Shmuel Halevi, *Turei Za'av, Yoreh Deah* 157:4 (stating that it is permissible and even required to surrender any criminal who is engaged in forbidden and dangerous activities, even if he was not singled out by the authorities. Such a criminal is regarded as if he were pursuing the Jewish community).

[68] The fugitive might have committed a crime in the past, according to Resh Lakish. The law of the pursuer, however, does not justify the surrendering of a fugitive for crimes committed in the past. Such crimes must be tried in a court of law. See Maimonides, supra note 31, at §5.

[69] See, e.g., S. Efrati, *Mi'gei Ha'harigah* 23 (1961). See also I. Robinstein, *The Holocaust and Halakhah* 31–34 (1976).

authorities."[70] Although the counterfeiter would be executed by the authorities his surrender is permissible. The law of the pursuer applies to the counterfeiter merely because he is endangering the public's lives, even though he had no intention to do so,[71] and was not going to commit a capital crime under Jewish law.

(7) The Grenade case. Rabbi A. Y. Karelitz discussed the following case.[72] A grenade was thrown into the midst of a group of people and is going to explode. One of the people seizes the grenade and is prepared to throw it away. He then realizes that a person is standing exactly where the grenade would land. Assuming that there is no other way to save the group except by throwing the grenade in the direction of the individual, is he allowed to kill the individual to save the group?

This case is different from the other pursuer cases, discussed previously. In all the other cases the pursuer was at least the indirect cause of a threat to the lives of others, even though in some of the cases the pursuer may not have been guilty of committing any offense. In the grenade case, the individual who is standing on the side is not even the cause of the problem. Nevertheless, because this case deals with the question of killing one individual to save others it is relevant to the pursuer issue.

At first glance, it would appear that the throwing of the grenade is not permissible. Comparing the grenade case with the fugitive case, Rabbi Karelitz argues that the surrender of the fugitive is permissible only because he was singled out by the outlaws (which turns the fugitive into a kind of a pursuer). By contrast, in the grenade case the throwing of the grenade should not be allowed because the individual was not singled out by anyone. Nevertheless, Rabbi Karelitz suggests that the throwing of the grenade may be permissible. As opposed to the fugitive case, where the rescue of the group is only incidental to the severe act of handing over the fugitive to the outlaws (which is equivalent to an act of killing), in the grenade case the throwing of the grenade is primarily an act of rescue while the killing of the individual is incidental to the act of rescue. Therefore, concluded Rabbi Karelitz, it may be permissible to throw the grenade in the direction of the individual.

This argument is problematic. Why is it permissible to consciously kill an innocent person just by defining the killing as an act of rescue? The defi-

---

70 See Rabbi Moshe Isserles (*Rema*), *Choshen Mishpat* 425:1.

71 See Rabbi Eliahu, *Biur Hagra, Choshen Mishpat* 425:11.

72 Rabbi Karelitz, supra note 67. In his description of the case the author speaks about an arrow being cast amidst a group of people. A grenade, however, would be a more realistic example.

nition of the act as one of rescue may indicate the good intention of the killer. It does not, however, change the fact that an innocent person is deliberately being killed. The individual in this case does not resemble a pursuer even remotely.

The above cases prompted some rabbis to believe that because Rabin's peace plan with the Palestinians would have presumably jeopardized many lives, he was to be considered a pursuer. However, an analysis of the law of the pursuer shows that this principle is not applicable to Amir's case. The arguments that support this conclusion are entirely different from those applied for the rejection of the necessity defense under Western law.[73] The distinctions between these two defenses and the inapplicability of the arguments, used against the necessity defense for the rejection of the pursuer defense, will be discussed in the next chapter.

The Pursuer Principle and the Necessity Defense

As discussed previously, the necessity defense under Israeli and Western law would not apply to Amir's case for a number of reasons: the lack of a relationship between the defendant and the people whose lives might have been jeopardized by Rabin's peace plan;[74] the availability of procedures for challenging wrong and dangerous governmental policies;[75] and the uncertainty of the danger generated by the peace plan.[76] All these arguments do not apply to a defense based on the law of the pursuer under Jewish law. The law of the pursuer is not limited to cases involving a relationship between the defendant and the people he was seeking to protect. It applies to any bystander. Likewise, although the defendant who raises the pursuer defense must show that he intended to prevent the death or severe injury to other people, he may not be required to prove that the danger was certain. A high likelihood of risk may suffice for the application of the pursuer principle. This is apparently the view of Rabbi Yishmael, one of the great *tannaitic* scholars (in the second century), who maintains that although the threat to the homeowner's life in the burglary case is not certain, it is permissible to kill the burglar to eliminate a possible threat to the homeowner's life.[77]

---

[73] See supra notes 13–28 and accompanying text.
[74] See supra notes 13–18 and accompanying text.
[75] See supra notes 19–24 and accompanying text.
[76] See supra notes 25–28 and accompanying text.
[77] See B. Talmud Yoma 85a. The Talmud cites Rabbi Ishmael stating that the permission to desecrate the Sabbath to save life, even where the threat is uncertain, derives from the burglary case, where the danger to the homeowner's life is not certain. Id. Although the Talmud rejected Rabbi Ishmael's view regarding the nature of the risk to the homeowner's life in the burglary

The argument that the necessity defense does not apply where other procedures for changing policies of a duly elected government are available, is based on the assumption that by providing those procedures the legislature implicitly indicated that those procedures should be the only measure for modifying governmental policies, and that the necessity argument should not justify illegal actions intended to obstruct the implementation of those policies. This indication of the legislature, however, may not affect the application of the pursuer defense under Jewish law.

Under Jewish law, the validity of the legislator's will and the law of the state is based either on the "king's prerogatives"[78] or the principle of *dina de'malchuta dina* ("the law of the state is the law").[79] However, the extent of the application of these principles and the question of whether these principles also apply to the state of Israel today, are subject to controversy.[80] In any event, one could make a forcible argument that under Jewish law the state cannot prohibit the performance of one of the most sacred duties of saving life. Although governmental policies may occasionally generate some danger to the people's lives, and Jewish law generally requires that people follow the orders of a legitimate government, this does not necessarily imply that a clearly faulty and dangerous policy would be immune against the application of the law of the pursuer.

Jewish legal sources do not indicate that the law of the pursuer does not apply to a defendant who acted against a government official or even the prime political leader in order to avoid fatal consequences resulting from the

---

case (holding that the risk is certain because of the presumption that the homeowner would confront the burglar and eventually will be killed), Rabbi Ishmael's understanding that the law of the pursuer applies even where the risk is uncertain was not challenged. See, however, infra note 151 and accompanying text, suggesting that Rabin may not be considered a pursuer even according to Rabbi Ishmael's view, because the discontinuation of the peace process might turn out to be as dangerous as the implementation of his peace plan.

78 See, e.g., Maimonides, *Mishneh Torah*, The Book of Judges, The Laws of the Sanhedrin 18:6, and The Laws of Kings 3:10; Maimonides, ibid., The Book of Torts, The Laws of Murderer and Preservation of Life 2:4; Rabbi Nissim, *Drush HaRan*, ch. 11; Rabbi H. Chayes, *Torat HaNevi'im* 43 (1958). See also 1 Elon, *Jewish Law: History, Sources, Principles* 55–57 (1994).

79 See B. Talmud Gittin 10b, Bava Kamma 113a, Bava Bathra 54b, Nedarim 28a; Maimonides, *Mishneh Torah*, The Book of Torts, The Laws of Robbery and Lost Objects 5:11; *Shulchan Aruch, Choshen Mishpat* 369.

80 See generally *Encyclopedia Talmudit* VII 295–308 (Zevin ed. 1981); S. Shilo, *Dina De'-Malchuta Dina* 131–184 (1978); M. Elon, supra note 78, at 64–74. C. Povarsky, "Legislative Power in the Jewish Legal System," *Jewish Law Report* 7–12 (Institute of Jewish Law, June 1991); J.D. Bleich, "Jewish Law and the State Authority to Punish Criminals," 12 *Cardozo L. Rev.* 829 (1991); A. Kirschenbaum, "The Sovereign Power of the State: A Proposed Theory of Accommodation," 12 *Cardozo L. Rev.* 925 (1991); C. Povarsky, "Jewish Law V. The Law of the State: Theories of Accommodations," 12 *Cardozo Law Review* 941 (1991).

implementation of governmental policies. On the contrary, biblical commentators have clearly indicated that the law of the pursuer applies even to a Jewish leader. For instance, the Bible relates the story of King Saul who was pursuing David, seeking to execute him[81] because of fear of David's growing popularity among the people.[82] On one occasion David had the opportunity of killing Saul, but refrained from doing so despite his comrades' advice.[83] According to some commentators, the justification for killing the king was the application of the law of the pursuer. By attempting to kill David, Saul was considered a pursuer, a status which could have justified his killing.[84]

The law of the pursuer was also applied to another Jewish leader, Samson the judge. Samson had killed many Philistines. Seeking revenge, the Philistines waged war against Israel. The Bible relates that a group of Israelites detained Samson and delivered him into the hand of the Philistines in order to save their lives.[85] According to commentators, the surrendering of Samson was based on the law of the pursuer.[86] The surrenderers believed

---

[81] See I Samuel 19:1, 15.

[82] Id. at 18:6–10, 29.

[83] Id. at 24:3–11.

[84] See Rabbi David Kimchi (*Radak*), commenting on I Samuel 24:11 (noting that David was permitted to kill Saul because the latter was a pursuer); *Ralbag*, commenting on I Samuel 24:5 (stating that "[a]lthough it was permissible [for David] to kill him [King Saul] because [the latter] was a pursuer, he [David, nevertheless] said 'G-d forbid that I do such a thing' . . ."). It could perhaps be argued that King Saul's battle with David was a personal matter, while Prime Minister Rabin's peace plan was a political matter. The tension between Saul and David, however, arose because of David's political and military activities which, Saul believed, were undermining his authority. These were political matters. In pursuing David, therefore, Saul functioned in his royal capacity rather than as an individual. Nevertheless, because there was no justification for King Saul's attempt to kill David, the former was considered a pursuer.

It should be noted that the killing of Saul by David could have been justified on the basis of the self-defense principle. See supra note 51 (discussing the distinction between the pursuer and self-defense principles). By applying the pursuer principle in this case, the commentators apparently wished to indicate that King Saul was also a pursuer; this would have entitled every one to kill him in order to save David.

[85] Judges 14:4–13.

[86] See Rabbi Meir Leivus Malbim, *Mikraei Kodesh*, commenting on The Book of Judges 15:11. It may be argued that Samson's actions against the Philistines, which triggered the Philistines' attacks against Israel, were Samson's private revenge for their ravishing of his wife, as Samson himself indicated. See Malbim, ibid. The war against the Philistine conquerors, however, was one of the nation's primary political strategies at that time. Scripture relates that the Philistines ruled over the Jewish people for forty years. See Judges 13:1. And when the Angel came to Samson's mother, in her pregnancy, advising her about the son she was to give birth to and his role as an Israelite leader, he said to her: "For, lo, thou shalt conceive and bear a son . . . and he shall begin to deliver Israel out of the hand of the Philistines." Id. Thus, Samson's wars against the Philistines were a national concern, even though Samson used his private grievance as an excuse for attacking them.

that because Samson's actions against the Philistines jeopardized the lives of the Jewish people, his surrender was justified.

Another Jewish leader who was assassinated based upon the law of the pursuer was Jehoiakim, King of Judea. King Jehoiakim rebelled against Nebuchadnezzar, the King of Babylonia.[87] *Midrash Rabbah*[88] recounts that when Nebuchadnezzar arrived in Jerusalem with his army, the members of the Great Sanhedrin (Supreme Court) inquired whether he intended to destroy the Holy Temple. Nebuchadnezzar replied that he had come to arrest Jehoiakim. The members of the Sanhedrin agreed to surrender the king to him. When they came to Jehoiakim, he asked them whether it was permitted to kill him in order to save their own lives. The members of the Sanhedrin replied that they were following the precedent set forth in the case of Sheva Ben Bichri.[89] King Jehoiakim was then delivered into the hands of Nebuchadnezzar, who executed him. According to one opinion, the members of the Sanhedrin first killed Jehoiakim and then delivered his corpse to Nebuchadnezzar.[90]

Although *Midrash Rabbah* does not mention the pursuer principle, the surrendering or killing of Jehoiakim was obviously carried out to save the lives of the Jewish people who were endangered by Jehoiakim's political policies. Moreover, the analogy between the cases of Jehoiakim and Sheva Ben Bichri indicates that the members of the Sanhedrin were applying the law of the pursuer in the case of Jehoiakim.[91] The cases of Saul, Samson and Jehoiakim indicate that the pursuer principle also applies to a Jewish leader who is jeopardizing Jewish life by his wrong and dangerous political policies.[92]

---

[87] II Kings 23:36–24:1.

[88] See *Midrash Rabbah*, Leviticus 19:6.

[89] See II Samuel 20:14–22 (relating the story of Sheva Ben Bichri who rebelled against King David and was hiding in the city of Avel Beth Hama'acha. Joab, the head of David's army, besieged the city and threatened to destroy it. The members of the city, then, beheaded Sheva Ben Bichri and threw his head over the wall of the city).

[90] Midrash Rabbah, supra note 88.

[91] Sheva Ben Bichri's killing was justified on the basis of the pursuer principle. See supra note 67 and accompanying text.

[92] It is true that the law of the pursuer does not apply where other means to stop the pursuer are available. The availability of other means, however, would prohibit the killing of a pursuer only where those means would effectively eliminate the danger. See supra note 31 (citing sources indicating that if the defendant could stop the pursuer by other means, the killing of the pursuer is not justified and the defendant may even be subject to a death penalty). The availability of legal procedures to modify government's policies, however, such as a non-confidence vote or election, does not mean that the defendant could actually avoid the "evil" by utilizing those procedures. Obviously, it is very difficult or virtually impossible for an individual to modify government's policies through ordinary procedures in a short period of time.

The inapplicability of the necessity defense, raised to justify offenses committed for the purpose of obstructing governmental policies, has also been based, under Western law, on the legislature's implicit indication that governmental policies cannot be considered evil as long as they were not legally reversed.[93] This indication, however, would not bar the application of the law of the pursuer in such cases under Jewish law. First, as discussed previously, the legislature's decision may not prevail over the paramount obligation of saving life. Second, the assumption that governmental policies cannot be evil was not accepted in Jewish law.

The underlying theory of the pursuer defense differs from that of the necessity defense. While the latter is based on a recognition of a need to choose between two evils, the former is based either on the preservation of life principle (where the offense was committed in order to save life) or the need to prevent a capital crime involving serious harm to innocent people.[94] The preservation of life principle sets aside all biblical commandments except three: idolatry, incest (including adultery) and homicide. In the case of a pursuer, however, homicide (the killing of the pursuer) is also permitted in order to save life. Thus, the defendant's action in pursuer cases is justified, not because he prevented a greater evil, but rather because he saved life or prevented the commission of a capital and harmful offense. Weighing and balancing evils would, therefore, be irrelevant under Jewish law in the context of the pursuer principle.

Furthermore, although Rabin's peace plan may have been supported by a majority of the Knesset, that does not necessarily mean that the plan was not destructive and dangerous, at least, from a Jewish political and legal perspective. The narrow majority of the members of the Israeli parliament who supported Rabin's plan included all of the Arab members. Israel is a democracy and Rabin's government whose existence depended on the Arab vote in the Parliament was a perfectly legitimate government. This, however, does not necessarily mean that the critical policy which involves the fate and safety of the Jewish people in Israel for generations to come, adopted by such a government against the strong opposition of perhaps a majority of the Jewish members of parliament, must be assumed to be good and harmless for the Jewish population. Consequently, the availability of procedures for modifying wrong and dangerous governmental policies would not preclude the application of the pursuer defense under Jewish law.[95]

---

[93] See supra notes 22–24 and accompanying text.
[94] See supra notes 35–40 and accompanying text.
[95] Although the arguments raised against the application of the necessity defense, under Israeli and Western law, may not work against the pursuer defense under Jewish law, nevertheless, the pursuer defense would not apply in Amir's case for other reasons, discussed below.

Discrepancies in Pursuer Cases

The analysis of the various pursuer cases may reveal some discrepancies and contradictions. A discussion of these problems will be helpful for the understanding of the pursuer principle in general.

(1) *The Pursuer's Culpability.* As shown above, the law of the pursuer has also been applied in cases where the pursuer was not about to commit any crime or at least a capital crime.[96] These cases seem to contradict the established principle according to which the law of pursuer applies only when the pursuer was about to commit a capital crime.[97]

(2) *The Bystander's Duty to Kill the Pursuer.* Whereas in the ordinary case of the pursuer (which involves a capital crime) everyone is obligated to kill the pursuer,[98] in the other pursuer cases, such as the informer, burglar and abortion cases, the killing of the pursuer is permissible, according to Maimonides, rather than mandatory.[99]

(3) *Different Terminology.* While in the ordinary pursuer case Maimonides uses the term *rodef*,[100] or pursuer, in other pursuer cases, such as the burglary and abortion cases, Maimonides uses the term *ke'rodef*, or "like a pursuer."[101]

(4) *The Burglary Case and the Preservation of Life Principle.* Under the preservation of life (*piḳuaḥ nefesh*) principle, one may desecrate the Sabbath in order to save life.[102] Rabbi Ishmael suggests that the biblical source of this principle is the law of the burglar. The law of the burglar, argues Rabbi Ishmael, justifies the killing of a pursuer to save the life of another. Surely, concludes Rabbi Ishmael, one may desecrate the Sabbath to save life.[103]

---

96 These include the cases of the informer, burglary, abortion, fugitive, bunker and the counterfeiter.

97 See supra note 40 and accompanying text.

98 See Maimonides, *Mishneh Torah*, The Book of Torts, The Laws of Murderer and Preservation of Life 1:6, 14. See also Sifre, commenting on Deuteronomy 25:12.

99 See Maimonides, *Mishneh Torah*, The Book of Torts, The Laws of Theft 9:7 (stating with respect to the burglar principle that "[e]very one has *permission* [*reshut*] to kill the burglar" (emphasis added)); Maimonides, ibid., The Laws of Wounding and Damaging 8:10 (stating that "[a]n informer may be killed anywhere, . . . and it is *permissible* to kill him before he has informed" (emphasis added)). A later authority, Rabbi Itzchak ben Sheshet, however, apparently maintains that there is an obligation to kill an informer. See *Responsa Rivash* 238 (discussing an informer case, *Rivash* indicates that one who refrains from killing the informer is guilty of violating the biblical commandment not to stand by the blood of one's neighbor). As to the abortion case, see Maimonides, supra note 61.

100 Maimonides, *Mishneh Torah*, The Book of Torts, The Laws of Murderer and Preservation of Life 1:6–8, 10–11, 15.

101 See Maimonides, supra note 55, at 9:9; See also Maimonides, supra note 63.

102 See B. Talmud Yoma 85a.

103 Id.

The analogy is problematic. As discussed above, one of the justifications for killing the pursuer is the prevention of a crime.[104] In the burglar case, the killing of the burglar is permissible to prevent the commission of a crime. In the case of the Sabbath no crime is being prevented by desecrating the Sabbath. How then can the permission to desecrate the Sabbath to save life be derived from the permission to kill the burglar?[105]

These problems may lead to the conclusion, discussed next, about the existence of two categories of pursuers.

Two Categories of Pursuer and the Equality Argument

It would appear that there are two categories of pursuers, derived from different sources and subject to different rules. The first category, which will be referred to as "the ordinary pursuer," is that of one who is about to commit a capital crime (even though he may not be responsible for it[106]), thereby inflicting serious injury or shame—not necessarily death—on another person. The ordinary pursuer principle is derived from the case of the rape of the betrothed woman, who may be saved even by killing the rapist.[107] Because the pursuer in this case is about to commit a capital crime seriously affecting the life of a victim, everyone is obligated to prevent the crime, even at the cost of the pursuer's life.

The second category of pursuer, which will be referred to as "the quasi pursuer" (or *ke'rodef*), is based upon the principle of the preservation of life. This includes the cases of the informer, the burglar, the abortion, the fugitive, the bunker, the counterfeiter and the grenade. Preservation of life is a justification for violating virtually any law. The preservation of life principle was derived from the following Scriptural text: "You shall therefore keep my statutes, and my judgments, which if a man do he shall live by them,"[108] which was interpreted to mean "to live by them and not to die by them."[109]

---

104 See supra notes 35–39 and accompanying text.

105 A similar question was raised by Rabbi Arieh Leib, *Gevurat Ari* (commenting on Yoma 85a). The burglary case, argues Rabbi Arieh Leib, is based on the pursuer principle rather than on a preservation of life principle. The latter principle does not apply in the burglary case because, according to the Talmud, one may not kill one person to save the life of another person. Consequently, the question of whether one is allowed to desecrate the Sabbath to save life, which concerns the preservation of life principle, cannot be inferred from the burglary case. Rabbi Arieh Leib did not resolve this problem.

106 For instance, a minor who is a pursuer is subject to the law of the pursuer, even though he is not responsible for his actions. See supra notes 44–48 and accompanying text.

107 See supra notes 49–50 and accompanying text.

108 Leviticus 18:5.

109 B. Talmud Yoma 85b.

The preservation of life principle in itself, however, does not justify the killing of a person, because one is not allowed to set aside the life of one person in order to save the life of another,[110] or as the Talmud puts it, metaphorically, "What makes you think that your blood is redder, perhaps his blood is redder,"[111] which means that one life does not take precedence over the life of another (hereinafter referred to as "the equality argument").[112] The preservation of life principle could, therefore, justify the killing of one individual to save another only when the equality argument does not apply. As shown below, in all quasi-pursuer cases the equality argument is not applicable, allowing the killing of the pursuer based upon the preservation of life principle.[113] Before we discuss the inapplicability of the equality argument in quasi-pursuer cases, the differences between the ordinary pursuer and the quasi-pursuer principles will be outlined.

---

110 See Mishnah Ohalot 7:6.

111 B. Talmud Sanhedrin 74a; Pesachim 25b; Yoma 82b.

112 The Talmud discusses the case of a man who was ordered by the governor of the town, under a threat of death, to kill an innocent person. The renowned talmudic scholar, Rava, who was consulted on this issue, ruled that one should rather die than kill an innocent person, because "What makes you think that your blood is redder, perhaps his blood is redder." Id. It is interesting to note that a similar approach was taken by the House of Lords in England in 1884, in the famous case of Regina v. Dudley and Stephens, 14 Q.B.D. 273 (1884). The Court agreed with Lord Hale's opinion that "if a man be desperately assaulted and in peril of death, and cannot otherwise escape unless, to satisfy his assailant's fury, he will kill an innocent person then present, the fear and actual force will not acquit him of the crime and punishment of murder if he commits the act, for he ought rather to die himself than kill an innocent." Id. at 283.

Whether a coerced killing of an innocent person is punishable under Jewish law is subject to debate. Maimonides holds that although the preservation of life principle does not justify the killing of an innocent person, if the order to kill was carried out under duress, the killer may not be subject to capital punishment. See Maimonides, *Mishneh Torah*, The Book of Knowledge, The Foundations of the Law 5:4; Tosafot, Yebamot 53b–54a, s.v. *Ein ones*. Other authorities, however, disagree. See Rabbi Y. Karo, *Kesef Mishneh*, commenting on Maimonides, ibid. (citing Rabbi Moshe HaCohen, *Remach*, who holds that a coerced homicide is punishable).

Maimonides' ruling does not apply in case of necessity, where no duress is involved. For instance, killing of a person in order to transplant one of his vital organs to save the life of the recipient would be punishable. Maimonides draws a clear distinction between duress and necessity with respect to punishment. Discussing the necessity defense, Maimonides states "[W]hen life is in danger, anything forbidden in the Torah may be used as a curative agent, except the practice of idolatry, unchastity or murder. Even to save life these offenses must not be committed. If a patient transgressed the prohibition and recovered, the court will sentence him to the punishment he deserves [*onesh haraui lo*]." See Maimonides, ibid. at 5:6.

113 Although the quasi-pursuer principle is based on the preservation of life principle, the principles are not identical. Quasi-pursuer cases involve the killing of one individual to save another, which may raise the equality argument, prohibiting the act. Preservation of life cases, however, for the most part, do not involve a homicide, and thus the equality argument does not come into play.

Distinctions Between the Two Categories of Pursuer

There are significant distinctions between the ordinary pursuer and the quasi-pursuer principles. First, while the ordinary pursuer is about to commit a capital crime (even if he may not be culpable),[114] the quasi-pursuer is not involved in a capital crime. Second, whereas the purpose of the ordinary pursuer principle is two-fold: to save the victim and to prevent the commission of a crime,[115] the purpose of the quasi-pursuer principle is merely to save the victim's life. Third, while the ordinary pursuer principle is derived from the rape case,[116] the quasi-pursuer principle is based upon the preservation of life principle.[117] Fourth, while the ordinary pursuer principle also applies when the pursuer's victim might be severely harmed or humiliated, but not necessarily killed,[118] the quasi-pursuer principle applies only when the killing of the pursuer would save human life. Fifth, whereas there is a legal duty to kill the ordinary pursuer,[119] the killing of the quasi-pursuer is permissible rather than mandatory.[120] Sixth, whereas the equality argument does not apply in ordinary pursuer cases because Scripture implicitly indicated (in the case of the attempted rape of the betrothed woman[121]) that when the pursuer is about to commit a capital crime, the life of the victim takes precedence, in quasi-pursuer cases the equality argument may not apply for a variety of reasons. The inapplicability of the equality argument in quasi-pursuer cases is a critical factor which must be considered in determining the permissibility of killing the quasi-pursuer, and will be discussed at length in the following chapter.

The Inapplicability of the Equality Argument in Quasi Pursuer Cases

The equality argument does not apply when the pursuer is about to commit a deliberate and harmful offense against a victim that would eventually jeopardize the victim's life. Although the pursuer is not committing a capital crime, because he is the guilty party, the life of the victim takes precedence. Examples of this principle are the cases of the burglar, the informer

---

114 Supra notes 35–48 and accompanying text.
115 Supra note 39 and accompanying text.
116 Supra notes 49–51 and accompanying text.
117 Supra notes 108–13 and accompanying text.
118 Supra notes 29–34 and accompanying text.
119 Supra note 98 and accompanying text.
120 Supra note 99 and accompanying text.
121 Supra notes 49–51 and accompanying text.

and the counterfeiter. The burglar intends to steal rather than kill. Nevertheless, because he is deliberately going to commit an offense and cause damage to the homeowner (stealing his property), thereby creating a threat to the life of the homeowner, the equality argument does not apply and everyone is allowed to kill the burglar. Likewise, the informer is about to deliberately commit an offense against the victim,[122] thereby causing him damage and eventually, though indirectly and perhaps even unintentionally, endangering his life. Therefore, the equality argument does not apply and the killing of the informer is justified. Similarly, the counterfeiter is committing a crime which could jeopardize the lives of the entire Jewish community. Although he is not committing a capital crime against the Jewish community, nevertheless, because he is consciously committing intentional and harmful crimes, the equality argument does not apply.

Also, the equality argument does not apply where the life of the victim is more valuable than the life of the pursuer. An example of this principle is the abortion case.[123] Because the life of the mother is more valuable than the life of the fetus, the equality argument does not apply and it is permissible to kill the fetus to save the mother's life on the basis of the preservation of life principle.[124] Likewise, the equality argument does not apply when the

---

[122] According to Maimonides, the informer must first be warned to desist from his wrongful act before he may be killed. See Maimonides, supra note 53. This indicates that to apply the law of the pursuer to the informer, the latter must be acting deliberately against his victim. The following example may illustrate the need for some degree of culpability on the part of the informer to apply the law of the pursuer. Suppose one is going to visit his wealthy friend, and is followed by gangsters who are seeking the wealthy person for the purpose of robbery. Although the visitor is endangering his friend's life, a bystander would not be justified in shooting him to save his friend's life. Because of his innocence, the law of the informer would not apply to the visitor.

[123] Supra notes 58–64 and accompanying text.

[124] The equality argument, however, would apply once most of the fetus emerged from the mother's body. At this point the child's life is as valuable as its mother's and cannot be killed on the ground of the preservation of life principle. See supra notes 58–59 and accompanying text. Likewise, the ordinary pursuer principle (which applies even where both lives, that of the victim and that of the pursuer, are equally valuable), will not apply to the child because he is not committing any crime; rather the threat to the mother's life is a result of a heavenly act. See supra note 60 and accompanying text.

It should be noted that the inapplicability of the equality argument in the abortion case does not necessarily imply that a fetus is not a person and that there is no obligation to preserve its life. On the contrary, it is permissible and even required to violate biblical precepts to save a fetus' life. Thus, a pregnant woman is allowed to eat on Yom Kippur if her fasting might jeopardize the fetus' life. See B. Talmud Yoma 82a; Rashi, ad loc. Likewise, it is permissible to desecrate the Sabbath to save the fetus' life. See B. Talmud Arakhin 7a–b (stating that if a woman died in labor, there is a duty to save the fetus even if it involves the desecration of the Sabbath). According to one interpretation, however, because the mother in this case died in her

choice is not between the life of the victim and the life of the pursuer, but rather between the death of both and the death of only the pursuer.[125] Examples of this principle are the cases of the fugitive and bunker.[126] Because the "pursuer" in this case will be killed anyway, no equality argument exists and the pursuer may be killed based upon the preservation of life principle.[127]

Lastly, the equality argument may not apply when the killing of the pursuer can be characterized as an act of rescue rather than an act of killing, as illustrated in the grenade case.[128] The killing of an individual to save the lives of other people would be justified in this case, not because it is perceived as an act of rescue, but rather because the equality argument does not apply when one commits a homicide in the midst of a rescue operation, and the killing could be characterized as an act of rescue. In the absence of the equality argument, the killing is permissible based upon the preservation of

---

pregnancy, the fetus is regarded as a newborn lying in a box. See Tosafot, commenting on B. Talmud Nidda 44a, s.v. *eiuh*.

Rabbi Ch. Soloveichick believes that the preservation of life principle does not justify the killing of the fetus to save its mother's life, because the fetus' life must equally be preserved. See Rabbi Ch. Soloveichick, *Chidushei Rabbenu Chaim Halevi*, The Laws of Murderer and Preservation of Life 1:9. No evidence, however, was presented in support of this argument. According to Rashi the fetus may be sacrificed to save its mother's life because it is not a person. See supra note 62 and accompanying text. This indicates that although the preservation of life principle also applies to a fetus, the fetus is not considered a person compared to its mother, and, consequently, the equality argument would not apply.

Moreover, discussing Maimonides' statement that an abortion is permissible to save the mother's life based on the law of the pursuer, Rabbi Soloveichick explains that although the mother is being pursued by heaven rather than by the fetus, the fetus is still considered a pursuer. The rule that for the application of the law of pursuer, the pursuer must actively endanger the life of the pursued, argues Rabbi Soloveichick, does not apply to a fetus. A fetus may be regarded as a pursuer merely by being the cause for its mother's critical situation, even though it does nothing. See supra note 63 and accompanying text. It is not clear, however, why the rule which requires a commission of an act for the application of the pursuer principle does not apply to a fetus. If a fetus is treated differently from a newborn with respect to the law of the pursuer, why can the fetus not be treated differently with respect to the preservation of life principle? Although the preservation of life principle also applies to a fetus, the equality argument may not apply to a fetus when it is competing with its mother for survival.

125 See, e.g., Rabbi Menachem Hameiri, *Beth Habechirah*, Sanhedrin 72b (stating that if one is ordered to kill an innocent person, and is warned that disobeying the order would result in the death of both of them, the killing is permissible. See also Rashi, commenting on Sanhedrin 72b, s.v. *yatza rosho*.

126 See supra notes 65–69 and accompanying text.

127 This argument may not apply in the bunker case according to Resh Lakish, who holds that the surrender of the fugitive, in the fugitive case, is permissible only if he was guilty. See supra note 66 and accompanying text. Since the child in the bunker case was totally innocent, his killing may not have been justified according to Resh Lakish.

128 Supra note 72 and accompanying text.

life principle. For instance, in the grenade case because the throwing away of the grenade is basically an act of rescue rather than of killing, the equality argument does not apply and it may be permissible to toss it away, even though another person would be killed.[129]

Solution of Discrepancies in Pursuer Cases

The discrepancies in the pursuer cases, discussed above,[130] may be resolved by applying the theory regarding the two categories of pursuers. One discrepancy concerns the nature of the pursuer's crime. While in some cases a capital crime is required in order to apply the pursuer defense, in others a capital crime is not required.[131] This discrepancy could be explained by drawing a distinction between the ordinary and quasi-pursuer categories. A capital crime is required for the application of the ordinary pursuer principle. Because ordinary pursuer cases do not necessarily involve a threat to the victim's life (e.g., the rape case), and do not necessarily require that the pursuer be culpable (e.g., the case of the under-aged pursuer), the pursuer principle would apply only if the pursuer is about to commit a capital crime. No capital crime on the part of the pursuer is required for the application of the quasi-pursuer principle, which always involves a threat to the life of the pursuer's victim.

Another discrepancy concerns the duty to kill the pursuer. This duty applies only to ordinary pursuer cases; it does not apply to quasi-pursuer cases.[132] Because in ordinary pursuer cases the pursuer is about to commit a capital crime, any bystander is duty-bound to kill the pursuer and save the victim. By contrast, in quasi-pursuer cases, the pursuer is not about to commit a capital crime. The only justification for killing the quasi-pursuer is to preserve the lives of others. But since one individual is going to be killed anyway (whether it is the pursuer or someone else), the preservation of

---

[129] This conclusion may depend on the interpretation of the equality argument. See infra note 150 and accompanying text. According to one interpretation, the equality argument totally eliminates the preservation of life excuse, and consequently, killing one person to save another is considered murder plain and simple. According to this interpretation, defining a homicide as an act of rescue would not justify it. According to another interpretation, because a person's life will be lost anyway, one is required to refrain from taking any action to save one at the expense of the other. Because of the severity of the act of killing, one is required not to be actively involved in the killing of one individual to save another. Although the killing may be excused it is not justified. According to the latter interpretation, where the act could be characterized as an act of rescue rather than killing, it may also be justified.

[130] See supra notes 96–105 and accompanying text.
[131] See supra notes 96–97 and accompanying text.
[132] See supra notes 98–99 and accompanying text.

life principle does not mandate the killing of the quasi-pursuer, but rather permits it.[133]

The distinction between the two categories of pursuers also explains the different terminology Maimonides uses in the context of the pursuer principle.[134] When discussing the ordinary pursuer case Maimonides uses the term *rodef* (pursuer), while when discussing cases of quasi-pursuer, such as the burglary and abortion cases, Maimonides accurately uses the term *ke'rodef* (literally "like a pursuer," or a quasi-pursuer).

The theory regarding the two categories of pursuer may also resolve the problem with Rabbi Ishmael's analogy between the burglar case and the preservation of life principle.[135] According to the above theory, the only reason for the license to kill a quasi-pursuer is the saving of his victim's life. Because the burglar case is based on the quasi-pursuer rather than the ordinary pursuer principle, the killing of the burglar is permissible, not to prevent the crime, but rather to save the homeowner's life. Rabbi Ishmael, therefore, rightfully drew the analogy between the burglar case and the permission to desecrate the Sabbath in order to save life.[136]

---

[133] Although the killing of the quasi-pursuer may not be mandated, it is not merely an excuse but rather a justification. Professor George P. Fletcher described the distinction between a justification and an excuse as follows:

> Claims of justification concede that the definition of the offense is satisfied, but challenge whether the act is wrongful; claims of excuse conclude that the act is wrongful, but seek to avoid the attribution of the act to the actor. A justification speaks to the rightness of the act; an excuse, to whether the actor is accountable for a concededly wrongful act. Fletcher, *Rethinking Criminal Law* 759 (Little, Brown and Co. 1987).

An example of a justification case is the execution of a criminal, or generally an act performed in accordance with instructions of a competent authority. Examples of excuse defenses are a defendant's claims of mistake of fact or insanity. If the claim is accepted, the defendant would generally be excused. Based upon Fletcher's distinction between justification and excuse, the quasi-pursuer defense, and certainly the ordinary pursuer defense, would be considered justifications. The killing of the pursuer in these cases is either permissible or mandated, or, in Western terminology, justified.

[134] See supra notes 100–101 and accompanying text.

[135] See supra notes 102–105 and accompanying text.

[136] It is true that whereas the burglar is engaged in committing a crime which would cause damage to the homeowner, in the case of the Sabbath nobody is about to commit a crime. This distinction, however, would not affect Rabbi Ishmael's analogy between the two cases. The commission of a harmful crime by the burglar is the reason for rejecting the equality argument. Once the equality argument is repudiated, the killing of the pursuer is sanctioned solely on the basis of the preservation of life principle. Based upon this analysis, one can easily infer from the burglary case, as Rabbi Ishmael did, that it is permissible to desecrate the Sabbath to save life just as it is permissible to kill the burglar to save the homeowner's life.

The Inapplicability of the Pursuer Principle in Amir's Case

Prime Minister Rabin's assassination was not justified, neither on the ground of the ordinary pursuer principle nor of the quasi-pursuer principle. Because Rabin was not going to commit a capital crime, the ordinary pursuer principle did not apply. To justify Rabin's assassination on the basis of the quasi-pursuer principle, the equality argument must first be repudiated. The quasi-pursuer cases, discussed previously (i.e., the cases of the burglar, the informer, the abortion, the fugitive, the bunker, the counterfeiter and the grenade), illustrate the circumstances under which the equality argument is inapplicable. None of those circumstances were present in Amir's case.

First, Rabin had no intention to commit an offense which would cause harm to Jewish people.[137] On the contrary, his intention was to save Jewish life, even though his plans might have proven to be disastrous. Second, Rabin's life was certainly as valuable as the life of any other person who might have been killed as a result of Rabin's policies.[138] Third, Rabin would have most probably lived out his years had he not been assassinated by the defendant. Even accepting the extreme assumption that Rabin's peace plan would have resulted in many Israeli casualties, the vast majority of the Jewish people, including Rabin himself, would most probably have survived.[139] Lastly, Rabin's assassination is certainly an act of killing rather than of rescue.[140]

But would the equality argument apply even when the killing of one person would save the lives of many? Should not the equality argument be dismissed in Amir's case, because by killing Rabin the defendant allegedly saved the lives of many people? The numerical factor might be significant for the application of the necessity defense under Western law, which is based on the "lesser evils" principle. Under this principle, one should be al-

---

[137] Whereas the pursuer in the burglar and informer cases intended to commit a harmful offense, thereby rendering the equality argument inapplicable, Rabin had no intention of committing an offense, and therefore the equality argument does apply.

[138] While the equality argument does not apply in the abortion case because the life of the mother is more valuable than the life of the fetus (see supra notes 115–116 and accompanying text), Rabin's life was as valuable as the life of any other person and therefore the equality argument would apply.

[139] While the fugitive and the child in the fugitive and bunker cases, respectively, would have died anyway and, therefore, the equality argument did not apply, Rabin's life was not at risk as a result of the peace plan, and, therefore, the equality argument did apply.

[140] Amir's case thus differs from the grenade case, where, according to *Chazon Ish*, the killing of an individual to save the group may be permissible, if the homicide could be regarded as an act of rescue rather than killing.

lowed to kill one individual to save many.[141] Under Jewish law, life is not measured by qualitative or quantitative factors. Therefore, the saving of many lives is not an excuse for taking one innocent life.[142]

Because none of the circumstances that might preclude the application of the equality argument exists in Amir's case, Rabin's assassination could not be justified on the ground of the preservation of life and quasi-pursuer principles. Consequently, on the basis of the equality argument, the assassination of Mr. Rabin was prohibited even assuming that his peace plan would have ended in failure resulting in many Jewish casualties.[143]

---

141 See, e.g., Model Penal Code §3.02, Commentary at 3 (1985) (adopted 1062) (stating that "[t]he life of every individual must be assumed in such a case to be of equal value and the numerical preponderance in the lives saved compared to those sacrificed surely establish legal justification for the act"). See 2 Paul H. Robinson, *Criminal Law Defenses* 64, n. 58 (1984) (noting that "[w]here the killing results in a net saving of life . . . [it] should be regarded as not merely excusing from punishment but as legally justifying"). See also G. Williams, *Criminal Law: The General Part* 740 (2d ed. 1961); "Wechsler & Michael, A Rationale of the Law of Homicide: I," 37 *Colum. L. Rev.* 701, 738–39 (1937).

142 See, e.g., Meiri, *Beth Habechirah*, Sanhedrin 72b (stating that the principle that one may not set aside the life of a person to save another, unless the first is a pursuer, also applies in a case where the lives of many people are at stake). The principle that an innocent person cannot be killed even to save many people may be deduced from Resh Lakish's view in the fugitive case. According to Resh Lakish, the fugitive may not be delivered into the hands of the outlaws unless he is guilty of a capital crime. See Supra note 66 and accompanying text. This implies that if the fugitive is innocent, he may not be delivered even though his surrendering would save the lives of many people.

Although according to Rabbi Yoḥanan the fugitive may be handed over even if he is innocent, this is not because the lives of many people take precedence over the life of one person, but rather because the fugitive would have been killed anyway, even if he were not surrendered. See Rabbi S. Yisraeli, "Risking Lives to Save Lives," 4 *Techumin* 136 (1983) (discussing the question of whether it is permissible to kill an innocent person to save many lives). See also Rabbi E. Waldenberg, 15 *Tzitz Eliezer* Ch. 70 (discussing the case of one who is driving a car and is approaching a crosswalk. Many people are on the crosswalk, crossing the street, but the driver is unable to stop the car. The only thing he can do is to pull the car to the side where one person is standing. Rabbi Waldenberg holds that the driver is not allowed to pull the car to the direction of the single person because it is not permissible to kill one person to save many). A similar approach was taken by the English House of Lords in the famous case of Regina v. Dudley and Stephens, 14 Q.B.D. 273 (1885). In this case survivors of a sunken yacht were floating in the open sea in a lifeboat. When they ran out of food and faced death by starvation, they killed one of them and fed on his flesh. They were convicted and sentenced to death. The court held that there is no justification to kill an innocent person even to save a number of people (the defendants were eventually pardoned by the Crown).

143 As mentioned previously, early commentators maintained that Saul was a pursuer because he attempted to kill David. See supra note 84 and accompanying text. Saul was apparently an ordinary pursuer because he was going to commit a capital crime. Although Saul believed that David was a usurper and deserved to die, this was obviously a mistake, as Saul

The Defendant's Punishment

Since Mr. Rabin was not to be considered a pursuer and his assassination was not justified, would Yigal Amir be subject to punishment under Jewish law?[144] Assuming—again, an extreme assumption—that Mr. Rabin's assassination indeed saved Jewish lives, would it affect the punishment of the assassin? An act may be prohibited and yet not punishable.[145] Moreover, under certain circumstances even a forbidden homicide may not be punishable. For instance, a homicide performed under duress, according to Maimonides, is not punishable even though it is prohibited.[146] This ruling is based on the principle of *ones rachmana patrei*, that is, the law exonerates one who commits an act under compulsion.[147]

---

himself admitted later. See I Samuel 24:17-23. Although because of his mistake Saul would not have been subject to capital punishment for killing David, he was, nevertheless, considered a pursuer. As discussed previously, the law of the ordinary pursuer applies even where the pursuer is not culpable. Thus, a pursuer who is a minor is considered an ordinary pursuer whose killing is justified, even though he is not culpable. See supra note 44-48 and accompanying text. Similarly, Saul would be regarded as an ordinary pursuer because he was about to commit a murder, even though he might not have been culpable.

Samson also may be regarded as a pursuer because he endangered the lives of the Israelites by his provocative actions against the Philistines. See supra note 86 and accompanying text. Likewise King Jehoiakim was treated by the Sanhedrin as a pursuer because he rebelled against Nebuchadnezzar, thereby jeopardizing the people's lives. See supra note 87-91 and accompanying text. Obviously, these two leaders were not going to commit homicide (or any other capital crime against the people), and therefore may not be regarded as ordinary pursuers. They were rather quasi-pursuers. Both cases, that of Samson and that of Jehoiakim, involved a demand by a powerful enemy (the Philistines or the Babylonians), to surrender the Israelite leader, threatening to destroy the country if the demand was not complied with. Because these two leaders would have been killed anyway (or, at least, this was the belief of the surrenderers), the equality argument did not apply, and the surrender was permissible on the basis of the preservation of life principle.

144 This chapter will not discuss all the aspects of the defendant's punishment under Jewish law. This would require an extensive discussion of Jewish penal law, criminal procedure and laws of evidence, which is beyond the purpose and scope of this work. Rather the discussion will focus on the punishment issue in connection with the necessity defense, that is, whether the necessity defense would exonerate the defendant from punishment.

145 Many biblical prohibitions are not punishable for one reason or another. For instance, a violation of a biblical commandment by omission (*lav she'ein bo ma'aseh*) is not punishable. See, e.g., B. Talmud Makkot 2b, 16a. Likewise, a violation of a negative commandment which is linked to a positive commandment (*lav hanitak le'aseh*) is not punishable. Id.

146 See Maimonides, *Mishneh Torah*, The Book of Knowledge, The Foundation of the Law 5:4 (stating that because "the transgression was committed under duress, [the transgressor] is not punished with stripes, and needless to add [that] he is not sentenced by a court to be put to death, even if he committed murder under duress"). See supra note 112.

147 See, e.g., B. Talmud Bava Kamma 28b and Nedarim 27a (stating that a betrothed woman who has been raped is not guilty of adultery because of *ones rachmana patrei*). See also supra note 112.

Would Mr. Amir's crime be regarded as an act performed under compulsion and not punishable? Maimonides distinguishes between two kinds of compulsion: duress and necessity.[148] If one kills an innocent person under duress he is not to be punished even though the act is prohibited. However, if one kills an innocent person because of necessity, he is to be punished.[149]

---

[148] See supra note 112 (for a discussion of the distinction between the duress and necessity defenses). Maimonides does not use the terms duress (in Hebrew—*korach*) and necessity (in Hebrew—*tzorech*). Rather, Maimonides uses the term *ones* or *onsin* for duress and the term *chola'im* for necessity. The concept of *ones* or *onsin* is broader than duress. It includes any situation which is beyond one's control. Thus, the term *onsin* is used in the context of the law of bailment, signifying a loss of an object under circumstances beyond the bailee's control and for which he is not responsible. See, B. Talmud Bava Metzia 93b (using the term *onsin* for an assault by armed robbers or wild animals). The term *onsin* was also used in the context of a conditional transaction. If the condition was not fulfilled under circumstances beyond the control of the party, it may not affect the transaction. See, e.g., B. Talmud Nedarim 27a (stating that if one agreed to give up certain rights if he does not appear in court on a certain date, and he missed the deadline because he could not cross a river, he does not lose his rights); B. Talmud Ketuboth 3a (ruling that if one divorces his wife on condition that he does not return from his journey within twelve months, and he could not return because of an illness, the divorce may not be valid, according to one opinion, because illness is considered an *ones*, and, therefore, the husband is regarded as though he did return to his wife). In both cases the Talmud derived the principle of *ones* from the case of the rape of the betrothed woman. The victim is acquitted from charges of adultery because of *ones*. See supra note 49 and accompanying text. This analogy indicates that the terms *ones* and *onsin* include any act performed against one's will and beyond his control, whether by duress or nature.

The term *onsin* used by Maimonides in the context of criminal activity and punishment, however, is limited to cases of duress (obviously, one is not responsible for an act performed by nature and beyond his control). The term *chola'im* mentioned by Maimonides means literally "diseases," and is used as an example of a necessity where one is compelled to violate the law under a *natural* threat to life. The term necessity generally has a broader meaning, including also the prevention of other grave consequences, not necessarily death. In this chapter, however, which deals with homicide, the term necessity is used in a narrow sense, including only the prevention of fatal consequences. Less severe consequences would certainly not justify a homicide.

[149] As an example of a necessity defense Maimonides mentions the case of killing a person to save the life of one critically ill (e.g., to use the slain person's organs for transplant purposes). See Maimonides, ibid. Another example is seizing the plank from a person in a stormy sea to save one's life and causing the other to drown.

The distinction between duress and necessity in homicide cases with respect to punishment, advanced by Maimonides, is not entirely clear. Many scholars questioned why killing for the purpose of saving the life of a critically ill person is different from killing an innocent person at the order of a brutal gangster threatening death. In both cases the killer acted under compulsion to save life. A number of theories have been suggested. According to one theory, the distinction is between external and internal compulsion. While duress constitutes an external compulsion, necessity constitutes an internal compulsion. External compulsion according to this theory negates free will. The coerced person is not exercising his own will, but rather the will of the coercer. By contrast, internal compulsion does not negate one's will. Although the person is pressured by the circumstances, he is able to deliberate and consider his options, and eventually arrive at a decision by exercising his free will. See Rabbi Meir Simcha Hacohen, *Or*

Mr. Amir was not under duress when he committed the horrible crime. The alleged saving of Jewish lives could at most be regarded as a necessity. Therefore, on the basis of Maimonides' ruling, the defendant would be subject to punishment.[150]

Conclusion

Amir's argument that Rabin was to be considered a pursuer may have been based upon two premises, one factual and the other legal. The factual premise postulates that by implementing his peace plan Rabin was jeopar-

---

Sameach, commenting on Maimonides, *Mishneh Torah*, The Book of Knowledge, The Foundation of the Law 5:6; Rabbi Moshe Feinstein, *Iggrot Moshe*, 4 *Even Haezer*, Ch.106. See also Ch. Povarsky, "The Intervention by Non-Jewish Courts in Jewish Divorces," *The Jewish Law Report* 1, 12–14 (August 1994) (discussing the effect of this theory on recent involvement by the New York State Legislature in Jewish divorces).

Another authority believes that there is a technical distinction between the two cases. While in the duress case the threat to the killer's life is imminent and certain, in necessity cases the threat is neither certain nor imminent. The defendant might not have died from the disease. Likewise, it is not certain that the killing would save the killer's life. See Rabbi Eliezer Segal Landau, *Yad Hamelech*, The Foundation of the Law 5:6, commenting on Maimonides.

According to both interpretations, Mr. Amir would be punished under Jewish law. Mr. Amir was not forced to commit the murder. He might have felt compelled to do so to save life, but this compulsion could at most be considered a necessity which would not exonerate him from punishment.

[150] The defendant's punishment, however, may depend upon the interpretation of the equality argument. According to Rashi, the equality argument totally rejects the preservation of life principle as a justification for killing an innocent person. The purpose of the preservation of life principle, argues Rashi, is to preserve life, but when the saving of the life of one person requires the killing of another, the net result is that life is not saved. Therefore, the preservation of life principle does not apply and the killing is prohibited. See *Rashi*, commenting on Pesahim 25b, s.v. *mai chazit*. According to Rabbi Ch. Soloveichick, this is also Maimonides' view. See Rabbi Ch. Soloveichick, *Chidushei Rabbenu Chaim Halevi*, The Foundation of the Law 5:1. In the absence of a justification, the defendant would be punished for killing an innocent person.

Other authorities, however, interpreted the equality argument to mean that because one life would be lost anyway one should refrain from taking any action. Because of the equality argument one should not interfere by actively terminating the life of one of them. See, e.g., Tosafot, commenting on Pesahim 25b, s.v. *af na'arah*; Tosafot, commenting on Sanhedrin 74b, s.v. *veha Esther*; *Chidushei Talmidei Rabbenu Yonah*, Sanhedrin 74a. The emphasis is on the active termination of one's life. A passive termination of one's life to save the life of another would be excused, according to these authorities, even where the passive termination of life could be regarded as an act of homicide. See Rabbi Soloveichick, ibid.

According to this interpretation, the equality argument does not totally reject the application of the preservation of life defense in homicide cases. Rather, because of the equality argument, the preservation of life principle does not justify an active homicide. It would, however, justify a passive homicide, and may perhaps excuse—not justify—even an active homicide.

dizing the lives of the Jewish people in Israel. The legal premise is that, although Rabin was not committing any crime against the Jewish people, and had no intention to harm anybody, rather sincerely believed that he was saving the people from great danger, he was still to be considered a pursuer because his action, allegedly, in fact did jeopardize people's lives.

The factual premise was not substantiated. Nobody can predict the consequences of a continued conflict with the Palestinians, which may involve other Arab countries and lead to a military confrontation in which nonconventional weapons might be employed. Equally unpredictable is the effect of the implementation of Rabin's peace plan on the lives and safety of the people. Thus, the factual basis of the pursuer defense is, to put it mildly, questionable. It is true that according to one opinion in the Talmud, the pursuer in the burglar case may be killed even though the threat to the homeowner's life is not certain.[151] In the burglar case, however, the killing of the pursuer eliminates entirely the risk to the homeowner's life, whereas Rabin's assassination did not necessarily eliminate the risk to the people's lives. A similar risk, although of a different form, might surface if the peace process were to be discontinued.

The analysis of the pursuer principle and the discussion of the various cases of pursuers in this work focused on the legal rather than factual aspects of Amir's defense. Because of the great interest of the public in this case and because of the complexities of the issues, it would be useful to briefly summarize our conclusions, both on the factual and legal levels.

Rabin could not be considered a pursuer because (a) there is no evidence that his peace plan would have jeopardized Jewish life more than a lack of a peace plan; (b) he certainly was not going to commit a capital crime, and (c) he did not commit any crime against the people and had no intention to cause any harm. Assuming his action would have jeopardized the people's lives, it would have been an indirect result of his actions.

It is true that the law of the pursuer has been applied even in cases where the pursuer was entirely innocent, and the danger to the lives of others generated by his actions was neither intentional nor direct. The application of the pursuer principle in these cases, however, was due to special circumstances which justified the killing of the pursuer: (a) the pursuer was about to commit a capital crime, even though he was unaware of it and was totally innocent; (b) the pursuer was about to commit an offense, being aware that his action would cause serious harm to others; (c) the pursuer would have been killed anyway; (d) the pursuer's life was not as valuable as the lives of those that might have died as a result of his actions,

---

[151] See supra note 77 and accompanying text.

and (e) the killing of the pursuer was basically an act of rescue rather than killing.

All these circumstances which would justify the killing of a person to save the lives of others were not present in the case of Prime Minister Rabin, and, consequently, according to Jewish law, there was no justification for his assassination.[152]

---

[152] As a final note, it is worthy to point out that a higher standard of morality in Jewish law requires that a pursuer is not to be killed even if his killing is permissible (provided his action does involve a capital crime, resulting in serious harm to others). The Jerusalem Talmud relates the story of Rabbi Yehoshua ben Levi, who was meeting with the prophet Elijah regularly. One day the prophet Elijah did not appear. It turned out that a fugitive who committed an offense was hiding from the authorities and found refuge in a Jewish community. The authorities demanded his surrender and threatened to destroy the entire community if he is not handed over. Rabbi Yehoshua ben Levi convinced the fugitive to surrender himself to the authorities. The prophet Elijah then stopped meeting with Rabbi Yehoshua. Elijah resumed the meetings only after much praying and fasting by Rabbi Yehoshua.

When Rabbi Yehoshua questioned the prophet about his absence, the latter responded rhetorically: "Do I show myself to informers?" (alluding to Rabbi Yehoshua's involvement in the surrendering of the fugitive). Rabbi Yehoshua defended himself by asking: "Did I not follow the Law?" The prophet answered, "[Yes indeed,] but is it also according to the laws of the pious?" Where Jewish law does not mandate the killing of an individual or his surrender to the authorities for execution, one should avoid doing so, even when this individual committed a crime and is jeopardizing the life of the entire community, and even where if not surrendered this individual would be killed anyway together with the entire community.

12

HIDDEN INTEREST AND RISK MANAGEMENT IN SIXTEENTH CENTURY MEDITERRANEAN COMMERCE

LAURENCE J. RABINOVICH*

This study examines some aspects of Jewish maritime trade in the sixteenth century, as revealed in the responsa literature. The scholars whose writings we shall examine lived under Ottoman rule which, during the sixteenth century, reached the pinnacle of its power and began, in the final quarter of the century, its slow decline.[1]

Quite apart from those considerations, the sixteenth century was a tumultuous and transitional time in Jewish history. The expulsion of Jews from Spain, the most cataclysmic event of Diaspora history until the Holocaust, continued to haunt Sephardic Jewry for generations. The exiles resettled in Amsterdam, Italy, North Africa and, most notably, Ottoman lands. Ashkenazic Jews were also on the move; following centuries of expulsion, crusades and blood libels, only a few pockets of Jews remained within the borders of France (now including Provence) at the dawn of the sixteenth century. Murderous rampages also decimated the Jewish communities in Germany.

Much of the remnant of Franco-German Jewry had relocated, by then, to Poland, Lithuania and neighboring lands. By the middle of the sixteenth century, Poland was home to two of the greatest halakhic authorities, R. Solomon b. Jechiel Luria (the Maharshal) and his kinsman, R. Moses b. Israel Isserles (the Rema). Yet it was a Polish scholar with a more modest reputation, Isaiah Menahem b. Isaac (also known as R. Mendel Menahem Avigdors,

---

* Partner, Schindel, Farman & Lipsius LLP, Esqs., 225 West 34th Street, New York, NY 10122.

[1] Among the histories which have been particularly helpful were, F. Braudel, *The Mediterranean and the Mediterranean World in the Age of Philip II*, tr. Sian Reynolds (New York, Harper & Row, 1972); S.A. Rosanes, *Divray Yemay Israel be-Togarma* (1930–1945) and several works by Bernard Lewis and Cecil Roth.

or Maharam), who revolutionized the halakhic approach to financial and credit transactions by publishing a new formula of the *hetter iska*, an arrangement permitting an investor to share in profits generated by a merchant.

Although Eastern European Jewry had already begun to increase in both size and scholarly achievements, the larger part of the Jewish people, and a clear majority of its leading scholars, lived within the Ottoman Empire in the sixteenth century, particularly after 1517 when the Ottomans captured Eretz Israel, Egypt and Syria. Jews, of course, had lived in the former Eastern Roman Empire since ancient times, and many of the communities in Asia Minor and the Balkans were centuries old. The influx of refugees from Spain and Portugal to the Ottoman Empire reinvigorated Jewish life in these communities, although not without creating social tensions.

Many of the arriving Sephardim were sophisticated merchants, of a different class and with different interests than the indigenous Jewish communities. Most of the leading rabbinic figures in Ottoman lands were also scions of Sephardic families including R. Joseph Caro (1488–1575), R. Moses di Trani (1500–1580) and R. Samuel de Medina (1506–1589). Merchants near and far, who plied their trade in the Mediterranean, sent halakhic inquiries to these and other scholars, seeking their rulings on the legality of a wide range of credit and consignment transactions utilized by contemporary merchants.

We will examine two particular types of these transactions:

1) the commenda and its halakhic cousin, the *iska*;
2) the cambio, or exchange, contract.

As we shall see, the contemporary rabbinic authorities carefully studied prevailing business practices in light of the legal precedent in halakhic sources.

The Iska

It would be difficult to overstate the obloquy directed by rabbinic writings at those who violate the Torah's usury prohibition.[2] The Torah's "zero tolerance" on this issue was, in fact, interpreted to apply not only to loans but to credit transactions in the commerce of goods and services as well.[3] A seller

---

[2] Ex. 22:24; Lev. 25:35–37; Deut. 23:20–21: Ez. 18:11–13; B.M. 61b ("those who lend on interest are compared to murderers"); R. Judah Loew b. Bezalel ("Maharal"), *Netivot Olam*, "*Netiv ha-Tzedakah*" Ch.6.

[3] Mishna Bava Metzia ("B.M.") 5:1.

may not evade the prohibition, for example, by permitting the buyer to defer payment on a purchase in exchange for paying a higher price.[4]

And yet, in spite of this (or, as some have suggested, because of it), halakhic authorities have also struggled with commercial realities, and attempted to permit business markets to operate in a manner consistent with the incentive for profit while not violating the halakha.

The first attempt by rabbinic authorities to address the concerns of commercial entrepreneurs was their recognition of the *"iska,"* an arrangement described in the Talmud (B. M. 104b). The *iska* (meaning business, or deal) permits a passive investor to share in the risks and, in the event of success, profits of the enterprise. Without the halakhic sanction of this arrangement, it could have been suspect as merely another variation of a usurious loan.

The creative solution was to view the *iska* as though it consisted of two parts. One half of the money transferred from the investor to the businessman is treated as a regular loan, while the second half is viewed as a bailment (the *rishonim* disagree as to whether the businessman-bailee has the status of a gratuitous bailee or salaried bailee).[5] The loan portion, of course, must be repaid in full on the due date, regardless of the outcome of the business transaction. A bailee, however, is not obligated to return the bailment in the event of accidental loss. Accordingly, if the business deal is unsuccessful, and the investment is lost, the merchant is not obligated to repay the bailment portion of the investment. The *iska*, then, is a mechanism for sharing risk.

Conversely, in the event the transaction leads to financial gain, the investor recoups his entire investment and is entitled to a share of the profit. For instance, in the standard *iska* (50% loan, 50% bailment), the investor would receive 50% of the profit, less a management fee owed to the entrepreneur for his efforts. While there is a good deal of controversy in the literature about how to calculate that fee, there is universal agreement that the entrepreneur must receive at least a little bit more than 50% of any profits.[6] That includes the 50% of the profit attributable to the loan portion of the *iska*, and a management fee for his efforts on behalf of the bailment portion. The Talmud itself speaks of a two-thirds share for the entrepreneur, and one-third for the investor in cases in which the risk was evenly split.

---

[4] Id. 5:2.

[5] Maimonides, *Yad ha-Ḥazaka, Sheluḥin ve-Shutafim* 6:2 takes the former view. Rabad, ad loc, and most others, adopted the latter view, which is accepted in the Shulhan Arukh, Y.D. 187:5.

[6] Rashi, s.v., *"kephoel batel,"* B.M. 68a; Tosafot, s.v. *"ve-Noten Lo,"* id. Without the management fee the arrangement would be forbidden because it would appear as if the entrepreneur was working without remuneration on the investor's portion, in exchange for receiving a loan.

Where the investor accepted two-thirds of the risk, he was entitled to half the profits (B.M. 68b–69a).

The term *"iska"* appears in a large number of responsa over the centuries, beginning in Geonic responsa and continuing up to and beyond the sixteenth century which we are examining. For instance, R. Samuel de Medina (1872 reprint, Yoreh De'ah Responsa 59) describes an *iska* in which the investor gave 1,000 ducats to the entrepreneur who traveled from the Ottoman Empire to Venice. At Venice, he purchased certain commodities which he sold in the course of his travels. When the merchant returned home, the investor demanded the return of the principal plus one half of the profits. However, the entrepreneur argued that the original agreement was void because it had provided for a fifty-fifty split of both profits and risk, an arrangement explicitly forbidden by the Mishna (B.M. 5:4). He wished to return only the principal and keep the entire profit for himself.

R. Samuel never entertains that clearly inequitable result. Instead, he turns to the talmudic models—the contract is rewritten into an agreement whereby the parties agreed to share any loss evenly, while two-thirds of any profit would go to entrepreneur. The responsum required the merchant to restore not only the principal, but one-third of the profits as well.

Another example of the traditional approach to the *iska* in sixteenth century responsa can be found in R. Joseph Caro's collection entitled *Avkat Rokhel* (Leipzig, 1859, no.136). The question is of general historical interest since it was posed by R. Isaac Ashkenazi, better known as R. Isaac Luria, the "Ari." Although his fame rests on his creative and original system of Kabbalah, Luria, at least during his stay in Egypt as a young man, studied halakha with the leading rabbis of Egypt, and engaged in commerce.

His query to R. Caro is in the form of a series of hypothetical scenarios involving the death of the entrepreneur, and the responsibilities owned by the entrepreneur's heirs to the investor, both in the event of total loss and in the event of profitable sale. Luria suggests that if the sea-going merchant dies en route, the heirs should be exonerated from repayment under the theory that the *iska* terminated immediately upon the death of the merchant.

R. Caro's responsa sets out the basic *iska* rules, adding that the death of the merchant does not relieve the heirs of the responsibility of restoring at least the loan portion of the *iska*. Conversely, in the event the heirs successfully complete the sales transaction, the profits are split with the investor in accordance with the terms of the *iska* agreement.

The *iska* arrangements described in these responsa are in the standard talmudic models. However, Geonic and Geniza sources show that no later than a few centuries after the close of the Talmud, Jews were experimenting with variations in the *iska*.

In addition, Jewish traders began utilizing an Arab institution known, alternatively, as the *mudāraba, qirād* or *muqārada* which later surfaced in Europe as the commenda. These contracts developed as an alternative to partnership which under Islamic law, as in the halakha, is created by compliance with a range of technical requirements.[7] The commenda was less formal and, no less importantly, not permanent; the commenda involved one particular transaction imposing no future mutual responsibilities. Commendas appear frequently in halakhic and Islamic sources; in Europe, where the commenda first appears in the tenth or eleventh century, it is credited by economic historians with contributing in large measure to robust growth of European maritime trade.[8]

The most striking difference between the *iska* and the commenda relates to who bears the risk of loss. In the classic *iska*, as we have seen, the merchant accepted one half of the risk of capital (i.e., the risk of loss). Maimonides accepted the principle that the parties could modify the terms so that the percentage of the *iska* which is a loan (for which the merchant bears responsibility) is greater than, or less than, fifty percent.[9] However, in nearly all scenarios, the merchant bears at least some of the risk of loss.

In the commenda, though, it is the investor who bears the entire risk of capital. If all or part of the investment is lost, the entrepreneur need not dip into his own savings to repay the investor. His sole investment is the risk of labor: if the commenda fails, he, unlike a salaried employee, receives no remuneration. The investor, not surprisingly, took the lion's share of any profits, three-fourths in most cases.[10]

In several of his responsa, Maimonides sanctioned—or at least enforced—the terms of commenda agreements between Jewish merchants. One questioner describes a "*qirād al-goyim*" (a *qirād* in the manner of non-Jews) in which the investor was to receive two-thirds of any profits. The cargo financed by the commenda was lost at sea. The investor himself drowned in a separate accident. His heirs (in this case a charity) sued the

---

[7] Abraham L. Udovitch, *Partnership and Profit in Medieval Islam* (Princeton University Press, 1970), 170 ff; Udovitch, "At the Origin of the Western Commenda: Islam, Israel and Byzantium," *Speculum*, 37/2 (April, 1962), 198–201.

[8] Id.; *Teshuvot Geonay Mizraḥ u-Ma'arav*, (ed. Müller, Berlin, 1888) responsa 224, 225, folios 61b–62a; R.S. Lopez, *The Commercial Revolution of the Middle Ages 950–1350* (Prentice Hall, Inc., NJ, 1971), 76–77.

[9] *Yad, Sheluḥin ve-Shutafim*, 6:5.

[10] Udovitch, "Origin," p. 199; N.J.G. Pounds, *An Economic History of Medieval Europe* (Longman Group Ltd., London and N.Y., 1974), 420–421.

entrepreneur. Maimonides unreservedly decreed that since the parties had arrange a *quirād*, not an *iska*, the entrepreneur was not obligated to pay any portion of the lost investment.[11]

R. Moses B. Isaac Alashkar (1466–1552), one of the leading halakhic jurists of the sixteenth century, appears to have been unaware of this responsum of Maimonides. A questioner from Tunis (where Alashkar had lived following the Expulsion from Spain) sought halakha guidance from Alashkar with respect to the types of *"iska"* apparently in use among North African Jewish traders:

> Reuben entrusted an *iska* to Simeon on condition that two-thirds of the profit would go to Reuben and the remaining third to Simeon. Or they agreed that Simeon would receive one-fourth of the profit and Reuben the remainder. And Simeon accepted no responsibility (i.e., none of the risk of loss). If the money is lost in a non-negligent manner, does Simeon bear any obligation, or is he completely exonerated since he accepted no responsibility?[12]

R. Moses concludes that Simeon does indeed bear a portion of the risk even though he accepted no responsibility in the contract. He notes that there are some early scholars who permitted this sort of arrangement. Citing at length from the Mishneh Torah of Maimonides, however, R. Moses concludes that Simeon, in return for a quarter of the potential profits, was obligated to assume one sixth of the risk of loss of the capital.

R. Moses does not cite the apparently contrary responsum of Maimonides, presumably because it was not available to him. It is also noteworthy that R. Moses refers to rishonim (early scholars) who permitted this type of arrangement, and not to contemporary scholars. Perhaps by the sixteenth century, Jewish traders in Italy and the Ottoman Empire had advanced into new types of contractual agreements and the commenda was no longer in common use. It is also possible, of course, that the commenda was so common that most merchants simply utilized commenda without seeking rabbinic sanction.

The responsa of the sixteenth century suggest a certain level of dissatisfaction by the contemporary merchants with traditional *iska*. These merchants, perhaps with the help of halakhically sophisticated advisors, created

---

[11] *Teshuvot ha-Rambam*, ed. Blau (Rubin Mass Ltd., Jerusalem, 1986), responsum 32, pp. 45–46. Blau translates *qirād* as *"iska."* The word *"qirād"* appears in a number of Maimonides' responsa (e.g. 25, 29,35). In responsum 91 (pp. 147–148) there is also a discussion of the non-Jewish type of *qirād*.

[12] *She'elot u-Teshuvot Maharam al-Ashkar* (Jerusalem, 1959), responsum 36.

variations of the *iska*. One such *iska*, quoted verbatim in a responsum of R. Moses di Trani, reads as follows:

> I, the undersigned ("Reuben") admit (i.e., agree) that following the collection by Simeon of the amount known to us from a certain party (literally, from a certain place), [with respect to] any further amount that he draws on my account, up to the amount of 500 ducats I declare that henceforth and hereafter I am willing to accept and be satisfied with the payment of only ten per every hundred, in a manner permissible by law, and he (Simeon) may invest the principal as he wishes and increase his account. All this was agreed on such and such date, etc.. I, Reuben, agree to all that is written above. And I, Simeon, agree to take (i.e., borrow) the above-referenced 500 ducats in the manner described above.[13]

The query posed to R. Moses notes that, in fact, Simeon took two hundred of the available ducats and invested them in merchandise. Unfortunately, the merchandise was lost and R. Moses was consulted when a dispute arose between Reuben and Simeon as to who was required to bear the loss.

Although neither the question nor the response explains what the perceived problem was, it is clear that his arrangement sounds dangerously like a loan at 10% interest. Presumably Reuben owned Simeon a certain undisclosed sum from a prior transaction which Simeon was to collect from a third party, perhaps Reuben's agent. In addition, Reuben made available a line of credit of five hundred ducats of which Simeon actually drew down two hundred.

R. Moses treats the agreement as a permissible *iska* by reading into the contract a provision the parties had neglected to mention. Reuben would be entitled to a "profit" of ten per hundred borrowed, but only if Simeon also profited no less than ten per hundred. Reuben's profit could never exceed Simeon's: If the estimate created an excess of only sixteen to a hundred, for instance, each party would be entitled to half of the profit. R. Moses feels justified in this reading of the contract because of the appearance of the word *"be-hetter"* ("in a manner permissible by law"). Without this additional term the contract would certainly have not been permissible.

Having so amended the contract, R. Moses' reading is quite plain. The opportunity for Simeon to earn ninety percent of the profit once a certain threshold had been crossed serves as an adequate substitute for the management fee ordinarily required. The risk of loss, therefore, is the standard

---

[13] *She'elot u-Teshuvot Mabit* (1861, reprinted in Israel, 1974), Vol.II, Part I, responsum 152, folio 41b.

fifty percent on each party. Thus Simeon is obligated to restore one hundred ducats to Reuben.

In a second responsum (Volume I, no. 244) R. Moses approved another *iska* which anticipates the *hetter iska*. The investor set out a remarkably strict set of conditions which the borrower/merchant would be obliged to follow in order to sustain the traditional *iska* split of fifty percent loan, fifty percent bailment. If the merchant failed to abide by any of the conditions (presumably the expected result) the entire risk of loss would pass to the merchant, and he would pay 10% of any profit to the investor. This ploy had been suggested by R. Israel Isserlein one hundred years earlier in a remarkable responsum that also foreshadowed the *hetter iska*.[14]

The eventual drafting of the *hetter iska* by R. Isaiah Menahem, and of the other variations of the *hetter iska* which followed, was not, therefore, a sudden and unexpected event. Centuries of experimentation lay behind its development. The responsa of the sixteenth century provide an open window onto the struggles of the rabbinic authorities of the time with the complex commercial transactions and the new legal approaches they required.

Hidden Interest And The Cambium Maritimum

The existence of a legal prohibition against taking or paying interest did not, of course, prevent individuals from nonetheless executing usurious contracts. The primary impediments for those willing to defy the law related to record keeping and enforceability. Jewish courts—and for that matter the non-Jewish courts, even in Renaissance Italy—would void any contract deemed usurious in any dispute brought before the court.[15]

While we cannot know how often businessmen sought to evade the usury strictures, we do know from the responsa literature that such attempts were made. For instance, in one matter brought before R. Samuel de Medina (Y.D. no.68), the lender presented a note bearing the borrower's acknowlegement of a debt for 305 ducats. The borrower, however, offered proof that the actual debt was 275 ducats, and claimed that it was a common practice in his city to disguise usury by misreporting the amount of the loan.

---

14 *Sefer Terumat ha-Deshen*, (Warsaw), responsum 302, folio 53b; Ṭur and Bet Yoseph, Yorah Deah Section 187. The original source may be Tosafot s.v. "*ha-Noten*," Bava Kama 102a.

15 Raymond de Roover, *The Rise and Decline of the Medici Bank, 1307–1497* (Harvard University Press, Cambridge, 1968). The assumption that Islamic courts refused to enforce usurious loan agreements has been questioned by Ronald C. Jennings, "Loans and Credit in Early 17th Century Ottoman Records," JESHA XVI (1973), 168–216.

R. Moses di Trani (Vol. I, no. 298) also discusses a case in which the loan document allegedly overstated the amount of the loan and included an interest payment.

A rather more sophisticated way of skirting the usury prohibition was developed by Italian merchants eager to earn profits without incurring the wrath of the Church. Although there has been some debate on the subject, economic historians have concluded that the theologians' views on what constituted usury strongly influenced European banking and credit practices until as late as the eighteenth century.[16]

As innovative and significant as were the contributions of Jewish traders to the spread of international commerce, these merchants could not but have been influenced by the practices of their far more numerous non-Jewish peers.[17] Since the latter were, in turn, influenced—constricted some may have thought—by Church doctrine, it was inevitable that the methods devised to evade Christian usury law would appear in Jewish legal sources.

The most striking example of such cross-influence was the exchange contract (called the cambio, letters (or bills) of exchange, *brieve van wissel* or *tratta*, in various local sources). The basic structure of the exchange is described in various contemporary documents. For our purposes, it is sufficient to describe the cambio as the receipt of money in one place, and its repayment at a later date in a different location and, most significantly, in a different currency. This type of arrangement facilitated credit transactions and reduced the need for merchants to travel with large amounts of money. The exchange from one currency to another, however, permitted the parties to mask an interest payment by purposefully undervaluing the foreign currency. In order to ferret out any usurious practice, the religious authority would need to be familiar with the precise exchange rates at a specific time. Ultimately, many theologians accepted the merchants' claim that the exchange transaction was not a loan transaction. Since there was no loan, there could, by definition, be no usury under Christian legal doctrine as interpreted by the Scholastics.[18]

---

16 de Roover, p. 10.

17 Focusing primarily on Genoese, Venetian and Sicilian archival documents, Eliyahu Ashtor has documented the involvement of Jews in international seaborne trade. Ashtor, *The Jews and the Mediterranean Economy: 10th–15th Centuries* (Variorum Reprints, London, 1983), ii–iii.

18 Raymond de Roover, "The *Cambium Maritimum* Contract according to the Genoese Notarial Records of the Twelfth and Thirteenth Centuries," in D. Herlihy, R.S. Lopez and Vsevolod Slassarev, eds., *Economy, Society and Government in Medieval Italy: Essays in Memory of Robert L. Reynolds* (Kent State University Press, 1969), 28, 29; de Roover, *Medici Bank*, 11; M. M. Postan, *Medieval Trade and Finance* (Cambridge, 1973), 13 ff; E.E. Power, "The Wool Trade in the Fifteenth Century," in E. Power and M.M. Postan, eds., *Studies in English Trade in the Fifteenth Century* (New York, Barnes & Noble, 1966), 64–68.

This limitation of usury law to straight loans is implicitly rejected in the Mishna[19] and, accordingly, rabbinic response to the development of the cambio is rather different than that of the Scholastics.[20] Among the earliest recorded examples of a cambio in halakhic literature is in a responsum of R. Isaac b. Sheshet Perfet (1326–1408).[21] This exchange contract was a *cambium maritimum* (a maritime cambio). In this type of cambio, the borrower utilized the capital that he borrowed to purchase goods which he personally accompanied aboard. The goal was to sell the goods at the foreign port. The loan would be repaid in the foreign currency under a pre-arranged exchange rate intended to return to the lender an amount in excess of what he had lent. The lender's profit, though, was not guaranteed; he did accept the risk of loss at sea.

In the Church's view, the risk accepted by the lender did not justify the interest payment.[22] As noted earlier, it was only the fact that the cambium was not considered a loan that saved it in the eyes of most Scholastics. From a halakhic perspective, however, this was a strange justification, indeed. In fact, under the halakhic view the only possible justification for this sort of transaction was the acceptance of risk by the lender.[23]

Accordingly, the question as presented to R. Isaac emphasizes the risk that the lender was taking; the currency exchange is only referred to once and is given no halakhic significance. The questioner sought guidance as to whether the risk acceptance was sufficient to justify the interest payment to the lender. R. Isaac's unequivocal response forbade the transaction; he con-

---

[19] Mishna Bava Metzia 5:1–2. As Professor Jacob Bazak points out in his careful review of sixteenth century sources, "Insurance Agreements for Sea Voyages (Cambium) in the Responsa Literature of the Sixteenth Century," *Sinai*, 75/1–2 (1974), 43–60, there are certain technical differences between straight loans and sales. I can not agree with him, though, that the responsa literature neatly divided cambios into loans (forbidden) and sales (permitted). He ignores, for instance, the size of the premium, which I take to be a crucial factor, at least for Maharashdam, Mabit and Alshekh.

[20] An extended discussion of the issue also can be found in Stephen M. Passamaneck, *Insurance in Rabbinic Law* (Edinborough, 1974), which contains a useful introduction, and detailed analyzes of various responsa relating to the halakhic viability of the cambio.

[21] *She'elot u-Teshuvot Rivash*, no. 308. In this responsum R. Isaac also discusses insuring the cargo with a third party, which he permits unreservedly. This appears to be the first halakhic reference to insurance in the modern sense, which developed as a result of the commercial revolution of the late thirteenth and early fourteenth centuries. Florence Edler de Roover, "Early Examples of Marine Insurance," *Journal of Economic History*, V (1945), 172–200.

[22] This is a central teaching of the papal canon *Naviganti* (1234) (*Corpus juris canonici, Decretales, Canon Naviganti of Gregory IX*, V, 19, 19). See, generally, John N. Noonan, Jr., *The Scholastic Analysis of Usury* (Cambridge, Harvard University Press, 1957).

[23] From the comments in de Roover, *Medici*, 11, it appears that the lay understanding of the Church's teaching was closer to the halakhic approach than to the Scholastic view.

cluded that the risk assumption, at least in this case, did not fall within the very narrow window suggested by some talmudic sources.

R. Samuel de Medina received numerous queries about cambio agreements, and his printed responsa return again and again to variations of the cambio. R. Samuel's consistently articulated view is that the cambio is completely forbidden, on a par with an explicit loan on interest (*ribbit ketsutsa*). He notes that other scholars felt that the cambio was objectionable only on the level of rabbinical prohibition, and that other scholars permitted cambio contracts, at least certain cambio types.[24] In addition, R. Samuel notes that "most of the merchants of Salonica trade and write cambios."[25] R. Samuel was, by then, the senior posek and communal leader of Salonica, but the use of the cambio was so widespread that he was obviously powerless to halt the practice. In fact, in one responsum (no. 70) he considers—though ultimately rejects—the possibility of justifying the use of cambio on the basis of its general acceptance as custom (*minhag*).

Responsum 220 contains other important historical nuggets, as well. R. Samuel relates that at the time that a sea trade route opened between Salonica and Egypt, presumably after the conquest of Egypt by the Ottomans in 1517, he learned from Salonica merchants who had been to Egypt, that the dayyan and rosh yeshiva in Egypt, R. David b. Solomon ibn Abi Zimra (better known by the acronym Radbaz) (1479–1573), permitted the use of cambios. R. Samuel, as is apparent from the language of his responsum, never saw Radbaz's responsa on the subject, which are quite explicit.

One cambio agreement cited in the responsum of Radbaz is similar to the cambio that R. Isaac b. Sheshet had forbidden.[26] Reuben borrowed money from Simeon which he used to purchase certain goods which Reuben was to carry abroad and attempt to sell. Simeon, who happened to accompany Reuben, accepted the full risk of loss at sea. Reuben was obligated to repay the principal, plus a pre-arranged premium, to Simeon, a certain number of days following the safe delivery of the goods to the foreign port. When the time came to pay, Reuben claimed, inter alia, that the arrangement was usurious.

Radbaz disagreed. He concluded that the arrangement violated neither biblical nor rabbinic norms, though he acknowledged that it did constitute

---

[24] *She'elot u-Teshuvot Maharashdam*, Yorah De'ah section number 220. The responsum was written after 1581 since R. Samuel adds "of blessed memory" when he mentions R. Joseph b. Lev who died in that year. R. Samuel himself died in 1589.

[25] Id.

[26] *She'elot u-Teshuvot Radbaz*, number 7. Professor Passamaneck, op. cit., argues (on page 40) that Radbaz accepted the view of Rivash. Responsum 7, however, suggests that Radbaz was far more willing to justify cambio arrangements.

an evasion of the usury prohibition. He notes that such cambios were commonly practiced by Jewish merchants. Radbaz does suggest that, for appearances' sake, two separate contracts be prepared, one for the loan, and a separate one referencing the premium in exchange for the acceptance of the sea risk.

R. Samuel, as we have seen, strenuously objected to this practice, calling it "a vulgar custom,"[27] and averring that the only disagreement among scholars was whether the arrangement was biblically prohibited, or only forbidden on the level of rabbinic structure. R. Samuel held, contrary to Radbaz, that breaking the transaction into two separate acts—1) Reuben borrowing money from Simeon, and 2) Simeon accepting legal responsibilities for the cargo en route in exchange for a premium—in no way solved the usury problem.

Citing talmudic and medieval authorities, R. Samuel noted that a borrower is not permitted to give any gift or consideration—such as free rental of a home—to the lender. Similarly, he reasoned, it would be impermissible for the borrower to rent a home from the lender at above market price; that would simply be a hidden interest payment for the loan. Similarly, paying a premium for the assumption of the risk of shipment in the cambio contract was simply hidden interest on the loan.

The amount of the premium that the lender is entitled to accept for the assumption of the risk is apparently crucial to R. Samuel's approach. In responsum 70 (Yoreh De'ah), for instance, Reuben borrowed money from Simeon and used it to buy goods. Simeon, the lender, agreed to accept the sea risk for the journey from Ancona to Salonica, in exchange for an unspecified premium (Responsum 221 references a premium of 20% per the term of the cambio. In responsum 218, the query refers to the practice of a 20% to 30% premium per the term of the agreement. In other words, if the cambio required repayment after six months, the annual premium could be as high as 60%.) Reuben, in responsum 70, acknowledged that he owed Simeon some premium for the assumption of risk, but argued that he should pay only the fair market value for insuring the journey. R. Samuel agreed.

However, it is important to note that R. Samuel did permit Simeon to collect the accustomed insurance premium. Any doubt on that score is resolved by examining the very next printed responsum, number 71 (Y.D.). There, in the absence of any proof that the premium was higher than the standard insurance rate, R. Samuel enforced a cambio agreement.

---

[27] *Maharashdam*, Y.D., number 70.

In light of that, Professor Passamaneck may have overstated the difference of opinion between R. Samuel and R. Moses di Trani on the appropriateness of using a cambio.[28] To be sure, in a responsum dealing with this issue, R. Moses concludes that the basic cambio arrangement does not violate halakhic norms even where (as it normally was) the cambio premium was clearly conditional upon the loan. However, he adds that this is so, "since he (the borrower) is not paying more than the suitable premium for the assumption of risk (by the lender)."[29] R. Moses would apparently agree with R. Samuel that a higher than standard premium would be forbidden on the ground of usury.

R. Moses Alshekh, another great scholar of the time, also accepted the basic view set out by R. Isaac b. Sheshet that the cambio was illegal because it was an attempt to conceal interest, and the premium charged for the assumption of liability was excessive. In responsum 2, for instance, he discusses a cambio in which the borrower agreed to a 28% return, whereas the market rate for insuring cargo was only 3%. Utilizing an analysis similar to that used by R. Samuel, R. Moses Alshekh ruled that the lender was not entitled to collect the cambio premium from the borrower.

Cambio agreements were still common among Jewish traders in the seventeenth century according to the testimony of R. Aaron b. Ḥayyim Abraham ha-Kohen Perahyah (d.1697), a successor of R. Samuel de Medina as chief rabbi of Salonica.[30] They eventually fade from the scene due, perhaps, to a variety of factors including the decline of Ottoman and Italian Jewries. The spread of the new *hetter iska* into the Mediterranean Jewish communities may also have lessened the dependance upon the cambio.[31] It is interesting to note, though, that a different type of exchange contract, the *mamran*, which received halakhic sanction, remained a popular method for Jewish credit transactions in Northern and Central Europe into the nineteenth century.[32]

---

28 Passamaneck, *Insurance*, 135.
29 *Mabit*, Vol. I, 6.
30 *Parah Mateh Aharon* (Amsterdam 1703), Part I, resp. 21.
31 See, e.g., *She'elot u-Teshuvot Ginat Veradim*, R. Abraham b. Mordecai Ha-Levi, 6:4.
32 *Mamran* contracts are exerpted in A. Gulak, *Otsar ha-Shetarot ha-Nehugim be-Yisrael* (Jerusalem 1926), 214 ff., and analyzed in Gulak, *Yesoday ha-Mishpat ha-Ivri* (Jerusalem, Dvir, 1923), pp. 142–145. Gulak traces the word *"mamran"* to the Latin *"memoriam,"* in the sense of record. It is no less plausible, according to Professor Gene Schramm of the University of Michigan, that *mamran* derives from the Hebrew *"temurah,"* or exchange. Abraham M. Fuss, "The Eastern European Shetar *Mamran* Revisited," in *Diné Israel* (Tel Aviv University, Vol. IV, 1973), LII–LXVII, summarizes the mechanics of the *mamran* and offers (courtesy of Professor Louis Feldman) yet another possible etymology: The Latin *membrana* (document).

13

Preventing Apostasy by Violating the Sabbath

Nahum Rakover[*]

Introduction

The question of whether it is permitted to violate Jewish law in order to rescue another from apostatizing to another faith raises the basic question of when it is permitted and when prohibited to violate the law in order to rescue another from a violation.[1] This question is dependent, to a great extent, upon reconciliation of certain discussions in the *Talmud*.

In the tractate *Shabbat* 4a, the *Tosafot* discuss a contradiction that arises from two talmudic passages concerning whether it is permitted to violate the law to rescue another from a violation. Whereas from the discussion in *Shabbat*, it appears that "We do not say to a person, transgress that your neighbor may benefit," in the tractate *Eruvin*, we find the principle that "People are willing to violate a minor prohibition in order to save another from a major prohibition."

The *Tosafot* propose various ways of resolving this contradiction. Two approaches restrict the source which **permits** one person to violate the law in order to rescue another from a violation. The third approach restricts the source that **prohibits** this:

(1) According to the first approach, the source that permits violation of a minor prohibition in order to rescue another from a major prohibition, applies only when the potential rescuer is **instrumental** in the other's transgression.

(2) According to the second approach, it is permitted to violate a prohibition only for the sake of an **important commandment** (*mitzvah rabbah*) or a commandment that relates to the **many** (*mitzvah derabbim*).

---

[*] Deputy Attorney-General, State of Israel; Professor of Jewish Law, Bar Ilan University.
[1] See Nahum Rakover, "Violation of the Law in Order to Preserve it," JLAS, VI 107ff. See also idem, "Hata Kedei sheTizkeh Atah O Ḥaverkha," *Tehumin*, XII (1991), 107ff.

(3) The third approach restricts the prohibition of violating the law in order to rescue another from a violation, to circumstances where the one to be rescued was guilty of a **wrongdoing**. Where the person to be rescued from transgression is guilty of no wrongdoing, however, it would be permitted to violate a commandment in order to rescue him.

The fact that the *Tosafot* offer three different resolutions of the contradictory passages poses the question of which approach is in fact operative. Is one permitted to rescue another from a violation only if the rescuer is instrumental in the other's potential violation of a prohibition? Or perhaps even if the rescuer was not instrumental in the other's potential violation it will be permitted to rescue him from violating an "important commandment." Or perhaps, it is **always** permitted except when the person to be rescued was actually guilty of some wrongdoing.

When considering the question of apostasy, in addition to clarifying which approach of the *Tosafot* is operative, we must ask whether apostasy falls into one of the categories discussed, or—owing to its seriousness—is a category unto itself and not subject at all to the approaches suggested by the *Tosafot*. Perhaps because of the severe penalty for apostasy or the fact that apostasy results in the apostate's complete alienation from the Jewish people, its status is unique among violations of Jewish law.

The Opinion of Rashba: The Sabbath May Not Be Violated

We open our discussion with a question put to Rashba[2] concerning a woman about to be coerced into apostasy.[3] Rashba was asked whether it is permitted to violate the Sabbath in order to rescue her. Rashba explains that the woman was removed forcibly from her home by a Jewish apostate and asks whether—according to the opinion that walking more than three *parsa'ot*[4] beyond the city limit violates a biblical prohibition—it is permitted to send a message on the Sabbath to her father, who lives in another city more than three *parsa'ot* away, and whether it is further permitted to bring him a government seal. Rashba wonders whether the case would be "like a possible danger to life, and thus constitute a basis for leniency (in permitting the Sabbath to be violated)."

---

2 *Resp. Rashba* VII:267.

3 See remarks of *Sefer Ḥasidim* (ed. *Mekitzei Nirdamim*) 125, concerning one who sees another who is about to apostatize—that it is desirable even to cast down a Torah scroll in order to prevent the many from an "**important** violation."

4 Sing. *parsah*; usually rendered "parsang" or "Persian mile." One *parsah* is believed to equal either 3,840 or 4,800 meters. Accordingly, three *parsa'ot* would equal either 11,520 or 14,400 meters.

Rashba's final question, "Would this be like a possible danger to life and thus constitute a basis for leniency...?" requires clarification. Is Rashba suggesting that apostasy is equivalent to loss of life[5] and that it is, therefore, permitted to violate the Sabbath to rescue a person from apostasy as it is permitted to violate the Sabbath to save human life? Or perhaps Rashba's question concerns the following "uncertainty:" just as in the case of danger to life, where the Sabbath is violated even when the danger is not certain, so too in the case of apostasy, the Sabbath is to be violated even when the danger is not certain—although apostasy is not equivalent to loss of life. The second way of interpreting Rashba may be supported by the wording of *Beit Yosef*,[6] who in quoting Rashba writes: "Does this uncertainty take precedence over observance of the Sabbath as uncertain danger to life overrides the Sabbath?"

Rashba, however, does not discuss this aspect of the question in his response. He responds rather that violation of the Sabbath does not appear to be permitted in this case, since rescuing a person from sin does not override the Sabbath. Thus, from Rashba's answer, it seems that rescue from apostasy is simply rescue from sin, and not equivalent to protecting human life.[7]

Rashba bases himself on the discussion in *Shabbat*, where it is concluded that Jewish law does not operate on the principle of "Transgress that your neighbor may benefit." Rashba adds that the authorization for one person to commit a minor violation in order to rescue another from a major violation applies only when the potential rescuer is ***instrumental*** in the other's transgression.[8] Clearly, Rashba does not take the view that "Transgress that your neighbor may benefit" does in fact apply unless the person to be rescued is guilty of a wrongdoing. Had this indeed been Rashba's view, he could have permitted violation of the Sabbath in order to rescue the woman from apostasy. The woman herself had done no wrong![9] On the other hand, Rashba does not take the other approach of the *Tosafot*. The *Tosafot*, it will be re-

---

5 It may be that where a person about to commit a transgression stands to incur capital punishment for his act—such as when he is warned by witnesses that the act he is about to perform is a capital offense—Rashba will indeed consider prevention of the transgression equivalent to protecting human life.

6 *Beit Yosef*, *Oraḥ Ḥayyim* 306.

7 See note 10 below.

8 Cf. Rashba's remarks in *She'elot uTeshuvot haMeyuḥasot laRamban* 252. There also, Rashba bases his opinion on the distinction whether the potential rescuer was instrumental in the serious transgression.

9 But see remarks of R. Ya'akov Reischer, author of *Shevut Ya'akov* I:16, cited below. R. Reischer understands Rashba to distinguish between a potential transgressor guilty of wrongdoing, and a potential transgressor who has done no wrong.

called, permitted transgression to rescue a person when an "important commandment" (*mitzvah rabbah*) is involved. Rashba, on the other hand, makes no mention at all of such a possibility[10] and does not assert that the woman is not to be rescued from apostasy, because rescue from apostasy is not an "important commandment." Thus, where an "important commandment" is involved, it is conceivable that Rashba would permit violation of the Sabbath.

R. Yosef Karo Disagrees, Permitting the Sabbath To Be Violated in the Case Entertained by Rashba

R. Yosef Karo, after citing Rashba's responsum in *Beit Yosef*,[11] notes that "in the first chapter of *Shabbat*, the *Tosafot* rule as does Rashba at the beginning of his response." Also concerning the *Tosafot*, R. Karo notes that afterward, for the commandment of procreation ("Be fruitful and multiply"), they permitted a violation, as this is "an important commandment." Moreover, R. Karo continues in an additional attempt at reconciling the discussions in *Shabbat* and *Eruvin*, the *Tosafot* write that only when the person to be rescued is guilty of wrongdoing do we not say "transgress that your neighbor may benefit;" however, when the person to be rescued has done no wrong, the *Tosafot* permit violation of a minor commandment in order to prevent another from violating a major one.

---

10 *Bi'urei haGra*, *Oraḥ Ḥayyim* 306:26, explains that Rashba is consistent with his understanding of the passage in *Shabbat*. There, Rashba does not consider releasing a person who is half slave and half free to be a violation of a biblical commandment. Rashba is thus not constrained (as are the *Tosafot*) to conclude that authorization to release the "half slave" is based on the principle that a relatively minor commandment may be violated for the sake of observing an important commandment.

R. Shaul Yisraeli in his article "*Piku'aḥ Nefesh beSakanah Ruḥanit*," *Teḥumin* II (1981) 27ff. at p. 33, suggests that the debate between Rashba and the *Tosafot* is based on a difference of opinion concerning the source for authorization to violate the Sabbath in order to protect human life. For Rashba, the source is the Leviticus 18:5, "And you shall observe my statutes and my laws: he who observes them shall **live by them**; I am the Lord"—the verse expounded in the Talmud by Shemu'el: "He shall live by them and not die by them." For the *Tosafot*, however, the source is Exodus 31:13, "And the children of Israel shall observe the Sabbath . . ."—which R. Shimon son of Menasiah expounds: "Violate one Sabbath for him, that he may observe many" (see *Yoma* 85b). For the *Tosafot*, then, the source is concerned primarily with spiritual rescue. Therefore, when an important commandment is involved, violation of a relatively minor one will be appropriate.

R. Yisraeli makes the same point in his article, "*haAliyah miRussia keGiderei Piku'aḥ Nefesh*," *Torah She-Be-Al Peh* XXXII (1991), 26ff., from p. 28. See also R. Avraham Sherman, "*Hilkhot Piku'aḥ Nefesh beSakanah Ruḥanit*," *Torah She-Be-Al Peh* XXV (1984), 96ff.

11 *Beit Yosef*, *Oraḥ Ḥayyim* 306. *Beit Yosef* was written by R. Yosef Karo (1488–1575), author of *Shulḥan Arukh*.

From here, R. Yosef Karo concludes that if rescue can indeed be permitted on the basis of an important commandment, "there is no more important commandment than rescuing the woman from being frightened into apostatizing." R. Karo further asserts that if not having done wrong is a basis for permitting a transgression in such cases, since the woman under discussion had done no wrong, it is permitted and obligatory to violate the Sabbath for her. R. Karo adds that where a person is not willing to violate the Sabbath in such a case, the court compels him to, as we find in the case of a half slave, whose owner can be compelled to free him on behalf of an "important commandment," such as procreation. It is even permitted to violate a Sabbath prohibition of biblical origin, since by comparison to apostasy, where the woman will violate the Sabbath for the rest of her life, such a prohibition is considered minor.

In *Shulḥan Arukh*[12] as well R. Yosef Karo rules that it is not only permitted but obligatory to violate the Sabbath to prevent apostasy (though in *Shulḥan Arukh*, R. Karo does not mention the basis for this ruling).

A Contradiction in the Opinion of Rema

Ascertaining the opinion of Rema in this matter is by no means straightforward. In response to R. Yosef Karo's ruling in *Shulḥan Arukh* (chapter 306),[13] Rema provides only a reference, "See chapter 328, paragraph 10 below."[14] There, in chapter 328, paragraph 10, we find: "When someone commits an important transgression (*aveirah gedolah*) under duress,[15] we do not violate the Sabbath in order to rescue him, see the end of chapter 306 above." What is the meaning of this comment? Does Rema wish to rule against R. Yosef Karo's decision? Does his term "important transgression" (*aveirah gedolah*) include apostasy? Is this why he refers the reader of chapter 306 to chapter

---

[12] *Shul. Ar. Oraḥ Ḥayyim* 306:14. See also *Bi'urei haGra*, ad loc., 26. According to *Bi'urei haGra*, it is not permitted unless the commandment is an important commandment **and** the potential transgressor has done no wrong. Thus, it is permissible to violate the Sabbath only in cases similar to the one under discussion where the woman was taken from her home forcibly and bears no guilt. This, however, is not the case described in *Shul. Ar. Oraḥ Ḥayyim* 328:10. There, although the commandment is an important one, the Sabbath may not be violated, "since there is no commandment more important than the Sabbath." *Bi'urei haGra* goes on to explain that only in a case such as that described in *Oraḥ Ḥayyim* 306:14, where violation of the Sabbath may succeed in returning the person to the Jewish people, do we not say that there is no commandment more important than the Sabbath.

[13] Rema, *Shul. Ar. Oraḥ Ḥayyim* 306:14.

[14] However, in the Cracow (1570) edition of *Shulḥan Arukh*, this reference does not appear. See R. Gavri'el Goldberg, "Nusaḥ haShulḥan Arukh veHagahot haRema," *Tzefunot* II:4 (Tammuz 1990) 87.

[15] See note 24 below.

328? If so, why does Rema refer the reader of chapter 328 back to chapter 306, where he has only a reference? (It is not clear, however, whether this reference was written by Rema himself or is a later addition.)

Some authorities have suggested correcting the text of Rema's comment in chapter 328 to read, "When someone is being forced to commit an important transgression (*aveirah gedolah*), on **whether** we violate the Sabbath in order to rescue him, see the end of chapter 306 above."[16] Such a correction would entail changing the Hebrew word *ein* (אין) to *im* (אם). This approach is problematic, however. If we accept it, Rema's comment in chapter 328 contains no ruling, only a reference to R. Yosef Karo's ruling in chapter 306. If so, why does Rema refer the reader of chapter 306 to chapter 328? (It should also be noted in this context that the text as it appears in contemporary editions of *Shulḥan Arukh* is the same text that appears in the very first printing of *Shulḥan Arukh* with Rema's comments.)

Other authorities suggest that Rema does not agree with R. Yosef Karo but rules, rather, according to the opinion of Rashba.[17] This approach is contradicted, however, by Rema's own comments in his work *Darkhei Moshe* on *Tur*. Rema's remarks are not found in the version of *Darkhei Moshe* printed in contemporary editions of *Tur*. They are to be found, however, in the full text of *Darkhei Moshe*, the *Darkhei Moshe haArokh*. There,[18] Rema writes on chapter 306, "Here is where *Beit Yosef* treats the matter of whether it is permitted to violate the Sabbath in order to rescue a person from transgression; it is relevant to chapter 328. See what I have written there." Indeed, in *Darkhei Moshe haArokh* on chapter 328, we find that Rema quotes *Beit Yosef* in full and expresses no reservations.

One is Obliged to Sacrifice His Life Rather than Apostatize; Thus Rescue from Apostasy is Rescue from Death

An interesting distinction between apostatizing, on the one hand, and other transgressions, on the other, is suggested by R. Mordekhai Yafeh, author of

---

16 See R. Yom Tov Lipman Heller's comments on *Levush* in *Malbushei Yom Tov*, *Oraḥ Ḥayyim* 328:13 (R. Heller is the author of *Tosefot Yom Tov*).

17 See the reference accompanying Rema's comment on *Shul. Ar. Oraḥ Ḥayyim* 328:10: "*Beit Yosef* in the name of Rashba." See also *Resp. Shevut Ya'akov* I:16. See also comments of R. Shemu'el Landau in a responsum appearing in *Noda biYehudah*, *Mahadura Tinyana*, *Even haEzer* 37. R. Landau mentions that in chapter 328, paragraph 10, Rema rules according to the opinion of Rashba. R. Landau refers the reader to *Taz* 306:5 and *Magen Avraham* 306:29 (*Taz* and *Magen Avraham*, however, do not write that Rema rules according to the opinion of Rashba; they rather explain Rema as taking a restrictive approach to the opinion of the *Tosafot*).

18 *Darkhei Moshe haArokh*, *Oraḥ Ḥayyim* 306, ad fin.

Levush.[19] R. Yafeh offers a novel explanation[20] that authorization to violate the Sabbath in the case of the woman about to be forced into idolatry is based on the fact that a person in such circumstances will be obliged to sacrifice his life rather than submit. Rescuing a person from idolatry, therefore, rescues him from death. The same principle applies equally to all other commandments which one is obliged to sacrifice his life rather than transgress.

One Forced to Commit Any Other Violation—It is Not Permitted to Transgress in Order to Rescue Him

In chapter 328,[21] the author of Levush repeats the same idea, asserting that one does not rescue a person who violates Jewish law under duress when rescue entails performing another transgression. When a person performs a forbidden act under duress, he is not held responsible for violating the law. For R. Yafeh, the basis for authorization to transgress in order to save a person from idolatry is not because doing so is **similar** to saving human life, but rather because it is **actually** saving human life, since one is obliged to sacrifice his life rather than violate the prohibition.

The Author of Malbushei Yom Tov Disagrees: Rescue is Not Permitted on the Basis of Death for Violation, But Rather on the Basis of the Persistence of the Prohibition

The author of *Malbushei Yom Tov*,[22] a commentary on *Levush*, rejects R. Yafeh's opinion. *Malbushei Yom Tov* holds that unless the violation is **persistent**—as is apostasy—the Sabbath may not be violated even to rescue a person from violating one of the three cardinal violations for which he is obliged to sacrifice his life rather than transgress. Violation of the Sabbath[23] is permitted only to rescue a person from apostasy or similar circumstances, in which he will live in violation of Jewish law for the rest of his life. In such a case, violation of the Sabbath is indeed considered "insignificant" by comparison. According to this opinion, it is the **persistence** of a violation that

---

[19] R. Mordekhai Yafeh (1530–1612) held rabbinic positions in Prague and Posen.

[20] *Levush, Oraḥ Ḥayyim* 306:14.

[21] *Levush, Oraḥ Ḥayyim* 328:13.

[22] *Malbushei Yom Tov* was written by R. Yom Tov Lipman Heller (1579–1654), an important rabbinic authority of the seventeenth century. R. Heller held rabbinic posts in Nikolsburg (Mikulov, Moravia) and Vienna.

[23] *Malbushei Yom Tov* on *Levush Oraḥ Ḥayyim* 328:13.

renders it severe and provides the basis for authorizing a one-time violation[24] of the Sabbath. However, the author of *Malbushei Yom Tov* concludes his comment with the assertion that the matter requires further study.

One Whose Transgression—Even Apostasy—Is Performed Under Duress Is Not to Be Rescued by means of Another Transgression

The author of *Bah* takes a different approach.[25] He cites the apparent contradiction between the two rulings: In chapter 306 of *Oraḥ Ḥayyim*, R. Yosef Karo rules that the Sabbath **must be violated**, when such a violation is required to rescue a person from apostasy, whereas in chapter 328, paragraph 10, Rema rules that "When someone commits an important transgression (*aveirah gedolah*) under duress, we do not violate the Sabbath in order to rescue him." "Since chapter 306 contains a reference to chapter 328, and chapter 328 contains a reference to chapter 306," *Bah* asserts, "both must be binding."

In his attempt to reconcile this contradiction, *Bah* distinguishes between one who violates the law under duress and one who violates the law willingly. When a person's violation is not committed under duress (but he is not considered guilty of wrongdoing, such as when we fear that a person will be frightened into apostatizing), it is permitted to violate the Sabbath to rescue him from idolatry. This is because rescue is itself an "important commandment." However, since the law exempts those who transgress under duress, when the transgression is performed under duress, even if the transgression is idolatry, the Sabbath may not be violated, since the law holds one who transgresses under duress guiltless.

We have already encountered the idea that the Sabbath may not be violated to rescue one who transgresses under duress, in the opinion of R. Mordekhai Yafeh, author of *Levush*. However, while R. Yafeh applied this principle to the violation of all commandments **except the prohibition of idolatry**, *Bah*, on the other hand, applies it to the prohibition of idolatry as well.

---

[24] See comments of *Bi'urei haGra*, *Oraḥ Ḥayyim* 306:14:26, summarized in note 12 above. The *Gaon* of Vilna seems to distinguish between apostasy and "an important transgression," as does *Levush*; however, The *Gaon*'s reason for permitting rescue from apostasy is "in order to return the person to the Jewish people," not the person's obligation to give up his life rather than transgress. Thus, the *Gaon* of Vilna seems to agree with *Malbushei Yom Tov*. In *Ḥayyei Adam* 68:12, R. Avraham Danzig rules that if a person is being forced to abandon the Jewish people and convert to another faith, every Jew is commanded to violate the Sabbath (if necessary) to save him.

[25] *Bah*, *Oraḥ Ḥayyim* 306, *ad fin*. See also note 34 below.

R. Yafeh, it will be recalled, held that where a person is compelled to commit an act of idolatry, we are commanded to rescue him, since he is obliged to sacrifice his life rather than transgress. *Bah* attributes no significance to the fact that one compelled to violate the prohibition of idolatry is obliged to sacrifice his life. In explaining his view, *Bah* asserts that even an idolatrous act, when performed under duress, is not considered a transgression, since the law exempts all transgressions performed under duress.

Since *Bah* holds that in an instance of duress one is exempt from transgressing the prohibition of idolatry, it is not entirely clear how *Bah* will explain the obligation to sacrifice one's life rather than perform an idolatrous act. Perhaps the commandment to sacrifice one's life rather than perform an act of idolatry is not based on the fact that an act of idolatry performed under duress is considered a violation, but rather upon an obligation to sanctify God's name under such circumstances. According to this reasoning, *Bah* would argue that although one who commits an act of idolatry rather than sacrificing his life fails to discharge his obligation to sanctify God's name, the law does not hold him responsible for violating the prohibition of idolatry. Since for the idolatrous act itself, the person is exempt—as he would be for any violation committed under duress—the Sabbath may not be violated on his behalf.

Nevertheless, where there is a chance that the person **will** sacrifice his life rather than violating the prohibition of idolatry, *Bah* will apparently agree with the author of *Levush* that the Sabbath may be violated in order to rescue him. This seems clear from *Bah*'s final remark that "the Sabbath is not to be violated to rescue one who would commit a violation under duress **as long as there is no danger to human life**."[26]

---

[26] *Mishnah Berurah* 328:31, quotes the ruling of *Levush*, but writes that if it seems that a person forced to commit one of the three cardinal transgressions will sacrifice his life, **it may be** that one must violate the Sabbath (if necessary) to rescue him. In *Iggerot Moshe, Yoreh De'ah* III:90, R. Moshe Feinstein discusses this opinion of *Mishnah Berurah*, offering a somewhat difficult explanation: Why does *Mishnah Berurah* write "it may be?" Since a person forced to commit a cardinal sin is **obliged** to sacrifice his life in order to sanctify God's name, there may be no obligation to rescue him in this case, since rescue will prevent sanctification of God's name. On a weekday, rescue **is** mandated, since, given the possible obligation to sanctify God's name, it is not certain whether it is obligatory or forbidden to rescue, and in situations of doubt concerning protection of human life, rescue is mandated. On the Sabbath, however, there is an additional factor: the prohibition of violating the Sabbath. Thus it is only "possible" (and not certain) that one must rescue on the Sabbath, since if rescue is not obligatory, it is forbidden (when it entails violation of the Sabbath). However, R. Feinstein concludes, it appears that violation of the Sabbath **is** mandated, since even when danger to life is not certain, the Sabbath must be violated to protect human life.

Rescue from Apostasy Takes Preference over Saving Human Life

Whereas Rashba does not discuss whether rescue from apostasy is equivalent to saving human life, we can nevertheless infer from his comments that he does not accept any such analogy. If he did, he would have permitted violation of the Sabbath in the case under discussion.

In an opinion of R. David haLevi, author of *Turei Zahav* (*Taz*),[27] however, we do find just this analogy. Trying to reconcile Rema's two comments, R. David haLevi distinguishes—as does his contemporary, the author of *Malbushei Yom Tov*—between apostasy under duress and a one-time transgression. However, in explaining the Rema's ruling, he adds a point not found in the opinion of *Malbushei Yom Tov*. *Taz* opens[28] by noting that in chapter 328, paragraph 10, Rema rules: "When someone commits an important transgression (*aveirah gedolah*) under duress, we do not violate the Sabbath in order to rescue him," while in chapter 306, where *Shulḥan Arukh* mandates violation of the Sabbath under such circumstances, Rema inserts a reference to chapter 328, paragraph 10. It would seem that Rema's ruling in chapter 328, paragraph 10, contradicts R. Yosef Karo's ruling in chapter 306, though Rema on chapter 306 issues no objection and merely refers the reader to chapter 328. *Taz* also notes that according to *Beit Yosef*, Rashba and the *Tosafot* disagree on whether it is permitted to violate the Sabbath in order to prevent apostasy.

To this problem, *Taz* responds that where apostasy is involved, as in chapter 306, and the potential apostate will remain an apostate (*mumar*) for the rest of his life, the *Tosafot* hold that the potential apostate must be rescued even if rescue requires violation of the Sabbath, **for this takes precedence over saving of human life**.[29] This rule does not apply, however, to the situation in chapter 328, where a person transgresses under duress on a one-time basis. Since in such cases the person is exempt of all responsibility for his act, the Sabbath is not to be violated to prevent a transgression.

---

[27] R. David haLevi lived from 1586 to 1667.

[28] *Taz, Oraḥ Ḥayyim* 306:5.

[29] *Resp. Besamim Rosh* 301, suggests a new perspective, asserting that the obligation to sacrifice one's life rather than violate a commandment is governed by the laws that govern the administration of capital punishment. As is known, authority to adjudicate capital matters ended once *semikhah* (full judicial authority originally granted to Moses and passed on to selected individuals in each generation) was no longer granted. Since that time, no one has the authority to sacrifice his life rather than violate a commandment. (The author of *Besamim Rosh* goes on to explain a case recorded in the *Talmud* [*Avodah Zarah* 27b], where persons did sacrifice their lives, as being an extraordinary decision [*hora'at sha'ah*], applicable only in that specific case, and not governed by ordinary legal principles.

From the opinion of *Taz* we understand that violation of the Sabbath is mandated to rescue a person from apostasy, even though once the person apostatizes, he will violate the commandments intentionally. Explaining this opinion, *Taz* asserts, "This takes precedence over saving human life."[30]

It is worthwhile examining *Taz*'s opinion that the Sabbath may not be violated for the sake of rescuing a person from transgressions other than apostasy. *Taz* advances two reasons: 1) In cases of duress, the Torah exempts the transgressor of all responsibility. 2) Since a person under duress transgresses but once, there is no reason to suspect that he will transgress again.

Explaining why the Sabbath may not be violated to prevent transgressions other than apostasy, *Taz* adds a new dimension to the reasoning that in cases of duress, the law exempts the transgressor of all responsibility. *Taz* emphasizes that the transgression occurs but once. Thus, the justification for not violating the Sabbath is based on two factors. From here, it might be possible to infer that if one of these factors does not apply, *Taz* would permit the Sabbath to be violated in order to rescue a person from transgression, **even when the transgression is performed under duress**. So, for instance, where a person is compelled, under duress, to transgress a commandment permanently, *Taz* might be willing to permit violation of the Sabbath to rescue him from transgression. On the other hand, what will be the opinion of *Taz* if a person stands to transgress of his own free will, not under duress? Here the reason, that one who transgresses under duress is exempt of all responsibility, does not apply. Perhaps *Taz* would permit violation of the Sabbath to rescue such a person.

Saving of Human Life Is Also For the Sake of Observing the Commandments

The parallel between protecting human life and rescue from apostasy appears in the opinion of *Magen Avraham*[31] as well. *Magen Avraham*, however, **does not** assert that rescue from apostasy is the equivalent of saving a life. *Magen Avraham* reasons that in rescue from apostasy, the principle, "It is preferable to violate one Sabbath for him, so that he may observe many Sabbaths," applies just as it does in protection of human life. Basing himself on this principle, *Magen Avraham* explains, as did *Beit Yosef*, that by comparison to apostasy and violation of the Sabbath for the rest of a person's life, one

---

[30] See Maharatz Ḥayyot, *Darkhei Hora'ah, Kol Sifrei Maharatz Ḥayyot*, VOL. I, P. 278.
[31] *Magen Avraham, Oraḥ Ḥayyim* 306:29.

violation[32] of the Sabbath is a minor matter.[33] Since persistent violation is the basis for authorization to violate the Sabbath, *Magen Avraham* concludes that if the person is to be compelled to commit even an act of idolatry just once, a Sabbath prohibition of biblical origin may not be violated in order to prevent the transgression. According to the *Talmud* (*Eruvin* 69b), *Magen Avraham* notes, violation of the Sabbath is tantamount to idolatry. So does *Magen Avraham* explain Rema's two comments on *Shulḥan Arukh*. (*Magen Avraham* also notes that Rashi, on *Ḥulin* 5a declares violation of the Sabbath to be graver than idolatry; however, *Magen Avraham* wonders what Rashi's source might be for such an assertion.) Further on in his comments, *Magen Avraham* takes exception to the opinion of *Bah*.[34] *Bah* holds that where a person stands to violate the law under duress, the Sabbath may not be violated to rescue him, since the law does not hold persons responsible for transgressions performed under duress. According to *Bah*, the question of violating the Sabbath is relevant only to rescue of one who stands to

---

32 See R. Shaul Yisraeli, "*haAliyah miRussia keGiderei Piku'aḥ Nefesh*," *Torah She-Be-Al Peh* XXXII (1991), 29ff., on the difference between the opinion of *Taz* and the opinion of *Magen Avraham* concerning the basis for the ruling.

33 *Magen Avraham* mentions *Beit Yosef* in this connection. *Beit Yosef*, however, states only that violation of the Sabbath is a minor matter when compared to apostasy. *Beit Yosef* does not mention the talmudic principle, "It is preferable to violate one Sabbath for him, so that he may observe many Sabbaths," which is stated with regard to protection of human life.

On whether authorization to violate the Sabbath is based upon this principle or on Leviticus 18:5, "And you shall observe my statutes and my laws: he who observes them shall **live by them**; I am the Lord;" and the ramifications of the two different sources, see note 10 above.

34 For further consideration of these issues, see R. David Pardo, *Resp. Mikhtam leDavid*, *Oraḥ Ḥayyim* 8 and 9 (the responsum of R. David Pardo). See also *Resp. Ḥatam Sofer, Even haEzer* 1:36, s.v. *Al Devar Gomer*, ad fin.: "*Magen Avraham* takes exception to *Bah*'s opinion. In my humble opinion, we do not permit a person to sin in order to rescue another from transgressing under duress, since in instances of duress, the transgressor is not held responsible."

See also R. Moshe Feinstein, *Iggerot Moshe, Oraḥ Ḥayyim* I:116, p. 180. R. Feinstein agrees strongly with the opinion of *Bah*, explaining that in the disagreement between Rashba and the *Tosafot*, we rule in accordance with the (strict) opinion of Rashba: only where the potential rescuer was instrumental in the other's transgression do we permit him to violate the Sabbath to rescue the potential transgressor from sin. According to R. Feinstein, we do not accept the opinion of the *Tosafot*, who hold that rescue is permitted **whenever** the potential transgressor is guilty of no wrongdoing. The ruling will be different, however, in a case involving violation of the Sabbath where it is feared that the person will be frightened into apostatizing and he will subsequently commit many serious offenses willingly. Here we rule according to the opinion of the *Tosafot*, that the Sabbath is to be violated if necessary to prevent the apostasy. These two rulings, R. Feinstein explains, do not contradict each other, as *Bah* has shown (see further remarks of R. Moshe Feinstein in the same responsum). See also R. Shaul Yisraeli, "*haAliyah miRussia keGiderei Piku'aḥ Nefesh*," op. cit. (note 10 above), p. 31.

See also *Resp. Sha'ali Tziyyon* 3:3, where the author attempts to justify *Bah*'s opinion. See also R. Moshe Feinstein, *Iggerot Moshe, Oraḥ Ḥayyim* I (ed. 1959), responsum 116.

transgress willingly. To this approach, *Magen Avraham* responds that chapter 328 of *Shulḥan Arukh* deals with persons who would transgress willingly. *Magen Avraham* cites a comment of Rema on chapter 329, paragraph 8. There Rema states: "See chapter 306 on whether it is permitted to violate the Sabbath in order to rescue one who [stands to transgress] under duress." From here it is clear that Rema believes chapter 306 to be dealing with transgression under duress.

Magen Avraham goes on to discuss whether authorization to violate the Sabbath will apply where a minor is being forced into apostasy. On the one hand, there is no biblical mandate to prevent minors from violating the law. On the other hand, the principle, "It is preferable to violate one Sabbath for him, so that he may observe many Sabbaths," would seem to apply in the case of a minor as well.[35]

Authorization to Violate the Sabbath to Prevent Apostasy in the Absence of Duress

R. Shemu'el ben R. David haLevi,[36] a student of *Taz* and author of *Naḥalat Shivah*, does not discuss the case of one who apostatizes under duress, but rather the case of one who apostatizes willingly.[37] R. Shemu'el also finds prevention of apostasy comparable to protecting human life, as we saw in *Taz*, and in R. Shemu'el's opinion, even though Rashba does not rule this way, "neither did Rashba decide to prohibit this, but rather concluded that the matter requires further study." However, R. Shemu'el's main innovation is his opinion that it is permitted to violate the Sabbath even to prevent a person from apostatizing **willingly**.

R. Shemu'el was asked concerning a father whose son disappeared. The father subsequently heard that the son had apostatized to Islam and fled. Thus, the father asked whether it is permitted to violate the Sabbath and pursue his son, on the chance that he may persuade him to return. Ruling that it is indeed permitted to violate the Sabbath in order to try to rescue the young man from apostasy, R. Shemu'el ben R. David haLevi makes the following points:

---

[35] See R. David Pardo, *Resp. Mikhtam leDavid, Oraḥ Ḥayyim* 8. See also R. Avraham Sherman, op. cit. (note 10 above), p. 102. See also *Magen Avraham*'s further comments, loc. cit., concerning walking beyond the distance permitted on the Sabbath in order to avenge one's father.

[36] R. Shemu'el ben R. David haLevi held rabbinic positions in Germany. He was born some time after 1624 and died in 1681.

[37] Responsa at the end of *Naḥalat Shiva*, responsum no. 83.

i. It is permitted to violate the Sabbath to save the life of one who is sick. In such case, we do not apply the principle, "We do not say to a person, transgress that your neighbor may benefit." Rather it is indeed permitted to violate the Sabbath for another's benefit.

ii. In the case of a sick person, it cannot be argued that it is permitted to violate the Sabbath on his behalf because he has not transgressed. "There is no death without sin;" hence, if a person's life is in danger, he cannot be guiltless. Thus, rescue is mandated even when the person to be rescued is guilty of wrongdoing.[38]

iii. If it is argued that apostasy is not equivalent to physical death and therefore not subject to the same principles, we must conclude *a fortiori* that it is mandated to violate the Sabbath in order to rescue a person from apostasy. Loss of life is only loss of life on this earth; apostasy, however, brings eternal death—loss of the world to come.[39]

iv. Rescue from apostasy is an "important commandment." As R. Yosef Karo writes in *Beit Yosef*: by comparison to apostasy, violation of the Sabbath is a minor offense.

v. "Violate one Sabbath that he may observe many"—one of the reasons invoked to justify violation of the Sabbath in order to protect human life—applies equally here.

vi. Even if the person has done wrong, as in the case of one who has apostatized willingly, his transgression can be considered as having practically occurred under duress or as the result of being incited to transgress, for he was in the grip of the human drive to engage in idolatry. In a short time he will regret his transgression. Thus being the case, R. Shemu'el argues, why should they not rescue him from apostasy?[40]

R. Ya'akov Reischer Disagrees: The Sabbath May Not Be Violated to Rescue One Who Apostatizes Willingly, and Rescue from Sin Is Not Equivalent to Rescue from Death

A serious campaign against the reasoning of the author of *Naḥalat Shiva* is undertaken by R. Ya'akov Reischer,[41] author of *Shevut Ya'akov*. R. Reischer was asked[42] concerning a case of one who intended to cause significant dam-

---

38 On this issue, see the objection of R. Ya'akov Reischer, author of *Shevut Ya'akov* below.
39 Holtzer, *Yelamed Da'at*, p. 298, discusses this line of reasoning.
40 Cf. *Tosafot, Shabbat* 4a, s.v. *veKhi Omerim*. See also my "Hata Kedei sheTizkeh, etc.," op. cit. (note 1 above), p. 120. See also R. Yisrael Aryeh Zalmanovitch, *Ḥayyei Nefesh* I, Introduction 22, and p. 16ff., concerning *Shevut Ya'akov*'s objections to the opinion of *Naḥalat Shiva*.
41 R. Ya'akov Reischer (d. 1733) was born in Prague, where he served as a rabbinic judge. He later became the rabbi of Reischer (Galicia), Worms, and Metz.
42 *Resp. Shevut Ya'akov* I:16.

age to the Jewish community by surrendering Jewish property to the non-Jewish authorities. The only conceivable way of preventing this was for one of the communal leaders to travel, in violation of the Sabbath, to try to dissuade the person from his evil intention. A Jewish legal authority had authorized the violation, and R. Reischer was later asked whether the authorization was correct.

R. Reischer rejects the ruling on two counts:

First and foremost, we do not violate the Sabbath in order to prevent loss of property.

Second, perhaps it will be argued that the Sabbath may be violated to protect a Jew for becoming a *moser*—one who surrenders the person or property of his fellow Jews to the non-Jewish authorities—and that becoming a *moser* is equivalent to apostasy. If this is the argument, we certainly do not say, "Transgress that your neighbor may benefit," since in the present case, the potential *moser* himself is guilty of wrongdoing.

Having established his basis for rejecting the ruling, R. Reischer suggests that perhaps the ruling was based upon the opinion of R. Shemu'el ben R. David haLevi, author of *Naḥalat Shiva*. R. Reischer proceeds to refute this opinion, adamantly asserting that R. Shemu'el ben R. David haLevi has taken it upon himself to rule against the opinions of Rashba, the *Tosafot*, and *Shulḥan Arukh*, not on the basis of law, but rather on the basis of his own faulty reasoning.

As mentioned, the author of *Naḥalat Shiva* bases his reasoning on the authorization to violate the Sabbath in order to protect human life and the principle "Violate one Sabbath that he may observe many." R. Reischer does not accept *Naḥalat Shiva*'s argument that there is no death without sin, and hence one who's life is in danger cannot be considered guiltless. "Sin," in this well known principle, R. Reischer asserts, refers to sin that is unintentional (*shogeg*). The situation is entirely different when (as in the case under discussion) a person is guilty of intentional wrongdoing. When one does transgresses intentionally, he intentionally harms his own soul.[43]

R. Reischer similarly rejects *Naḥalat Shiva*'s *a fortiori* argument that if it is permitted to violate the Sabbath in order to preserve life in this world, it must certainly be permitted to violate the Sabbath to rescue a person from eternal death. If it is argued that, "it is worse to cause a person to transgress

---

[43] But see *Mishnah Berurah* 254, *Sha'ar haTziyyun* 40. The author of *Mishnah Berurah* holds that "wrongdoing" includes *shogeg* (i.e., unintentional wrongdoing), where the person should have taken precautions against finding himself in a situation where he would be likely to transgress. For further discussion of R. Ya'akov Reischer's opinion, see *Yelamed Da'at*, p. 295ff.; and R. Yisrael Aryeh Zalmanovitch, *Ḥayyei Nefesh*, I, Introduction, and p. 16ff.

than to kill him," it is also true that even as regards extremely serious transgressions, one is permitted to transgress rather than give up his life. Thus, protection of life has weightier status than rescue from sin. When a person knowingly forfeits his life in the world to come, we certainly do not say, "Transgress that your neighbor may benefit." For he has wronged himself by choosing death over life.[44] Every man has two paths open to him, and the Bible commands us to choose life. As to the principle that one who causes another to sin is worse than one who kills him, this is simply a statement that the penalty for causing another to sin is a severe one.

Thus, R. Reischer concludes, the ruling to permit violation of the Sabbath in the case under discussion was a serious error.[45]

Support for the approach that restricts violation of the Sabbath exclusively to cases where apostasy is under duress and does not permit violation of the Sabbath to rescue one who would apostatize willingly may be found in a comment by the *Gaon* of Vilna.[46] The *Gaon* of Vilna also distinguishes between apostasy and "an important commandment." Referring to *Shulḥan Arukh*'s authorization in chapter 306 to violate the Sabbath to rescue a person from apostatizing under duress, the *Gaon* asserts[47] that the authorization applies only in cases such as the one cited, not in cases such as described in chapter 328, paragraph 10, even though the violation is "great:" "For there is no greater commandment than observance of the Sabbath."

This does not apply, however, to the case in chapter 306, where the matter involves "keeping the potential apostate as a member of the Jewish

---

[44] R. Yeruham Yehudah Leib Perlman (also known as *haGadol miMinsk*), *Or Gadol* 1, p. 16, s.v. *Hinei Nitba'er*, writes concerning R. Reischer: "From here it would seem that he might hold that where a sick person brought danger upon himself by his own negligence, we may not violate the Sabbath for him, see *Semak* comments ad loc. The matter requires further study." Concerning rescue of one who brings danger upon himself, see also his remarks above and below the passage quoted here.

R. Moshe Feinstein *Iggerot Moshe*, *Oraḥ Ḥayyim* I:127, demonstrates that even where a person's own negligence has placed him in danger, we are obliged to violate the Sabbath on his behalf. R. Feinstein rejects attempts to prove the opposite on the basis of *Magen Avraham* 245:14. See also R. Eliezer Waldenberg, *Tzitz Eliezer* VIII:15:4.

[45] R. Yehi'el Mikhel haLevi Epstein, *Arukh haShulḥan*, *Oraḥ Ḥayyim* 306:25, distinguishes between rescue from a one-time violation of the Sabbath and rescue from a situation that will affect a person for the rest of his life. Concerning the latter case, R. Epstein finds it preferable to violate the Sabbath once rather than leave the person to violate the Sabbath for the rest of his life—as in cases of protection of human life. R. Epstein concludes, "The matter requires further study if she herself has done wrong. Each individual case must be judged on its own merits."

[46] R. Eliahu, the *Gaon* of Vilna (1720–1797), is recognized as the outstanding rabbinic scholar of recent generations.

[47] 259 *Bi'urei haGra*, *Oraḥ Ḥayyim* 306:26. See note 10 above.

people (*lehavi'ah likhlal Yisra'el*)."[48] Thus, the *Gaon* does not emphasize the persistence of the transgression of one who would apostatize. The crucial factor according to the *Gaon* seems to be the person's complete alienation from the Jewish people.

As for willing apostasy, the *Gaon* writes explicitly that the authorization to violate the Sabbath applies only in cases of duress: "And it is not permitted except when the person has done no wrong and the commandment is great. . . ."[49]

Conclusion

Should authorization to violate the Sabbath to prevent apostasy be governed by the normal principles concerned with rescue from transgression, or should apostasy be considered equivalent to loss of life, which must be prevented even at the expense of violating every commandment of the Torah?

As we saw in the case of a woman forcibly abducted for the purpose of causing her to apostatize, Rashba refused to authorize violation of the Sabbath in order to rescue her. Though Rashba in his response raises the possibility of a parallel between the case under discussion and possible danger to life (*sefek nefashot*), he does not actually discuss this possibility. In accordance with the normal principles governing rescue from transgression, Rashba concludes that the Sabbath may not be violated.

Based on the same principles, R. Yosef Karo comes to the opposite conclusion, mandating violation of the Sabbath in the case discussed by Rashba. R. Karo explains that in order to prevent violation of an "important commandment," where the person to be rescued has done no wrong, it is permitted to transgress; when compared with apostasy, violation of the Sabbath must be considered a minor offense. Rema's opinion on the matter is not entirely clear, as two of his comments on *Shulḥan Arukh* seem to contradict one another.

A novel opinion in this matter is advanced by the author of *Levush*, who suggests that apostasy be considered equivalent to loss of life, given that one is obliged to sacrifice his life rather than commit idolatry. For this same

---

48 However, the *Gaon* of Vilna might rule that if the commandment superseded is not observance of the Sabbath, it is permitted to violate that commandment to prevent violation of an important commandment that is less encompassing than the prohibitions involved in apostasy.

49 See B. Landoi, *haGa'on heḤasid miVilna*, p. 68, nt. 25, writes in the name of the *Gaon* of Vilna, that if a potential apostate went of his own accord, he is guilty of wrongdoing, and the Sabbath may not be violated to rescue him (from the *Gaon* of Vilna's commentary on the opinion of the *Tosafot*).

reason, it will be permitted to violate the Sabbath not only to prevent apostasy, but even to prevent a single act of idolatry or any other act for which one is obliged to sacrifice his life. This applies, of course, only to situations where a person is in real danger of dying. Where it is certain that the person will not give up his life to avoid apostatizing, it would not be permitted to violate the Sabbath to rescue him.

In a further innovation, the author of *Levush* finds that where a person would transgress under duress, it is not permitted to transgress in order to rescue him (unless he would transgress one of the three cardinal sins). This is because the law does not consider acts performed under duress to be transgressions. The author of *Malbushei Yom Tov* has another view. He emphasizes the persistence of an apostate's transgression as the basis for permitting transgression of the law to prevent apostasy. In the case of a one-time violation, however, even where the transgression is a serious one, such as idolatry, it will not be permitted to violate the Sabbath to rescue him. Violation of the Sabbath is not considered a minor offense that can be superseded in order to prevent another one-time transgression.

Concerning the author of *Leduc*'s opinion on one who transgresses under duress, *Bah* holds that even when the transgression is idolatry, if the person performs the forbidden act under duress, it is prohibited to transgress in order to rescue him from sin. His act is not considered a violation, since the law does not hold persons responsible for acts performed under duress. (However, if the person chooses to sacrifice his life rather than transgress, it might be permitted to transgress in order to rescue him.)

The difficulty of equating prevention of apostasy with protecting human life lies in the fact that the potential apostate is in no danger of dying. In this connection, *Magen Avraham* notes that concerning protection of human life it is said, "Violate one Sabbath for him that he may observe many Sabbaths." Protection of human life, then, also seems to be based upon rescue from sin. In apostasy as well, it would seem proper to violate the Sabbath in order to rescue another from violating the Sabbath for the rest of his life. When the spiritual implications of physical rescue are considered, the distinction between physical rescue and spiritual rescue becomes blurred.

The analogy between protecting human life and preventing apostasy was greatly expanded by the author of *Naḥalat Shiva*, who concludes that even when someone apostatizes **willingly** it will be permitted to violate the Sabbath in order to rescue him. This opinion was strongly rejected, however, by the author of *Shevut Ya'akov*, who emphasizes that although it is said that "one who causes another to sin is worse than one who kills him," this principle applies only with regard to divine retribution and does not imply the legal equivalence of sin and death.

14

Consecutive Gifts

Yosef Rivlin[*]

The test case[1]

Mr. A and Mrs. B, each previously married, have together three children: his son—a; her son—b; and their common son—c. In his deathbed declaration, Mr. A bequeathed his property to his wife, and after her death, the property will pass on, in this way: two thirds to his son—a, and one third to their son—c. After c's death the property will pass to his son—a. The husband died and the wife used the property. She gave a gift of one half of the property to her son—b, against her late husband's wishes. Afterwards she married Mr. D, her third husband. In her deathbed will she bequeathed the remaining half of the property to her brother—E. It is clear that her previous husband's son—a, and their common son—c, object to this act.

Some questions arise: 1. Is a will valid which leaves property to someone drawn up on condition that on the testatee's death the property will pass to another? 2. What kind of right has the first beneficiary during his lifetime? 3. Is the wife entitled to give a gift to her son? 4. Is the wife permitted to make a will? 5. How does her new marriage affect her right to the property? 6. What are the second beneficiary's rights? 7. What will happen to the property if Mr. A's son dies before their common son?

Background

If a person bequeaths his property in a deathbed declaration to someone, and stipulates that after the death of the first beneficiary, the property will pass on to another and not to the first beneficiary's children, what kind of

---

[*] Department of Talmud, Bar-Ilan University.
[1] I would like to thank the participants of the conference, especially Prof. J. Bazak, Prof. B. Lifshitz and Dr. D. Sinclair, for their helpful comments.

right has the first in it? Is it a right of ownership or only a right of usufruct? Some legal systems deal with such a case, and provide some solutions. Roman law offers two approaches: 1. The ownership of the property passes immediately to the second beneficiary [or the last one] while the first beneficiary receives only the right of usufruct. 2. The beneficiaries have complete ownership but not simultaneously. Each one of them has full right during the period that the property belongs to him, but the ownership of the first beneficiary is on condition that he leaves the property to the second. This obligation was at the beginning only a moral one, but later it became mandatory. The solution offered by English law is quite complex, and is similar to the first approach in Roman law. Each of the beneficiaries has an immediate right in the property: the first has the right to enjoy it now, and the second has the right to enjoy it later.[2]

The sources

Several Tannaitic texts deal with this case: "Whoever says: 'Field X (be given) to A, and when A dies to B, and when B dies to C;' the first eats the fruits and when he dies they shall be given to the second and when he dies they shall be given to the third."[3] The main question here is: Is A an owner or only an usufructuary? If A is a usufructuary, who is the owner? Is ownership immediately vested in B, so that even should he die before A, his (B's) heirs would receive the property? Opinions differ on this question, and there are three solutions: I. "If the second dies before the first has died, the first eats the fruits and when he dies they shall be given to the third." II. "When the first dies the fruits shall revert to the heirs of the donor." III. "The goods shall revert to the heirs of the first."[4] These three solutions represent three opinions on the exact right of each beneficiary. On this point we have some opinions of scholars of Jewish law: Yaron's point of view is that the first solution seems to be the one most in accordance with the probable wishes of the testator. Nothing justifies the assumption that he intended to make C's rights depend upon prior enjoyment by B.[5] Other scholars accept another idea, but they are in dispute on another point. Gulak, Shilo and

---

[2] See: S. Shilo, "Split Ownership Rights in Property in Talmudic Law," *Dine Israel*, 12 (1984-1985), 173–195, especially in pp. 186–189.

[3] Tos. BB. 8:4, Zuckermandel, p. 409; Lieberman, pp. 156–157. See also: R. Yaron, *Gifts in Contemplation of Death*, Oxford, 1960, p. 202.

[4] See: Lieberman, ibid.

[5] Yaron, supra n. 3, 202–204.

Englrad held that in Jewish law there exists an ownership for a limited period. Albeck thinks that an ownership must be unlimited.[6] To return to the texts mentioned above, we can see that the latter two texts held that it is a condition stipulated by the testator, that C's right depends upon prior enjoyment by B. This opinion was not accepted by the first text. The two texts are divided on the question of what kind of right has the first beneficiary?

Maimonides accepts the third solution: "If the second dies during the lifetime of the first the estate goes to the heirs of the first." This means that the first has full ownership.[7]

The first beneficiary's right

As mentioned, the view that the first beneficiary is an owner with full rights was accepted as law. This right includes the power to alienate, with some limitations. The first one is a moral one, according to Abaye's words: "Who is a cunning Knave? He that advises to sell goods. . . ."[8] The power of alienation is also restricted in that the beneficiary cannot dispose the property by a "deathbed declaration." Maimonides derives from the Talmud another distinction: "If he sold or gave to his son or to one of his heirs, he has done nothing."[9]

If we come back to the test case mentioned above, we can surmise that such a will is valid, according to Jewish law. Immediately after his death his property passes to his wife. She is allowed to use the property in her lifetime as she desires. On her death, the property will pass on to the children according to the husband's will: two thirds to his son and one third to their common son. From the moral aspect, she is prohibited from selling or giving the property away and doing any act which will thwart her husband's wish. But it is only a moral obligation. However, if she did sell or give the property, the act is valid. Indeed, in two cases the act is invalid: (1) if she gave the property to her own natural son; (2) if she disposed of the property by a deathbed declaration.

When a woman marries, all her property passes to her husband's ownership. According to the Talmud, this is regarded as a purchase by her husband.[10] As mentioned above, she also has no permission to sell the prop-

---

6 See: Shilo, supra n. 2, 188–189, n. 74. See also: J. Rivlin, *Inheritance and Wills in Jewish Law*, Bar-Ilan University Press, (in press), Part II, Chapter 6.
7 Maimonides, *Zekhiya u-Mattanah* 12:7.
8 TB. BB 136b–137a.
9 Maimonides, ibid., 9–10.
10 *Ma she-Kantah Isha Kanah Baalah*, BT Nazir 24b; Sanhedrin 71a; Gittin 77a–b.

erty; but if she does so, the act is valid. The property now belongs to the husband and the consecutive gifts are interrupted.

We shall pay attention to the fact that, in our case, as the gift to her son was void, her husband will also win this portion. It means that on her marriage, all her property passes to the husband. On his death, all this property will pass on to his heirs, and nothing will pass to her previous husband's heirs. But if she does not marry, then on her death the property will be divided according to her husband's will: two thirds to his son and one third to their common son. According to the will's terms, the gift to his son is without conditions; it is an absolute gift that allows him to do with it whatever he wishes. This is not the case with the other beneficiary, their common son; his gift is under a condition that on his death, the property will pass to the husband's son. His right in the gift is like the right that his mother had. He can use it, but has no permission to sell it; but if he does sell it, the sale is valid.

If in the meantime his brother, who gets the property in the future, dies, the property will remain in the hands of the last beneficiary's heirs. The case will be similar if the second beneficiary dies in the lifetime of the first beneficiary. In our case, if the common son dies before his mother, the property will remain with her other heirs.

The Identification of the first beneficiary

Jewish law has different solutions as to the identification of the first beneficiary. For instance, if the first beneficiary is the testator's heir: a son among his sons, or if he has no sons, a daughter among his daughters, the heir's acceptance stops the consecutive bequests, and after the first beneficiary's death, the estate will pass to his, the first's, heirs. Returning to our case, if the property were bequeathed first to his son and afterward to the wife, or first to their common son and then to his son, we would say that "an inheritance has no interruption" ["*Yerusha ein la hefsek*"] and the gift to one of his heirs is an absolute gift. The property remains in the hand of the first beneficiary for life, and on his death it passes to his heirs and not according to the will.[11]

The dictum "an inheritance has no interruption" does not apply when the testator uses the term of a gift and not of inheritance, according to some scholars. Many of them think that if the testator gives the estate to his heir and says explicitly that he intends to give it as a gift and not in the category

---

11 TB. BB 129b. Maimonides, ibid., 4. See also: Rivlin, supra 6, chapter 2.

of an inheritance, he can stipulate consecutive gifts. This instruction does not work in the case of a healthy person's will, only in the case of a gift in contemplation of death. Another exception is when the testator wills his property to his embryo as the first beneficiary, and after him to another. The property will pass to the other on the first's death. There is not any change in the above mentioned instructions, in the case that the second beneficiary is also his son.[12]

In connection with the previous problem, we must add that a healthy man's will with the formula of "from today and after death," is like a regular gift and not regarded as a gift of an ill person.

Some practical implications

To return to our case by replacing the protagonists: The wife willed to her husband. Does the law change? We must remember that according to Jewish law, the husband inherits his wife, but the wife does not inherit the husband.[13] Therefore, in the previous case, the husband drew up a will for someone who does not inherit him. But in this case the wife arranges a will for her heir, and as we know, "an inheritance has no interruption," so the property remains in the hands of the husband and will not pass on to others as written in the will. It is true that there is a dispute about this. Some scholars understand that this instruction applies only in a biblically sanctioned inheritance [inheritance *de-Oraita*], but not in the case of a wife's inheritance where her status is only *de-Rabanan*. Most of the scholars hold that the status of the inheritance between husband and wife, is only *de-Rabanan*. Therefore, in our case, there is no difference whether the husband or the wife willed.[14]

It is customary today to arrange mutual wills between couples.[15] Now we have to join our two cases into one: If the husband dies before his wife, the property will pass on to her, and if she pre-deceases him, the property will pass on to him. In every case, after the death of the surviving heir the property will be divided into two portions: the greater one will pass to the remaining son, and the smaller one to their common son. After the common son's death the portion will revert to the heir of the surviving heir. We must pay attention to one very important subject. Generally, mutual

---

12 Maimonides, ibid., 5–6; Rivlin, ibid.
13 M. BB. 8:1–2.
14 Rivlin, ibid.
15 About Mutual Wills in Israeli Law, see: S. Shilo, *The Succession Act—1965*, Jerusalem, 1988, pp. 325–326. About Jewish law, see: Rivlin, ibid., Part III, Chapter 3.

wills are regarded as "healthy people's wills" where the instruction mentioned above is not operative. If one may take a practical point of view, we must remember that in the case of a healthy person's will an act of acquisition is needed and has to be written in the will that the time of validity is one hour before death.

15

Inheriting the Crown in Jewish Law: The Question of Rabbinic Succession

Jeffrey I. Roth[*]

> ... Moses and Aaron went first, Nadab and Abihu walked behind them, and all Israel followed, and Nadab and Abihu were saying: "When will these two old men die and we assume authority over the community?"[1]

I

"Succession" is a universal problem, arising from the need to determine who comes next when a position of leadership falls vacant. "Inheritance" is one possible solution, determining the next occupant of a position by identifying and installing the heir of the deceased one. Inheritance may take many forms and there are any number of alternative solutions, such as combat among the rivals, casting lots, consulting an oracle, rotation in office, popular election, and merit-based appointment. A society may rely on a combination of procedures to resolve questions of succession.

Aaron's sons, Nadab and Abihu, expected to inherit positions of authority when Moses and Aaron died, but in the course of Jewish history, a number of noteworthy offices were allocated according to principles other than inheritance. For example, the Priest Anointed for War, who had the task of rallying the troops before they went into battle,[2] required a striking appearance and had to possess high oratorical skills to inspire valor and steadfastness for combat.[3] He was selected from among the priests for these qualities and not because of his lineage[4] and his post did not descend to his heir.[5] Similarly, the earliest leaders of Israel in the Promised Land, the Bibli-

---

[*] Associate Professor of Law, Touro College Law Center, Huntington, New York.
[1] *Midrash Rabbah: Leviticus (Ahare Mot)* XX, 10 (J. Israelstam trans., London: Soncino Press, 1983), 260–261.
[2] Deuteronomy 20:2–4.
[3] *Sefer Ha-Ḥinukh*, No. 526.
[4] R. Abraham b. Mordecai ha-Levi, *Ginat Veradim, Yoreh Deah*, 3:8.
[5] *Sifra, Tsav*, ch. 5, ¶ 1 and *Yoma* 72b–73a.

cal Judges,[6] were charismatic warriors who stood down when the crisis that prompted their appointment receded.[7] Selected for their strength, wisdom and fear of Heaven, the Judges neither acquired their offices from their fathers nor did they pass their posts on to their sons.[8] Again, when a member of a sanhedrin died and had to be replaced,[9] he was succeeded, not by his son, but by the foremost among the pupils who sat before the court in semicircular rows, each in an assigned place according to his ranking as a scholar.[10]

In citing these alternatives to inheritance there is no intention to suggest that the procedures for succession are wholly discretionary under Jewish law. On the contrary, specific verses in the Torah mandate inheritance for the offices of king and High Priest and a third verse excludes the Priest Anointed for War from this principle.[11] But no biblical verse expressly speaks to the matter of rabbinic succession,[12] creating some leeway in establishing the legal principles that should govern it. How the authorities of Jewish law exercised this discretion is the focus of our inquiry.

---

[6] As used in this connection, the term "Judge" (Heb. *shofet*) has a broad connotation akin to "ruler" or "governor." See K. Whitelam, *The Just King: Monarchical Judicial Authority in Ancient Israel* (Sheffield, 1979), 52. After the Israelite monarchy was established and governmental roles specialized under a central royal adminstration, the term acquired a narrower sense relating specifically to the administration of justice. Id., 59.

[7] R. Abraham Bornstein, *Avney Nezer, Yoreh Deah*, No. 312, §52. By contrast, Don Isaac Abravanel, *Perush al ha-Torah*, Introduction to the Book of Judges, believes there was no break in continuity between the Judges.

[8] Don Isaac Abravanel, *Perush al ha-Torah*, Introduction to the Book of Judges. Note the people's request to Gideon in Judges 8:22 ("Rule thou over us, both thou, and thy son, and thy son's son also . . .) which he declines ("I will not rule over you, neither shall my son rule over you; the Lord shall rule over you.") Id., 23.

[9] See R. Obadiah Bertinoro, Commentary on the Mishnah, *Sanhedrin* 4:4, s.v. *hutzrehu lismokh*.

[10] Mishnah, *Sanhedrin* 4:4; see also Maimonides, *Mishneh Torah, Sanhedrin* 1:7–8.

[11] The biblical verses are Deuteronomy 17:20 (king)—see *Sifre, Piska* 162 and *Horayot* 11b; Leviticus 6:15 and 16:32 (High Priest)—see *Sifra, Tsav*, chap. 5, par. 2 and *Aḥarey Mot*, chap. 8, par. 5; and Exodus 29:30 (Priest Anointed for War)—see *Sifra, Tsav*, chap. 5, par. 1 and *Yoma* 73a.

[12] Whether the rules regarding rabbinic succession are from the Torah (*mi-d'oraita*) or rabbinic enactments (*mi-derabbanan*) is a subject of dispute. Compare R. Yom Tov Algasi, *Simḥat Yom Tov*, No. 6 (rules are from the Torah, citing *Sifre, Parshat Shoftim*) with *Magen Avraham, Oraḥ Ḥayyim* 53:25 (rules are rabbinic enactments, based on custom dating from the time of Hillel). Algasi concedes that the rules are not expressly stated in the Torah but derived by way of *midrash*.

The upshot of the dispute is practice that, in cases of doubt, will favor inheritance by the heir over another candidate. Jewish law requires stringency in applying a law that is possibly from the Torah (*safek d'oraita le-ḥumra*). Under this principle, if there is doubt concerning who is entitled to succeed to a post, the heir or someone else, the heir should be appointed, for if he is denied the appointment when he is in fact entitled to it, a possible Torah norm will have been violated. See *Ginat Veradim, Yoreh Deah*, 3:8.

II

Reasoning by analogy could not dictate a definitive answer to the question of rabbinic succession because plausible analogies point in opposite directions. On the one hand, with regard to the functions of their office, rabbis resemble both the Judges who judge Israel according to *halakhah*[13] and the Priest Anointed for War who through preaching and exhortation inspires the people to perform *mitzvot*. If these considerations govern, then rabbis should be selected based on their fitness for their posts without regard to their lineage. On the other hand, appointment to a rabbinic post is a sacred appointment (*minui shel kedusha*) like that of the High Priest,[14] and a rabbi in some communities enjoyed authority as the master of the place (*mara d'atra*) that made him almost a ruler.[15] If these factors govern, then by analogy rabbinic posts, like priesthood and monarchy, should pass by inheritance.

Inheritance of rabbinic posts may serve a number of salutary purposes. By making the former rabbi's heir his presumptive replacement, it may reduce disputes over succession and preserve communal peace.[16] Unlike candidates from the outside whose credentials and personal qualities will be unknown, the rabbi's son will be known to the community.[17] If his father has groomed him to succeed, then he will be familiar with the community's problems, issues and personalities and able to function effectively very soon after taking office.[18] Transitions in outlook and religious practice will tend to

---

[13] Unlike kings who judge according to the needs of the hour (*hora'at sha'ah*). See Don Isaac Abravanel, *Perush al ha-Torah*, Introduction to the Book of Judges.

[14] R. Moses Sofer, Responsa, *Oraḥ Ḥayyim* 12 (holding appointment of rabbi, unlike that of king, is a sacred appointment) and *Avney Nezer*, No. 312, §34 (disagreeing with *Ḥatam Sofer* as to king but not as to rabbi and holding both are sacred appointments).

[15] R. Moses Sofer, Responsa, *Oraḥ Ḥayyim* 13; *Avney Nezer, Yoreh Deah*, No. 312, §§51–55 ("Rabbis today have the law of a king").

[16] *Ginat Veradim, Yoreh Deah* 3:8 (citing *Rashba, Kol Bo* and *Beit Yosef*).

[17] See the responsum of R. Saul b. R. Heschel involving application of a *takkanah* that imposed stricter requirements on rabbinic appointees from outside the community whose impartiality as judges vis-a-vis their relatives in the town could not be known; the responsum is printed in Asher Ziv ed., *She'elot u-Teshuvot ha-Rema* (1970), pp. 518–519.

[18] See R. Elijah b. Hayyim (*Ranah*), Responsa, No. 98 (stating community would never have appointed an outsider as its rabbi if it had known that the incumbent's son, who was familiar with the community and its affairs, was qualified to succeed his father).

Some communities viewed the problem from a different perspective and had a practice of appointing **only** outsiders to succeed their rabbi. They feared that a local candidate with relatives in the town would either be legally disqualified from judging certain lawsuits in which his relatives were parties or would be partial towards them. See Jacob Katz, *Tradition and Crisis: Jewish Society at the End of the Middle Ages* (B. D. Cooperman, trans.) (New York: N.Y.U. Press, 1993), 129. Rabbi Yair Hayyim Bachrach (*Havot Yair*, 1637–1702), in the introduction to his book *Kelaley Etz ha-Ḥayyim*, printed in the 1834 edition of his responsa following No. 238, states that his son was rejected as his successor by the leaders of his community citing this practice.

be gradual and moderate, the son having absorbed the attitudes and practices of his father.[19] Further, it has to be conceded that open competition to fill a vacancy will not necessarily guarantee that the best qualified candidate will be chosen, for common experience demonstrates that any selection process, even one that is ostensibly merit-based, is fallible and subject to extraneous influences.

Still, some will always find the notion that rabbis should inherit their positions counterintuitive. Surely, they will argue, as the *Maharashdam* did, that a rabbi's successor should be the candidate best qualified to provide the highest level of Torah scholarship and Torah leadership to the community, whether that person is his son or someone else.[20] The idea that Jewish law would prefer lineage over merit, and pass over a better qualified candidate in favor of the decedent's heir,[21] seems a striking departure in a tradition that posits high achievement in Torah-learning as a paramount value.

---

[19] These possible advantages of inheritance will not be present in every case and should not be overemphasized. If, for example, the heir spent his formative years away from his father and his community, e.g. studying at a distant yeshiva or living with his out-of-town in-laws, then he will not be well-known at home nor will he be familiar with local problems there. Further, he is quite liable to have fallen under the influence of his *rosh yeshiva* and to have absorbed his religious outlook and practices, which may differ radically from his father's.

[20] R. Samuel b. Moses Medina (*Maharashdam*), Responsa, *Yoreh Deah*, No. 85 ("... for a rabbi and leader of the nation of Israel must be an expert in Torah law, whether in monetary matters ... divorce and marriage ... or any of the other prohibitions in the Torah ... for it is written, 'Justice, justice shalt thou pursue' [Deut. 16:20]—follow a proper court ... As our sages said [*Yoma* 72b], 'There are three crowns ...' and the crown of Torah is not an inheritance, let anyone who wishes to take it [come and take it] ...").

[21] A celebrated instance in which a community passed over a more qualified candidate in favor of the decedent's heir occurred in France in the 16th century when a rabbi died and left a minor son. The townsfolk settled on a prominent scholar, R. Moses Alsheikh, as their new rabbi. However, another scholar who lived in the community, Maharash Alkabetz, argued that the community should wait until the prior rabbi's son came of age (reached *bar mitzvah*) and then appoint him. In support of his view he cited a ruling by Maimonides that where a king dies leaving a minor heir, we hold the kingdom for him until he comes of age. *Mishneh Torah, Hilkhot Melakhim* 1:7. By analogy, he argued, the same procedure should apply to rabbinic appointments. This argument carried the day and the decision to appoint R. Alsheikh was rescinded. *Ginat Veradim, Yoreh Deah* 3:8.

Later authorities were divided in their reactions to this incident. Some cited it with approval to support the notion that an heir is preferred even when a greater scholar is available, for surely Moses Alsheikh was more learned than the child who displaced him. *Sefer Devar Moshe*, No. 1; *Avney Nezer, Yoreh Deah* No. 312, §39. In another view, the community's conduct was beyond the letter of the law (*lifnim meshurat ha-din*); that is, it was under no legal obligation to hold the post for the heir until he came of age but it wished to do so. *Hekrey Lev, Oraḥ Ḥayyim*, Part I, No. 18. Still others denied that a community may choose to wait for a minor to come of age. Rather it should appoint someone else as rabbi immediately. There is no assurance that the minor will grow up to be a qualified scholar and the community may not leave the father's post vacant in the interim. "*A*" v. *Selection Board for the Ashkenazic Chief Rabbi of City "B" and the Reli-*

If we turn to the very first case of rabbinic succession in Jewish history, we find this sentiment reenforced. A midrash relates that Moses, just prior to his death, argued that his sons should inherit his glory. However, the Holy One, Blessed be He, informed him, "Your sons sat idly by and did not study the Torah."[22] Instead, Joshua was selected as his successor.[23]

Despite this, a consensus developed among the *Aharonim*, the late authorities of Jewish law, that favored the inheritance of rabbinic posts by qualified heirs. This is exemplified by a ruling of Rabbi Moses Isserles (*Rema*) concerning a rabbi who is established in a town:

> [E]ven his son and his son's son forever have priority over others as long as they fill their fathers' place in fear of Heaven and are somewhat learned.[24]

Two requirements qualify the right to inherit a rabbinic post. First, the heir must possess certain minimum qualifications: fear of Heaven and a little learning.[25] If he does possess them, he is entitled to the post even

---

gious Council of City "B", 11 P.D.R. 97 (5738), at 107. The French community could do so only because their town was an exceptional place where many qualified scholars resided. They could handle halakhic matters while waiting for the heir to mature. Further, we hold the throne for a minor only because the Torah requires it. Id. R. Yom Tov Algasi recommended that a community appoint a temporary rabbi while the heir is a minor and then, when he comes of age, install the heir if, but only if, he has become a qualified sage. *Simhat Yom Tov*, No. 6.

22 *Midrash Rabbah: Numbers (Pinchas)*, XXI, 14 (J. Slotki, trans., London: Soncino Press, 1983), 840–841.

For the *Hatam Sofer* it seemed unlikely that Moses would have asked for his sons to succeed him if he had believed they were unqualified. That God denied the request and that Joshua succeeded are, for the *Hatam Sofer*, strong proofs that inheritance does not apply to rabbinic succession. See his Responsa, *Orah Hayyim*, vol. 1, No. 12. Others countered this argument by suggesting that Moses was unique in the annals of Jewish history, having himself served in three capacities as priest (during the consecration of the Tabernacle), king and rabbi, so that no general rules could be derived from the circumstances surrounding the selection of his successor. *Divrey Malkhiel*, Part IV, No. 82; *Avney Nezer, Yoreh Deah*, No. 312:40–42.

According to another midrash, earlier in his career—at the Burning Bush—Moses had requested of God that kings and priests descend from him. But God denied his request, for monarchy had already been assigned to David and his heirs and the priesthood to Aaron and his heirs. *Midrash Rabbah: Exodus (Shemoth)*, II, 6 (S. Lehrman, trans., 1983), 57; see also *Zevahim* 102a.

23 Numbers 27:15–23.

24 *Shulhan Arukh, Yoreh Deah* 245:22. The passage continues: "But in a place where it is the custom to appoint a rabbi for a fixed term or where it is the custom to appoint whomever they wish, they have the right to do so." Id.

25 Id.; see also *Divrey Malkhiel*, Part IV, No. 82 (to qualify as successor, an heir must be a scholar but need not be as great as his father). That the heir must be qualified for the post in order to inherit it is derived from *Sifra, Tsav*, ch. 5, ¶ 2 ("... when he fills his father's place he has priority over all others, but if he does not fill his father's place, let another come and serve in his stead.") and from the circumstances related in the Talmud regarding the succession of Gamaliel to the post of *nasi* upon the death of his father, Rabbi Judah, *Ketubot* 103b.

if there is a better qualified candidate available.²⁶ Second, the community's consent to the appointment is required.²⁷ No compulsion is applied to force them to consent, but they remain under a legal obligation to appoint the heir.²⁸

Given the need to establish his qualifications and to obtain the community's consent, some construe the heir's right to be a preference (*zekhut kedimah*) rather than an inheritance (*yerusha*).²⁹ The heir is preferred over other candidates and has a right to be considered ahead of them but not necessarily to obtain his father's post in all events.

The Vilna Gaon found support for the Rema's ruling in a midrash in *Sifre*.³⁰ The midrash draws an analogy from monarchy in favor of inheritance for all leadership positions in Israel. Commenting on Deuteronomy

---

26 See e.g. R. Hayyim Amarillo, *Sefer Devar Moshe, Oraḥ Ḥayyim, Hilkhot Shatz*, No. 1; see also supra, note 21.

Some carve out an exception to this rule where the differences in scholarship between an heir and a rival candidate are so vast that the heir is not even in the same league as the other candidate, holding that in such cases the community is free to reject the heir and to appoint the greater scholar. *Ginat Veradim, Yoreh Deah* 3:7 (attributing this view to the *Maharashdam*); but see *Sefer Devar Moshe, Oraḥ Ḥayyim, Hilkhot Shatz*, No. 1 (stating this is view of *Ginat Veradim* only, whereas *Maharashdam* denies inheritance applies to *keter Torah* at all).

27 Rabbi Moses Schick (*Maharam Shik*), Responsa, *Yoreh Deah*, No. 22; see also R. Isaac b. Moses of Vienna, *Or Zaru'a*, No. 115, quoting a letter of R. Moses b. Ḥasdai Taku (13th cent.), who writes of a case where the heir of a deceased rabbi was not acceptable to the community as his father's successor. The heir was qualified in Torah learning but had not attained the level of his father. Rabbi Moses wrote that the community should accept him, "for they have no other learned person available and fit to take his place." But it was also incumbent upon the heir (*shurat ha-din u-mishpat*) to appease the community, to go from door to door to make himself beloved to them. There is no mention in the letter of any right on the part of the heir to inherit his father's position.

28 For a good discussion of this point, see the opinion of the rabbinical court in *"A" v. Selection Board for the Ashkenazic Chief Rabbi of City "B" and the Religious Council of City "B"*, 11 P.D.R. 97 (5738), at pp. 100–106; see also R. Ephraim Weinberg, *Al Devar Yerusha be-Rabbanut, Ha-Torah ve-ha-Medinah* 9/10 (5718–19), 493–4 (citing *Minḥat Yeḥiel, Beit Yitzhak*, and *Maharsham*).

29 E.g. R. Joseph Hazzan, *Ḥekrey Lev, Oraḥ Ḥayyim*, Part I, No. 15 ("The inheritance of positions is nothing but a preference.") The Rema also states the rule in terms of priority rather than inheritance. *Yoreh Deah* 245:22 (". . . even his son and his son's son forever have priority over others . . .").

30 R. Elijah of Vilna, *Be'ur HaGra, Yoreh Deah*, 245:22, Par. 38. He also cites as sources for the Rema's ruling *Tosefta, Shekalim* 2:15 ("Whoever takes precedence in inheritance takes precedence in positions of authority, so long as he follows the custom of his forefathers.") and *Ketubot* 103b ("Simeon my son [shall be] *ḥakham*, Gamaliel my son [shall be] *nasi* . . ."). Whether the latter passage applies to rabbinic succession was questioned by the *Ḥatam Sofer* who held inheritance in the case of the *nasi* was an aspect of *keter malkhut* rather than *keter Torah*; see infra note 48.

17:20 which reads, "so he may prolong his days in his kingdom, he and his children, in the midst of Israel," the *Sifre* states:

> **He and his children** . . .—if he dies, his son will reign in his place. This applies only to kings; whence do we learn that this applies also to all leaders of Israel. . . ? From the verse, . . . **in the midst of Israel**—anyone who is in the midst of Israel, his son will fill his place.[31]

It is important to note that the midrash does not expressly mention rabbis. Although the phrase it uses, "all leaders of Israel" (Heb. *kol parnesey Yisrael*), is a broad and inclusive one, all conceded that some positions, including the Priest Anointed for War and the office of Judge,[32] were not inherited by sons. Hence the phrase "all leaders of Israel" could not have been intended literally to cover every office in Israel.[33] The Ḥatam Sofer interpreted the midrash in light of its context, a discussion of monarchy, and confined the midrashic rule of inheritance to similar positions of leadership that exercise dominion over Israel.[34] These positions were distinguishable from sacred offices, like that of High Priest and rabbi, and this would explain why a *second* verse was needed to mandate inheritance for the High Priest specifically (but not rabbis), for without the second verse one could not derive inheritance of a sacred office from a verse that deals with royal succession.[35]

---

[31] *Sifre, Piska* 162 (Reuven Hammer trans., New Haven: Yale Univ. Press, 1986, pp. 194–95).

[32] See supra notes 3–9 and accompanying text.

[33] See R. Shneur Zusha Reise, "*B'inyan Yerushat Hezkat Rabbanut*," Ha-Maor 5:9 (5714), 10–11.

[34] R. Moses Sofer, Responsa, *Oraḥ Ḥayyim*, No. 13 (citing *Magen Avraham, Oraḥ Ḥayyim*, § 53, ¶ 25).

[35] Id. The *Ḥatam Sofer* conceded that in the modern era, when a rabbi is obligated to serve the community's needs and receives compensation, the rabbinate is no longer purely a sacred calling but has aspects of public service. Given this change in function and status, he held the analogy drawn from royal succession had become apt and rabbinic posts in the modern era, like the monarchy, should pass by inheritance to heirs. However, he held, the rule of inheritance should *not* govern succession to the post of Chief Rabbi since he must be a greater scholar than the country's other rabbis who will look to him for leadership. Id.

In his position on the chief rabbinate, the *Ḥatam Sofer* acknowledges that lineage cannot serve as a direct proxy for Torah learning and that where superior scholarship is an essential requirement of the post, rabbinic succession must be governed by an assessment of the candidates' scholarly attainments rather than by inheritance. This was always true in the case of the *gadol ha-dor*, the recognized greatest halakhic authority of his generation to whom other rabbis turned to answer their most perplexing legal questions. This position, although an informal one, possessed a high degree of authority in the Jewish legal system, but no-one argued that it could or should pass by inheritance.

By citing the *Sifre* as a source for the rule of inheritance, the Vilna Gaon indirectly reveals the absence of this midrash from the Talmud. Not only is the midrash absent, but in the Talmud, the very scriptural words on which the midrash bases the rule of inheritance, "in the midst of Israel" (Heb. *bekerev Yisrael*), are used as the source for a totally different *halakhah, viz.*, that a king, although himself the son of a king, must be anointed when a dispute arises over his accession to the throne.[36] Whether it is proper to derive two legal rules from the same words in a single Biblical verse is open to question, and the editors of the Talmud may have omitted the midrash deliberately because they rejected its rule of inheritance for "**all** leaders of Israel," believing inheritance should be confined to the two positions, monarch and High Priest, where the Torah expressly requires it.[37] Rabbi Joseph b. Ḥayyim Ḥazzan, in his work *Ḥekrey Lev*, first notes that the rule regarding inheritance of rabbinic posts is absent from the works of many early authorities (*Rishonim*)—he mentions the *Rif*, the *Rosh*, the *Ṭur* and the *Beit Yosef*—and then suggests the omission might have been based on this reasoning.[38] By contrast, he writes, those early authorities who do cite the rule in their works, including Maimonides,[39] the

---

36 *Horayot* 11b, *Keritot* 5b.

37 Interestingly, this was the Karaite position, that based on Scripture, lineage determined succession only for the monarchy and priesthood. See Sidney Hoenig, "Filial Succession in the Rabbinate," *Gratz College Annual of Jewish Studies* 1 (1972), 15 (citing Solomon b. Yeruham).

38 *Ḥekrey Lev, Oraḥ Ḥayyim*, Part I, No. 15.

39 Maimonides, *Mishneh Torah, Hilkhot Melakhim* ("The Laws of Kings") 1:7, reads as follows:

> Not only the monarchy but every office and appointment in Israel passes by inheritance to his son and his son's son forever, provided that the son fills his forefather's place in wisdom and fear of Heaven.

Josef Karo cites the midrash in *Sifre* as the source for this rule. *Kesef Mishnah*, ad loc.

Maimonides also states the rule in *Hilkhot Keley ha-Mikdash* ("Laws of Temple Vessels") 4:20 as follows:

> When the king or High Priest or one of the other appointees dies, his son or other proper heir is appointed in his place.... We learn [from Scripture] that the monarchy is an inheritance, and the same rule applies to every office in the midst of Israel, that he who acquires it does so for himself and his descendants.

Neither of the rulings mentions rabbis expressly.

The question arises why Maimonides repeats the rule twice in his code since each time he states it broadly enough to cover all offices in Israel. Further, the rule does **not** appear a third time in his treatise dealing with Torah sages, *Hilkhot Talmud Torah*. From this pattern one might argue that Maimonides accepts the rule of inheritance only for *keter malkhut* and *keter kahuna*, hence its inclusion in his treatises dealing with kings and priests, but he rejects the rule for *keter Torah*, hence its absence from the treatise on Torah sages. The broad language he used in the cited passages may be explained as Maimonides' merely having adopted the wording of the *midrashim* on which the rulings are based without intending to cover rabbinic succession. For

Rashba,[40] and *Sefer ha-Ḥinukh*,[41] are prepared to derive two *halakhot* from the same words in a single biblical verse.[42]

The *Ḥekrey Lev*'s observation leads quite naturally to the following question: If the Talmud rejects the midrash, then what is its approach regarding succession to positions of Torah leadership? One way to begin to

---

the suggestion that Maimonides did not consider rabbinic posts an "office," "position" or "appointment" as those terms are used in his code, see A. Grossman, "From Father To Son: The Inheritance of the Spiritual Leadership of the Jewish Communities in the Early Middle Ages," *Zion* 50 (5745) (Heb.), p. 190, n. 3. However, based on these passages in *Mishneh Torah*, Maimonides is generally cited in the halakhic literature as one of the *Rishonim* who apply the rule of inheritance to rabbinic positions, as the *Ḥekrey Lev* cites him here.

[40] Responsa, No. 300. The case involved an elderly cantor who wished to appoint his son as his assistant. Some in the community opposed the son's appointment, claiming his voice was not suitable. The Rashba held that the cantor's right to name whomever he wished as his assistant was expressly granted to him in his *takkanah* of appointment and that it is fitting for a father to turn to a son for assistance. Further, every lifetime appointee has the implied right to name an assistant, even where his contract is silent, for surely he will on occasion become ill or need to travel and hence require a temporary substitute. Now there may come a time when because of the father's age or infirmity, he will never be able to resume his duties and his replacement will be permanent rather than temporary. In such a case, the Rashba writes, the correct rule (*shurat ha-din*) gives the son priority, and this is the custom (*minhag*) in many communities respecting cantors: sons follow their fathers in office. This practice is consistent with an important principle (*kelal gadol*) of the Sages: that in all matters of appointment, if the son is qualified, he has priority over all others, including those who are equal to him in ability and even those who are greater.

In this responsum, the Rashba treats three separate issues: first, appointing a temporary replacement and second, appointing a permanent replacement—both while the father is still alive—and third, succession to the post upon the father's death. Only the first issue was involved in the situation presented to the Rashba. His views on the second were offered gratuitously and his brief comment on the third provided support for his position on the second, viz. that it is proper to appoint a son when a father needs a permanent replacement. Thus, although the Rashba acknowledges the principle that sons have priority in matters of appointment, the responsum does not specify how he might weigh all the various factors involved in applying the principle in a given situation.

There is another difficulty in interpreting the responsum. The *Aḥaronim* noted the Rashba's references to law (*din*) and custom (*minhag*) and were at a loss to explain why he mentioned both. For some attempted explanations, see e.g. *Ḥekrey Lev, Oraḥ Ḥayyim*, Part I, No. 20 ("custom" to permit son to replace father while he is alive; "law" for son to succeed at death); *Ḥatam Sofer*, Responsa, *Oraḥ Ḥayyim*, No. 12 (by "law," inheritance applies to posts of kings and High Priests; by "custom" to posts of rabbis and cantors); *Maharsham, Da'at Torah*, Y.D. *Hilkhot Sheḥitah* 1:81 (by "law," inheritance applies to positions of authority, like king; by "custom" to positions that lack communal authority, like cantor or kosher slaughterer).

[41] No. 493.

[42] *Ḥekrey Lev* himself decided the matter in favor of the inheritance of rabbinic posts, resolving the problem he raised by demonstrating how the two rules—the one regarding inheritance of positions and the other regarding the anointing of a king whose throne is disputed—can be derived by taking each word in the phrase *bekerev Yisrael* separately as a basis for one of the rules. *Ḥekrey Lev, Oraḥ Ḥayyim*, Part I, No. 15.

fashion an answer is to consider its attitude towards the "heirs apparent," that is, the sons of the sages. The Talmud does not express a high opinion of them. It asks, why is it not common for scholars to have sons who are scholars? There follow five answers: Rabbi Joseph said, "That it might not be maintained, the Torah is their legacy." Rabbi Shisha said, "That they should not be arrogant towards the community." Mar Zutra said, "Because they act high-handedly against the community." Rav Ashi said, "Because they call people asses." And Rabina said, "Because they do not first utter a blessing over the Torah."[43] Thus, the Talmud offers five answers but no dissent from the underlying proposition. It regards a family in which more than three generations are scholars as nothing less than miraculous.[44] This reenforces the importance of Rabbi Yossi's admonition in *Avot*, "Make yourself fit to study Torah, for it is not yours by inheritance."[45] In fact, the entire tractate *Avot* may be read as an argument against hereditary succession in matters of Torah leadership, for by depicting an intellectual genealogy of the sages it demonstrates that Torah is transmitted from teacher to student, master to disciple, rather than from father to son.

In the talmudic era, despite dynastic tendencies on the part of some of the sages who regarded being a scholar as a craft which they could transmit to their sons,[46] positions of Torah leadership were not inherited.[47] It is true

---

[43] *Nedarim* 81a (I. Epstein trans., London: Soncino Press, 1936, pp. 252–3).

[44] *Bava Metzia* 85a ("R. Parnakh said in the name of Rabbi Johanan: One who is a sage whose son is a sage and whose grandson is a sage—the Torah will not cease from his descendants forever," citing Isaiah 59:21 as a prooftext).

[45] *Avot* 2:12.

[46] G. Alon, "The Sons of the Sages," in *Jews, Judaism and the Classical World* (I. Abrahams trans. 1977), 436–457; see also Albert Baumgarten, "The Politics of Reconciliation: The Education of Rabbi Judah the Prince," in E. P. Sanders et al., eds., *Jewish and Christian Self-Definition* (1981), vol. II, p. 213, and Stuart A. Cohen, *The Three Crowns: Structures of Communal Politics in Early Rabbinic Judaism* (Cambridge, 1990), 240–243.

[47] See e.g. Rashi, *Gittin* 60b, who gives the order of succession to the post of *rosh yeshiva* at the academy in Pumbeditha as follows: Rav Yehuda, followed by Rabbah, Rav Yosef, Abaye and Rava. These were among the outstanding scholars of their era whose merit, rather than lineage, must have been the determining factor in their appointments, for none of their fathers had served as *rosh yeshiva* before them. Nor did their sons succeed them in office although some of them left learned sons. *Divrey Malkhiel*, Part IV, No. 82, noted that Rav Yehuda, Rabbah and Abaye left sons who were scholars but did not become *roshei yeshiva*. The only son of a *rosh yeshiva* in Babylonia in the talmudic era who succeeded to the post his father held was Mar the son of Rav Ashi. There is no evidence of inheritance in a single instance of father-to-son transmission of an office, for it is just as likely in such cases that the son was selected on his own merit as the best candidate available at the time to replace his father. Further, Mar did not become *rosh yeshiva* at Sura immediately upon Rav Ashi's death but only decades later after at least two other scholars had occupied the chair. It is questionable whether we should consider as a case of "inheritance" a son's eventual accession to an office his father once held which, however, is preceded by the service of a number of nonrelated individuals in the post.

that from the time of Hillel and after, the position of *nasi*, president of the assembly of scholars in the Land of Israel, did pass by inheritance, but this was an innovation instituted by the sages to commemorate the Davidic monarchy during the period of Hasmonean rule,[48] for the *nasi* exercised political as well as spiritual authority and traced his lineage to the House of David.[49] The basic norm is reflected in the practice before Hillel when the post of *nasi* did not pass from father to son.[50]

The Talmud's approach to the question of succession to Torah leadership positions is better exemplified by the tradition of "the three crowns."[51] The first, the crown of monarchy, was acquired by David and his descendants forever. The second, the crown of priesthood, was acquired by Aaron and his descendants forever. And what of the third, the crown of Torah? It is available to anyone who wishes to take it. In some formulations, the crown of Torah is referred to as "abandoned property" (Heb. *hefker*),[52] which is not intended to suggest discarded property having no value, but rather ownerless property, hence available, in the public domain so to speak, for all who wish to take it.

This characterization of the Torah crown as available to all operates on two levels. On one level, it is simply an invitation to everyone to come and study.[53] On a second level, however, the tradition has implications for succession to positions of Torah leadership. This can be inferred from the context, for the tradition juxtaposes the crown of Torah, on the one hand,

---

48 R. Moses Sofer, Responsa, *Oraḥ Ḥayyim*, No. 12 (stating view that inheritance in the case of the *nasi* should be considered an aspect of *keter malkhut*, the crown of monarchy, rather than *keter Torah*, the crown of Torah); see also *Magen Avraham*, *Oraḥ Ḥayyim* 53:25 (stating view that inheritance did not apply to *keter Torah* as a matter of law but, after Hillel, only as a matter of custom).

49 *Ketubot* 62b (stating Rabbi Judah ha-Nasi was a descendant of one of David's sons).

50 See Mishnah, *Hagigah* 2:2.

By contrast, according to the *Maharam Shik*, Responsa, *Yoreh Deah*, No. 228, the basic norm is reflected in the practice **after** Hillel when the post of *nasi* was inherited. The rule of inheritance was suspended prior to that time, perhaps out of respect for Moses whose sons did not inherit. In the generations immediately following the death of Moses, the appointment of the Biblical Judges was made subject to a proviso that their sons would **not** inherit when their terms expired.

51 *Yoma* 72b; see also Mishnah, *Avot* 4:4; *Avot de-Rabbi Nathan*, ch. 41; *Midrash Tanḥuma, Parshat Va-Yakhel*, §8; Maimonides, *Mishneh Torah, Talmud Torah* 3:1.

52 E.g. Rabbi Israel Isserlein, *Terumat Ha-Deshen, Pesakim u-Ketavim*, §128.

53 *Divrey Malkhiel*, Part IV, No. 82 (interpreting the passage as an invitation to study; since appointment to office requires the community's consent, it would be inappropriate to say of communal office, "let anyone who wishes come and take it."); in this vein, see also *Midrash Tanḥuma, Parshat Va-Yakhel*, §8 ("And why was the Torah given in the desert? To teach just as the desert is ownerless [and available] to all, so the words of Torah are ownerless as to all who wish **to learn.**").

with the crowns of monarchy and priesthood, on the other. While those offices pass by inheritance to the descendants of David and Aaron respectively, positions of Torah leadership are available to all without regard to lineage. Let anyone who is learned in the Torah come and apply. A number of authorities over the centuries interpreted the tradition of the three crowns this way and, in their works, disputed the notion that rabbinic posts are inheritable.[54] But their position is the minority point of view among the *Aharonim* who achieved a widespread consensus favoring the inheritance of rabbinic posts, consistent with the Rema's ruling cited earlier.

III

The late-developing consensus in favor of inheritance is noteworthy in light of the lack of support from the Talmud, the absence of the rule from the works of many *Rishonim*, and the cogent arguments against inheritance of rabbinic positions.[55] Further, it runs counter to the trend towards professionalization of the rabbinate which stresses, among other things, the fitness of the candidate for his post based on objective merit-based criteria, certified independently by a reliable ordination (*semikhah*). Can we suggest a reason for the development of the consensus, in this fashion and at precisely this

---

[54] R. Israel Isserlein, *Terumat Ha-Deshen, Pesakim u-Ketavim*, §128 ("The crown of Torah **and its authority** are lying ownerless for all who wish to acquire them"); R. Samuel b. Moses Medina (*Maharashdam*), Responsa, *Yoreh Deah*, No. 85; R. Moses Sofer, Responsa, *Orah Hayyim*, Nos. 12–13; see also R. Saul Israeli in his minority opinion in *Rabbinical Council of Tel Aviv-Jaffo v. Rabbi "A"*, 10 P.D.R. 38 (5735), at pp. 41–50 (distinguishing between rabbinic posts possessing a communal leadership aspect that do pass by inheritance and those that function purely in the realm of halakhic decision-making, *keter Torah*, and hence do not pass by inheritance).

As noted above, note 35, the *Hatam Sofer* modified his original position against inheritance in the case of rabbinic posts, other than that of Chief Rabbi, in the modern era. For a discussion of his change of heart and the reasons for it by his son, Rabbi Shimon Sofer, see Yaakov Vais, *Rabbanut u-Kehila be-Mishnat Maran ha-Hatam Sofer Zal* (Jerusalem, 1987), 150–154.

[55] See e.g. A. Grossman, op. cit. supra note 39, at pp. 201–204 (criticizing inheritance, as practiced in Babylonia in relation to the position of *gaon*, on the following grounds: it led to the appointment of some who were not of the highest caliber; it resulted in elderly incumbents, short tenures, and high turnover; and it fostered an atmosphere of passive learning and lack of motivation among students who did not have the correct lineage).

For an early critique of hereditary succession as practiced in Jewish communities that ignored the requirement that an heir be fit for his post, see the excerpt from the medieval commentary on *Midrash Rabbah*, Numbers 3:4, published in Marc Saperstein, "The Earliest Commentary on the *Midrash Rabbah*," in I. Twersky, ed., *Studies in Medieval Jewish History and Literature* (1979), 283, 288–290.

time? It is possible to do so provided we take into account developments in relation to rabbinic compensation occurring at the same time.[56]

By the fifteenth century, Jewish law had undergone a sea change on the propriety of rabbis' accepting compensation, departing from the traditional position that a sage's knowledge of Torah should be placed at the disposal of the community free of charge. In the Talmud, this tradition was attributed to Moses who instructed the people to teach the Torah to future generations without compensation just as he was privileged to learn it at Sinai.[57] Rabbi Zadok's admonition in the Mishnah,[58] never to use the Torah as "a spade with which to dig," was explained by Hillel's comment that anyone who derives a material profit from the words of Torah will perish from the world.[59]

Maimonides in his day argued for the continuing relevance of the tradition.[60] For him, the ideal scholar was one who labors in the Torah without compensation while he toils at a secular trade to earn his living. But the harsh realities of Jewish life in the Middle Ages conspired against the classic ideal. In straitened economic circumstances, no one was willing to serve as a religious functionary without compensation.[61] In addition, if the ancients possessed the ability to study Torah and toil at a trade and to succeed at both, contemporary scholars who tried to combine the two endeavors would succeed at neither.[62] Left to the attention of part-time scholars who had to interrupt their studies each day for trade, there was the danger that the Torah would be forgotten.[63] The problems confronting Israel in the diaspora were not part-time problems. Jewish communities required the services of a rabbinate that ministered full-time to their pressing needs. This would be possible only with a professional rabbinate that, forsaking the earnings to be gained from commerce, looked instead for their livelihoods to the Jewish communities whom they served.[64]

By the fifteenth century, compensation had become the norm. Once rabbis began to receive salaries and fees, they began to compete for lucra-

---

[56] The discussion in the six paragraphs that follow is based on conclusions developed at length in a companion article. See Jeffrey I. Roth, "Three Aspects of the Rabbinate: Compensation, Competition and Tenure," *Drake Law Review* 45 (1997), 569–624.

[57] *Nedarim* 37a.

[58] *Avot* 4:5.

[59] Id.

[60] Commentary on the Mishnah, *Avot* 4:7 (J. Kapah ed. 1963, pp. 288–291); see also *Mishneh Torah, Hilkhot Talmud Torah*, chs. 1–3 passim.

[61] R. Isaac b. Moses of Vienna, *Or Zaru'a*, No. 113.

[62] R. Simon b. Zemah Duran, *Tashbetz*, Part I, No. 147; see *Berakhot* 35b.

[63] Joseph Karo, *Kesef Mishneh, Talmud Torah* 3:10.

[64] *Tashbetz*, Part I, No. 147.

tive appointments. For the first time, rabbis leveled the charge of trespass, *hasagat gevul*, against colleagues who invaded their economic territory, a charge that hitherto had been lodged only by merchants and tradesmen against newcomers who opened competing business concerns in their town.[65] When such a charge was presented to Rabbi Israel Isserlein, head of the Talmudical academy in Neustadt, in the celebrated Anshel-Bruna matter,[66] he rejected it. In his view, the crown of Torah and the authority it confers are "*hefker*" for all who wish to take them.[67] Rabbinic fees, he wrote, "are an embarrassment to us and we have to strain to find legal grounds to accept most of them."[68] Compensation with such uncertain legal justification could never rise to the level of a livelihood whose "boundaries" had to be respected by other scholars.

However, as time passed and rabbinic compensation became entrenched, one can detect in the halakhic literature the embarrassment that Rabbi Isserlein had so candidly expressed dissipating, generation by generation. A century after his ruling, the Rema ruled that a new scholar arriving in a town may deprive the established rabbi of his fees "to a certain extent only"[69] but not entirely—a limitation that was absent from Rabbi Isserlein's ruling. In this fashion, the Rema raised the status of rabbinic compensation to the level of a legitimate livelihood entitled to some legal protection against encroachers. The *Shakh* went further, stating the custom is not to permit a newcomer to deprive an established rabbi of his fees **at all**.[70] The Ḥatam Sofer declared that rabbinic salaries no longer cause embarrassment.[71] He held the Rema's ruling was superseded in our times when communities hire a rabbi like an employee and are obligated to pay him a salary. In his view, anyone who siphons fees away from an established rabbi is an evil-doer.[72]

---

[65] See Mordecai Breur, *The Rabbinate in Ashkenaz During the Middle Ages* 20–21 (1976) (Heb.) (noting that the charge of *hasagat gevul*, trespassing against another's economic boundaries, was never leveled by one rabbi against another until they began to receive salaries and fees, and that such accusations were most prevalent during the fifteenth century, when accepting compensation became the norm).

[66] In 1454, Rabbi Israel Bruna immigrated to Regensburg upon leaving his rabbinical post in Brunn when the Jews were expelled from the city, intending to continue his rabbinic practice in his new town, but upon arrival, a scholar who lived in Regensburg, Rabbi Anshel, attempted to prevent him from acting as a rabbi in the town. See Roth, supra note 56, 588–591.

[67] Rabbi Israel Isserlein, *Terumat Ha-Deshen, Pesakim u-Ketavim* § 128.

[68] Id.

[69] *Yoreh Deah* 245:22.

[70] R. Shabbetai b. Meir Ha-Kohen, *Siftei Kohen, Yoreh Deah* 245, Par. 16.

[71] R. Moses Sofer, Responsa, Vol. 6, Ḥoshen Mishpat No.21.

[72] Id.

At the same time, it was widely held that a rabbi, once appointed, was entitled to retain his position for life.[73] Lifetime tenure complemented and supplemented halakhic developments in relation to compensation and competition, for once a rabbi's salary was legally sanctioned and insulated from competition, tenure guaranteed him the ability to enjoy the benefits of office for the longest possible time: the remainder of his life.

With the material profile of the rabbinate contoured in this fashion, inheritance of positions becomes the logical next step. It represents an attempt to extend the benefits of the office beyond the incumbent's life to the next generation by passing the post to his heir at his death. The *Maharam Shik* put it this way: "This is part of the compensation of leaders in Israel—they benefit in that their sons will be leaders after them."[74] Instead of engaging in ordinary trade or commerce and building up a large estate with accumulated wealth that they could bequeath to their heirs, rabbis bequeathed their positions.

Thus, once the rabbinate had become associated with property through the receipt of salaries and fees, rabbinic positions acquired some of the characteristics of property, such as descendibility to the next generation. Something which began as *hefker* became in the end a sort of quasi-property, for a property interest developed in the rabbinic appointment itself.

IV

In the preceding section, the term "quasi-property" was used to suggest that halakhic authorities never completely equated rabbinic positions with ordinary property. For example, they ruled an incumbent could not transfer his post to a third party by sale or gift.[75] If early authorities sometimes drew broad parallels between property and office for purposes of inheritance,[76]

---

[73] E.g. Rema, *Shulḥan Arukh, Yoreh Deah* 245:22 (end); and R. Yehiel Epstein, *Arukh ha-Shulḥan, Yoreh Deah* 245:28; see Roth, supra note 56, 601–608.

[74] R. Moses b. Joseph Schick, Responsa, *Yoreh Deah*, No. 228.

[75] *Ḥekrey Lev, Oraḥ Ḥayyim*, Part I, No. 20 (citing *Mordecai*); *Avney Nezer, Yoreh Deah*, No. 312; *Maharsham*, Responsa, vol. 4, No. 53.

In the prohibition against selling rabbinic positions it is plausible to see a delayed condemnation of a practice common towards the end of the Second Temple period when the office of High Priest was transferred by sale and the incumbent changed as often as once a year, defeating the rule of inheritance. Cf. G. Alon, op. cit. supra note 46, at pp. 65–68 (stating families of High Priests regarded the office as their property which they could sell or lease).

[76] E.g. Rashi, *Horayot* 11b, commenting on Deut. 17:20, wrote, "This indicates it [the monarchy] is an inheritance for them, like a father's estate that passes to his sons," and Maimonides, *Mishneh Torah, Hilkhot Keley ha-Mikdash* ("Laws of Temple Vessels") 4:20, ruled, "Anyone who has priority for purposes of inheriting property also has priority for purposes of [inheriting] the decedent's office," based on *Tosefta, Shekalim* 2:15.

later authorities tended to be more guarded in their statements. They perceived that the rules governing inheritance of office and property would differ in some respects. This was clear from the Torah itself, for if succession to office was to be treated exactly the same as inheritance of property, then the rules that govern the latter would have sufficed for both. There would have been no need for additional verses in the Torah to specify inheritance for the king and High Priest.[77] It became a recurrent theme in the responsa of the *Aharonim* to delineate the differences between the two types of inheritance.[78]

But the fine distinction between property and quasi-property could be lost on the heirs who sometimes attempted to take the notion of office-as-property to what seemed to them its logical conclusion. For example, since a decedent's property is divided among his heirs while his office passes to just one of them, the excluded heirs might claim monetary compensation from the one who received the appointment.[79] Where none of the heirs wished to follow their father in office, they still might wish to receive the fees he customarily collected or demand a payment from the new appointee, claiming they were entitled to a monetary equivalent as their inheritance in place of the office which they declined.[80] In advancing claims of

---

77 *Hekrey Lev, Orah Hayyim*, Part I, No. 15.

78 See e.g. R. Hayyim Hezekiah Medini, *Sedey Hemed, Hazakah be-Mitzvot*, §7, ¶61 (property: heirs divide it; office: one heir acquires it to the exclusion of all the others); R. Yom Tov Algasi, *Simhat Yom Tov*, No. 6 (property: daughter inherits where there are no sons; office: daughter never inherits); R. Joseph Hazzan, *Hekrey Lev, Orah Hayyim*, Part I, No. 16 (property: even an evil-doer will inherit; office: heir must fear Heaven to qualify to inherit). In *"A" v. Selection Board for the Ashkenazic Chief Rabbi in City "B"*, 11 P.D.R. 97 (5735), discussed infra in Part V, the court noted three additional distinctions: (1) property: the heirs' rights arise upon their father's death; office: the heir's right to succeed arises at the moment his father is appointed to his post; (2) property: no one can oppose the rightful heirs' inheritance; office: community opposition will prevent an heir from succeeding; (3) property: even a minor or a fool inherits; office: heir must be fit to serve in order to succeed.

79 See R. Catriel F. Tecoresh, "*Yerusha be-Misrah Tzeburit*," *Shevilin* 31–32 (5739), 96–101, reporting the case of a town official who died and whose sons did not want his post but whose son-in-law wished to be appointed. The sons did not object to his appointment but sought damages as compensation for not assuming the father's office. Asked to resolve the matter by the town council, Rabbi Tecoresh rejected the sons' claim for damages, reasoning that office, unlike property, passes to just one heir, and that the excluded heirs succeed to nothing: neither the office nor any right to compensation as a substitute.

The post at issue was not described in any detail but it was not a rabbinic position nor did the incumbent occupy a position of communal leadership. In an interesting portion of his paper, Rabbi Tecoresh, a member of the Chief Rabbinate of Israel, expressed the view that a daughter might inherit such a post and transfer it to her husband, "for it is the common practice of mankind to seek the assistance of relatives." Id., 98.

80 See R. Shneur Zusha Reise, "*B'inyan Yerushat Hezkat Rabbanut*," *Ha-Maor* 5:9 (5714), 10–11, discussing a case in which a rabbi who supervised the *kashrut* of the community's butch-

this sort, the heirs were treating their father's position exactly as property, seeking to divorce the emoluments of the office from its functions and to inherit the former or a monetary equivalent while declining to perform the latter. Halakhic authorities who considered claims of this type properly rejected them as overreaching by the heirs.[81] Yet it is possible to see their claims for a cash substitute for the office as a direct and perhaps inevitable[82] extension of the notion that office is a sort of property that descends from one generation to the next like an inheritance.

V

To conclude our study of rabbinic succession we consider two trends that in the modern era are affecting the inheritance of rabbinic posts with markedly contrasting results.

Under the prevailing pattern in the diaspora, the rabbinate has acquired the trappings of a modern profession.[83] Typically rabbis no longer serve for life as "rulers" of their towns, provinces or countries. Often a rabbi's community has been reduced to the single congregation that interviewed him, hired him and employs him pursuant to contract. These circumstances tend to undermine the notion that a rabbi, upon his appointment, acquires for his descendants a right to succeed him. Unlike the leaders of Israel whose offices descend to their heirs, the ordinary employee or hired worker occupies

---

ers died and his heirs had no desire to serve in his post. However, after their father's death, they claimed the right to continue to collect his customary fees as part of their inheritance. In the meantime the community hired someone else to perform these functions. Rabbi Reise expressed his displeasure at the heirs' conduct, stating that he had never heard of a similar case in which the heirs lived elsewhere, declined to perform the functions of office, and still wished to collect the fees. He advised the heirs to submit the matter to religious adjudication (*din Torah*) or binding arbitration to prevent the Divine name from being profaned (*ḥillul ha-Shem*).

81 See the preceding two notes.

82 In the introduction to a study of succession to high office in many societies, the anthropologist Jack Goody noted, "The process of socialization inevitably puts pressure on the modes of inheritance and succession to coincide, despite the essential differences between the transfer of property and office . . ." Jack Goody, ed., *Succession to High Office* (Cambridge, 1966), 28. Further, he observed that inheritance of positions is never purely automatic and that some element of choice is always present even in hereditary systems. "High office generally demands some particular qualities for its incumbents," he wrote, and "[e]lements of election and appointment occur even in the most rigidly hereditary systems." Id., 4 and 13. In requiring of the heir a little learning, fear of Heaven and the community's consent, Jewish law tends to confirm these observations.

83 The development of the modern rabbinate since the period of Emancipation is surveyed in Simon Schwarzfuchs, *A Concise History of the Rabbinate* (Oxford: Blackwell Pubs., 1993), chs. 7–11.

a post that is not inherited.[84] As Rabbi Yehiel Epstein observed in his late code of law, "It appears to me that the son has no priority [to succeed as rabbi], even where he fills his father's place [in learning and fear of Heaven], for it is the father that they wanted to hire and not the son . . ."[85] Given these changes in the nature of the rabbinic vocation, the logic of the situation has altered in a way that makes inheritance an inappropriate way to fill vacancies.[86]

By contrast, with the establishment of the State of Israel and the creation of a host of official positions staffed by members of the rabbinate, the rule of inheritance is experiencing something of a renaissance. In Israel, fixed terms of office and compulsory retirement tend not to be insisted upon in the case of rabbis.[87] Their appointments thus become *de facto* appointments for life. When a rabbi dies while in office the circumstances are ripe for his heir to come forward and claim the vacant post by right of inheritance. In two cases where the community demurred, the disappointed heirs sought a resolution of the matter in the rabbinical courts where they achieved a measure of success.

---

[84] There is a longstanding debate in Jewish law concerning which communal religious functionaries are to be regarded as leaders of Israel whose offices pass to their heirs and which are merely hired workers whose posts are not inherited. Cantors and religious slaughterers are often, but not always, assigned to the second category. See *Ḥekrey Lev, Oraḥ Ḥayyim*, Part I, No. 15; *Maharsham, Da'at Torah*, Y.D. Hilkhot Sheḥitah 1:81; and R. Catriel Tecoresh, op. cit. supra note 79, at pp. 100–101. That rabbis in the modern era have become mere "employees" of their congregations and should also be consigned to the second category are conclusions halakhists are understandably reluctant to reach. Note that offices in the second category may still be accorded inheritance rights by custom, if not by law. See supra note 40.

[85] *Arukh ha-Shulḥan, Yoreh Deah* 245:28. The passage concludes, "Still, if the son fills his father's place in Torah and fear [of Heaven], why should he be less preferable than anyone else?"

[86] The heads of the Hasidic rabbinic dynasties remain exceptions to these observations. The *tsadik* or *rebbe* cannot properly be equated with the rabbis who are the subjects of our study and whose authority is based on Torah scholarship. As Schwarzfuchs noted, "The Hasidic dynasties had created a new type of authority, which was based not on Talmud learning but on descent." Op. cit., at 133.

It is interesting to note that hereditary succession was not an original feature of the Hasidic movement. Its founders in the eighteenth century bequeathed their positions, not to their sons, but to their foremost pupils. Thus, the Baal Shem Tov was succeeded by his pupil, R. Dov Baer, who was succeeded in turn by his disciples, R. Levi Yitzhak of Berditchev, R. Shneur Zalman of Ladi, and the brothers Zischa and Elimelech of Lizensk, each of whom gave rise to his own strain of *Ḥasidut*. See R. Ephraim Weinberg, "*Al Davar Yerusha be-Rabbanut*," Ha-Torah ve-ha-Medina 9–10 (5718–19), 496.

[87] This factor was noted and played a role in the outcomes of both of the rabbinical court cases that will be discussed in the following paragraphs. See *Religious Council of Tel Aviv-Yaffo v. Rabbi "A"*, 10 P.D.R. 38 (5735), at p. 51, and *"A" v. Selection Board for the Ashkenazic Chief Rabbi of City "B" and the Religious Council of City "B"*, 11 P.D.R. 97 (5738), at p. 99.

In the first case, *Religious Council of Tel Aviv-Yaffo v. Rabbi "A"*,[88] the father had served until his death as head of the Sabbath and Sabbath Boundaries Department of the local rabbinate. The Israeli Chief Rabbinate certified his son as qualified for the post. However, the local religious council wanted to hold an open competition to fill the vacancy. It claimed that the son was not qualified, and further, that the position was not one that passed by inheritance.

In its split decision, two members of the panel held for the son.[89] On the issue of qualifications, they ruled the heir must be deemed presumptively fit based on the Chief Rabbinate's certification. The local religious council had the burden of proving the heir unfit, a burden it had not yet met at the time the case was heard.[90]

The majority also held that the post in question was one that passed by inheritance. The local religious council had argued that although the father was a rabbi, his function was that of an administrator, supervising his department, checking the Sabbath boundaries and ensuring that no labor was performed in violation of the Sabbath. The son countered by arguing that in addition to his administrative duties, his father had functioned as a rabbi, deciding halakhic questions relating to Sabbath observance and Sabbath boundaries (*eruvin*).

The majority was satisfied that the father had exercised rabbinic functions in deciding halakhic questions relating to matters within the purview of his department. But even if he had not, they held, the post would pass to his heir for inheritance governs succession to all offices in Israel. It is not limited to positions of authority but applies equally to offices that accord honor but not authority to the incumbent.[91]

One member of the panel, Rabbi Saul Israeli, dissented. While he agreed with his colleagues that the father had exercised rabbinic functions, he believed this fact was inimical to the son's claim. In his view, to the extent the father engaged in halakhic decision-making, he wore the mantle of *keter Torah* (the crown of Torah). But the crown of Torah does not pass by inheritance.[92] Now if, in modern times, according to the *Ḥatam Sofer*, rabbis, in addition to deciding halakhic matters, act also for the public welfare as

---

[88] A decision of a three judge panel of the Rabbinical High Court of Jerusalem, reported at 10 P.D.R. 38 (5735).

[89] Id. at pp. 50–61 (majority opinion by R. Mordecai Elijah and concurring opinion by R. Eliezar Goldschmidt).

[90] Id., 59.

[91] Id., 51, 59.

[92] Id., 42–50 (citing *Yoma* 72b, *Maharashdam*, *Magen Avraham* and *Ḥatam Sofer*.)

leaders of their communities and in this capacity acquire also the mantle of *keter malkhut* (the crown of monarchy), then surely inheritance applies only to the post of rabbi of a town who indeed rules his community. By contrast, the post of someone like the claimant's father, a functionary who did not exercise communal leadership and, in deciding religious questions, wore the crown of Torah only, does not pass by inheritance.[93]

The two person majority was itself split on the issue of altering the rule of inheritance by regulation. Rabbi Elijah held the town religious council may change the rule prospectively by properly enacted rabbinic regulation so that all future appointments could be limited to the incumbent and not pass to heirs.[94] Rabbi Goldschmidt questioned whether the town's religious council, even acting with the addition of all the local rabbis and rabbinical judges, was sufficiently representative of the community to exercise the authority to alter its customs by regulation.[95] There was no need for them to resolve the question because both agreed that any such regulation could only operate prospectively and would not affect the outcome of the case.

The second case, *"A" v. Selection Board for the Ashkenazic Chief Rabbi of City "B" and the Religious Council of City "B"*,[96] was decided three years later. Here the father had served as chief rabbi of a city for thirty years prior to his death. A son claimed he was entitled by right of inheritance to appointment as his successor. He sued in the district rabbinical court to enjoin the town's religious council and its selection board from appointing anyone but him to fill the vacant post. Further, he sought an order enjoining any other candidates from stepping forward to offer their names for consideration.

The court held not much discussion was necessary to establish an heir's right to succeed to his father's rabbinic post in view of the consensus

---

[93] Id.

[94] Id., pp. 59–60.

[95] Id., pp. 60–61.

[96] 11 P.D.R. 97 (5738), a decision of the district rabbinical court of Petaḥ Tikvah. The case was heard before a three judge panel of Rabbis S. Karelitz, M. Solti, and Y. Meshorer. Rabbi Solti passed away during the deliberations and the parties agreed to accept the judgment of the remaining two. Id., 115. The reported opinion is unsigned.

There is no mention by the judges here of the Rabbinical High Court's opinion in the *Rabbi "A"* case, decided three years earlier, an omission no doubt based on the lack of a doctrine of binding judicial precedent in Jewish law. See M. Elon, *The Principles of Jewish Law* (Jerusalem: Keter Pub. Co., 1975), 115–117. Each judge has a personal obligation to address the legal questions in a case according to his own lights and apply his conclusions to the facts presented as he deems proper. Still, wholly apart from the issue of the bindingness of precedents, one may question whether failing to acknowledge a decision rendered three years earlier by judges in the same court system dealing with the same legal issues and sources is a sound way to develop a coherent jurisprudence on this or any other issue before the rabbinical courts.

among the *Aharonim* on this point, provided the heir is qualified.[97] In this case, where the father had served for life, upon appointment he acquired the post as an inheritance for his descendants in perpetuity. The court cited the statement of the rule in Maimonides' code, *Hilkhot Melakhim* 1:7, and noted the consensus interpreting this passage to encompass rabbinic positions (*keter Torah*).[98]

Still, the heir's right to inherit the post was dependent upon the community's consent to his appointment.[99] The attorney for the respondents had argued that a majority of the community did not consent. In reviewing the submissions in the case, the court found evidence of opposition to the heir but no evidence of local support. The heir characterized the opposition as merely political or emanating from persons unworthy of determining who is fit to serve as a rabbi. The court rejected this characterization for there was opposition from the members of the religious council and the selection board and they were surely qualified to make this judgment.[100]

But the court went further, holding that even if the opposition were "merely political," as the heir claimed, it would block his appointment.[101] It derived its conclusion from a close reading of a passage in the *Maharam Shik*.[102] He states there is no right to inherit a post where a community does not consent, and no legal compulsion is used to force it to consent, but a community should consent to the succession of a rightful heir and so long as it does not, it is not acting properly under Torah law. Regarding the *Maharam Shik's* comment that in such a situation the community "is not acting properly under Torah law," the court reasoned as follows: he cannot be referring to a case where the community rejects for legitimate reasons, e.g. where the heir is **not** qualified to serve because he lacks fear of Heaven, for such a one is not entitled to the post by Torah law and the community will be acting correctly when it rejects him. Rather, the *Maharam Shik's* comment must be addresssed to a community that rejects a perfectly qualified heir, refusing to consent to his appointment "for reasons of its own." In such a case, since the heir is entitled to the post under Torah law, the community is not acting properly. Still, its opposition vitiates the right of inheritance and the town is free to appoint another.[103]

---

[97] 11 P.D.R. 99.
[98] See supra note 39.
[99] 11 P.D.R. 100.
[100] Id.
[101] Id.
[102] Responsa, *Yoreh Deah*, No. 228.
[103] 11 P.D.R. 100.

Since the case involved appointment as chief rabbi of a city, the court had to consider the position of the *Ḥatam Sofer*. He denied the rule of inheritance applied to the post of chief rabbi of a country, for the occupant of such a post must be greater in learning than his colleagues and lineage alone cannot ensure this.[104] The religious council claimed that there resided in its town rabbis and scholars whose stature and attainments were greater than that of the heir. The court held this fact would not alter their decision.[105] In their view, the *Ḥatam Sofer's* position is limited to a case where the chief rabbi commands a rabbinic hierarchy which he heads. In such a case the chief must be greater than his subordinates who are obligated to follow his directives. But this principle has no application to the chief rabbi of a town who is not in a direct chain of command with respect to other rabbis in the town. The heir's right to inherit is not impeded by the fact that greater scholars reside in the town for they do not take orders from him.

Apparently the heir did not live in the town and was not well-known to the residents. The court ruled he should make an attempt to become known to them and secure their consent to his appointment. It ordered the religious council to make arrangements for a visit by the heir and gave him two months to appear. If the heir failed to appear, or if after the visit the opposition persisted, his claim to inherit the post would be dismissed. Whether the heir was qualified for the post and whether the opposition emanated from "a majority" of the community were questions to be decided by a competent *beth din* (rabbinical court) convened for this purpose.[106]

The decisions in these two cases demonstrate the continuing vitality in Israel of both the consensus view that rabbinic positions pass by inheritance and the minority view that they do not, at least where the rabbi wears the crown of Torah only. It is equally clear that an heir may never assume his father's office without first obtaining the community's consent to his appointment. Further there appears to be some scope for the community's power to abrogate the rule of inheritance by regulation, provided it is enacted by a religious body that is sufficiently representative of the community as a whole. Taken together, the decisions in these two cases suggest the possibility of applying the rule of inheritance to rabbinic posts in Israel in a manner that is consistent with the aspirations of the State to be both Jewish and democratic.

---

104 See supra note 35.
105 11 P.D.R. 114–115.
106 Id., 115.

VI

Our study of rabbinic succession has shown that over the course of Jewish history, the authorities of Jewish law debated whether the crown of Torah (*keter Torah*) should pass from father to son by inheritance. For the most part they resisted this notion for it was evident to them that the qualities most essential to the rabbinic vocation—fear of Heaven, knowledge of Torah and the ability to apply it in the world—are not inherited traits. It was only in the latest period, after the rabbinate became salaried and rabbinic posts were associated with property, that a consensus developed in favor of inheritance. Still, each generation called forth a prominent dissenter, such as Rabbi Israel Isserlein in the 15th century, the *Maharashdam* in the 16th century, the Ḥatam Sofer two centuries later, and Rabbi Saul Israeli in recent times, who continued to argue that high achievement in Torah learning and not lineage must determine who shall wear the crown of Torah and exercise its authority over the community.

We have also seen that descent alone never guarantees the heir's succession. He must demonstrate his own fitness for the post—his fear of Heaven and a little learning—and he must obtain the community's consent to his appointment. Still, his status as heir confers some advantages. He has a right to be considered first among the candidates for a post. He should be preferred in cases of doubt and where the candidates are equal. Even when the candidates are unequal, the community rests under an obligation to accept the heir although he may be the lesser scholar. These preferences based on descent, which may induce a community deliberately to appoint a less qualified individual as its rabbi, we regard as a singular anomaly in a tradition that in most other contexts places Torah learning at the apex of its scale of values.[107]

In the modern era, the changing nature of the rabbinate presents a challenge to the notion that rabbinic positions should descend by inheritance, at least in communities where a rabbi is considered an employee of his congregation. By contrast, in the State of Israel, in response to the claims of heirs seeking the official posts their fathers held until death, rabbinical court judges have revived the rule of inheritance. As this dichotomy of approaches suggests, new chapters in the debate over rabbinic succession are sure to be written.

---

[107] Mishnah, *Peah* 1:1.

16

Genetics and Jewish Law

Daniel B. Sinclair*

Introduction

The aim of this article is to outline the approach of Jewish law to some of the areas of legal and ethical concern created in the wake of recent developments in genetics. The issues discussed are the recognition of hereditary diseases in the *halakhah*; genetic screening; the abortion of genetically defective fetuses; gene therapy; the control of genetic information and the question of genetic determinism.

The Recognition of Hereditary Diseases in the Halakhah

A simple illustration of the recognition of hereditary diseases is the talmudic recommendation that a man not marry into an established family of lepers or epileptics on the grounds that the disease may be passed on to his offspring. The occurrence of three cases of this type of disease in a family constitutes sufficient evidence that it is a hereditary one.[1]

A more complex instance of heredity and genetics in halakhic literature is the case of bleeding to death as a result of circumcision. The Talmud rules that the third son of a family in which two male children have already met such a fate may not undergo the ritual. The deaths of his brothers serve to establish the fact that the mother is from a family of "profuse bleeders" and the third son must not be exposed to a similar fate.[2]

---

* Professor of Jewish Law, Tel-Aviv College of Management Law School.
[1] *Yev.* 64b; Y. Katznelson, *Hatalmud Vekhomat Harefuah* (Berlin, 1928), 230–231; R. Shlomoh Zevin, *Leor Hahalakhah* (Tel-Aviv, 1957), 188.

[2] *Yev.* 64b; *Shulhan Arukh, Yoreh Deah* 263:2. The general principle is that as long as there is any danger to the child's life, the circumcision is suspended until such time as he is out of danger. It is also possible to suspend it entirely if such a step is warranted on medical grounds, see *Resp. Noda Biyehuda, Yoreh Deah* no. 165; *Resp. Divrei Malkiel* 3 no. 74; *Nishmat Avraham, Yoreh Deah* 263:4; S. Rappaport, "Defining Danger to Life in the Context of Circumcision" (Heb.), *Halakhah Urefuah* 1 (1980), 283–291.

Now, it is generally assumed that the cause of such circumcision fatalities is hemophilia,[3] which is a hemorrhagic disease resulting from a deficiency of anti-hemophilic globulin factors. Hemophilia is transmitted by a sex-linked recessive female gene and its effects are confined, almost exclusively, to male children. The subsequent discussion of this ruling in halakhic literature would, in fact, appear to turn on a point of genetics. According to Maimonides, it is the third son of the same woman who is not to be circumcised but not of the father, i.e. if the father of two male children who died at circumcision marries another woman, he will, indeed, be obliged to circumcise the son of that marriage.[4] A decision along these lines was recorded by R. Alexander Susslin Hacohen, a fourteenth century Ashkenazic scholar, who wrote as follows:

> I was asked concerning a man who had lost two sons as a result of circumcision, and then his wife died. He married another woman and when she gave birth to a son, I ruled that he should be circumcised. . . . and this was done, and the boy lived.[5]

In addition to Maimonides' ruling, R. Hacohen also cites the talmudic view that embryonic blood is supplied by the mother and not by the father, in support of his decision.[6] Blood diseases, therefore, are passed on exclusively by the mother and hence, the prohibition on the circumcision of the third son applies only to her issue and not to that of her husband.

A different approach, however is adopted by R. Manoah, a medieval Sephardic authority, who maintains that the prohibition also applies to the third son of the father.[7] It would appear that his reason is that in matters of life and death, ritual law invariably gives way to the need to preserve human life and this is certainly the way in which R. Manoah's view is understood by later codifiers.[8]

In the light of genetic science, however, it is evident that the Maimonidean view is correct, since the carrier of the fatal gene is the mother and if the father remarries, there is no reason to suspect that his third son will be the victim of any hemorrhagic disease. Today, of course, the whole issue is

---

[3] See Katznelson (n.1 above), 226–233; *Encyclopaedia Hilkhatit Refuit* 3 (ed. A. Steinberg, Jerusalem, 1982), 683–685; F. Rosner, *Medicine in the Bible and the Talmud* (Ktav, N.J., 1995), 43–49.
[4] *Laws of Circumcision* 1:18.
[5] *Sefer Ha'agudah, Perek Rabbi Eliezer*, no. 164.
[6] *Nid.* 31a. Also see *Turei Zahav, Yoreh Deah* 263:2.
[7] *Beth Yosef, Yoreh Deah* 263, s.v. *vekhatav R. Manoah*.
[8] See *Rema, Yoreh Deah* 263:2.

a purely academic one, since the establishment of any potentially fatal genetic condition will suspend the obligation to circumcise until such time that there is no longer any risk to the life of the person concerned.[9]

The debate is, nevertheless, of academic significance in that it serves as an indication of the recognition and significance of fairly complex aspects of heredity and genetics in the *halakhah*.

An area in which modern genetics has had a direct impact upon the *halakhah* is that of niece marriages. According to the Talmud, it is a virtuous act to marry a niece,[10] and the proof-text is the biblical verse "and hide not from your own flesh."[11] Amongst the reasons given for the recommendation of this practice is the idea that it combines similarity of background with marital love, thereby providing a recipe for a successful marriage.[12] This ruling is incorporated into the glosses of R. Moses Isserless on the *Shulḥan Arukh*, although the question of whether it applies to the daughters of a brother, as well as those of a sister, remains an open one.[13]

In the *Will of R. Judah the Ḥasid*, a thirteenth century pietistic work, the practice of niece-marriages is frowned upon.[14] No reason is given for this disapproval in the *Will* itself, but there is little doubt that it is based upon the highly original beliefs held by the medieval pietist group known as the *Ḥasidei Ashkenaz*, of which R. Judah was the prime exponent.[15] Although the halakhic status of this *Will* is a matter of debate,[16] its rulings were nevertheless taken seriously by a significant number of Ashkenazic authorities.[17]

In a collection of responsa published in 1877, R. Elijah Klatzkin reports the finding of a number of eminent physicians that niece-marriages are much more likely to lead to the birth of defective children than marriages between genetic strangers.[18] R. Klatzkin accepts this evidence and explains that whilst defective children may be born to genetically unrelated spouses, the chances of such a child being born are much higher when relatives

---

9 See *Resp. Hagri Herzog, Yoreh Deah*, no.83.
10 *Yev.* 62b–63a; *Sanh.* 76b.
11 Isaiah 58:7. Also see Maimonides, *Laws of Forbidden Intercourse* 2:14.
12 *Maggid Mishneh, Laws of Forbidden Intercourse* 2:14.
13 *Even Haezer* 2:6 and 15:25.
14 *Zava'at Rabbi Yehuda Heḥasid*, no.22.
15 See G. Scholem, *Major Trends in Jewish Mysticism* (NY, 1940), 80; H. Soloveitchik, "Three Themes in Sefer Ḥasidim," *Association for Jewish Studies Review* 1 (1976), 311.
16 See *Resp. Noda Biyehuda* 2, *Even Haezer*, no. 79; *Resp. Divrei Ḥayyim, Even Haezer*, no. 8.
17 See sources in n. 15 above.
18 R. Klatzkin cites "the book of rules for preserving health (hygiene) by Rickeles who provided statistical evidence for his findings." He also mentions the "*Real Encyclopaedia of Medical Science* published by Eilenberg" and observes that inbreeding amongst animals also leads to the birth of defective young.

intermarry. In order to justify deviating from talmudic law on this point, R. Klatzkin relies upon the *Will of Judah the Ḥasid* and argues that the talmudic obligation to marry a niece only applies to those who are motivated to do so solely by a desire to support their own family members. If the motivation to marry a niece falls short of this purely altruistic intention, then it loses both its virtue and the Divine protection afforded to those who carry out the commandments in a sincere fashion.[19] When R. Judah the Ḥasid "saw that the generation was at a low level and people were marrying for the sake of beauty only, he commanded that no man marry his niece, because of the dangers arising from this practice to his children."[20]

R. Klatzkin's responsum provides the basis for the decision of R. Eliezer Waldenberg, a modern Israeli authority, to the effect that niece-marriages ought to be avoided on eugenic grounds.[21]

In the light of the above, it is evident that the *halakhah* is concerned to avoid genetic diseases in the same way that it mandates medical therapy in general.[22] The problem, of course, is that the specter of mass genetic engineering looms behind every discussion of human genetics and there is a vital need to establish the parameters of legitimate therapy in this area. Any halakhic approach to genetic therapy would be strongly concerned with the establishment of such parameters and the preservation of the line between the relief of suffering and the desire to achieve perfect offspring using genetic knowledge and techniques. This point will be taken up in greater detail in the discussion of the abortion of genetically defective fetuses below.

Genetic Screening

Any genetic screening program raises a number of ethical as well as *halakhic* issues e.g. the need to avoid stigmatization and discrimination; the need to close the gap between diagnosis and treatment, especially in the case of late-onset conditions such as Huntington's Chorea; the preservation of confidentiality; the importance of education regarding the significance of the results of the screening and the necessity for counseling and follow-on care.[23] The halakhic response to these issues is based upon the need to

---

[19] A similar argument is used to account for the fact that *halizah* takes priority over Levirate marriage (*Yev.* 39b).

[20] *Resp. Even Harosha*, no. 31.

[21] *Resp. Ziz Eliezer* 15 no. 44. Also See *Yad Ramah, Sanhedrin* 76b; *Appei Zutra, Even Haezer* 2:6.

[22] See D. Sinclair, "Non-Consensual Medical Treatment of Competent Individuals in Jewish Law," *Tel-Aviv University Studies in Law* 11 (1992), 227–243.

[23] These concerns are of a general nature and figure in most of the recent literature on human genetics, see *Our Genetic Future* (British Medical Association, Oxford University Press,

strike a balance between the principle of personal dignity and the requirements of public welfare, and it is noteworthy that the Tay-Sachs screening program involving young Ashkenazi Jews of marriageable age received the sanction of major rabbinical figures in North American Jewry. Tay-Sachs disease is a single-gene defect and a child born with it begins to suffer from weakness at about six months of age. This is followed by progressive mental and motor deterioration, blindness, paralysis, dementia, seizures, and death by the age of four years. There is no cure for Tay-Sachs syndrome. The condition is restricted, almost exclusively, to Ashkenazi Jews and a test prior to marriage is a simple means of determining whether the prospective couple both carry the defective gene. If they do, there is a twenty-five per cent chance that their offspring will be stricken with the disease. The screening of American Jews, including the strictly observant and Hasidic communities, for Tay-Sachs has resulted in a dramatic drop in the number of babies afflicted with the disease. The success of this scheme lies in the sound educational background to the screening and the care taken, at the insistence of the rabbinic authorities, to ensure the confidentiality of the results. It may, therefore, be concluded that genetic screening for therapeutic purposes is not halakhically objectionable provided it conforms to the laws regarding the disclosure of private matters and the obligation to preserve human dignity.[24]

Abortion of a Genetically Defective Fetus

The issue of aborting a genetically defective fetus in Jewish law came into sharp focus in relation to Tay-Sachs disease. Modern authorities have grappled with this issue and reached diametrically opposed results.

According to R. Eliezer Waldenberg, it is permitted to abort a Tay-Sachs fetus until the seventh month of pregnancy.[25] R. Moses Feinstein, on the other hand, wrote a responsum in which he argued that the abortion of a Tay-Sachs fetus was tantamount to murder.[26] The issue, therefore, is a matter of debate amongst the authorities.[27]

1992), 188–209; T. Wilkie, *Perilous Knowledge* (London, 1994), 97–133; *Human Genetics: The Science and its Consequences* (Science and Technology Committee, House of Commons, HMSS, London 1995).

[24] See F. Rosner, "Tay-Sachs Disease : To Screen or Not to Screen," in *Jewish Bioethics* (Ed. F. Rosner and J.D. Bleich, NY, 1979), 178.

[25] *Resp. Ziz Eliezer* 13 no. 102; 14 no. 100.

[26] *Resp. Iggrot Moshe, Ḥoshen Mishpat* 2 no. 69.

[27] See *Resp. Lev Aryeh* 2 no. 32; *Nishmat Avraham, Ḥoshen Mishpat*, no. 425; *Resp. Mishneh Halakhot* 5 no. 233; 6 no. 14; *Encyclopaedia of Jewish Medical Ethics* 2 (Heb.), (ed. A. Steinberg, Jerusalem, 1991), 89–90.

Whilst a detailed analysis of this debate in the context of abortion *halakhah* is clearly beyond the scope of the present article,[28] there are a number of points arising from it which ought to be considered in the context of a discussion of genetics and Jewish law. According to R. Waldenberg, the mental torture undergone by a mother who has no choice but to stand by and watch her child deteriorate and die is sufficient to justify a lenient decision. In terms of the problem posed by the gap in time between the proposed abortion and the birth of the child, R. Waldenberg is able to rely on earlier precedents according to which it is permitted to abort a *mamzer* fetus on the grounds of the "shame, disgrace and trauma" which will be experienced by the mother at the birth of her tainted offspring.[29] There is a clear analogy between the *mamzer* fetus and a genetically defective one since in both cases the threat to the mother is not a direct and immediate one to her life or physical health and the focus is definitely on the fetus rather than on the mother. Of course, it is also true that a Tay-Sachs child will definitely die by the age of four and as a result, it is arguable that it is a human *terefah*, i.e., an individual suffering from a fatal condition, the killing of whom carries less serious consequences in terms of criminal sanctions than that of a viable person.[30] Indeed, it has been suggested by another halakhic authority that the early death of the Tay-Sachs victim is the primary halakhic justification for permitting abortion in these cases.[31] R. Waldenberg, however, insists that the justificatory principle in relation to Tay-Sachs lies in the halakhic doctrine of feticide and in particular, in the concept that a fetus is not a legal being.[32] In this respect, R. Waldenberg's ruling is applicable to any genetic disease and not only Tay-Sachs and is, therefore, of direct relevance to genetics in general.

In fact, R. Waldenberg is also prepared to sanction the abortion of a fetus with Down's Syndrome on the "basis of the same sources and arguments used in relation to Tay-Sachs."[33] The human factors underlying his permissive ruling in relation to Tay-Sachs are also applicable with regard to Down's Syndrome and he mentions a case of an ultra-Orthodox couple who had already had two such children, both of whom died in their first year or so of life. The wife suffered from nervous shock and refused to co-

---

28 See D. Sinclair, *Tradition and the Biological Revolution* (Edinburgh, 1989), 93–98.

29 See, *Resp. Rav Paalim, Even Haezer*, no. 4; *Encyclopaedia Hilkhatit Refuit* 2 (ed. A. Steinberg, Jerusalem, 1991), 87.

30 See Sinclair (n. 28 above), 19–45.

31 See *Resp. Lev Aryeh* 2 no. 32, endnote.

32 See *Resp. Ziz Eliezer* 9 no. 51; 13 no. 102; D. Sinclair, "The Legal Basis for the Prohibition on Abortion in Jewish Law," *Israel Law Review* 15 (1980), 126–127.

33 *Resp. Ziz Eliezer* 14 no. 101.

habit with her husband for fear of giving birth to another sick child. Matrimonial harmony was restored only by assuring her that if she were to become pregnant, the fetus could be tested for any genetic defects and if necessary, aborted. It is in this type of case that R. Waldenberg recommends the application of his reasoning in the Tay-Sachs case to other genetic defects.

R. Waldenberg mentions the argument made on Kabbalistic grounds that the birth of defective children must be accepted on the grounds that it is a form of Divine punishment or an opportunity afforded to a transmigrated soul which requires it to spend some time on earth before it may enter in to the world of souls. According to R. Waldenberg, however, this type of argument constitutes an unjustified Kabbalistic intervention into the halakhic process and is certainly inapplicable in the context of the prevention of disease.[34]

R. Feinstein, on the other hand, is prepared to sanction an abortion only in a case of a direct and immediate threat to the mother's life and he is, therefore, totally opposed to the abortion of genetically defective fetuses and to any testing of them for defective genes. His responsum has been analyzed at length by the present writer elsewhere and it would appear that it is shaped by moral as well as halakhic factors.[35]

The parameters of therapeutic abortion in a genetic age are, therefore, still unclear and it is the task of halakhists in this area to develop guidelines in order to clarify the situation.

Another significant point arising out of the Tay-Sachs debate is that neither R. Waldenberg nor R. Feinstein appeared to have felt constrained by the traditional time-limit of forty days and three months in their decisions. Indeed, R. Waldenberg, who permits the abortion until the seventh month, clearly states that these limits are of secondary significance only and have no direct bearing on whether or not to sanction an abortion in a particular case.[36] It is arguable, therefore, that there may not be strong halakhic insistence on early genetic testing of fetuses as opposed to such testing later on in the pregnancy. In terms of pre-natal screening, this point is significant,

---

[34] See *Resp. Ḥatam Sofer, Oraḥ Ḥayyim*, no. 51; *Ḥiddushei Ḥatam Sofer al Hatorah*, Exodus 21:19. It is noteworthy that R. Waldenberg also uses other Kabbalistic ideas in order to refute this argument, e.g., the idea that the sixth millennium is, according to the Zohar, the era of wisdom and there is therefore a mystical mandate to use science and technology in this era, especially for the purpose of curing disease and improving the human condition.

[35] See Sinclair, *Modern Jewish Biomedical Law* (forthcoming) Chapter 1.

[36] R. Waldenberg cites *Resp. Havat Yair*, no. 31 to the effect that these time limits are "merely inclinations of the mind," lacking any basis in normative *halakhah*; see however, J.D. Bleich, "Abortion in Halakhic Literature" in *Jewish Bioethics* (n. 24 above), 169, no.34.

since a test such as chorionic villus sampling may be carried out as early as eight weeks but is associated with a relatively high risk of spontaneous abortion. The more well-established method of amniocentesis has a much lower risk of miscarriage but can only be carried out in the second trimester. On the basis of the Tay-Sachs responsa, it would seem that there would not be any compelling halakhic reason for choosing chorionic villus sampling over amniocentesis, since the abortion aspect ultimately depends upon the criterion of maternal welfare, not the status of fetal development.

The diametrically opposed views of R. Waldenberg and R. Feinstein reflect two emerging schools of thought in relation to the application of halakhic doctrine to contemporary bioethical issues. The view represented by R. Waldenberg is based upon the premise that medical therapy is a positive value and that there is nothing inherent in any area of the *halakhah* which militates against the use of genetic techniques in a therapeutic context. R. Feinstein may very well be concerned with the possible misuse of these techniques and their application in non-therapeutic contexts. As already observed, the question of the parameters of legitimate medical therapy have yet to be drawn in a definitive fashion and the issue is, therefore, of an ongoing nature.[37]

Gene Therapy

In principle, gene therapy would appear to be no different from any other form of medical therapy, and hence permissible in terms of Jewish law.[38] In contrast to somatic cell therapy, the simplest form of which is the replacement of faulty genes with properly functioning ones, e.g., the replacement of stem cells in the bone marrow bearing the hemophilia gene with cells containing normal genes; germ-line therapy involves the manipulation of the genetic code of future generations. Genetic alteration of the germ-line has almost universally been rejected at least for the time being, and the reasons include the lack of scientific knowledge with regard to its long-term effects; the problems involved in carrying out the necessary research on embryos and the possibility that other techniques, e.g., preimplantation, are capable of achieving the same therapeutic goal, albeit in a less scientifically dramatic fashion.[39] It is noteworthy that in its 1995 Report, the Science and

---

37 See Sinclair (n. 35 above).

38 See A. Rosenfeld, "Judaism and Gene Design," in *Jewish Bioethics* (n. 24 above), 401; F. Rosner, "Genetic Engineering and Judaism" in *Jewish Bioethics* (n. 24 above), 417–419.

39 See *Our Genetic Future*, n. 23 above, 185–188; Wilkie, (n. 23 above), 152–158. Also note Wilkie's comments on the darker side of the prospects offered to society by somatic-cell gene therapy.

Technology Committee of the House of Commons recommended that "the current prohibition on manipulating the genetic structure of a human embryo should remain, and there should be no manipulation of a human germ-line at any stage without the approval of the Gene Therapy Committee."[40]

In terms of Jewish sources, there is a particularly dramatic talmudic passage in which King Hezekiah is informed that it is not within his authority to determine the fate of future generations and to prevent a son being born to him who was destined to undo all his good work in spreading the word of the Lord in Israel.[41] Now, although the future defect in this case is of a moral rather than a physical nature, the principle of "what have you to do with the secrets of the All-Merciful" articulated in this passage may be of some value in shaping a response to the issue of germ-line therapy in the context of the scientific uncertainties with which it is surrounded. The biological fate of future generations ought not to be determined by their ancestors unless there are very good and well-proven reasons for so doing.

The Control of Genetic Information

The list of pressing ethical issues surrounding contemporary research in human genetics includes the patenting of DNA, the restriction of employment on the basis of genetics, and the insurance of those afflicted with defective genes or unfavorable genetic predispositions. The concerns raised in relation to the patenting issue range from a principled opposition to the ownership of living matter to worries about the effects of patenting upon scientific co-operation and patient protection.[42] The extent to which employers should be entitled to a full genetic profile of potential employees is also a moot point. This question arises not only in relation to the protection of the public but also to the protection of the workers themselves. Clearly, any workplace screening would have to be carefully monitored and closely regulated in order to avoid serious breaches of privacy and unjust discriminations.[43] The right of insurance companies to require genetic information from potential clients is also a thorny issue. The ramifications of genetic profiling for health insurance premiums are clear and fairly immediate. The regulation of the genetic information made available to insurance

---

40 See *Our Genetic Future*, ibid., 185; Wilkie, ibid., 158–165.

41 *Ber.* 10a.

42 *Our Genetic Future* (n. 23 above), 218–226; Wilkie (n. 23 above), 93–96; *Human Genetics* (n. 23 above), 64–73.

43 *Our Genetic Future*; ibid., 232–233; Wilkie, ibid., 127–129; *Human Genetics*, ibid., 77–78.

companies requires striking a delicate balance between considerations of privacy and those of economic expediency.[44] As yet, little progress has been made in finding solutions to any of these problems.[45]

The existence of copyright and patent in Jewish law is itself a matter of debate. Although there is no direct reference to these concepts in classical Jewish law, the biblical prohibition on landmark-removal[46] has been cited as an indication that the protection of intellectual property is recognized by the *halakhah*, and it was, indeed on this basis that printers' rights received protection from the 16th century onwards.[47] Assuming that patenting is a halakhically valid enterprise, the question arises as to whether or not it is possible to take out a patent for genetic material. One of the issues which naturally presents itself for discussion in this context is the ownership of a person's body. The majority of authorities maintain that people hold their bodies in trust from God and hence cannot be said to own them.[48] There is, however, a minority view according to which a person does have a right to his own body.[49] It is also possible that an individual may be able to exercise a right to biological matter under the provisions relating to quasi-ownership in Jewish law.[50] Finally, it is noteworthy that the Mishnah mentions the sale of hair as a legitimate method for raising the necessary funds to cover one's financial obligations.[51] There would appear, therefore, to be some basis for raising the question of the patenting of DNA in a halakhic context.

Employment and insurance involve issues such as confidentiality and privacy which were raised above. The development of an integrated halakhic approach to all of these issues involves elements drawn from several different branches of Jewish law and the halakhists of the future will undoubtedly be involved in the enterprise of providing solutions for both these and related problems cast up by modern biotechnology.

Genetic Determinism and Jewish Thought

The notion that human behavior is determined by genetics is a popular one and has manifested itself in relation to both criminality and sexual orienta-

---

44 *Our Genetic Future*, ibid., 233; Wilkie, ibid., 125–127; *Human Genetics*, ibid., 77–82.
45 See G. Annas, L. Glantz, P. Roche, *The Genetic Privacy Act and Commentary* (Boston, 1995).
46 Deuteronomy 19:14.
47 See R. Isaac Herzog, *The Main Institutes of Jewish Law* 1 (London, 1965), 127–136; M. Elon, *The Principles of Jewish Law* (Jerusalem, 1974), 344–346.
48 *Resp. Rosh*, no. 68:10; *Tur, Ḥoshen Mishpat*, no. 384; R. Shlomo Zevin (n. 1 above), 318.
49 R. Saul Yisrael, "The Kibiyeh Incident in the Light of the Halakhah" (Heb.), *Hatorah Vehamedinah* 4–6 (1953–54), 106.
50 See N. Shulman, "Genetic Modification," *Le'ela* (September, 1994), 20.
51 *Ned.* 9:5 *Ned.* 65b; *Shab.* 6:1.

tion.⁵² It is, however, abundantly clear that as yet, there is little scientific basis for any claimed link between gene variants and abnormal behavior and that, in any case, a genotype does not necessarily make a phenotype. In the words of the Science and Technology Committee of the House of Commons:

> Our awareness of the power and intellectual excitement of genetic science does not imply a belief that we are merely 'programmed by our genes.' Human nature is a product of the interaction between genes and environment which is subject to uncertainty.⁵³

This would certainly appear to be the position in the Jewish tradition. The Talmud records the view that "everything is in the hands of heaven except the fear of heaven,"⁵⁴ i.e., a person's qualities are fixed by nature but his moral qualities depend upon his own choice. A vivid illustration of this idea is the legend of the portrait of Moses cited by R. Israel Lipschutz in his commentary on the Mishnah.⁵⁵ According to this legend, an Arabian king heard about the great exploits of Moses and sent an artist to paint a portrait of the celebrated divinely inspired leader of the Israelites. Upon the artist's return, the portrait was handed over to the king's physiognomists for the preparation of a character analysis of Moses. The results were totally negative and the great leader emerged as a thoroughly evil individual. The king was dissatisfied with the results and decided to visit the Israelite camp in order to check on the accuracy of the portrait. The visit confirmed the artist's claim that his portrait was a faithful reproduction of Moses's face and the king concluded that the fault lay with his physiognomists. Prior to leaving the camp, however, the king informed Moses of the events which had caused him to make his visit. Moses then assured the king that his physiognomists were as precise as his artist and that by nature he was even worse than the picture they had painted of him. Without a concerted effort to overcome the evil proclivities to which nature had disposed him, Moses would never have become the servant of God and the greatest prophet in

---

52 "The Genetic Revolution," *Time*, January 17, 1994, p. 39; "Search for a Gay Gene," *Time*, June 12, 1995, p. 52.

53 See *Human Genetics* (n. 23 above) 22.

54 *Ber.* 33b.

55 *Tiferet Yisrael, Kid.* 4:14. In fact, the earliest versions of this story in Jewish sources contain no reference to Moses whatsoever, and the source is probably a passage in Cicero's *Tusculan Disputations* (London, 1927), 4 no. 80; see S. Leiman, "R. Israel Lipschutz and the Portrait of Moses Controversy," in *Danzig : Between East and West* (ed. I Twersky, Harvard University Press, 1985), 49.

Israel. This legend clearly expresses the notion that free will reigns supreme even in the context of a natural disposition. It may therefore be concluded that the establishment of a genetic predisposition would not in any way affect the theological doctrine of moral choice which is at the very heart of traditional Jewish thought.

17

REFUSING THE MILK OF HUMAN KINDNESS

HANNAH GELDWERTH-SPRECHER, JD & STANLEY SPRECHER, MD*

The highly incendiary issue of body fluids found a prominent place in Israeli news during the year 1996. Images were broadcast over news services throughout the world of a rioting Ethiopian community in Israel inflamed by the discovery that Israeli blood banks were secretly discarding standard Ethiopian blood contributions.

Within several weeks of these disturbances, the Israeli media reacted with disdain to a reported ruling by Rabbi Ovadiah Yosef, among other rabbinic leaders, that enjoined the *Charedi* community from receiving blood from donors who were not adherents to religious law—*Shomrei Torah Umitzvot*—except in situations of immediate *Pikuach Nefesh*. This ban had not been promulgated as a health precaution—the *Charedim* affirmed that they fully recognized that blood banks are capable of screening for those exposed to viral agents—but rather as a preventive measure to preclude any **spiritual** contamination transferred through the blood of a secular Jew.

Israel's reporters and commentators condemned the *Charedim* for their perceived racism, which seemed reminiscent of Nazi superiority theories. Representative of these are the words of Ze'ev Chafets in the January 25, 1996 issue of the Jerusalem Report:

> When I heard this, I said to myself—well, what could I say? Here are two of the world's leading rabbinical authorities [Rabbi Ovadiah Yosef and Rabbi Mordechai Eliyahu] neither fringe nor fanatic, at the peak of their intellectual and spiritual powers. And they have a clear answer to the question that has plagued me since my bar mitzvah-boy days. Real Torah Judaism is found neither in good deeds nor in humble faith. It certainly has nothing to do with something so simplistic as the golden rule. No. Real Torah Judaism is a scientifically based doctrine of racial purity, Jews have one, superior kind of blood, the rest of humanity has another.

---

* In addition to practicing their respective crafts of attorney-editor and physician, the authors maintain an active interest in the Responsa literature, both past and current.

In this paper we will examine the basis for and veracity of the Israeli media's highly critical reportage and place this issue in the context of an earlier warning regarding the dangers involved in the transfer of body fluids—a previously unpublished 18th century admonition to Jewish parents to avoid the practice of giving their infants to Gentile wet nurses for their early nutrition.

The author of this warning, Mordechai Gumpel Schnaber HaLevi (known later in his life as Dr. Georg Levison), was an eighteenth-century physician, the son and grandson of rabbis, who achieved great success as a medical practitioner in three countries.[1] He was the second Jew ever to receive the title of professor without having to undergo baptism as a prerequisite.[2] He wrote medical treatises in English, German and Swedish and edited two medical journals in Hamburg. Surprisingly, he was able to accomplish all this while remaining a Torah-committed Jew, publishing several volumes of *Chiddushei Torah* and using the wealth he had acquired as an eminent physician to endow a trust fund for needy Torah scholars and the elderly poor of Hamburg. This outstanding exemplar of *Torah im Derekh Eretz* proved that it is possible to successfully combine and integrate Torah observance and secular education. Yet, while well-known and celebrated

---

1 We have used the following sources to delineate the life of Schnaber-Levison (throughout this paper we will be using "Levison" and "Schnaber-Levison" interchangeably): H.J. Schoeps, "Gumpertz Levison-Leben und Werk: Eines Gelehrten Abenteurers des 18 Jahrhunderts," *Zeitschrift fur Religions-und Geistesgeschichte* 4 (1952), 150–61; H.M. Graupe, "Mordechai Gumpel (Levison)," *Bulletin des Leo Baeck Institute* 5 (1962), 1–12; C. Roth, "The Haskalah in England," *Essays Presented to Isaac Brodie* (London, 1967), 367–68, and C. Roth, *History of the Great Synagogue* (London, 1950), 130, 152; D. Ruderman, *Jewish Thought and Scientific Discovery in Early Modern Europe* (New Haven, 1995), 332–68; M.N. Rosenfeld, *Jewish Printing in Wilhermsdorf* (London, 1995), pp. VII–VIII; E. Shochet, *Im Chilufei Tekufot: Reishit HaHaskalah beYahadut Germaniah* (Jerusalem, 1960), 199–241; L. Lewin, *Jahrbuch der Judisch-Literarischen Gesellschaft* IX (1911), "Judische Aerzte in Grosspolen" (Frankfurt am Main: 1912), 14, 25–29, 35, 54. Ruth P. Goldschmidt-Lehmann's entry on Levison in her study, *A Bibliography of Anglo-Jewish Medical Biography*, p. 59, Supplement to *Koroth, vol. 9*, Jerusalem, 1988, repeats an error also found in *Encyclopaedia Judaica*, Vol. X, p. 857, that can be traced to E. Carmoly, *Les medicins Juifs*, 217–219 in which Levison is listed as having been baptized. This claim is certainly incorrect. In fact, Levison received his medical degree from Marischal College in Aberdeen, Scotland, because it was the only institution of its kind that permitted Jews and Christian nonconformists to matriculate. See the article by Kenneth E. Collins, *Jewish Medical Students and Graduates in Scotland, 1739–1862*, in *Jewish Historical Studies: Transactions of the Jewish Historical Society of England*, 29, 1982–1986, pp.75–96, London, The Jewish Historical Society of England, 1988. Collins, however, is mistaken in stating that Levison served as court physician to King Gustave III of Sweden.

2 Although Schoeps, p. 150, claims that Levison was the **first** unbaptized Jew to be named professor, this honor is in fact due Jacob Mantino, named Professor of Medicine to the Sapienza in Rome, by the Pope in 1539. See H. Vogelstein, *Jewish Community Series: Rome* (Philadelphia: JPS, 1940), 245–246.

in his own generation, Levison has long since been relegated to obscurity. Perhaps he was destined to suffer the fate of obscurity because he was an anomaly. He was too committed to traditional Judaism to suit the tastes of the *Maskilim* of the period, and the *Torah im Derekh Eretz* movement would not come into being until nearly half a century after Levison's death.

Mordechai Gumpel Schnaber HaLevi was born in 1741 in the city of Berlin where his father, Rabbi Yehudah Leib, was a *dayan*. Young Gumpel studied Torah under the direction of Rabbi David Frankel, the Chief Rabbi of Berlin.[3] After concluding his Torah studies in Berlin, he moved on to Rabbi Yonatan Eybeschutz's Beit Midrash in Hamburg. Later on in his career, Schnaber would run afoul of the synagogue authorities in charge of the Great Synagogue in Duke's Place in London, and would draw upon the fact that he had studied under these two great Torah luminaries as a way of defending his honor and good name. Indeed, he claimed that he had received *semikhah* at the age of fourteen from both these authorities.[4]

Gumpel Schnaber immigrated to England where he became a disciple of the celebrated eighteenth-century English physicians, William and John Hunter. In London he was to enjoy outstanding success, although controversy would dog his steps. As his reputation grew, he came to the attention of the philanthropist and later British Prime Minister, William Cavendish-Bentinck, 3rd Duke of Portland, who appointed Schnaber to the post of Attending Physician at the General Medical Asylum the Duke had established in London.[5] For professional purposes he changed his name to Georg Levison, and it was under this name that he authored two well-received treatises, "An Essay on the Blood" (London, 1776), dedicated to William Hunter and "An Account of the Epidemical Sore-Throat" (London, 1778), dedicated to the Duke of Portland. Both of these works were later

---

[3] One of his fellow students was the young Moses Mendelssohn. Gumpel seems to have had little respect for Mendelssohn, claiming that he was moved to compose his own commentary to *Kohelet* after seeing what a poor job Mendelssohn did in his attempt at explicating this enigmatic work. Mendelssohn's commentary to *Kohelet* was published in Berlin in 1769, not bearing any attribution as to its authorship, but apparently it was widely known who the author actually was. Gumpel's personal copy of Mendelssohn's commentary to *Kohelet* is in our possession, and it contains extensive critical glosses.

[4] This claim is undoubtedly an exaggeration. Typically, at least ten years of rigorous Torah study was required before one was granted *semikhah*.

[5] The Duke of Portland was highly influential, and it was certainly a coup for Schnaber-Levison to have attained his good will and patronage. William Cavendish-Bentinck, 3rd Duke of Portland, devoted much of his time and money in the service of the public good. He was active in politics and held several cabinet posts. He served twice as prime minister, once as a Whig and, several years later as a Tory, often earning the wrath of his monarch, George III, because of his policies and proposals.

translated into German, and subsequently into Swedish. Schnaber-Levison did not neglect his Hebrew studies either, publishing *Ma'amar HaTorah VeHachokhma* in 1771. It was one of the few non-liturgical works produced by the newly resurrected (in 1770) Hebrew press of London.

His professional success was marred, however, by personal tragedy. Aaron Franks, the ninety-year-old *Rosh HaḲahal* of the Great Synagogue, the main Ashkenazi synagogue in London, had Schnaber-Levison publicly expelled on the grounds of unbecoming conduct.[6] Schnaber-Levison answered these charges in a pamphlet he published entitled *Tokhachat Megulah* (London, 1774). His enemies responded in kind, with a vicious attack published under the title *Teshuvot HaPrushim*.[7]

His career took another turn in the summer of 1779, when August Nordenskjold, a young Swedish scientist, came to London to have his work on Alchemy translated into English. He let rooms at the residence of Schnaber-Levison and so greatly interested his host in his project that Schnaber-Levison helped prepare the English edition, "A Plain System of Alchemy," for publication. Nordenskjold, in turn, was equally taken with Schnaber-Levison and persuaded him to sail for Stockholm for a personal introduction to King Gustave III. In a series of meetings with the Swedish monarch, Schnaber-Levison convinced the King to establish a royal hospital in Stockholm for the purpose of providing medical care for the needy while at the same time serving as a venue for the practical training of young physicians—a teaching hospital. In this proposal, Levison was simply importing the London model of teaching hospitals to Scandinavia, where the concept was still unknown. According to Schnaber-Levison's plan, the most interesting and most difficult cases confronting the hospital's staff would be collected annually and published for the edification of the medical community. At one of their meetings King Gustave bestowed upon Schnaber-Levison the title of Professor of Medicine.

Unfortunately, Levison was forced to return to England because a financial crisis at the Duke of Portland's General Medical Asylum threatened its existence. While back in England, Schnaber-Levison made an enemy of

---

6 What this "unbecoming conduct" actually involved remains unclear. It has been suggested that Schnaber-Levison's *Ma'amar HaTorah VeHachokhmah* proved too controversial for the Orthodox community in London. In addition, he had left Germany under a cloud: he had been arrested in Breslau on suspicion of murder and after a period of incarceration, he was released. Apparently, this episode became known to the London Jewish community and contributed to his unpopularity.

7 Both pamphlets are known by virtue of single remaining copies in the British Library, where, ironically, they are bound together, bearing Accession Number 1982 d 3. Among the accusations in the latter pamphlet is the assertion that the Breslau murder charges were in fact true, but influential family connections succeeded in quashing the indictment.

a young German count, ultimately leading to a duel between the two antagonists. The outcome of the duel was unfavorable for the German count, but the repercussions for Schnaber-Levison were also severe.[8] The scandal reached the ears of King Gustave, and Schnaber-Levison's Swedish project was terminated. Nevertheless, he maintained cordial relations with the Swedish royal court, and wrote a two-page dedication to King Gustave III at the opening of a commentary to *Kohelet* that he authored in 1784. Moreover, Schnaber-Levison served, by royal appointment, as the physician to the Swedish diplomatic corps resident in Hamburg.

In 1782 Schnaber-Levison returned to his native Germany where he established a highly successful medical practice in Hamburg. In addition to maintaining his clinical practice, he published several well-received medical texts containing approbations and laudatory reviews by Johann Christian Theden, the Surgeon General of Prussia. He also edited two medical journals in Hamburg.

As he had done in London, his attention to Torah studies continued, despite his obviously hectic work schedule. In 1784 he published the above mentioned commentary to *Kohelet* which carries the title *Tokhachat Megillah*, in 1792 he published a lengthy analysis on the *Shelosh Esreh Yesodei HaTorah* of the Rambam entitled *Yesod HaTorah*, and in 1797 his opus posthumous *Solet Minchah Belulah* appeared, containing Schnaber-Levison's *Chiddushei Torah* on *Tanakh* and *Shas*. All these works were published in Hamburg-Altona.[9]

---

[8] By the late eighteenth century, dueling was illegal in England. According to English law, the winner of a fatal duel was viewed and was culpable to the same extent as a willful murderer. In practice, however, the participants rarely saw the inside of a courtroom, let alone a prison or the gallows. Possibly because duelists were for the most part members of the aristocracy, landed gentry, or the military's hierarchy, they had the means to evade the legal consequences of their actions. Yet, there were consequences. The state, clergy and intelligentsia were all vocal in their condemnation of dueling, and their revulsion had a strong effect on public opinion. By Schnaber-Levison's day, dueling had definitely fallen into disrepute. In order to avoid the legal ramifications of their actions, the winner as well as the loser of a duel (if he survived) were often forced into exile until the scandal faded from the law's and the public's collective memory. Often, this took several years.

[9] Unlike his German medical works, which had received approbations from the Prussian Surgeon General, Schnaber-Levison's *Yesod HaTorah* was his only *Sefer* to contain any *Haskamot* from notable rabbis of his time.

These *Haskamot* were written by Rabbi David Breslau, Chief Rabbi of Munster; Rabbi Moshe Meisel, Chief Rabbi of Weislitz; and Rabbi Zvi Hirsh Mirels of London, Chief Rabbi of Schwerin.

Rabbi David Breslau, son of Rabbi Michel HeChasid MiBreslau, is remembered today mainly for the many *She'elot* he had posed to Rabbi Yaakov Emden—ten in all—published with Rabbi Emden's *Teshuvot* in *She'ilat Ya'avetz*, Part II—#68, 69, 72, 116, 117, 118, 119, 121, 122, 123. No other correspondent even approaches this number.

Relevant to our discussion is the *Ma'amar Machazeh Shaddai*, which is a manuscript in a highly fragmentary state,[10] in the collection of the Jewish Theological Seminary (Enelow Memorial Collection #2481). The microfilm of this document in the Jewish National University Library Institute for Manuscripts (#28734) bears the identification of the author as Schnaber-Levison. Our reading of the manuscript in conjunction with what is known about Schnaber-Levison corroborates this identification.

Throughout the manuscript, Schnaber-Levison intersperses discourses on Jewish topics with various medical theories and techniques. These range from the commonplace in 18th century medicine such as anatomical dissections that he has conducted, therapeutic administration of mercury for the treatment of venereal disease and a reference to the disorder "Hypochondriack", which is the 18th century term for severe melancholy or depression;[11] to innovations that were developed by Schnaber-Levison such as sur-

---

While little is known of Rabbi Moshe Meisel, Rabbi Zvi Hirsh Mirels is noted for his family ties. He was born in London, where his father, Rabbi Aaron ben Meshulam Zalman, is thought to have served as rabbi of the Hambro Synagogue (see Cecil Roth's *History of the Great Synagogue*, 130, n. 4.) Rabbi Aaron's sister, Sarah Mirels, was married to the Hakham Zvi, making Rabbi Zvi Hirsh Mirels first cousin to Rabbi Yaakov Emden. (Incidentally, Rabbi Emden's son Meshulam succeeded his uncle, Rabbi Aaron, as rabbi of the Hambro Synagogue.)

What is especially interesting about Rabbi Mirels' *Haskamah* is his declaration that in addition to his own positive assessment of Levison's work, his kinsman, Rabbi David Tevel, Chief Rabbi of Lissa, had also read with approval portions of *Yesod HaTorah*. Rabbi Mirels states that only Rabbi Tevel's reluctance to issue approbations to new works prevented him from joining in the published *Haskamot*. Rabbi Tevel is acknowledged as one of the staunch opponents of *Haskalah*. Indeed, it was his *Shabbat HaGadol Derasha* of 1782 that is considered the opening salvo in the polemic against the agenda of Mendelssohn and Weisel, conducted by the *Gedolim* of Europe at the end of the eighteenth century. If Schnaber-Levison's work passed muster in the eyes of Rabbi Tevel, one can be certain that it is free of any taint of *Haskalah*. Another indication that Schnaber-Levison should be assigned to the traditional camp is the oneiric quality (using J. Le Goff's formulation as quoted by J.M. Davis in *Leo Baeck Institute Yearbook* XXXVII 1993, "The Cultural and Intellectual History of Ashkenazic Jews 1500–1750: A Selective Bibliography and Essay," p. 347) of much of the material in the *Ma'amar Machazeh Shaddai*, and in the *Solet Minchah Belulah*.

10 Ruderman, p. 346, in listing all the known works of Levison, was the first scholar to publish this attribution, i.e., that the author of this manuscript is Levison. The manuscript begins with page 29 and continues to page 32. Thereafter there is a gap until page 93, and nothing remains after 97. The page size is quarto, and the handwriting is in a typical 18th-century Ashkenazi script.

11 There was the perception that this ailment affected Jews to a greater degree than what might be expected on a statistical basis. The legal and social disabilities that Jews suffered under were assumed to be the cause of the malady's prevalence. See, for example, the testimony of an eighteenth-century Lorraine physician, M. Le-Jau, in a memoir entitled "Remarks on the Diseases of the Jew" published in the *Bulletin of the History of Medicine*, 1993, 67:248–281 by H. Mitchell and S. Kottek. Dr. Jonah Jeiteles, the noted Jewish physician of late eighteenth-century Prague also suffered extensively from depression, a fact made public in the biographi-

gical removal of a parasite from the limb of a child by utilizing a microscope to aid in locating the infestation, and the fashioning of a prosthetic palate to enable a congenital syphilitic to speak. In the realm of medical theory he is also innovative. For example, he critiques the traditional view among physicians that pigs were the animals with the anatomy and physiology that most closely resembled human characteristics. Galen, for example, had done all his anatomy studies on pigs. Schnaber-Levison disagrees and claims that primates bear a stronger similarity to humans, which is, of course, the prevailing theory today. He also enthusiastially embraces the theory of internal human combustion, which had just been promulgated by the eighteenth-century English physician, Thomas Beddoes.[12]

These discussions are followed by an analysis of the talmudic account of the punishment meted out to the Emperor Titus. Schnaber-Levison attempts to rationalize the Talmud's narrative with the medical knowledge at his disposal. His approach to the story lies midway between the opposing views held by Azariah DeRossi and the Maharal. Azariah DeRossi saw the story as a fiction designed to hearten the Jewish masses with the conviction that God takes revenge upon His enemies.[13] The Maharal, by contrast, accepts the veracity of the Talmud's account, but assigns a deeper meaning to each aspect of its retelling.[14] As a medical scientist, Schnaber-Levison is initially puzzled by the description of Titus' malady: how could a creature as large as a sparrow or dove exist inside the Emperor's brain? He resolves this seeming impossibility by explaining that in reality the creature inhabiting Titus' brain was only a tiny parasite. Yet the Rabbis of the Talmud examined it under a microscope (of their own invention)[15] and consequently it appeared as large as a sparrow or dove. He then turns his read-

---

cal sketch of his life prepared by his son, Jehuda Jeiteles, entitled *Benei HaNe'urim* (Prague, 1821), 54–55.

12 This practitioner claimed that many diseases resulted from a derangement in the process of internal human combustion, and that cures could be effected by therapeutic administration of various gases and vapors. Although his "pneumatic medicines" were unsuccessful in curing anyone, his efforts ultimately contributed to the development of respiratory therapy and the practice of anesthesia. Another curious by-product of this theory was the belief that the cause of sudden death in alcoholics was a spontaneous internal conflagration.

13 See *Me'or 'Einayim, Imre Binah*, 1:16.

14 See *Be'er HaGolah*, 137–138, and *Chiddushei Aggadot*, Part II, 108.

15 A similar claim about the invention of the telescope was made by the celebrated Italian Jewish physician of the Renaissance, Abraham Yagel, who was the second Jew (after Delmedigo, a direct disciple of Galileo) to describe the telescope recently invented by Galileo. Yagel maintains that Rabban Gamliel had devised a comparable instrument, which allowed him to see up to two-thousand cubits (see *Talmud Bavli Eruvin* 43b), cited by D. Ruderman in his book, *Kabbalah, Magic, and Science* (Cambridge:Harvard University Press, 1988), 98.

er's attention to his own experiences with the microscope, recounting several surgical cures he had effected with the aid of that instrument.[16]

What is especially noteworthy for the purposes of this paper is his long discussion about the behavior of wealthy, urban German Jews who send their infants out of the home to be nursed by rural Christian wet nurses. He notes that this common practice inflicts significant harm on these infants in diverse ways:

The transmission of infectious diseases, particularly the venereal diseases, since not enough attention is paid to the health of the wet nurse. He records many instances in which he was called upon to treat serious infectious diseases that had been transmitted from the wet nurse to the infant in her charge.[17]

Second, he finds the danger of physical trauma: Schnaber-Levison believes that many of these infants are unknown victims of child abuse.[18] He maintains that it is common for the wet nurse herself or someone in her household to deal with the annoyance of an infant's prolonged crying by beating the child. These violent actions lead readily to head injuries with resultant deafness or blindness and are responsible as well as for multiple fracture deformities.

And finally there is the infliction of spiritual trauma: the diet of the Gentile wet nurses includes non-kosher food, therefore every Jewish child in their care is exposed to the spiritually contaminating effect of *neveilot u'treifot*.

To Levison, the spiritual trauma was the most serious of the dangers. While his theories regarding child abuse and the transfer of disease were considered innovative in his day, his views on the spiritual trauma involved have a long *Halakhic* history and, as we will see, a direct link to the issue of blood transfusions.

---

[16] Rabbi Yaakov Emden, in his work *Iggeret Bikkoret*, second edition (Altona, 1765), 19a, also discusses medical applications utilizing the microscope.

[17] See Janet Golden, *A Social History of Wet Nursing in America* (New York:Cambridge University Press, 1996), 143–6, documenting the extent of the problem recognized by 19th-century physicians who warned against the dangers of wet nurses transmitting tuberculosis and venereal diseases to the infants in their care. Schnaber-Levison was ahead of his time in this regard as well.

[18] It should be pointed out that while the medical literature credits Ambroise Tardieu's 1860 article as the first to discuss child abuse, and the first recorded case of child abuse in America did not take place until 1874 (see M. Heins, "The Battered Child Revisited," *Journal of the American Medical Association* (1984), 251:3295–3300). However, general medical and lay recognition of this problem was virtually absent until 1962 when Dr. H. Kempe and associates published a landmark article in JAMA (cited by Heins.) Schnaber-Levison deserves recognition as the actual discoverer of this important syndrome, and his analysis of the neurological and orthopedic injuries sustained by the victims of child abuse is in full accord with contemporary observations.

The rabbinic literature discusses the issue of the permissibility of using Gentile wet nurses in three instances: *Talmud Bavli Yevamot* 114a and *Avodah Zarah* 26a, and *Tosefta Shabbat* Chapter 10. After incorporating the commentaries and analyses of these rabbinic sources by the *Rishonim*, three approaches to this issue emerge:

First is the position of the Rashba and of the Meiri,[19] which essentially permits the utilization of a Gentile wet nurse even when an equally acceptable Jewish wet nurse is readily available. According to this approach, eschewing a Gentile wet nurse in favor of a Jewish one is seen only as a *midat chasidut*—an extraordinary act of piety, rather than a matter mandated by law. In the words of the Rashba, "but it is a *midat chasidut* to nurse children with Jewish milk since the character of Jews is more subdued, because they are accustomed to performing mitzvot and they are merciful and modest by nature. Therefore their milk will induce a similar good nature in their recipient." The Rashba then cites the *Midrash Shemot Rabbah* I:25 that since Moses was destined to speak directly to God, it was not fitting for him to be nursed by an Egyptian and so God worked matters in such a way that insured that he would be nursed by a Jew—his own mother.[20]

This opinion of the Rashba is echoed by the great Provencal rationalist and follower of Maimonides, the Meiri, who writes: "although there is not the slightest bit of prohibition in being nursed by a Gentile, nevertheless it is a *midat chasidut* as much as possible to be nursed by a Jew."

---

19 Both sources are found in their respective commentaries to *Yevamot* 114a.

20 The Rashba might also have cited the following charming midrashic story repeated by Tosafot, Talmud Bavli Avoda Zara, 10b, "AMAR LEI." This midrash, also found in Jellinek's *Beit Midrash* (Vol. 6, 130–131) and Rav Moshe Hadarshan's *Bereishit Rabbati* (86–87 of the Albeck edition), is commenting on the great friendship between Rabbi Yehudah HaNasi and the Roman Emperor Antoninus and begins with the words "Milk contaminates and milk purifies." According to the midrash, there had been a Roman decree prohibiting circumcision in effect at the time of Rabbi Yehudah HaNasi's birth. His parents refused to submit to the decree and secretly had the infant circumcised. Unfortunately, their act was discovered, and the family, including the newborn child, was summoned to the court of the Roman emperor to face judicial proceedings. While in Rome, the wife of Severus, a high court official, befriended Rabbi Yehudah HaNasi's mother, sympathized with her plight and agreed to switch her own uncircumcised son with the Jewish child for the duration of the trial. When the family appeared before the emperor, the infant impostor was examined, was found to be uncircumcised and the parents of Rebbi were exonerated. During the proceedings, Rabbi Yehudah HaNasi's mother had the opportunity to nurse the Roman baby, who grew up to be the Emperor Antoninus, and the midrash credits his having been nursed by a Jewish woman for his strong kinship with, and admiration for, the Jewish people. *The Talmud Yerushalmi*, in fact, states that Antoninus ultimately converted to Judaism.

Second is the position of the Ritva[21] who maintains that choosing a Gentile wet nurse when a Jewish one is available is an *issur d'Rabbanan*— a violation of a rabbinic ordinance.

The third position is that of Rabbeinu Chananel[22] who sees the issue as an *issur d'orayta*—that it is a violation of a biblical law to choose a Gentile wet nurse over an available Jewish one, provided of course, that this results in no danger to the welfare of the child.

The normative *Halakhah* is in accord with the Rashba's position since the Rema in *Yoreh De'ah* 81:7 codifies the ruling in conformity with the Rashba: "milk of a Gentile is equivalent to the milk of a Jew but nevertheless a child should not be nursed by a Gentile if milk of a Jew is available, because a Gentile's milk "*metamteim*" (obstructs) the heart and gives rise to a bad nature." The Rema's comment should not be taken as being motivated by a racist ideology of "Jewish superiority." This is proven by the Rema's next line where he states that even a Jewish mother who must eat non-kosher food for medical purposes should avoid nursing her child for as long as her diet includes non-kosher items.[23]

Armed with this background material, we can now return to our original problem, the matter of blood transfusions. When the first media reports surfaced that their rabbinic authorities forbade *Charedim* from utilizing the blood of secular Jews, our first impression was that this represented another aspect of the media's demonization of *Charedim* in the wake of the assassination of Israeli Prime Minister Yitzchak Rabin. However, when accounts of this *psak* appeared in the *Charedim*'s own media,[24] it then became a matter to be taken more seriously. According to a popular *Charedi* newspaper, Rabbi Yehoshua Steinberger, head of the organization "Medicine and Halakha" (*RAFAH*), declared that Rabbi Ovadiah Yosef had indeed issued such a ban. As a result, Rabbi Steinberger was negotiating with representatives from the Ministry of Health to insure that methods would be instituted to keep *Charedi* blood separate from the supplies of the general public. He explained there was a powerful religious dimension involved in spurning blood from secular Jews:

---

[21] See Ritva's Commentary to *Masekhet Yevamot* (Jerusalem:Mosad Harav Kook, 1986) 1586, n. 101. The Maharshal in his *Yam Shel Shlomo* on *Yevamot* 114a rules in accord with the Ritva.

[22] Cited by the *Nemukei Yosef* to *Yevamot* 114a.

[23] It is evident from this last comment of the Rema that the spiritually polluting effect of non-kosher food is not mitigated by its being *Halakhically* permitted. This point is however subject to a dispute among many *Halakhic* authorities. For an excellent summary of the differing views on this issue see A. I. Rubin, "In the Matter of Obstructing the Heart and Mind Through the Ingestion of Forbidden Foods [Heb.]," *Mesorah* 11 (1994), 61–71.

[24] *Panim Chadashot*, Gilyon 386, Adar 10, 5756, p. 19.

the Kabbalah compares blood to the soul. Alien blood flowing through the circulatory system of a person can imprint the evil characteristics and sins of the donor and can thus stain the soul of the recipient. The recipient of blood from one who ate non-kosher food causes impurity in the recipient. Furthermore, one who angers often—his blood has a tendency to boil. If such blood is then infused into a calm person, it will cause the recipient also to become easily angered.

After reading this account, we had to see this ruling for ourselves. Here things became "curiouser and curiouser." For despite all these claims about what he had ruled, a direct examination of Rabbi Yosef's published responsum (*Yabiya Omer* vol. 8, *Choshen Mishpat siman* 11, p. 492) which was printed in Jerusalem in 1995, revealed that in fact Rabbi Yosef never issued the ruling that he was being excoriated for by the secular media. He never remotely banned the use of blood from non-observant Jews or Gentiles. He explicitly states "there is certainly no prohibition whatsoever in the use of such blood." He merely reiterates the basic position of the Rashba that if there is no urgency and it is possible to delay the transfusion, then it is a *midat chasidut* to receive transfusions from *Shomrei Torah uMitzvot*. Rabbi Yosef deduces from the Rashba's position regarding Gentile wet nurses, that a blood transfusion from a non-observant Jew can cause similar spiritual damage to the recipient as does the milk of a Gentile wet nurse to her Jewish charge. He bases this opinion on the Talmud Bavli *Bekhorot* 6b which states that blood is transformed into milk—blood is the source for milk, and if the by-product can cause spiritual damage, then certainly the source can as well. Yet, following the Rashba, he sees no actual prohibition on its use.

Interestingly, most of Rabbi Yosef's responsum is actually devoted to rebutting the opinion of a twentieth-century Sephardi *posek*, whose views on the subject of transfusions and transplants are much more stringent than his own. Rabbi Ovadiah Hadaya ruled[25] that a Jew who is totally blind is still not permitted to receive a corneal transplant from a Gentile. Rabbi Hadaya maintains that although the blind person is exempt from *mitzvot* and would again become subject to *mitzvot* with restoration of sight, nevertheless, the world through Gentile eyes is entirely that of the *Sitra Achara* , and consists of thieving, murder, fornication and other grave sins, which will result in the Jewish recipient pursuing an evil lifestyle, just as the donor would be prone to do. It is therefore preferable, in the eyes of Rabbi Hadaya, for a Jew to be blind in **this** world so that he might enjoy the light of the World to Come. Furthermore, since all Jewish souls are interconnected, transplanting

---

25 Volume 6 of *Teshuvot Yaskil Avdi* (*Yoreh De'ah siman* 26:6), (Jerusalem, 1969).

a Gentile body part into a Jew results in spiritual damage to the entire *Klal Yisrael*. The individual who receives such a transplant will likely not merit bodily resurrection because of the alien admixture.

Rabbi Yosef finds Rabbi Hadaya's formulations extreme, since by prohibiting the use of a Gentile cornea, Rabbi Hadaya's ruling would consign a Jew in need of corneal transplants to permanent blindness. That needy Jew would be denied all alternatives: receiving a corneal transplant from a Jew is prohibited by most *poskim* because of the prohibition against defiling a Jewish corpse and Rabbi Hadaya's ruling would block corneal transplants from Gentiles as well.[26]

It is obvious then, that Rabbi Yosef's ruling is entirely prosaic and represents no innovation to merit the media attention and opprobrium it received. In fact it wasn't even new: although the responsum is not dated, its appearance in print in May of 1995 indicates that it predates, by at least one year, the date it came to the media's attention, and reiterates six centuries worth of *Halakhah* on the subject of wet nursing as its basis—hardly meriting the reaction it received.

Moreover, it is our contention that the prohibition, be it rabbinic or *midat chasidut*, against the use of Gentile wet nurses in the care of Jewish babies was never practically observed. It is only the Ritva who records that in the locale in which **he** lived, Gentile wet nurses were not used. In other areas of Jewish settlement Gentiles were used unrestrictedly in this capacity. We have evidence of this from a perusal of Solomon Grayzel's well-known book, *The Church and the Jews in the XIIIth Century*[27] which contains numerous exhortations by Christian prelates warning against the practice of having Christian women serve as wet nurses in Jewish homes. The Third Lateran Council of 1179 and the various Councils of Montpellier, Paris, Narbonne and Tarracona as well as The Regulations and Synod of Worcester dating from 1195–1240 all specifically prohibit Christian women from serving as wet nurses to Jews under the threat of anathema, excommunication and the denial of Christian burial. Pope Innocent III complains to the archbishop of Sens and the bishop of Paris in a letter dated July 15, 1205 that, as evidence of Jewish insolence and contempt, the Jews who use Christian wet nurses for their infants' care force them to "pour their milk into the latrine

---

[26] Rabbi Hadaya's harsh views regarding Gentiles is even more extreme than that of the nineteenth-century noted *posek*, the Chatam Sofer. In his commentary to Talmud *Bavli Shabbat*, folio 86b, the Chatam Sofer writes that one cannot rely on the medical information provided by contemporary physicians in deciding matters of *Halakhah*, since physicians are taught the medical physiology of Gentiles, which differs from the physiology operative in Jews.

[27] (New York: Sepher-Hermon Press, 1966), 2nd edition, see under "nursing" in Index.

for three days" after they had taken in "the body and blood of Jesus Christ" on Easter.[28] In 1233, Pope Gregory IX complained of the practice in his correspondence, and in 1272, the Bishop of Olmutz informed the newly elected Pope Gregory X, in a kind of State of Christendom missive, that the practice was widespread in Bohemia and Hungary.

Among the Jews of medieval Europe, even the *Chasidei Ashkenaz*, the proponents of extreme piety, who might be expected to castigate their fellow Jews for not observing the *midat chasidut* ban on Gentile wet nurses, do not live up to expectations on this issue: in Section 672 of *Sefer Chasidim* there is an episode about an encounter between a *Chasid* and an ordinary Jewish householder. The *Chasid* inquires why the Jew employs two Gentile wet nurses who hate each other. The householder responds that their mutual hatred insures that they will never cooperate in stealing from the home, but would quickly inform on each other. The *Chasid* warns him that their enmity presents a graver danger: one of the nurses might murder the infant in the charge of the other nurse so that the second might be blamed for its death.

In the 18th century, we have Levison's deeply felt testimony that this practice was widespread among the wealthy city dwellers in Germany. We also have the words of Rabbi Hezekiah Da Silva, writing in his *Pri Chadash*[29] (published in Amsterdam in 1692), that among the Jewish communities he was familiar with, "go out and see that this recommendation by the Rema to refrain from using Gentile wet nurses is not followed." As for Eastern European Jewry, we take note of Tzvi Hirsh of Vilna writing in *Beit Lechem Yehuda*[30] (Zolkiew, 1733) that "The custom of the world [*minhag olam*] is to be lenient in the use of a Gentile wet nurse even when a Jewish wet nurse is readily available." Now, it is evident that in the situation described by Levison, i.e., Jewish children sent to lodge in the rural homes of their Gentile wet nurses, these nurses did not restrict their diets to kosher food. Similarly, there is no mention in these other, earlier sources of any stipulation being made that these wet nurses could only eat kosher food for the duration of their employment. Indeed, from the 1205 letter of Pope Innocent III cited earlier we learn that nursing was temporarily suspended only after ingesting the Eucharist, and not after eating ordinary non-kosher food.

As for the twentieth-century, through anecdotal evidence, we are aware that the practice of using Gentile wet nurses was still customary among Orthodox Jews in prewar Europe. A number of our female relatives attest that they were nursed by Gentile wet nurses. What is especially noteworthy

---

28 Grayzel, 114–17.
29 *Yoreh De'ah* 81:7.
30 *Yoreh De'ah* 81:7.

is that these relatives were from a prominent **Hasidic** family. Followers of Hasidism always placed great stress on avoiding any trace of non-kosher food. One of the major points of strife between the emerging Hasidic movement of the late eighteenth-century and the organized Jewish community, i.e., the *Kehillah,* was the refusal of Hasidim to utilize the services of the community-appointed ritual slaughterers [*shochetim*] and butchers for fear that they were not meticulous enough in weeding out non-kosher meat. Instead, Hasidim ate only meat prepared by *shochetim* who were also adherents of their movement. The most prominent Hasidic leader of the mid nineteenth-century, the *tzaddik* of Sanz, declared[31] that the wave of secularism that engulfed so much of European Jewry could be traced to the carelessness of the community-appointed *shochetim*. By providing their unsuspecting customers with meat that was not really kosher they polluted them spiritually and thus allowed them to be subject to the heresies of modernism. Hasidim, on the other hand, were largely spared this blight of secularization because they patronized only truly pious, i.e., Hasidic, *shochetim*.

There is also printed twentieth-century *Halakhic* material that conforms fully with this position—a 1951 *psak* issued by Rabbi Jacob Breisch[32] who finds no prohibition whatsoever, not even a *midat chasidut*, in accepting blood transfusions from a Gentile. Rabbi Breisch quotes an oral teaching he had received from the Belzer Rebbe—that when a person is very ill, the evil inclination finds it difficult to induce this person into performing the usual sins of appetite and desire. So instead, he induces the sick person to seek out *chumrot* [stringencies] that would actually interfere in his recovery so that his victim violates the positive commandment of *"vechai bahem"*— "... and you shall live [by the Torah]."

Thus, throughout the history of the Diaspora—in both Sephardi and Ashkenazi communities—even with the codified *Halakhah* considering it a *midat chasidut* to avoid Gentile wet nurses—as a practical matter, it does not seem that it was widely followed. There was certainly no question that a blood transfusion, wherein life or health are at stake, would be similarly seen and accepted by all, even by Rabbi Yosef whose ruling is situated fully in this mainstream tradition of idealizing an act as *midat chasidut* but placing no practical consequences on the person in need.

Why, then, has this issue resurfaced? And why have the predominantly Ashkenazi *Charedim* suddenly embraced a *"psak Halakhah"* of the Sephardi Rabbi, Ovadiah Yosef—whose opinions they have largely ignored or even vilified? The answer, we believe, is simple. Israeli *Charedim* are not afraid of

---

31 *Divre Chaim, Yore De'ah,* Section I, siman 7.
32 *Tshuvot Chelkat Yaakov,* vol. 2, siman 40.

the racist label—they have rarely been troubled by public relations concerns—but they *are* afraid of AIDS and other diseases contracted through tainted blood. A request to the Ministry of Health to separate *charedi* blood from supplies of the general population for health reasons would be met with outrage and could prove to be illegal as well. But accommodation based on religious grounds has many precedents.

Thus, the *Charedim* have cloaked their real and temporal concerns under the guise of religious imperative, hoping to receive a more sympathetic response from Israeli authorities. Some in the *Chasidic* community in the United States, well aware of the issues at stake, have begun to follow suit by raising religious concerns regarding the use of non-Orthodox donors as sources for transfusions. While we understand and share every individual's desire to insure a safer blood supply, we cannot condone a misrepresentation of the *Halakhah* to achieve these goals.

# 18

The (Double) Vision of the Divine Picnic (Acts 10:1–11:18): The History of New Testament Kashrut III

Peter Zaas*

> ... ὅσοι μὲν γὰρ θέλουσιν ὑπὸ τοὺς αὐτοὺς ἡμῖν νόμους ζῆν ὑπελθόντες δέχεται φιλοφρόνως, οὐ τῷ γένει μόνον, ἀλλὰ καὶ τῇ προαιρέσει τοῦ βίου νομίζων εἶναι τὴν οἰκειότητα. τοὺς δ ἐκ παρέργου προσιόντας ἀναμίγνυσθαι τῇ συνηθείᾳ οὐκ ἠθέλησεν.
>
> ... As many, on the one hand, who wish to come and live under our same laws, [our lawgiver Moses] receives with an open heart, believing that kinship is not only a matter of race but also of choice. On the other hand, he did not wish happenstance passers-by to be joined into our way of life.[1]
>
> Josephus, Contra Ap., II. 210

Since biblical times, Jews had considered that the canopy of God's providence, and therefore His law, covered all the nations, not only His chosen people. The laws of the TaNaKh, of which Josephus is so proud, explicitly included the *gar toshav*, the alien resident.[2] But, except for those laws which specifically apply to the *gar toshav*, the precise ways in which non-Jews are obliged to observe God's laws remain vague until well through the Tanaitic period, and even then assume a very minor role in Jewish legal thinking.

Certainly the condition of Gentiles under God's Torah was not of great moment to the Jews of Roman Judea and its extensive diaspora, who were preoccupied with determining how they themselves were to understand the law, given the rapid changes that were occurring in Jewish life in this period. The condition of Gentiles under the law went largely ignored while Jews wrestled with more critical legal issues, whose terms are becoming well-established: Is there an Oral Torah to observe alongside a Written? What is

---

* Siena College, Loudonville, NY 12211.
[1] All translations in this paper are the author's.
[2] As in Ex. 12:49: תורה אחת יהיה לאזרח ולגר הגר בתוככם

the extent of its authority, and how may its requirements be derived? What should be the response of one group of Jews to another whose legal interpretation it finds reprehensible? Under what legal theory should the Temple be administered?

But still the question of the role of Gentiles vis-à-vis the Jewish law was never entirely off the table in the Second Temple Period. Certainly some of the disputes facing Jews in the first-century had to do with the status of Gentiles under the Torah. Some of the considerations of these disputes were theoretical: What laws must a Gentile perform in order to be considered righteous? Some of them were practical: What types of commerce were forbidden with Gentiles? In the "practical" column, we might place the question "How should Gentiles behave who wish to worship God?"

This latter question lay at the center of the self-definition of the small group of Jews gathered under the supposed messiahship of Jesus of Nazareth in the latter half of the first century CE. As their message of this Jesus' resurrection found more fecund reception among Gentiles than among Jews, however, the question of how, or even whether, to incorporate these Gentiles into the community came very much to the forefront. Eventually, the question became moot, as the Christian community came to define itself as something very different from Judaism.

The very question of when Christianity should be considered a Gentile rather than a Jewish phenomenon may be answered with reference to the question of the observance of Jewish law among the followers of Jesus. To consider oneself obliged to observe the laws of the Jews is to relate oneself to Judaism; to consider these laws as the laws of others is to cease to locate oneself within the Jewish community.

In a series of papers presented before this body[3] I have attempted to begin to map out one area of separation of the nascent Christian community from Judaism—not from "normative" or "mainstream" Judaism,but from Judaism itself. In two studies, "Paul and the הלכה" and "Jesus as Sadducee," I described New Testament texts dealing with questions of dietary laws, examining passages from Paul (I Cor. 8–10) and "Mark" (Mark 7) respectively. The present study continues this course of interest, to examine a third author, "Luke," whose book of Acts describes the transformation of the Jesus movement from a tiny Jewish sect proclaiming his-

---

3 "Paul and the הלכה: Dietary Laws for Gentiles in I Corinthians 8–10," in S. M. Passamaneck and M. Finley, eds., *Jewish Law Association Studies VII. The Paris Conference Volume* (Atlanta: Georgia, Scholars Press, 1994) 233–245; "What Comes out of a Person is What Makes a Person Impure: Jesus as Sadducee" in E. A. Goldman, ed., *Jewish Law Association Studies VIII. The Jerusalem 1994 Conference Volume* (Atlanta: Georgia, Scholars Press, 1996) 217–226.

tory's end to a Gentile movement set to play its own role in the history of the Roman empire.

These three authors each represent different moments in the history of the nascent Christian movement. Paul deals with the practicalities of bringing a Jewish message, however far from the mainstream, to Gentiles in the middle years of the first century CE. The anonymous author of the Gospel of Mark, writing on the eve of the First Jewish Revolt, tries to explain an essentially Jewish movement to an audience of Gentile readers, for whom too close a concern with Judean politics is an obstacle. Luke, writing during a time when the issue of Gentile membership in the Christian community had been resolved,[4] tries to describe this resolution in irenic terms.

In the pericope I examined in Mark's Gospel, 7:1–23, the evangelist records a controversy about whether or not impurity is conferred by eating without first washing the hands. In this discussion, Jesus is shown first to take a "Sadducean," i.e., anti-oral-law position, and then take a "moralizing" position, that while it is what comes out of a person that makes him or her impure, he is talking about sins, rather than about bodily discharges. These discharges pass not into the heart, but into the stomach, and thence down the latrine. Jesus was thereby, according to the evangelist

... καθαρίζων πάντα τὰ βρώματα

declaring every food pure (Mark 7:19).[5]

As I described in my paper for the Jerusalem 1994 conference,[6] the pericope in Mark shows a certain confusion or, more precisely, a rewriting of

---

[4] Acts is notoriously difficult to date, to the extent that commentators often ignore the question of dating almost entirely. I accept the attribution of authorship to an anonymous fellow-traveler with Paul, writing long after the Pauline journey in which he participated, after the composition of the Gospel of Luke c. 90. For a brief, but balanced, discussion of the date of composition of Acts, cf. H. Conzelmann, *Acts of the Apostles. A Commentary on the Acts of the Apostles,* trans. J. Limburg, A. T. Kraabel, and D. H. Juel, ed. E. J. Epp with C. R. Matthews. Hermeneia series. (Philadelphia: Fortress Press, 1987), xxxiii.

[5] The verse is textually problematic. The Cantabrigiensis (D), which has discharges flowing into the ὀχετός, "bowel" (?), thinking that it is the bowel which καθαρίζει πάντα τὰ βρώματα "purifies every food." A few mss. have the finite verb in the third person, καθαρίζον, "they purify every food," a few have it in the middle, καθαρίζεται, "every food is purified," but the vast majority of authorities (א, A, B, L, W, Δ, Θ among the uncials) provide the participle, understanding that grammatically it was Jesus "declaring every food pure." V. Taylor, *The Gospel According to St. Mark* 2 (London: The MacMillan Press Ltd., 1966) 344–5n. B. Metzger, *A Textual Commentary on the Greek New Testament* (London and New York: United Bible Societies, 1971) 95 and n.

[6] "Jesus as Sadducee," op. cit.

the historical narrative to reflect the changing understanding of what issues are involved in food laws as the church becomes more and more Gentile in its self-understanding. Mark's narrative begins with Jesus expressing an understanding of purity (not *kashrut* but *tahorut*) that is antagonistic to the Pharisaic extensions of the purity code beyond the terms of the written Torah. It concludes, in an added section, with Jesus moralizing the purity code, perhaps following the lead of John the Baptist. The evangelist's comment cited above which suggests that inasmuch as bodily discharges do not cause impurity, any food might be eaten, does not follow from the legal discussion of the pericope, but instead reflects the evangelist's concern to let his Gentile audience know that they were not obliged to follow the dietary laws of the Jews. An audience for whom debates about "written-Torah-purity" vs. "oral-Torah-purity" were no longer of moment was still concerned about issues of dietary law.

The passage under consideration in this paper, "Luke's" account of the dual visions of Cornelius and Peter in Acts 10:1–11:18, provides an impressively parallel case of the same phenomenon. This author, writing late in the first century, looks back upon the "Gentilization" of the church, retrofitting stories about the resolution of old issues with the solutions to newer ones. Examining this process in detail gives us another perspective on the growing alienation of Christians from the concerns of Jewish law, the growing realization that "Christianity" is now something very different from "Judaism."

Luke's narrative in 10:1–11:18 is remarkably complex, a good example of the great gifts of this storyteller.[7] The narrative, involving as it does interlocking visions which bring the two principle actors in the story together, must be compared to the immediately preceding narrative in Acts 9, another story in which carefully-timed visions bring together the characters in the story, in that case Paul and Ananias, the pious Jewish Christian from Antioch.

In the section under consideration here, the first vision is sent to one Cornelius, "a Centurion of the Italian Cohort," who is described as both εὐσεβής, "pious,"[8] and φοβούμενος τὸν θεὸν σὺν παντὶ τῷ οἴκῳ αὐτοῦ, "worshipping God with all his household," (10:2) that is to say, he is a Gentile who worships the God of the Jews.[9] This Cornelius is told in his

---

[7] C. H. Talbert, *Literary patterns, theological themes, and the genre of Luke-Acts* (Missoula, Montana: Scholars' Press, 1974) is the best discussion of Luke's narrative art, although he does not discuss this particular pattern.

[8] The adjective, or a cognate, is used in Acts of Cornelius, a soldier from his staff (10:7) of the gathered brethren (3:12), and of the Athenians who worship an "Unknown God" (17:23).

[9] The identity of the "God-worshipers" is notoriously problematic, to the extent that a number of scholars doubt that they had any identity at all. Cf. A. T. Kraabel, "The Disappear-

vision to summon Peter, and gives the address where he can be located in Jaffa.

As Cornelius' emissaries are traveling from Caesarea to Jaffa, Peter has his vision, timed by the author to be finished the moment the emissaries arrive. Peter, who is hungry after his morning prayer, has a vision to do with food: He sees the heavens opened, and "a vessel descending, something like a great cloth, being lowered by its four corners to the earth" (10:11).

This is the vision of the divine picnic, and it is a picnic whose menu contains all the creatures of creation, except for the fish:

ἐν ᾧ ὑπῆρχεν πάντα τὰ τετράποδα καὶ ἑρπετὰ τῆς γῆς καὶ πετεινὰ τοῦ οὐρανοῦ.

In it were all the four-footed beasts, and the creeping things of the earth, and the birds of the sky (10:12).

Along with this replete menagerie comes a *bat kol*, which instructs Peter to

Ἀναστάς, . . . , θῦσον καὶ φάγε.

Rise, . . . sacrifice,[10] and eat (10:13).

Peter demurs, citing his lifelong Torah-observance,

Μηδαμῶς, κύριε, ὅτι οὐδέποτε ἔφαγον πᾶν κοινὸν καὶ ἀκάθαρτον.

"Never, Lord, for I never ate anything unfit and impure!" (10:14)

focusing, understandably, on the non-kosher animals in the vision, as the commentators note.[11] The response of the *bat kol* seems definite:

---

ance of the 'God-fearers,'" Numen 28 (1981) 113–126 and idem, "Synagoga Caeca: Systematic Distortion in Gentile Interpretations of Evidence for Judaism in the Early Christian Period," in J. Neusner and E. S. Frerichs, eds., *"To See Ourselves as Others See Us," Christians, Jews, "Others" in Late Antiquity* (Chico, California: Scholars Press, 1985) 227–228.

10 θύω normally means "sacrifice," although commentators are usually drawn to the notion that Peter is asked to slaughter his meat, not sacrifice it. Haenchen, ad loc, asserts that the word should be translated "slaughter," citing Strack-Billerbeck to the effect that θύω = שחט, offering the objection that unclean animals cannot undergo *sh'chita*, then arguing that the passage obliterates the distinction between clean and unclean anyway. But in Luke and Acts the verb only once carries the meaning of "slaughter," in the parable of the Prodigal Son in Luke 15,where it is used of the fatted calf which the prodigal's father orders slaughtered in his joyful feast; otherwise it always takes the normal Greek meaning "sacrifice," of the paschal sacrifice in Luke 22:7; of Aaron's sacrifice to the golden calf, Acts 7:41, 2; in our passage and its reprise in Acts 11:7; and of the sacrifices to Zeus which Paul and Barnabas prevented in Lystra, Acts 14:13, 14.

11 Commentators at least since Lake and Cadbury cite Ezechiel's demurral Μηδαμῶς, κύριε, in 4:14 LXX, where the prophet responds to another divine demand to eat something improper, here barley cake baked on human dung. K. Lake and H. J. Cadbury, in F. J. Foakes

Ἃ ὁ θεὸς ἐκαθάρισεν σὺ μὴ κοίνου.

"What God has purified you must not make unfit!" (10:15)

The vision, presumably with its oral interpretation, is repeated three times, and Peter is pondering its meaning just as the messengers from Cornelius arrive at the house where he is staying.

What Peter thinks the vision means we learn after he arrives at Cornelius' house. Greeted worshipfully by the centurion, Peter tells him to rise, that he is only a human being. Entering the house, he encounters a sufficient crowd to make a brief speech (he will make a longer one momentarily) in which he reveals the vision's meaning:

ὑμεῖς ἐπίστασθε ὡς ἀθέμιτόν ἐστιν ἀνδρὶ Ἰουδαίῳ κολλᾶσθαι ἢ προσέρχεσθαι ἀλλοφύλῳ· κἀμοὶ ὁ θεὸς ἔδειξεν μηδένα κοινὸν ἢ ἀκάθαρτον λέγειν ἄνθρωπον· 10.29 διὸ καὶ ἀναντιρρήτως ἦλθον μεταπεμφθείς. πυνθάνομαι οὖν τίνι λόγῳ μετεπέμψασθέ με;

You know how wrong[12] it is for a Jewish man to cling to or to gather together with a member of another nation. But God has shown me that I should not call any human being impure or unclean. So when you sent for me, I came without any objection. May I inquire then regarding what purpose you have sent for me? (Acts 10:28-29)

God has apparently shown Peter that it is no longer forbidden–by Torah or by tradition–for Jews to associate closely with[13] Gentiles. That is to

---

Jackson and K. Lake, eds., *The Beginnings of Christianity. Part 1: The Acts of the Apostles IV: English Translation and Commentary* (repr.: Grand Rapids, Michigan, Baker Book House, 1979) 115n.

12 ἀθέμιτος carries the connotations of both "terribly wrong" and "unlawful." The word appears in the NT only here and in I Pet. 4:3, ἀθεμίτοις εἰδωλολατρίαις, "with wanton acts of idolatry." In Josephus it is ἀθέμιτος to place any image of a living creature in the Temple, BJ 1:650; for the Essenes to taste of their breakfast before the *b'racha*, BJ 2:131; either to take up arms or to make a peace treaty on the Sabbath, BJ 4:100; for Ananus to attack the Zealots inside the Temple with unpurified troops, BJ 4:205; for Jews to take up arms against Jews, V 26:4 and to leave the Temple doors open at night, C. Ap. 2:120.

13 The two verbs that describe what was formerly forbidden and what is now permitted are interesting. κολλάομαι is used in Luke-Acts to refer to the dust that clings to the feet of the apostles, Lk 10:11; to the indenturing of the prodigal son to an owner of swine, 15:15; of becoming joined to the church, Acts 5:15, 9:26, 17:34; to Philip's joining the Ethiopian eunuch's chariot, Acts 8:29. Nearly all the other NT occurances of the verb use it to translate דבק, as in Matt 19:5 and twice in I Cor. 6. Which of these meanings expresses what Jews were formerly forbidden, and are now permitted, to do with Gentiles? If κολλάομαι is too specific, προσέρχομαι is too general; "approach" is the normal meaning. Lake and Cadbury, op. cit., translate as "visit the house" of a Gentile, without offering any justification. Likewise, Haenchen, op. cit., offers

say that the author portrays Peter as interpreting a vision consisting of a commandment to eat previously-forbidden animals as in fact permitting him to associate with the Gentile Cornelius.

Does Peter eat with Cornelius? The passage is remarkably silent on the subject. After the Gentiles received the "gift of the holy spirit" (10:45), marking for Peter their readiness for baptism, the members of Cornelius' entourage request that he "remain with them for several days" (10:48), but there is no description of what arrangements he made for his meals. He is accused of eating with Gentiles by "those of the circumcision," once he returns to Jerusalem,

> Εἰσῆλθες πρὸς ἄνδρας ἀκροβυστίαν ἔχοντας καὶ συνέφαγες αὐτοῖς.
>
> You have gone to uncircumcised men and eaten together with them (11:3);

but Luke's narrative nowhere states directly that their accusation is true.[14]

In our treatment of the discussion of food and purity in Mark 7, we observed that Mark inserts a blanket revocation of all dietary laws into a discussion nominally about whether Jesus' followers need to follow Pharisaic or Sadducean laws of purity. Of the passage, I wrote

> Mark's account captures a moment in history in which the Christian community had not yet decided the extent to which biblical laws concerning purity and food applied to it.[15]

Mark decides that the way to apply the Torah to a community of Gentile Christians who no longer feel bound by it is to moralize it, creating a

---

"visit." Precisely **what** Luke thinks used to be forbidden and is now permitted remains mysterious. For a recent summary of the question of Jewish-Gentile table-fellowship in this period see P. J. Tomson, *Paul and the Jewish Law: Halacha in the Letters of the Apostle to the Gentiles* (Minneapolis, Minnesota: Fortress Press, 1990) 230–236.

14 How is this story connected with the similar–but very different–episode in Gal. 2:11f?

Ὅτε δὲ ἦλθεν Κηφᾶς εἰς Ἀντιόχειαν, κατὰ πρόσωπον αὐτῷ ἀντέστην, ὅτι κατεγνωσμένος ἦν. πρὸ τοῦ γὰρ ἐλθεῖν τινας ἀπὸ Ἰακώβου μετὰ τῶν ἐθνῶν συνήσθιεν· ὅτε δὲ ἦλθον, ὑπέστελλεν καὶ ἀφώριζεν ἑαυτόν φοβούμενος τοὺς ἐκ περιτομῆς.

When Cephas came to Antioch, I opposed him to his face, for he was condemned by his actions. For before certain people came from James, he ate with the Gentiles. But when they came, he stood back and separated himself, fearing those of the circumcision (Gal. 2:11–12).

Tomson, op. cit., 222–230 discusses the passage in Galatians at length, but with only cursory attention to the story in Acts. Of course, the two accounts are opposite; in the present narrative Peter is accused of eating with Gentiles but does not back down.

15 "Jesus as Sadducee," op. cit., p. 217.

system of "moral purity" to replace a system of religious purity. In such a system, where what makes a person impure is not what he or she ingests but by what sins he or she exhibits, all foods are indeed "pure:" purity no longer has anything to do with food.

Luke's narrative in Acts 10 is directly comparable to the pericope in Mark 7, but the issues have altered in the intervening generation between the two authors. For Luke, the issue of Torah-observance has been resolved in the natural law/Noachide law formulation of the Apostolic Degree, itself perhaps an artifact of the irenic aims of this author. The new issue no longer has to do with how the church decided whether the Oral Torah must be observed alongside the Written, but how it decided that there were no longer any legal or traditional barriers separating Jews and Gentiles. Luke's narrative illustrates how the issue came to be defined not as what you ate, but with whom.

We may thus see Luke's account of the vision of the divine picnic as another stage in the development of Christian kashrut (or anti-kashrut), a development that represents one of the measures of separation between the community of Jesus' followers and the community of Jews. It is not the final stage. Luke still envisions some measure of difference between Jewish Christians and Gentiles. But he is looking forward to the final stage, in which Jews and Christians inhabit entirely different communities, the separation complete.

Text and Translation

10.1 Ἀνὴρ δέ τις ἐν Καισαρείᾳ ὀνόματι Κορνήλιος, ἑκατοντάρχης ἐκ σπείρης τῆς καλουμένης Ἰταλικῆς, 10.2 εὐσεβὴς καὶ φοβούμενος τὸν θεὸν σὺν παντὶ τῷ οἴκῳ αὐτοῦ, ποιῶν ἐλεημοσύνας πολλὰ" τῷ λαῷ καὶ δεόμενος τοῦ θεοῦ διὰ παντός, 10.3 εἶδεν ἐν ὁράματι φανερῶς ὡσεὶ περὶ ὥραν ἐνάτην τῆς ἡμέρας ἄγγελον τοῦ θεοῦ εἰσελθόντα πρὸς αὐτὸν καὶ εἰπόντα αὐτῷ, Κορνήλιε. 10.4 ὁ δὲ ἀτενίσας αὐτῷ καὶ ἔμφοβος γενόμενος εἶπεν, Τί ἐστιν, κύριε; εἶπεν δὲ αὐτῷ, Αἱ προσευχαί σου καὶ αἱ ἐλεημοσύναι σου ἀνέβησαν εἰς μνημόσυνον ἔμπροσθεν τοῦ θεοῦ. 10.5 καὶ νῦν πέμψον ἄνδρας εἰς Ἰόππην καὶ μετάπεμψαι Σίμωνά τινα ὃς ἐπικαλεῖται Πέτρος· 10.6 οὗτος ξενίζεται παρά τινι Σίμωνι βυρσεῖ, ᾧ ἐστιν οἰκία παρὰ θάλασσαν. 10.7 ὡς δὲ ἀπῆλθεν ὁ ἄγγελος ὁ λαλῶν αὐτῷ, φωνήσας δύο τῶν οἰκετῶν καὶ στρατιώτην εὐσεβῆ τῶν προσκαρτερούντων αὐτῷ 10.8 καὶ ἐξηγησάμενος ἅπαντα αὐτοῖς ἀπέστειλεν αὐτοὺς εἰς τὴν Ἰόππην.

10.9 Τῇ δὲ ἐπαύριον, ὁδοιπορούντων ἐκείνων καὶ τῇ πόλει ἐγγιζόντων ἀνέβη Πέτρος ἐπὶ τὸ δῶμα προσεύξασθαι περὶ ὥραν ἕκτην. 10.10 ἐγένετο δὲ πρόσπεινος καὶ ἤθελεν γεύσασθαι. παρασκευαζόντων δὲ αὐτῶν ἐγένετο ἐπ' αὐτὸν ἔκστασις 10.11 καὶ θεωρεῖ τὸν οὐρανὸν ἀνεῳγμένον καὶ καταβαῖνον σκεῦός τι ὡς ὀθόνην μεγάλην τέσσαρσιν ἀρχαῖς καθιέμενον ἐπὶ τῆς γῆς, 10.12 ἐν ᾧ ὑπῆρχεν πάντα τὰ τετράποδα καὶ ἑρπετὰ τῆς γῆς καὶ πετεινὰ τοῦ οὐρανοῦ. 10.13 καὶ ἐγένετο φωνὴ πρὸς αὐτόν, Ἀναστάς, Πέτρε, θῦσον καὶ φάγε. 10.14 ὁ δὲ Πέτρος εἶπεν, Μηδαμῶς, κύριε, ὅτι οὐδέποτε ἔφαγον πᾶν κοινὸν καὶ ἀκάθαρτον. 10.15 καὶ φωνὴ πάλιν ἐκ δευτέρου πρὸς αὐτόν, Ἃ ὁ θεὸς ἐκαθάρισεν σὺ μὴ κοίνου. 10.16 τοῦτο δὲ ἐγένετο ἐπὶ τρις καὶ εὐθὺς ἀνελήμφθη τὸ σκεῦος εἰς τὸν οὐρανόν.

10.17 Ὡς δὲ ἐν ἑαυτῷ διηπόρει ὁ Πέτρος τί ἂν εἴη τὸ ὅραμα ὃ εἶδεν, ἰδοὺ οἱ ἄνδρες οἱ ἀπεσταλμένοι ὑπὸ τοῦ Κορνηλίου διερωτήσαντες τὴν οἰκίαν τοῦ Σίμωνος ἐπέστησαν ἐπὶ τὸν πυλῶνα, 10.18 καὶ φωνήσαντες ἐπυνθάνοντο εἰ Σίμων ὁ ἐπικαλούμενος Πέτρος ἐνθάδε ξενίζεται. 10.19 τοῦ δὲ Πέτρου διενθυμουμένου περὶ τοῦ ὁράματος εἶπεν [αὐτῷ] τὸ πνεῦμα, Ἰδοὺ ἄνδρες τρεῖς ζητοῦντές σε, 10.20 ἀλλὰ ἀναστὰς κατάβηθι καὶ πορεύου σὺν αὐτοῖς μηδὲν διακρινόμενος ὅτι ἐγὼ ἀπέσταλκα αὐτούς. 10.21 καταβὰς δὲ Πέτρος πρὸς τοὺς ἄνδρας εἶπεν, Ἰδοὺ ἐγώ εἰμι ὃν ζητεῖτε· τίς ἡ αἰτία δι' ἣν πάρεστε; 10.22 οἱ δὲ εἶπαν, Κορνήλιος ἑκατοντάρχης, ἀνὴρ δίκαιος καὶ φοβούμενος τὸν θεὸν μαρτυρούμενός τε ὑπὸ ὅλου τοῦ ἔθνους τῶν Ἰουδαίων, ἐχρηματίσθη ὑπὸ ἀγγέλου ἁγίου μεταπέμψασθαί σε εἰς τὸν οἶκον αὐτοῦ καὶ ἀκοῦσαι ῥήματα παρὰ σοῦ. 10.23 εἰσκαλεσάμενος οὖν αὐτοὺς ἐξένισεν.

Τῇ δὲ ἐπαύριον ἀναστὰς ἐξῆλθεν σὺν αὐτοῖς καί τινες τῶν ἀδελφῶν τῶν ἀπὸ Ἰόππης συνῆλθον αὐτῷ. 10.24 τῇ δὲ ἐπαύριον εἰσῆλθεν εἰς τὴν Καισάρειαν· ὁ δὲ Κορνήλιος ἦν προσδοκῶν αὐτούς συγκαλεσάμενος τοὺς συγγενεῖς αὐτοῦ καὶ τοὺς ἀναγκαίους φίλους. 10.25 ὡς δὲ ἐγένετο τοῦ εἰσελθεῖν τὸν Πέτρον, συναντήσας αὐτῷ ὁ Κορνήλιος πεσὼν ἐπὶ τοὺς πόδας προσεκύνησεν. 10.26 ὁ δὲ Πέτρος ἤγειρεν αὐτὸν λέγων, Ἀνάστηθι· καὶ ἐγὼ αὐτὸς ἄνθρωπός εἰμι. 10.27 καὶ συνομιλῶν αὐτῷ εἰσῆλθεν καὶ εὑρίσκει συνεληλυθότας πολλούς, 10.28 ἔφη τε πρὸς αὐτούς, Ὑμεῖς ἐπίστασθε ὡς ἀθέμιτόν ἐστιν ἀνδρὶ Ἰουδαίῳ κολλᾶσθαι ἢ προσέρχεσθαι ἀλλοφύλῳ· κἀμοὶ ὁ θεὸς ἔδειξεν μηδένα κοινὸν ἢ ἀκάθαρτον λέγειν ἄνθρωπον· 10.29 διὸ καὶ ἀναντιρρήτως ἦλθον μεταπεμφθείς. πυνθάνομαι οὖν τίνι λόγῳ μετεπέμψασθέ με; 10.30 καὶ ὁ Κορνήλιος ἔφη, Ἀπὸ τετάρτης ἡμέρας μέχρι ταύτης τῆς ὥρας ἤμην τὴν ἐνάτην προσευχόμενος ἐν τῷ οἴκῳ μου, καὶ ἰδοὺ ἀνὴρ ἔστη ἐνώπιόν μου ἐν ἐσθῆτι λαμπρᾷ 10.31 καὶ φησίν, Κορνήλιε, εἰσηκούσθη σου ἡ προσευχὴ καὶ αἱ ἐλεημοσύναι σου ἐμνήσθησαν ἐνώπιον τοῦ θεοῦ. 10.32 πέμψον οὖν εἰς Ἰόππην καὶ μετακάλεσαι Σίμωνα ὃς ἐπικαλεῖται Πέτρος, οὗτος ξενίζεται ἐν οἰκίᾳ Σίμωνος βυρσέως παρὰ θάλασσαν. 10.33 ἐξαυτῆς οὖν ἔπεμψα πρὸς σέ, σύ τε καλῶς ἐποίησας παραγενόμενος. νῦν οὖν πάντες ἡμεῖς ἐνώπιον τοῦ θεοῦ πάρεσμεν ἀκοῦσαι πάντα τὰ προστεταγμένα σοι ὑπὸ τοῦ κυρίου.

10.34 Ἀνοίξας δὲ Πέτρος τὸ στόμα εἶπεν, Ἐπ' ἀληθείας καταλαμβάνομαι ὅτι οὐκ ἔστιν προσωπολήμπτης ὁ θεός, 10.35 ἀλλ' ἐν παντὶ ἔθνει ὁ φοβούμενος αὐτὸν καὶ ἐργαζόμενος δικαιοσύνην δεκτὸς αὐτῷ ἐστιν. 10.36 τὸν λόγον [ὃν] ἀπέστειλεν τοῖς υἱοῖς Ἰσραὴλ εὐαγγελιζόμενος εἰρήνην διὰ Ἰησοῦ Χριστοῦ, οὗτός ἐστιν πάντων κύριος, 10.37 ὑμεῖς οἴδατε τὸ γενόμενον ῥῆμα καθ᾽ ὅλης τῆς Ἰουδαίας, ἀρξάμενος ἀπὸ τῆς Γαλιλαίας μετὰ τὸ βάπτισμα ὃ ἐκήρυξεν Ἰωάννης, 10.38 Ἰησοῦν τὸν ἀπὸ Ναζαρέθ, ὡς ἔχρισεν αὐτὸν ὁ θεὸς πνεύματι ἁγίῳ καὶ δυνάμει, ὃς διῆλθεν εὐεργετῶν καὶ ἰώμενος πάντας τοὺς καταδυναστευομένους ὑπὸ τοῦ διαβόλου, ὅτι ὁ θεὸς ἦν μετ᾽ αὐτοῦ. 10.39 καὶ ἡμεῖς μάρτυρες πάντων ὧν ἐποίησεν ἔν τε τῇ χώρᾳ τῶν Ἰουδαίων καὶ [ἐν] Ἰερουσαλήμ. ὃν καὶ ἀνεῖλαν κρεμάσαντες ἐπὶ ξύλου, 10.40 τοῦτον ὁ θεὸς ἤγειρεν [ἐν] τῇ τρίτῃ ἡμέρᾳ καὶ ἔδωκεν αὐτὸν ἐμφανῆ γενέσθαι, 10.41 οὐ παντὶ τῷ λαῷ ἀλλὰ μάρτυσιν τοῖς προκεχειροτονημένοις ὑπὸ τοῦ θεοῦ, ἡμῖν, οἵτινες συνεφάγομεν καὶ συνεπίομεν αὐτῷ μετὰ τὸ ἀναστῆναι αὐτὸν ἐκ νεκρῶν· 10.42 καὶ παρήγγειλεν ἡμῖν κηρύξαι τῷ λαῷ" καὶ διαμαρτύρασθαι ὅτι οὗτός ἐστιν ὁ ὡρισμένος ὑπὸ τοῦ θεοῦ κριτὴς ζώντων καὶ νεκρῶν. 10.43 τούτῳ πάντες οἱ προφῆται μαρτυροῦσιν ἄφεσιν ἁμαρτιῶν λαβεῖν διὰ τοῦ ὀνόματος αὐτοῦ πάντα τὸν πιστεύοντα εἰς αὐτόν.

10.44 Ἔτι λαλοῦντος τοῦ Πέτρου τὰ ῥήματα ταῦτα ἐπέπεσεν τὸ πνεῦμα τὸ ἅγιον ἐπὶ πάντας τοὺς ἀκούοντας τὸν λόγον. 10.45 καὶ ἐξέστησαν οἱ ἐκ περιτομῆς πιστοὶ ὅσοι συνῆλθαν τῷ Πέτρῳ, ὅτι καὶ ἐπὶ τὰ ἔθνη ἡ δωρεὰ τοῦ ἁγίου πνεύματος ἐκκέχυται· 10.46 ἤκουον γὰρ αὐτῶν λαλούντων γλώσσαις καὶ μεγαλυνόντων τὸν θεόν. τότε ἀπεκρίθη Πέτρος, 10.47 Μήτι τὸ ὕδωρ δύναται κωλῦσαί τις τοῦ μὴ βαπτισθῆναι τούτους, οἵτινες τὸ πνεῦμα τὸ ἅγιον ἔλαβον ὡς καὶ ἡμεῖς; 10.48 προσέταξεν δὲ αὐτοὺς ἐν τῷ ὀνόματι Ἰησοῦ Χριστοῦ βαπτισθῆναι. τότε ἠρώτησαν αὐτὸν ἐπιμεῖναι ἡμέρας τινάς.

11.1 Ἤκουσαν δὲ οἱ ἀπόστολοι καὶ οἱ ἀδελφοὶ οἱ ὄντες κατὰ τὴν Ἰουδαίαν ὅτι καὶ τὰ ἔθνη ἐδέξαντο τὸν λόγον τοῦ θεοῦ. 11.2 ὅτε δὲ ἀνέβη Πέτρος εἰς Ἰερουσαλήμ, διεκρίνοντο πρὸς αὐτὸν οἱ ἐκ περιτομῆς 11.3 λέγοντες ὅτι Εἰσῆλθες πρὸς ἄνδρας ἀκροβυστίαν ἔχοντας καὶ συνέφαγες αὐτοῖς. 11.4 ἀρξάμενος δὲ Πέτρος ἐξετίθετο αὐτοῖς καθεξῆς λέγων, 11.5 Ἐγὼ ἤμην ἐν πόλει Ἰόππῃ προσευχόμενος καὶ εἶδον ἐν ἐκστάσει ὅραμα, καταβαῖνον σκεῦός τι ὡς ὀθόνην μεγάλην τέσσαρσιν ἀρχαῖς καθιεμένην ἐκ τοῦ οὐρανοῦ, καὶ ἦλθεν ἄχρι ἐμοῦ· 11.6 εἰς ἣν ἀτενίσας κατενόουν καὶ εἶδον τὰ τετράποδα τῆς γῆς καὶ τὰ θηρία καὶ τὰ ἑρπετὰ καὶ τὰ πετεινὰ τοῦ οὐρανοῦ. 11.7 ἤκουσα δὲ καὶ φωνῆς λεγούσης μοι, Ἀναστάς, Πέτρε, θῦσον καὶ φάγε. 11.8 εἶπον δέ, Μηδαμῶς, κύριε, ὅτι κοινὸν ἢ ἀκάθαρτον οὐδέποτε εἰσῆλθεν εἰς τὸ στόμα μου. 11.9 ἀπεκρίθη δὲ φωνὴ ἐκ δευτέρου ἐκ τοῦ οὐρανοῦ, Ἃ ὁ θεὸς ἐκαθάρισεν σὺ μὴ κοίνου. 11.10 τοῦτο δὲ ἐγένετο ἐπὶ τρίς, καὶ ἀνεσπάσθη πάλιν ἅπαντα εἰς τὸν οὐρανόν. 11.11 καὶ ἰδοὺ ἐξαυτῆς τρεῖς ἄνδρες ἐπέστησαν ἐπὶ τὴν οἰκίαν ἐν ᾗ ἦμεν, ἀπεσταλμένοι ἀπὸ Καισαρείας πρός με. 11.12 εἶπεν δὲ τὸ πνεῦμά μοι συνελθεῖν αὐτοῖς μηδὲν διακρίναντα. ἦλθον δὲ σὺν ἐμοὶ καὶ οἱ ἓξ ἀδελφοὶ οὗτοι καὶ εἰσήλθομεν εἰς τὸν οἶκον τοῦ ἀνδρός. 11.13 ἀπήγγειλεν δὲ ἡμῖν πῶς εἶδεν [τὸν] ἄγγελον ἐν τῷ οἴκῳ αὐτοῦ σταθέντα καὶ εἰπόντα, Ἀπόστειλον εἰς Ἰόππην καὶ μετάπεμψαι Σίμωνα τὸν ἐπικαλούμενον Πέτρον, 11.14 ὃς λαλήσει ῥήματα πρὸς σὲ ἐν οἷς σωθήσῃ σὺ καὶ πᾶς ὁ οἶκός σου. 11.15 ἐν δὲ τῷ ἄρξασθαί με λαλεῖν ἐπέπεσεν τὸ πνεῦμα τὸ ἅγιον ἐπ' αὐτοὺς ὥσπερ καὶ ἐφ' ἡμᾶς ἐν ἀρχῇ. 11.16 ἐμνήσθην δὲ τοῦ ῥήματος τοῦ κυρίου ὡς ἔλεγεν, Ἰωάννης μὲν ἐβάπτισεν ὕδατι, ὑμεῖς δὲ βαπτισθήσεσθε ἐν πνεύματι ἁγίῳ. 11.17 εἰ οὖν τὴν ἴσην δωρεὰν ἔδωκεν αὐτοῖς ὁ θεὸς ὡς καὶ ἡμῖν πιστεύσασιν ἐπὶ τὸν κύριον Ἰησοῦν Χριστόν, ἐγὼ τίς ἤμην δυνατὸς κωλῦσαι τὸν θεόν; 11.18 ἀκούσαντες δὲ ταῦτα ἡσύχασαν καὶ ἐδόξασαν τὸν θεὸν λέγοντες, Ἄρα καὶ τοῖς ἔθνεσιν ὁ θεὸς τὴν μετάνοιαν εἰς ζωὴν ἔδωκεν.

A certain man in Caesarea, by the name of Cornelius, a centurion of the Italian Cohort, a pious man who worshipped God together with all his household, performing many acts of charity for the whole people, and praying to God constantly, suddenly saw in a dream a messenger of God, around three o'clock in the afternoon, coming to him and saying, "Cornelius!" Staring at him in fear, he said, "What is it, Lord?" He said to him, "Your prayers and your acts of charity have ascended as a memorial before God. Now, send a man to Jaffa, to summon a certain Simon who is called 'Peter.' He is staying with a certain Simon the tanner, who lives along the sea. When the angel who was speaking to him left, he called two of his servants and a pious soldier from among those who served him, and having told them everything, he sent them to Jaffa.

The next day, while they were approaching the city on their journey, Peter went up to the roof to pray, at about noon. He became hungry and wished to eat. While they were preparing his meal, a trance fell upon him, and he saw the sky opening, and a vessel descending, something like a great cloth, being lowered by its four corners to the earth. In it were all the four-footed beasts, and the creeping things of the earth, and the birds of the sky. A voice came to him, "Rise, Peter, sacrifice and eat!" But Peter said, "Never, Lord, for I never ate anything unfit and impure!" The voice a second time said to him, "What God has purified you must make unfit!" This happened a third time, and the apparatus was directly taken up into the sky.

As Peter was pondering the meaning of the vision that he saw, behold, the men who were sent by Cornelius to seek the house of Simon stood by the gate, and heard them asking if Simon called "Peter" was staying inside. While Peter was reflecting on the vision, the Spirit said to him, "Look, three men are seeking you. Rise, go down and travel with them, without concern, for I have sent them. Peter, having gone down to the men, said "Behold, I am the one whom you seek. What is the reason for your visit?" They said, "Cornelius the centurion, a righteous man, a God-worshiper, about whom the whole Judean nation gives testimony, was directed by a holy angel for you to be summoned to his house, and to hear what you have to say." And inviting them inside, he put them up for the night.

Rising on the next day, he went with them, and some of the brothers and sisters from Jaffa accompanied him. The following day, he arrived at Caesarea. Cornelius was there to greet them, having invited his relatives and intimate friends. When Peter entered, Cornelius approached him and, falling at his feet, began to worship him. But Peter raised him up, saying "Get up! I am merely a human being." While he was speaking with him, he went inside and found that many had gathered together. He said to them, "You know how terribly wrong it is for a Jewish man to be joined or to gather together with a member of another nation. But God has shown me that I should not call any human being impure or unclean. So when you sent for me, I came without any objection. May I inquire then regarding what purpose you have sent for me?" Cornelius said, "Four days ago, around this time, I was praying during the ninth hour in my house, and behold, a man in shining garments was standing before me, and he said, 'Cornelius, your prayer has been heard, and your acts of charity have been remembered before God. Send, therefore, to Jaffa, and call upon Simon, who is called "Peter," who is staying at the house of Simon the Tanner along the sea.' So I sent for you immediately, and you have come graciously. Now we are all gathered before God to hear all the things that you have been commanded by the Lord."

Peter opened his mouth and said, "I truly perceive how impartial God is, but in every nation the one who fears him and performs righteous works is acceptable to him. You know the word which he sent to the children of Israel, preaching the good news of peace through Jesus Christ, the one who is the Lord of all people, the story which occurred throughout all of Judea, starting from Galilee after the baptism which John proclaimed, Jesus of Nazareth, whom God anointed with the holy spirit and with power, who traveled about performing miracles and healing all of those who were oppressed by the Devil, because God was with him. And we were witness of all of the things which he did both in the land of the Judeans and in Jerusalem. And they destroyed him, hanging him on a tree. God raised this man on the third day, and made him visible, not to all the people, but to us whom God had chosen as witnesses, who ate and drank together with him after he raised him from the dead. And he appointed us to proclaim to the people and to testify that this one is the one whom God appointed as a judge between the living and the dead. All the prophets testify about this man, that all who trust in him receive through his name a pardon from sins. While Peter was speaking these words, the holy spirit fell upon all who were hearing the speech. Those circumcised believers who had come with

Peter were beside themselves, because the gift of the holy spirit had been poured out even upon Gentiles. For they heard them speaking in tongues and glorifying God. Then Peter said, "Is there anyone who is able to withhold the water, so that these people may not be baptized, when they have received the holy spirit even as we have?" So he ordered them to be baptized in the name of Jesus Christ. And they wished him to remain with them for several days.

The apostles and the brothers and sisters who were residing in Judea heard that the Gentiles had received the word of God. When Peter went up to Jerusalem, those of the circumcision challenged him, saying "You have gone to uncircumcised men and eaten together with them." Peter began to describe the events in order, saying, "I was praying in the city of Jaffa, and I saw a vision in a trance, something descending like a great sheet, lowered by four corners from the sky, and it came to me. Upon it I saw, when I looked closely, the four-footed animals of the earth, and the beasts, and the serpents, and the birds of the sky. And I heard a voice speaking to me, 'Rise, Peter, sacrifice and eat.' I said, 'Never, Lord because an unclean or impure thing has never gone into my mouth.' A second time, a voice answered from the sky, 'What God has purified, you must not call unclean.' This happened a third time, and it was suddenly snatched up again to the sky. Behold, immediately three men arrived at the house where we were, sent from Caesarea to me. The spirit told me to go with them without drawing any distinctions. There came with me also these six brothers and we came to the man's house. He told us how he saw the angel standing in his house and saying, 'Send to Jaffa and escort Simon, called Peter, who will say words to you by which you will be saved, you and all your household.' When I began to speak, the holy spirit fell upon them, just as it did upon us at the beginning. I remembered the word of the Lord, as he said 'John baptized you with water, but you will be baptized with the holy spirit.' So if God gave the same gift to them as he did to us who trusted in the Lord Jesus Christ, how was I able to stand in the way of God? Hearing these things, they became silent, and they glorified God, saying 'God has given even to the Gentiles the repentance that leads to life.'"